HISTORICAL RECORDS OF RANDOLPH COUNTY, ALABAMA 1832-1900

Compiled by

MARILYN DAVIS BAREFIELD

Copyright 1985

by

Marilyn Davis Barefield
1108 South 28th Street, Apt. 1
Birmingham, Alabama 35205

Other books by the author

BUTLER COUNTY IN THE NINETEENTH CENTURY

OLD CAHABA LAND OFFICE RECORDS
& MILITARY WARRANTS, 1817–1853

OLD ST. STEPHENS LAND OFFICE RECORDS
& MILITARY WARRANTS
AMERICAN STATE PAPERS, PUBLIC LANDS, VOL. I

OLD SPARTA & ELBA LAND OFFICE RECORDS
& MILITARY WARRANTS, 1822–1860

OLD TUSKALOOSA LAND OFFICE RECORDS
& MILITARY WARRANTS, 1821–1855

ALABAMA MORTALITY SCHEDULE 1850

CLARKE COUNTY, ALABAMA, RECORDS
1814–1885

PICKENS COUNTY, ALABAMA
1841–1861

CEMETERIES OF JEFFERSON COUNTY, ALABAMA
VOLUME ONE

BUTLER COUNTY, ALABAMA, OBITUARIES

Southern Historical Press, Inc.
c/o The Rev. Silas Emmett Lucas, Jr.
P.O. Box 738
Easley, South Carolina 29641–0738

ISBN 0-89308-548-0

TABLE OF CONTENTS

"Early Days in Randolph County" by General B.F. Weathers	Page	1
"Randolph County, Alabama, 62 Years Ago, The Red Man's Home, the White Man's Eden" by J.M.K. Guinn	Page	9
"Randolph County" by William Wallace Screws	Page	95
Probate Notices from The American Eagle	Page	100
Probate Notices from The Randolph Enterprise	Page	105
Register of Deaths in Randolph County	Page	115
Alabama State Gazeteer and Business Directory 1887-1888	Page	143
Probate Notices from The Jacksonville Republican	Page	148
1850 Mortality Schedule	Page	157
Randolph County Post Offices and Postmasters	Page	159
Probate Notices from The Randolph Toiler	Page	161
Civil War Pensioners of Randolph County	Page	164
Wills and Deeds of Randolph County	Page	183
Index	Page	200

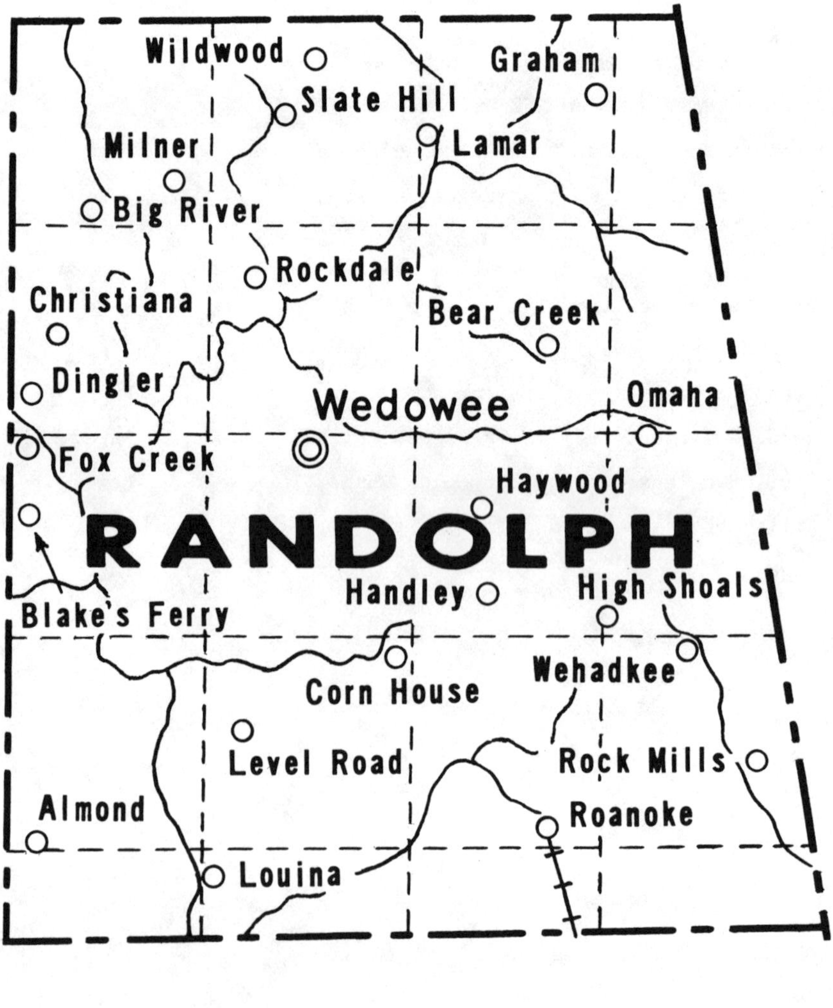
Wildwood
Graham
Slate Hill
Milner
Lamar
Big River
Rockdale
Christiana
Bear Creek
Dingler
Wedowee
Omaha
Fox Creek
Haywood
RANDOLPH
Handley
High Shoals
Blake's Ferry
Wehadkee
Corn House
Level Road
Rock Mills
Almond
Roanoke
Louina

HISTORICAL RECORDS OF
RANDOLPH COUNTY, ALABAMA
1832 - 1900

INTRODUCTION

Randolph County is one of the counties in Alabama which has suffered the loss of probate records. This disaster occurred in 1896 when the courthouse burned destroying all of the records up to that time. This book is a compilation of some early records of the county in an effort to make the existing material readily available for research.

Included are three histories written on the county as follows, "Early Days in Randolph County" by General B.F. Weathers, "Randolph County, Alabama, 62 Years Ago, The Red Man's Home, The White Man's Eden" by J.M.K. Guinn and "Randolph County" by William Wallace Screws.

Three early newspapers of the state, The Jacksonville Republican, The American Eagle and The Randolph Enterprise provided marriages, obituaries, probate notices and advertisements for the time period from 1841 to 1875 and from 1895 to 1897.

In the Department of Archives and History in Montgomery, Alabama were found the Registers of Deaths beginning in 1886. These records from 1886 to 1897 are included in this book. Names of the deceased, date of death, place of birth, age at death, sex, color, marital status, occupation, cause of death, place of death, place of burial, with the last space being reserved for the name of the physician, mid-wife or head of the family, are given in the ledgers for each person.

The 1850 Mortality Schedule for Randolph County, The Alabame State Gazeteer and Business Directory 1887-1888, Randolph County Post Offices and Postmasters, Civil War Pensioners and a few Wills and Deeds complete the records. The book ends in a section of pictures of old houses and buildings in the county.

I would like to express my gratitude to Mr. Ben McDonald who spent a good portion of one day guiding me around the county and to Mr. and Mrs. John B. Stevenson for their many courtesies.

The map on the opposite page was reproduced by Mr. Frank H. Temple of Montgomery, Alabama, from an 1886 Railroad and County Map of Alabama by H.C. Hudgins & Co. of Atlanta, Georgia.

Marilyn Davis Barefield

The Shoals in Rock Mills

EARLY DAYS IN RANDOLPH COUNTY
by
Gen. B.F. Weathers
Roanoke Leader - 10/14/1931-1/13/1932

The basis of this series of articles is personal knowledge, history and tradition orally delivered by the first settlers of the county of Randolph and the town of Roanoke.

Randolph County was established by an act approved December 18, 1832 and was carved out of the last Creek cession. The county was named to honor John Randolph of Virginia. John Randolph was born in Petersburg, Virginia in 1773, and entered Congress in 1799. He was a member of one house or another of that body with the exception of two or three short interruptions until his death in Philadelphia on May 23, 1833. He was minister to Russia in 1830 for a few months. He possessed much talent and culture and was one of the most popular men of any age.

Randolph County has an area of 600 square miles. The County is well watered with many fine springs. In the early days the creeks, springs, and rivers were clear and full of fish. The forest had plenty of game.

The population is thus placed on the records: in 1860 - whites, 18,132; blacks - 1,927; the assessed value of real estate was $765,969; personal property $116,163, a total of $882,332. The cash value of farm lands $62,032 acres improved; 189,044 acres unimproved worth $620,331.

In 1860 just before the war, the value of livestock including 1,313 horses, 835 mules, 9,860 cattle, 7,485 sheep, 14,819 hogs was $370,810.

In 1860 the farm production was 48,587 bushels of wheat, 264,448 bushels of corn, 20,707 bushels of oats, 38,902 bushels of potatoes, 125,066 pounds of butter, 12,992 gallons of molasses, 7,670 pounds of tobacco, 2,246 bales of cotton, 13,262 pounds of wool. The value of animals slaughtered was $119,803 and farm products were valued at $718,695.

The surface of Randolph County is broken and hilly intersected by fertile valleys which lie well for small farmers. Metamorphic rock, everywhere visible, reveals in nature's language the fact that this country lies within the primary system of creative matter.

Wedowee, the seat of justice since 1836, is a village the name of which means the Rolling Waters in the Muscogee tongue. It was changed to McDonald in 1839, but resumed its present name three years later.

Louina was a village named for Louina, a wealthy Indian, the wife of Nicahargo. She had two negro slaves, twenty-five horses, one hundred cattle and much silver money. It is said that when she left, she had her money in sacks, put them on her pony and the sacks were so heavy the pony gave down under them.

The first courts were held at Blake's Ferry - then called Triplett's or Young's, ten miles west of Wedowee. Wehadkee (White Water) is the site of the Rock Mills Cotton Factory.

State Senators of Randolph County: In 1834-William Arnold; 1838-William B. McClellan; 1839-George Reese; 1843-James E. Rouse; 1845-Jeff Falkner; 1847-Seaborn Gray; 1851-John T. Heflin; 1853-Henry M. Gay; 1857-R.S. Heflin; 1859-R.S. Heflin; 1863-R.T. Wood; 1865-M.R. Bell. Names of Representatives: 1837-Thomas Blake; 1838-William McKnight; 1839-F.R. Adrine; 1843-F.F. Adrine; 1849-Wyatt Heflin; 1842-Jeremiah Murphey; 1843-Wyatt Heflin; 1844-James F. Allen; 1845-Wyatt Heflin; 1847-William Wood and C.J. Ussery; 1849-R.S. Heflin and C.D. Hudson; 1851-Rob Pool and John Reeves; 1853-W.P. Newell and John Goodin; 1855-W.H. Smith and R.J. Wood; 1857-W.H. Smith, A.W. Denman and Isaac S. Weaver; 1859-F.M. Murray, F.M. Ferrell and J. Hightower; 1861-C.J. Ussery, A.W. Denman and James Aiken.

North Alabama is a fine section of the state. Four counties lie on the north side of the Tennessee River - Lauderdale, Limestone, Madison and Jackson, the latter named in honor of Pres. Jackson. The Tennessee River valley is level, has fine farms east of Decatur and west of Tuscumbia. North Alabama has produced many very able men. Its first settlers were from Virginia, Tennessee, North Carolina and Georgia. Madison County was the second county formed in the state. No other county in the state has produced more men of talent. Huntsville has one of the finest springs in Alabama.

About thirty miles of the Memphis and Charleston Railroad runs through the county. Huntsville was the first town in the state to be incorporated. This was in 1811. The first newspaper published within the limits of the state was the Madison Gazette in Huntsville. It was first printed in 1812. The first bank also was established there in 1819.

The first legislature of the state was held in Huntsville which was then the seat of justice. It was founded in 1806 by John Hunt who came from Tennessee. The town was first named Twickenham. It now has a hotel of the same name. On December 23, 1859 the name was changed to Huntsville by an act dated November 25, 1811. The Convention that framed the Constitution for the would-be State met in Huntsville in July 1819.

One of the most distinguished men of Huntsville was Leroy Pope Walker. He was a native of Madison County, a son of R.W. Walker. He was born in 1817 and was thoroughly educated. He read law under Judge Hopkins, was admitted to the bar and at once removed to Canton, Mississippi. He practiced there with but little promise for a short time, then returned and located at Belleforte, Jackson County, A year later he removed to Moulton and became the partner of the Hon. D.G. Legon in 1843 and in 1844 he represented Lawrence County in the House, but the year after removed to Lauderdale. That county elected him to the House in 1847 and he was made Speaker. In 1848 he was a Cass elector for his district and for the State at large for Pierce and Buchanan. In 1849 he was re-elected to the House, but the year after was elected Judge of the Circuit Court. This position he held nine months, then resigned it. In 1853 he again represented Lauderdale but in 1855 made his residence at Huntsville where he afterwards lived and became the partner of Messrs. R.C. Brickell and Septimus D. Cabaniss.

In 1860 Leroy Pope Walker was a delegate to the historic

Charleston Convention and when the State seceded he was sent as a committee to Tennessee where his speech before the Legislature urging cooperation was able and eloquent. He had just returned when in February President Davis summoned him to a place in the cabinet of "The" storm cradled nation that failed.

To the duties of this high position Mr. Walker brought inexperience, but this was to a great extent if not fully compensated by zeale and energy. The task of organizing and equipping armies almost without materials and with resources limited to the patriotic ardor of the people was a herculean one. His labors were incessant and when he resigned in the Autumn of 1861 his health was shattered. The exact motive for his retirement from the Cabinet is not known, but the belief is general that the self-confidence of Mr. Davis first exhibited itself in the War Office and that Gen. Walker had too much respect for the responsibilities and dignity of his position to let it be subordinated to a mere clerkship.

Gen. Walker was censored for his speech in Montgomery when announcing the fall of Fort Sumter. His utterances were being regarded as official but Mr. Stephens in his "War Between the States" practically exonerates Gen. Walker. He was commissioned as Brig. Gen. on his retirement and ordered to report to Gen. Bragg and was placed in command in Mobile, but held it only a short time. In the spring of 1862 he resigned his commission because he was not assigned to duty. The following year he was appointed Judge of a military court and served to the close of the war. After that time he practiced his profession very successfully in Huntsville.

In 1874 George Houston of Limestone County was elected governor. The legislature passed a bill ordering the state constitution convention in 1875. In the spring of that year delegates in every county were elected. A little later they met in Montgomery and organized by electing Leroy Pope Walker as President of the Convention. They were in session 28 days. There were ten Representatives, three of them negroes. I'm the only living member of that Convention. Gen. Walker was about five feet and ten inches high with less than medium flesh and a fair complexion. His appearance and manners indicated culture and refinement. As an orator he earned his greatest fame. Gen. Walker first married a lady from Mississippi. His second wife was the daughter of the Hon. W.D. Pickett of Montgomery.

Back to Randolph and Roanoke. The first settlers came from Georgia in 1832. Among them were William McClendon, J.M. Baker, James Hathorn, and Hugh Hathorn. Willie McClendon located where the Simm's residence now stands in Roanoke. Just across the West Point Road on the east from the Simm's house, J.M. Baker and McClendon had a store house - a log house. The door was on the side fronting the West Point Road. They sold dry goods. On the side of the road where the high school building stands, a little log house stood. In that groceries were sold. The articles kept there were a barrel of Dexter Whiskey, a sack of coffee, a bag of brown sugar, a box of tobacco, bar lead, gun flints, a keg of powder and some other articles. In that store also was a post office. Postage of letters was five cents and wafers to seal them. Goose quills were used to make pens.

Wiley McClendon was a Primitive Baptist minister. He liked to fish and chew tobacco. He had four or five slaves. His wife was a Longshore. Lelan Allen, a Missionary Baptist minister, was his brother-in-law. Tim Pittman was also a brother-in-law. His wife was a Longshore.

Tim Pittman was probate judge of the court from 1860 to 1865. He was a strong advocate of the Confederate cause. Brade Hand was the county treasurer. Things got so warm in Wedowee that they both left the state and moved to Cedartown, Georgia, and lived and died there.

In 1834 Jim Furlow came from Georgia and built a house at the crossroads---the road from Rock Mills to Louina and the Wedowee and West Point Road. It became the nucleous for the town of Roanoke. Wiley McClendon built where John Radney's office is. He sold dry goods. Baker and Hutchins built where the Post Office is. Dr. W.E. White and brother were where A.M. Awbrey's store is, Norred and Davis where W.H. McMurray is, Wes Thomaston where the old Post Office was. He sold groceries. The McDonald Hotel was built where Yates Motor Co. is. The Masonic Lodge where Guy Hanley's hardware store stands. In 1832 James Hathorn lived where the Widow Pool recently died. Hugh Hathorn lived and died here and was buried near his house. It was one of the best houses in Roanoke and stood for many years. Bath Thornton had a batch of negroes. The first church built in Roanoke was a Methodist. It stood in what is now the cemetery of Roanoke. The house was a frame building and was given by Wiley White a Methodist minister. Later a new building was built where the high school building stands.

Roanoke's first Baptist Church stood on the north side of High Pine Creek where the bridge crosses the creek on the Wedowee Road. I remember how it was built. Two logs were laid on the ground at each end and a post stood about ten feet high.

On top was a split log weather boarded with boards riven out of pine. It had a dirt floor and logs for seats. When Benager Goss came to Roanoke from Heard County, Georgia, a Missionary Baptist preacher, he moved the church to Roanoke and built where it now stands and for years he was the preacher. The First Baptist Church of Roanoke never changed from its first location.

Isham Thornton came from Troup County, Georgia and built on a lot adjoining that of the Baptists. His house was the first house painted in Roanoke. He made buggies. He built a little corn mill and wool factory on the creek where the Louina Road crosses. Griff Wilson ran the wool factory. Mr. Thornton moved to Lineville and died there. He was a very useful man and a good citizen.

W.B. Nichols bought the place. He was the father of Park Nichols and was a clerk in Dr. White & Brothers dry goods store. In 1859 they built a new store house the same year Baker & Mickle built where the Post Office is. Dave Manley was their clerk.

The Baker family came from Newton County, Georgia in 1832. Dr. Davis and the Nichols came from Macon, Georgia in 1852. Davis' wife died soon after. His second wife was a Gillispie, the sister of Mrs. Baker and of Crawford Gillispie, a noted Methodist preacher of Galveston, Texas in 1866.

Mrs. Baker and her father moved to Texas. She had two boys. They came to be noted and honorable men of Texas - Jean and Oscar. Their father was killed in Roanoke in August, 1862 by Israel Moore, a very stout man.

The men of the town had the habit after supper of meeting and talking until bedtime. The Baker's house was on the Ed Mickle lot. Mrs. Mickle was not at home at the time Baker was killed, but her sister was and she tried to keep Baker at home knowing that Moore was in town and mad. It was a bright moonlight night. Moore was in front of the White store of Busing Baker. When he saw Baker coming up he, with his knife open, made at him. Baker was not armed but picked up some rocks and threw one at Moore and which struck him on the face cutting a gash, but did not stun him. Moore made a lunge and struck Baker over the collar bone cutting the main artery. He was soon dead.

Dr. White heard the racket and found Baker dead and Moore laying on his back. Dr. Davis came up and examined Moore and found a bullet hole in the back of his head. "No use to place a guard over him. He will soon be dead." He was picked up and laid on the porch of Bill Davis' grocery. Moore lived all night but never spoke.

The trouble between the two men grew out of the sale of some negroes. Baker had loaned Moore several hundred dollars and took a lien on some negroes. In a settlement Baker bought the negroes. Moore was not satisfied with the price paid. It ended in the death of both men. Dr. Davis was appointed administrator of the Baker Estate.

When the war came up John A. Moore went to Richmond and was appointed quartermaster. He had to make a bond of $20,000. Baker and Mickle went on his bond. In the spring of 1862 Moore came by Roanoke and deposited with Baker and Mickle $20,000. They bought cotton with the money and had it on hand when the war closed. After the death of Baker, M.J. Mickle and Dave Manley formed a partnership and sold dry goods. Their storehouse stood where the Post Office is. Mickle lived in a house where now John Faucett's residence stands. Dave Manly lived where Frank Harper is. In 1852 Sam Jones and Fletcher Haynes, a sadler, had a store on Rock Mill Street where Dr. Yates now lives. They sold family groceries. Bill Wood, a blacksmith, had four acres of land. In 1874 W.D. Mickle and B.F. Weathers bought the place from Wood. Jim Anderson lived where Belcher's barn is.

He made buggies. He built a workshop where the Simm's store is. It had three stories and was of octagon shape. It had 32 windows. The dug-out basement was a blacksmith shop, the second floor a workshop, and the third floor was where he sand papered and painted his buggies. Anderson sold his place to a man named Stewart and moved to Montgomery, Alabama. Stewart sold the place to J.M.K. Guinn who sold the shop to Weathers in 1859.

I boarded at Bill Mickle's and went to school to John A. Moore. He had about forty students. I know of only one other person now living who went to that school and that is Mrs. Sue Pate of Wedowee. A great many of the boys went to the war.

In 1860 John A. Moore taught school at Pine Knot near W.D. Nichols. Moore and his family lived in one of Nichol's houses. Moore's wife was a Widow Smith. She was the mother of Hoyt Smith who became well-known. My wife and Hoyt went to school together at Pine Knot. It is said that Hoyt walked from Roanoke to Oxford, Alabama where he went to school. From Oxford he went to New York City and studied law. He was sent to London, England to adjust some business matters and later became the king's advisor.

Hoyt's mother was a Defrees - a very intelligent woman. Hoyt had his named changed from Smith to Defrees. The family home was in Randolph County near Lineville (then in Randolph). John A. Moore's father was John A. Moore of Georgia, a horse racer and gambler. He lived about six months with his wife and was arrested. His wife married a man named Skinner. They had a son, Jim Skinner, a half-brother of John A. Moore. He also came to Roanoke. He was in my company and was killed in the Battle of Shiloh.

In the fall of this year John A. Moore went to San Francisco, California. He had two daughters who were teachers in high school in San Francisco.

In Roanoke Jim Emory's residence stood where the Presbyterian Church is. Tomlin Wilf ran a blacksmith shop. Riley Fields was a blacksmith. Agga Rose, a tailor by trade, had a little shop where W.A. Hanby's brick store later stood. Agga would get drunk. Bill Davis set a trap in front of Agga's door and baited it will a flask of whiskey. Agga came out of his shop and stood for some time, then took his jacket off and said, "I can whip the man who set this trap." Someone told him the man was gone.

About 1845 Jack Hanley moved to Louina. He was the father of W.A. Hanby. They came from Heard Co., Georgia. W.A. Hanley was born December 15, 1834 in Heard Co. His mother before marriage was a Miss Tomby. In 1845 and for several years he brought the mail from Louina to Roanoke, a bare-footed boy. A man named Donald ran a stage from West Point to Wedowee. He bought the mail on that line and travel also. W.A. Hanley got what education he had in the Louina School.

He was a clerk in Barber's store in 1860. He went to Wesabulgo and opened business for himself. He was wounded in Murphresboro and resigned. His brother, F.N. Hanley, then became Capt. of the Company.

In 1870 W.A. Hanley was nominated to Congress without solicitation on his part. He was elected by a large majority. In 1868 he came to Roanoke and made it his home until his death.

The first schoolhouse stood back of Turberville's residence. The teachers who taught in that building were McComb, Ed Connelly, John A. Moore, John T. Smith and Harper Cole.

John T. Smith made up a Company and left Roanoke the fourth day of July 1861. He was killed in the Battle at Sharpsburg.

Peter Mitchell bought the old school house and had it fitted up for a dwelling. In 1873-4 a new schoolhouse was built. It cost $6,000. $5,000 had been subscribed: A building committee of five was elected: W.A. Hanley, Dr. White, Sam Fausett, M.J. Mickle and B.F. Weathers - five. W.A. Hanley was made chairman of the committee. Mr. Hanley donated the lot. A rock post was placed at each corner. The committee advertised for bids. R.M. Greene, the lowest bidder, got the contract and agreed to furnish all of the material and complete the house, for which he was to get $5,000. The committee agreed to advance to him money to enable him to get pay for material and labor. W.B. Taylor and A Mr. Stevens were furnishing the lumber. Guin fell down on his contract before the building was completed.---all money gone, so W.A. Hanley, Dr. White and B.F. Weathers made a note to the West Point Bank for $1,500 and made a contract with Nath Davis to complete the building. Certificates of stock were issued. The building was kept insured for the benefit of the stockholders. John P. Shaffer was placed in charge of the school. Mr. Shaffer was a good organizer. He soon built up a fine school. He had a great many boarders from LaGrange, West Point and other places. Prof. Erdman of LaGrange, Georgia was the teacher of music.

Mr. Shaffer was in charge of the Roanoke school for several years. He was a most excellent school teacher...a fluent speaker with much humor, big hearted and sympathetic. After several years work he asked to be relieved and resigned.

George Stevens of Rock Mills took charge of the school. The night before the second term was to begin the schoolhouse burned. The stockholders met and passed a resolution to give their insurance to the rebuilding. They had $3,000 that went into the new building. It was brick with a slate roof. Coon McPherson had the contract. Another teacher in the meantime had been in charge of the school; Stevens, Dr. Blake, Pinkard, Garrison, J.D. and Ben Moore and L. Jones.

In 1887 the railroad from Opelika to Roanoke was completed. In 1888-9 Bedford Ponder built the Roanoke Warehouse. In 1890 he organized the first bank in Roanoke. In 1894 he sold his stock to Wimberly who later sold out to Fred Vaughan.

In 1879 the first brick house in Roanoke was built by W.A. Hanley. Fred Wagner was contractor. Hill, Hardy and Co. built a brick store adjoining the Hanley house. In 1866-7-8 Weathers & Pate sold dry goods.

In 1874 Weathers was appointed postmaster. Capt. Thompson of Stroud rode the mail from West Point Georgia to Wedowee. Bill Culpepper rode the mail from Rowena to Franfort, Georgia. In 1876 Weathers & Mickles store was robbed and $500 worth of goods stolen.

About 1890 Morgan Schuessler came to Roanoke and engaged in the supply business. A.J. Driver bought cotton for him. In 1892 Morgan Schuessler died. Major and Bob Schuessler then came. They located where Dr. Yates store is. Bill Ussery came from High Shoals. He ran a hotel on the second floor of the Hanley House for several years. A man named Clemmons ran it for a while before Ussery.

The Roanoke Cotton Mill was built about 1900 by a stock company. Harvey Enloe became superintendent. He came from West Point, Georgia and had been with the mill up to the present.

Henry Knight came from Dadeville. Pinkard and Griffin came from Opelika as dealers in Hardware. Reed and John Carlisle came from Chambers County and did a supply business. The Awbreys came from Heard Co., Georgia. W.H. Brittain came from Troup Co., Georgia. Dr. Trent and Frank Harper came from Rock Mills.

Frank Harper is the biggest peanut dealer in the county. W.W. Campbell and J.C. Wright came from Tuskeegee to Roanoke. They were bankers and owned the oil mill, acid plant, ice factory and Roanoke Cotton Warehouse. Their business in Roanoke was extensive.

The Stevenson family came to Roanoke over forty years ago. John B. Stevenson was a noted Methodist minister. He had four sons - Leon, Olin, Worth and Henry. The latter is a Methodist preacher; W.W. a doctor; Olin and Leon are very prominent newspapermen, well-known in the State of Alabama. The family came from North Alabama, the father from Tennessee.

Up to 1860 Roanoke was the fighting place of the bullies on Saturdays. Rus Duke was the Captain of the Jackson Allen Co. Ike Broughton was Captain of the High Pine Company. The two companies would meet in Roanoke on Saturday, drink, fiddle and dance until about 3 p.m. By that time they had got good and mellow and wanted to show their skill in fighting. Someone would make a ring, roll up his sleeves and bawl out that he was the best man on the hill. No quicker than said someone would accept his challenge.

They would knock and beat each other sometimes till bloody. When one said he had enough that ended the fight. They would go in the grocery, wash their faces, take a drink and shake hands in good fellowship.

In front of the Masonic Building was an oak tree and a horse block. Boy-like I would stand on the horse block so I could see the men fight. They were not mad -- they wanted to show their strength. They didn't want to kill each other. The man who had a weapon on his person was considered to be a coward. Fighting was cruel fun. The men in those days were much stronger than in this age. Up to the war in 1861, men did not go armed. But now, it is a common thing. Some attend church with a pistol in their hip pocket. It is a disgrace for anyone. It is a constitutional right for us to have firearms for our protection, but we should use them in the right way.

THE END

The reader is cautioned to keep in mind that this reminiscense was written many years after the events occurred, and there are probably some inaccuracies.

An old home of the Heflin family built in the mid-1800s in the Louina Community. Courtesy of the Birmingham Public Library.

RANDOLPH COUNTY, ALABAMA, SIXTY-TWO YEARS AGO
THE RED MAN'S HOME, THE WHITE MAN'S EDEN

by

J.M.K. Guinn

1894 - 1896

Reproduced with permission
of the
Birmingham Public Library
1984

Transcribed by
Library Project 3529
Works Progress Administration
Under Sponsorship of the Birmingham Library Board
Birmingham, Alabama
1937

Foreword

This history of Randolph County, Alabama ran serially in the Wedowee "Randolph Toiler" from December 6, 1894 to March 13, 1896. The author, J.M.K. Guinn and his brother were editors of the Toiler. This is a transcript of a copy lent the Birmingham Public Library by the State Department of Archives and History, Montgomery. The work was done by Library Project 3529, Works Progress Administration under the sponsorship of the Birmingham Library Board.

RANDOLPH
SIXTY-TWO YEARS AGO
THE RED MAN'S HOME
THE WHITE MAN'S EDEN
J.M.K. GUINN

Written for The Toiler

Alabama was admitted to the Union, December 14, 1819, and South western, West, North and North eastern sectional territory, where accessible to navigable water courses, was rapidly settled. Thirteen years afterwards (March 2, 1832,) a treaty was formulated with the Creek Indians through Chief McIntosh, which shortly after cost his life. And on December 18, 1832, all this territory was organized into new counties, Randolph being one of them; and almost the entire eastern part of Alabama was the home of the Red Man-a perfect Eden-in length North and South more than 200 miles, width averaged 75 miles. North rugged and mountainous gradually descends toward the South into rolling formation of valleys and flat, low stretches to the Chattahoochee river. Northeast rich deposits of gold, copper, iron and mica; clear bold springs, branches, creeks and rivers; fine timbers, fertile soil, mild climate, pure air and good health.

In Randolph county sixty-two years ago the river, creek and branch bottoms and their hillsides were covered with reed, cane and cane-brakes, in valleys and hills with grass and vegetation two and three feet high, the high flat ridges and hills with pine, oak, hickory, chestnut and chinquapin promiscously; hickorynuts, acorns, chestnuts and chinquapins could be found plentiful after the woods were burned in March and April. We have raked up a hat full within a yard's space.

The chinquapin grew in forests sometimes for miles in length and as thick as a plum orchard, but not so high with limbs, bent into umbrella shape loaded down with fruit, and when ripened, the grandest and most interesting sight the eye ever beheld.

Grapes (summer) grew in rich hollows and on hillsides, and baskets full have been gathered in December and January.

Walnuts, hazlenuts, red and black haw were plentiful.

Whortle and gooseberries, when not burned over in the fall and winter, were never failing crops, on which men, beast and bird lived luxuriously.

New ground (land cultivated the first year) made fine corn, wheat, oats, potatoes, pumpkins, and watermelons grew to perfection, cotton but little planted.

Horses needed no feed unless worked. Cattle wintered well, their owners drove great herds to market and kept the people supplied with money. Hogs kept fat in the woods and the supply of meat was bountiful.

Game was plentiful; sometimes as many as 15 or 20 deer could be seen herded together; a large drove of wild turkeys was a common thing; squirrels (gray and fox), opossums and rabbits were numerous; wild ducks, pigeons and black birds came in flocks and wintered here.

Fish of all kinds, sizes and qualities filled the creeks and rivers, and could be seen 8 and 10 feet deep swimming and darting about; and last, the little bee, with its rich deposits stored away in mountain oak and pine, though plentiful, hard to find.

With all these good things to eat and enjoy, the pioneers had the wolf, cat, fox, opossum, mink, owl, hawk, as well as the cruel revengeful Indians and dishonest treacherous white men to watch.

What thought can interest you more than that to read about the Red man's home and the White man's Eden, and as it comes from the hand of God?

County Established

Number Two

Written for The Toiler.

The General Assembly, in 1832, passed an act establishing Randolph County, as follows, to wit: That all that tract of county bound as follows, to wit: Beginning at a point where the line dividing Townships 16 and 17 cross the line dividing Ranges 8 and 9, East of the Meridian of Huntsville; thence along said boundary down to the line dividing Coffee's and Freeman's Survey; thence due West along said line to the aforesaid line dividing Ranges 8 and 9; thence along said line due North to the beginning; shall constitute one separate and distinct county to be called and known by the name of Randolph. Approved December 18, 1832.

Randolph County at that time embraced Townships 17, 18, 19, 20, 21 and North fractional part of 22, and Ranges 9, 10, 11, 12, 13 and 14. The latter two being fractional on account of the Georgia State line of the East. This made the county about 31½ miles North and South, 24¼ on North end and 30 1/3 on the South end; an average of 27 3/8 miles wide, with an area of 862 5/16 square miles or 551,880 square acres.

Randolph County is situated on the Coosa Land District, which is all that tract of country east of the Meridian of Huntsville, with township line running East and West and numbered from North to South from 1 to 22; and range lines running North and South and numbered from West to East, from 1 to 14.

The line dividing Randolph and Chambers counties is the line dividing Coffee's and Freeman's Survey and makes Township 22 fractional.

A Township is six miles square, bound on North and South by township lines and on the East and West by range lines, and with 36 sections each one mile square; containing 640 acres divided into 16 quarter sections or 80 acre lots.

Sections in a township are designated by numbers commencing at the northeast corner and run from 1 to 36 consecutively; sections are divided into quarter sections, thus: NE¼ NW¼ SW¼ and SE¼.

Range one is a true meridian line east from Huntsville and runs north and south; all range lines or sub-division lines running north and south are parallel, and with the same variations. Surveyors generally corner at Section 36 and run north: this is supposed to give them the correct variations of that section and range line. It is said, by old surveyors, the variations change every fifty years from east to west and vice versa.

The Coffee and Freeman line dividing Randolph and Chambers counties is neither township nor a sectional, but a made line, and that gives fractional townships, fractional quarter sections which are designated by letters A,B,C, etc. The line dividing Alabama and Georgia is another made line with a variation of about 1/5 of a mile to the section west of north running north, this also gives fractional townships, sections and quarter sections. Little and big Tallapoosa rivers gives fractional quarter sections; so it happens these fractions are some times larger than quarter sections, but generally smaller. T. 21, R. 13, Sec. 1, contains only 0.17 of an acre; T. 21, R. 14, Sec. 3, contains only 2.97 acres. Robert W. Higgins entered Sec. 1, T. 21, R. 13, and Benjamin Zachary entered S. 3, T. 21, R. 14.

In 1868 the General Assembly in establishing new counties cut off Township 17 on the north to Cleburne and Range 9 on the west to Clay. Now the county from north to south is 25½ miles in length and an average of 21 3/8 miles wide with an acre of 545 1/16 square miles or 348,840 acres.

There was a treaty made March 2, 1832, with the Creek Indians which gave to each Indian a half Section 320 acres to be selected and located by him; with this the United States reserved the 16th sections for school purposes and the rest was subject to entry.

ORGANIZATION
Number Three

Written for The Toiler.

The time of the County's advent into existance and organic sisterhood, is one of the most important historical characteristics of her future.

It is conceded where there is an existance there was a beginning. Therefore, in order to be as accurate as the facts will justify, in the absence of recorded evidence, it will be necessary to use circumstantial evidence when it will throw light on the point desired to be established, especially as to time of organization.

The first official and authentic evidence we find is the act of the legislature establishing the County's boundary, and approved December 18, 1832.

The second is a power of attorney given by John Camp, of Randolph County, Alabama, to Neil Furgerson of Carroll County, Georgia and dated January 9th, 1833. Attested: Archibald Sawyer, J.C.C.

These two recorded official acts we think, will establish the time of the county's organization, and her legal and official executive control and jurisdiction. The law provided that the legislature should elect these judges, but in case of vacancy the governor appointed them. Just when Judge Sawyer was sworn into office is a mere matter of conjecture; however it must have been between December 18, 1832, and January 9, 1833, an interval of 22 days. The legislature having the power to elect these judges, being then in session, and having passed an act designating the boundary, and names given to Benton, Talladega, Randolph, Chambers, Coosa, Tallapoosa, Russell, Macon, Barbour and Sumpter counties, it suggests itself as reasonable to suppose the candidates for County Court Judges were present then, or had on file an application asking the election and were notified and went immediately to Tuscaloosa, the State Capital, and were sworn in.

There was no railroad in Alabama then, nor is it reasonable to suppose any post office in this wild unsettled territory; besides it would take a person by private conveyance (horseback) three to four days, and perhaps longer, as there was only one wagon or any other kind of road, and that was the McIntosh Trail, in this section of country. To go from Tuscaloosa at that time would have been on an Indian or cow trail route.

There was no member from any one of these counties in the legislature, for they were not organized then; but there may have been, and no doubt were representative petitioners sent from each, and Judge Sawyer may have been, and more than likely was one of them. Otherwise, these representative commissioners may have returned bringing the Judge's commission or notified him and he went immediately to Tuscaloosa and was sworn in. But, still, we are not justified in saying whether Judge Sawyer was sworn in, in December, 1832, or January, 1833. There was, so far as we know, no one authorized by law officially, to administer an oath or qualify Judge Sawyer here at that time and the Judge had to go somewhere else to be qualified. We suppose December, 1832, and at Tuscaloosa.

THE COUNTY SEAT

Number Four

Written for The Toiler.

This subject has elicited no little discussion as to the identical place where the first court was held, and it had been questioned as to who was wrong.

It takes facts to make history-traditions and suppositions are not always facts; but our readers must indulge us if we should have to use some traditions as facts, to get a seat for the county, or else leave her standing first on one foot and then on the other until 1835. It is not reasonable to suppose though, young, active and frolicsome she did not sit down somewhere, whether under a tree, on the grass or a rock; for either would have been commodious, while her other and special wards domiciled in hollow trees and under wagon beds for safe keeping and quick delivery.

The first County Seat was at or near Hedgeman Triplett's ferry on the Big Tallapoosa river, the present Blake's ferry, ten miles west of Wedowee.

Commissioners Court, April Term, 1834: "It is ordered (by the court) that Hedgeman Triplett gets the establishment of a ferry boat on the Tallapoosa river at or near the County seat in Randolph County." Attested: George McKaskle, Willis Wood. Archibald Sawyer, J.C.C., William Vardeman, Clerk.

While the above is official evidence of a County seat somewhere "at or near", it does not locate definitely and we introduce tradition, which says, "The first court was held on the bank of the river at Triplett's ferry under a large oak tree; that Judge Sawyer set on a log and leaned against the tree while presiding, and that tree is of course the first county seat."

Another tradition is handed down to us and says: "The first court was held under a large mulberry tree near Triplett's house, which was more than one hundred yards southwest of the ferry; that Triplett furnished the court with seats and grub, and that was the county seat."

A third tradition says: "The first court was held on the flat rock a mile west of Triplett's ferry and this was the county seat."

Now let us see if the minutes of the April term of the Commissioner's court, 1834, when carefully read in connection with the traditions won't reconcile as to time and place and establish the first court and county seat. There were three courts, viz: County, Commissioner's and Circuit; the first County Court was held February, 1834, and the first Circuit Court was held April 15, 1834. An act of the legislature, 1832-3 says: "The County Courts shall be holden on the 3rd Mondays in June and November each and every year; courts of roads and revenue February, May and September and December; Circuit Court shall commence on the fourth Mondays after third Mondays in March and September." Now, if there was a Circuit Court held in 1833, it would have been held on the 14th day of October, only four days after the first Circuit Clerk and Sheriff had entered on duty, and no jury drawn nor papers served, and it is not reasonable to suppose a Circuit Court was held under these circumstances in 1833. There had been no County nor Commissioners Court held prior to that time, no jurors drawn nor no one to do so until October 10th, four days prior to the time designated by law to hold a Circuit Court. These facts justify us in saying there was no Circuit Court held in 1833.

THE COUNTY SEAT

Number Five

Written for The Toiler:

The law made provision for two commissioners to locate the County Seat; in the absence of any act of theirs we take the minutes of the Commissioners Court. There was no point designated in these minutes other than indefinitely "at or near" Triplett's ferry.

The County Court was the first court held, and that was November, 1833, and under the oak tree that stood on the west bank of Big Tallapoose river at Triplett's ferry; and why? The character and habits of the Judge and Sheriff of that court could not have desired or needed more or better accommodations that the shade and shelter of a large tree, for whatever held, it was in the open air and outside of any building. Under all circumstances, it is reasonable to believe Hedgeman Triplett, County Surveyor and owner of the ferry, had the only house in miles of there, and furnished the Court with what accomodations he had.

There were only two cases docketed for trial at this court: Ibba Taylor vs James B. Jones, and Ibba Taylor vs Silas Taylor;

both suits were dismissed at defendant's cost. John W. Rutton was security for cost; with Archibald Sawyer, an old bachelor as Judge, William Hightower, Sheriff; A.O. Nix and ___ Freeman, Attorney. A Philadelphia lawyer couldn't make believe that court went a mile to sit on a rock instead of the grass at the ferry. No, not ten steps further than the fulfillment of the requirements of the law did that honorable court go. The law said "at or near," and here sit and sat the first court of Randolph County.

The tradition that claimed the first court held under the mulberry tree was doubtless the first Commissioners Court held, and that was February, 1834. But it would be very plausible and reasonable to believe the first Circuit Court Judge would select the flat rock as a more suitable place to hold his court, and we are persuaded to believe that this was done, and that court was held April 15, 1834. The minutes of the Commissioners Court says, "at or near." This left it discretionary with the court which designated no one certain place anywhere near the ferry. With these facts, the supposition corroborates the tradition, viz: The first court was County Court, and was held November, 1833, under a large oak on the west bank of Big Tallapoosa river at Hedgeman Triplett's ferry. The first Commissioners, but second court, was held February, 1834, under a large mulberry tree at or near Hedgeman Triplett's dwelling house, south about 100 yards from the ferry. The first Circuit, but third court, was held on the flat rock one mile west of the ferry in April 1834. The character of the courts, the probable attendance, the time of year held and the conditions of the weather had much to do with the place located. The records show as facts one, if not two, terms of the County Court, November 1833, and June 1834, two terms of the Commissioners Court February and April, 1834, and one term of the Circuit Court, April, 1834, at or near Triplett's ferry; but does that fact within itself establish a county Court or oak tree county seat, a Commissioners Court or Mulberry tree County District, a Circuit Court or Flat Rock County Seat. We have failed up to the present to find any name for the county seat: it is rather suggested, however, to call it "Tripplett's." We find there was an act for the organization of certain counties, approved January 12th, 1833, which made it the duty of the citizens of such counties as shall not have had commissioners appointed by the legislature, to locate the seat of justice in their respective counties, to elect said commissioners. Section 8 of said act is as follows: "And be it further enacted, that the Commissioners for the counties aforesaid, shall locate the county seat of justice of said counties respectively, at or near the center of said counties, if practicable, if not, at the most eligible point, not exceeding six miles from the center of said counties." Tripplett's ferry was more than six miles from the center. There were no Commissioners appointed by the legislature for Randolph County, neither was there an election held as provided, on the first Monday of March, 1833. There may have been an election for these Commissioners in August, at the time the first county officers were elected in 1833, as we find the Clerk of County and Circuit Courts and Sheriff were elected then.

We are inclined to think there was only one Circuit Court held at the flat rocks, and the county seat was moved to Wedowee some time during the summer of 1834. Our reasons for believing so are these: The law required the county seat within 6 miles of the center. Tripplett's ferry was more than that, while Wedowee was within one and a half miles of the center. No one had the right to locate or remove it but the Commissioners. There was but one house at or near the ferry while there was an Indian town and several white: Joseph Benton, Asa Hearn and others at Wedowee.

EARLY DAYS---COUNTY SEAT MOVED TO WEDOWEE

First Court at Wedowee Held in an Indian Chief's Wigwam

Number Six

Written for The Toiler.

Some time in the fall of 1834 or spring of 1835 the county seat of Randolph County was moved to Wedowee.

Tradition says: The first court held at Wedowee was held in Wedowee's wigwam; a chief at the time, lived in the Indian village half mile northeast of the present town of Wedowee. We suppose from what tradition says, his name originally was Wah-wah-nee or swift runner, Wah-hah-tah-nee or the fast runner, Wah-kee-bah-nah or the hard runner and Wah-wah-shee or the quick runner. Tradition, however, gives the following interpretations to the name Wedowee: First, rain or falling water, second; rolling or swift water; third, swift running water. We find it was written by some Wa-daw-wee; others Wid-o-wee. Wah-wah-nee, swift runner, a chief from which the creek took its name, and the town from the creek, it seems to be conceded. Wah-wah-nee, or swift runner, would, in our opinion, characterize the name of a chief Indian, and at the same time describe the creek clearly and exactly, for it is a swift runner. Rain or falling water does not describe the character of the creek, other than clear and pure. Rolling or swift water would do very well as a description of the creek but not so well for the name of man.

We found, seven years after Wedowee had been located and named, race tracks near the town said to have been used by the Indians. These race tracks were on the lower bottom field of Mr. William Traylor's, the east and lower end of these race tracks were not far from the spring and ran within a few paces of the present cotton house on the creek, and the west or upper end stopped near where a walnut tree now stands. These race tracks suggest another good reason for the name "swift runner." To the south of these race tracks on a ridge, and opposite and north of the "ten foot hole," there was about 100 feet square, smooth and hard as a floor apparently, where it is said, the Indians had their brand dance.

At the time tradition says the first court was held, the Indians were friendly with the whites. As you know there had been a treaty made with the Creeks on January 24, 1826, and a part of them had gone west. On March 2, 1832, the other Creeks in Alabama and the Muskogees of Georgia made their last treaty with the United States. Rolly and Chilly McIntosh signed this last treaty. In the treaty of March 24, 1832, it was provided the creeks should be paid for their lands, except half sections which were set apart for each head of family, to be selected by themselves on which they were to reside until their final departure west, the reserve then to be subject to sale by the United States and the proceeds to be paid to them the same as the other lands. The treaty provided protection in person and property. Under these considerations it would be very reasonable to suppose a court was held in Wah-wah-nee's wigwam. J.W. Bradshaw, who lives near Wedowee said to us a few days since: "I was at the first and last Circuit Court ever held in the Courthouse at Wedowee." Knowing he came to Wedowee in 1836, and there had been Circuit Courts held at

Triplett and Wedowee, as the records show, we were about to question his recollection, for his word is unimpeachable, when we happened to think it was a sell, of which he delights in, and sure enough it was, for he qualified the "first" and "last" court with the phrase "in the Courthouse." There was no Courthouse in Wedowee until after March 14, 1836. The town was surveyed and platted by Hedgeman Triplett, December 1st, 1835, and the first sale of town lots was March 14, 1836. The first lot sold was 13, on which Dr. J.R. Hood's dwelling now stands. It was bid off by W.H. Cunningham, Circuit Court Clerk, William Hightower, then Sheriff, bid off at the same sale lot 108 and during 1836 a log Courthouse was built on this lot, near where R.T. West's store stands at present. So, J.W. Bradshaw was no doubt correct when he said: "I was at the first Circuit Courts ever held in the courthouse at Wedowee." We quote J.W. Bradshaw again; he says: "The minutes of the court were kept on bark." At first, we thought he was talking through his hat, but when we began to think about how few white families there were here, no post office in the county and the nearest trading point perhaps, at Wetumpka, then in Montgomery County, how strict the United States laws were over trade agents who were under $5,000 bonds and the little use they had for writing papers, we decided to believe him. Imagine, if you please, how far from any where but home these people were and how many other things more needful than paper and you will believe him too. This accounts for the missing official records in the Clerk's office.

FIRST COURT HOUSE A LOG CABIN WITH DIRT FLOOR

JAIL BUILT IN 1839, AT A COST OF $1,000
CONTRACT, LET FOR A NEW COURT HOUSE IN 1839

Number Seven

Written for The Toiler.

Under the treaty of March 24, 1832, Che-wasti-hadjo held the north half section 3, township 20, range 11, on which the Indian village was situated. Judge Archibald Sawyer entered the east ½ southwest, and west ½ southwest ¼ southeast ¼ section 3, township 20, range 11, October 5, 1836, on which the town of Wedowee was then located. The legislature in December, 1832, in the act establishing the boundaries of the new counties, you should remember, made provision for two commissioners to locate the county seats. We have no official information as to whom or when these commissioners were elected yet it is reasonable to suppose such were elected at the August election in 1833; and temporarily located Triplett's ferry as the county seat, afterwards finding it was not near enough (within six miles) to the center of the county, and after the April term of the Circuit Court held near Triplett on the Flat rock, selected Wedowee. The supposition is that the court held in Wah-wah-nee's wigwam was the October term of the Circuit Court in 1834. It was, at least, one step towards higher civilization-from a rock to a wigwam-not only with the red man but white pioneers. It was an honor, no doubt, Chief Wah-wah-nee and his people appreciated and certainly an act of kindness and liberality to the honorable court. We can't tell where the courts were held in 1835; if not held in Wah-wah-nee's wigwam or some other wigwam or white man's house, most likely out under a tree in the open air. For while the commissioners had selected the present location, the town was not platted until December 1, 1835, nor lots sold until March 16, 1836. The spring term of the Circuit Court held afterwards was in April, and no doubt in the new court house. Sheriff Hightower's duty was to secure a place

18

for the court and as he owned the lot on which the house was built, and in the absence of any record or other evidence or information, the county paid for it. It must have been a private investment without dimensions or accomodations specified more fully than, "it was for the use of the court." With dirt floor, three holes cut for windows and one for a door, without a shutter to either, no seat for the clerk or seats for the jury. Another and higher step or object lesson of civilization from an Indian wigwam to a pioneer's cabin. What need for door shutters, seat for jurors or table for clerk with a bachelor judge, clerk and Sheriff and the proceedings of the court kept on hickory and poplar bark with lead pencils and the prisoners jailed in a hollow tree or wagon bed turned bottom up--Sheriff Hightower bossing the job? We find the following order of the Commissioners Court:

February Term, 1837

It is ordered by the court that the Sheriff (Willis Wood) be instructed and required to have such repairs made to the court house as seems most necessary, viz: A Judge's seat, clerk's table and seats for the accommodation of the jury and with a good and substantial door shutter, and that said work be completed by the Circuit Court next ensuing and that he present his account to the next term of this court for allowance.
William McKnight)
William Mullaley) Comm.
Thomas Blake   )

Hundreds of The Toiler's readers may imagine the pioneer fathers were old fogies when they read about a dirt floor, court house without shutters to door or seats to sit on. We won't think anything strange if they do, for there are but few of them who know anything about pioneer life and inconveniences. "Maybe so" when we tell you, you won't "think so." There was no saw nor grist mill nearer than Dickson's, the old Jacob Eichelberger, and now James McCosh mill in the extreme south east corner of the county. We don't know whether Dickson sawed lumber then or not. The business and dwelling houses were built out of logs or slate 6 or 8 feet long, split timber fashion and wattle in. Whip saws that two good hands would cut 300 feet of plank per day, with broad axes in the hands of skilled laborers were a great help toward building until saw mills run by water were introduced. Jacob Peeler put in a mill one mile east and at the present W.W. Dodson mill place, and sawed lumber and ground corn and wheat and new frame houses went up all about.

Congress passed an act, approved July 2nd, 1836, locating and establishing the following mail routes: From Franklin, Heard county, Georgia to Wedowee, to Talladega; from Jacksonville via White Planes and Boiling Springs, to Wedowee, from LaFayette, via White Plains, to Jacksonville. An act approved July 7, 1838, the following route were established: From Montreal, via Wedowee, to Carrollton, Georgia; from Hickory Level, via Adrian's ferry to Arbacooche Gold Mines, and Canal Gold Mines, to Franklin, Ga.

At the September term, 1837, of the Commissioners Court an order was passed to advertise town lots for sale on October 30th. This notice was ordered published in "The Southern Register," at Jacksonville, Alabama and the "Columbus Sentinel": at the same term a contract was let to build a new jail. (Hightower's hollow poplar tree jail was too small to facilitate the dispatch of business and comfort of its inmates we suppose). Leonard W. Young bid off the contract at $1,000. Jeff Faulkner and Jeptha V. Smith,

County Building Commissioners, reported the completion and acceptance of the jail December 14, 1839. At the August term 1839, a contract for building a court house let. Hightower's court house, like his jail, couldn't accomodate the court and facilitate business. Isaac Baker bid it off at $2,000, to be completed by August, 1840. It was received September 5th, 1840. At the May term, 1839, there was an order to advertise another sale of town lots in the Jacksonville Republican; that grand and true patriot, James F. Gran, was it's editor.

On January 1st, 1840, that true and tried, first and most faithful of all county judges, Archibald Sawyer, retired to private life after serving from January 1st, 1833 to January 1st, 1840, seven long, honest, faithful years, and so far as we know or the official records show, honored, loved and respected in public and private life. With his retirement, a name associated with him from the first to the last official act ceased to be officially recognized as the county seat---it was Wedowee.

Andy Burnham, county judge and McDonald, county seat January 1st, 1840.

RANDOLPH'S COUNTY SEAT
NAME CHANGED FROM WEDOWEE TO MCDONALD
FIRST COUNTY OFFICIALS

And some leading citizens receive our attention in this issue.

Number Eight

Written for The Toiler.

We told you in number seven series that Wedowee had been changed to McDonald on January 1st, 1840. Now we tell you by whom and why it was done.

There was a keen, shrewd, well-educated young man who had a great deal of curiosity, ambition and adventure in his make-up with plenty of energy and sport which he never allowed to lie dormant. This young man's name was Francis M. Perryman. He held a position which brought him in contact with all classes, and of course his inventive genius led him to play on the credulity of the curious. His first step was to change High Pine to Roanoke; then Chulafinne, and being successful, he petitioned the Post Master General to change Wedowee to McDonald. Of course, the citizens were wrathy, but ignorant of the course of relief. They were not up to the ways of petitioning, nor did they know why the names of these post offices had been changed. The joke is too good to keep. Finally letters to their congressman began to visit Washington and in one was a request to have McDonald changed back to Wedowee. This of course lead to the exposure which brought before the people a petition with a large number of names asking and praying for the change. Every man, woman, boy and negro that was known to young Frank was on that petition. He had every post office in the county named to suit his own fancy. His first petition was an experiment more through curiosity than anything else. Finding a key to unlock Uncle Sam's post office officials, he utilized it; so you now know why the change in the name of your county seat was made.

We find when Jeff Faulkner entered the office of Judge of County Court, his first official act recognized Wedowee as the name of the county seat, and from that time since it still goes as Wedowee. It was just four years, and during Judge Andrew Burnham and John D. Bowen's judgeship McDonald was the name. We drop Wedowee and her courts for a few weeks in order to introduce to you the men who filled the various county officers from her earliest days down to the present.

Judge of the County or Orphan's Court, Archibald Sawyer, an old bachelor who lived at Sawyers ferry, Oakfuskee, was elected Judge by the General Assembly December 18th, 1832, qualified and entered on duty about January 1st, 1833. He was a man of rough frontier or pioneer habits, had a good common business education, honest and upright in his dealings and stood favorable with his people. He was one of the first settlers and had been a soldier in the Indian wars. He was afterwards a Colonel in the State Militia and took pride in battalion muster. He was generous to a fault, and made donations to the Masonic Lodge which bears his name today. His grave can be seen at the Masonic cemetery and was the first interred in honor of its donator. His brother, Joe, a bachelor also, lived several years afterwards and to his death with J.W. Guinn, and died at Homer, Angelina county, Texas. Being only a boy when the judge died we know but little of his many good deeds and traits of character and will try to get some one more and better acquainted and qualified to furnish us with a fuller publication.

His last official connection with the county judgeship ended December 31st, 1839.

RANDOLPH'S COUNTY OFFICERS

From 1833 to 1892

Number Nine

Written for The Toiler.

Judge of County or Orphans Court:

Archibald Sawyer, January 1st, 1833, Andrew Burnham succeeded him January 1, 1840.
John D. Bowen, January 1st, 1843.
Jefferson Falkner, January 17, 1844.
John Reaves, August 18, 1845.
James W. Guinn, January 1, 1846; and held until May 23, 1850.

By an act of the legislature this court was abolished and Courts of Probate were substituted.

Judges of Probate Court

Joseph Benton, elected May 23, 1850.
Joseph Curry, May 20, 1856.
T.L. Pittman, May 13, 1862.
R.S. Heflin, August 5, 1865.
W.W. Dodson, February 20, 1868.
D.L. Davis, November 7, 1874.
S.E.A. Reaves, August 20, 1880.
T.J. Thomason, August 26, 1886.
A.J. Weathers, November 4, 1892.

County Court Clerks

William Vardeman, January 1st, 1833. (He was removed by the

County Court April 14, 1834.)
W.H. Cunningham, April 14, 1834.
Jefferson Falkner, October 26, 1835.
W.H. Cunningham, Deputy, January 20, 1839.
W.M. Buchanan, January 14, 1839.
C.W. Slatham, October 2, 1843; he held until May 23, 1850, when the office was abolished.

Circuit Court Clerks

Johnathan Camp, elected August and qualified October 8, 1833, to succeed himself.
W.H. Cunningham, October 31, 1834.
W.H. Wood, December 6, 1848.
John L.C. Donner, January 23, 1849.
R.T. Smith, February 22, 1852.
John Reaves, September 6, 1853.
H.H. Wise, August 12, 1864.
W.E. Connelly, August 27, 1865.
H.H. Wise, November 13, 1865.
J.H. Davis, Jr., March 14, 1867.
R.H. Bolt, February 12, 1868.
John T. Owens, December 11, 1876.
O.H. Perryman, August 13, 1880.
J.W. Stewart, August 20, 1886.
B.J. Ford, August 12, 1892.

Sheriffs

William Hightower, October 8, 1833.
Willis Wood, October 11, 1836.
Sylvanus Walker, October 26, 1839.
Robert Caskey, was elected on 1st Monday in August, 1842, but by some hokus pokus he did not qualify until later.
Samuel Carpenter, October 1842.
R. Coskey, March 18, 1844. He was allowed ex-officio from October 1842, for his full term.
W.P. Newell, September 14, 1845.
Almond P. Hunter, September 7, 1848.
Joel T. Morrison, February 22, 1850.
Wilson Falkner, April 28, 1853.
J.M. Hearn, September 23, 1853.
A.W. Denman, August 14, 1854.
Wilson Falkner, August 10, 1856.
John V. McKee, August 14, 1860.
Larkin Breed, August 11, 1863.
Linsey McKee, August 3, 1865.
S.E. Jordan, June 22, 1867.
Jenkins Bennett, November 15, 1871.
Robert Merrill, November 7, 1874.
J.B. Amos, December 20, 1874.
W.C.S. Robertson, August 15, 1877.
M.V. Mullins, August 14, 1880.
Wilson L. Ayers, August 25, 1884.
R.H. Ford, August 16, 1888.
Robert Willoughby, August 9, 1892.

Number Ten

Written for The Toiler.

Tax Assessors

The taxes were assessed and collected by the same persons who were appointed by the Commissioner's Court until 1841.

Richard Jones, May 1834.
William Hightower, Sheriff, June, 1835.
Willis Wood, Sheriff, May, 1837.
Sylvanus Walker, Sheriff, May, 1838.
A.P. Hunter, 1839.
Hugh Harris, elected, August, 1841.
George C. Powell, assistant, 1842.

The law was changed and assessor appointed in battalion districts in 1843: John Hanna, district 1; Hugh Montgomery, 2; Thomas Gilland, 3; R.W. Caskey, 5; James F. White, 6; Samuel Carpenter, 7; James M. Pittman, 8; Samuel T. Owens, 9; James M. Hornsby, 10; James Duke, 11.

1844

Micajah Goodwin, W.G. Falkner, J.H. Allen, Andrew Burnham. The law was changed and office made elective in 1845.

Elijah Humphries elected April, 1845. The law was changed in 1848 and district assessor appointed.

W.F. Caldwell, July, 1848.
Harrison Crow, January 1848.
W.A. Striplin, July, 1848.
Harrison Crow, January, 1849.
R.L. Robertson, January, 1849.
Joseph Savage, January, 1849.
W.F. Caldwell, February, 1849.
Law changed again.
W.H. Spruce, April, 1850.
E.M. Burgess, February, 1851.
D.A. Perryman, August, 1853.
W.T. Wood, August, 1854.
J.C. Burson, August, 1855.
William Ingram, August 1857.
W.A.C. Busbee, August, 1863.
R.L. Robertson, November 1865.
W.H. Cofield, November, 1871.
C.W. Eichelberger, November, 1874.
John Y. Irvin, August, 1877.
Rufus Forester, August, 1884.
J.H. Radney, Assistant Commissioner of Taxes, 1884.
M.P. Pittman, elected August, 1888.
M.P. Stewart, elected August, 1892.

Tax Collectors

Richard Jones, May, 1834.
William Hightower, Sheriff, June, 1835.
Willis Wood, Sheriff, May, 1837.
Sylvanus Walker, Sheriff, May, 1838.
Hugh Harris, elected 1841.

George C. Powell, vice, Hugh Harris resigned in 1842.
W.B. Campbell, 1843.
Elijah Humphries, March, 1844.
William Johns, March, 1852.
Peter Powell, August, 1855.
W.W. Weathers, August, 1857.
W.A.J. Swann, August, 1863.
Warren Armstrong, March, 1865.
John Coston, January 1867.
W. Wood, August, 1868.
C.B. Nichols, November, 1871.
J.H. Davis, February, 1873.
T.J. East, November, 1874.
J.H. Radney, August, 1877.
A.J. Cheeves, March, 1891.
W.A. Radney, August, 1891.
J.M. Kitchens, August, 1892.

NUMBER ELEVEN

Written for The Toiler.

COUNTY TREASURERS

W.H. Cunningham, appointed, 1834.
W.G. Faulkner, December, 1835.
J.W. Stallings, August, 1838.
Joseph Benton, August, 1841.
Isaac Baker, May, 1850.
C.W. Statbane, February, 1853.
W.J. Taylor, August, 1854.
B.J. Hand, August, 1857.
Henry Walls, August, 1863.
B.J. Hand, appointed, November, 1863.
H.H. Huckeba, August, 1865.
F.F. Adrian, November, 1865.
William Colwell, February, 1868.
F. Ricke, November, 1874.
S.E.A. Reaves, August, 1877.
John T. Owens, August, 1880.
M.V. Mullins, August, 1884.
J.M. Bell, August, 1888.
J.H. Barsh, August, 1892.

COUNTY SURVEYORS

Hedgeman Triplett, 1834-8.
Martin H. Wordsworth, 1839-45.
John McPherson, 1840-48.
James McPherson, 1844.
Joseph Curry, January, 1849-54.
F.M. McMurray, December, 1849-57.
R.D. Kennedy, January, 1852-54.
N.N. Ligon, August, 1856.
C.M. Amos, August, 1857-69.
John D. Barron, August, 1858.
John M. Hendricks, August, 1859-60.
W.H. Cofield, August, 1862.
W.M. Perryman, August, 1863.
W.W. Wilson, February, 1868.
Joseph Swint, November, 1874-89-92.
O.H. Perryman, February, 1878.
W.W. Kidd, February, 1881.

Number Ten

Written for The Toiler.

Tax Assessors

The taxes were assessed and collected by the same persons who were appointed by the Commissioner's Court until 1841.

Richard Jones, May 1834.
William Hightower, Sheriff, June, 1835.
Willis Wood, Sheriff, May, 1837.
Sylvanus Walker, Sheriff, May, 1838.
A.P. Hunter, 1839.
Hugh Harris, elected, August, 1841.
George C. Powell, assistant, 1842.

The law was changed and assessor appointed in battalion districts in 1843: John Hanna, district 1; Hugh Montgomery, 2; Thomas Gilland, 3; R.W. Caskey, 5; James F. White, 6; Samuel Carpenter, 7; James M. Pittman, 8; Samuel T. Owens, 9; James M. Hornsby, 10; James Duke, 11.

1844

Micajah Goodwin, W.G. Falkner, J.H. Allen, Andrew Burnham. The law was changed and office made elective in 1845.

Elijah Humphries elected April, 1845. The law was changed in 1848 and district assessor appointed.

W.F. Caldwell, July, 1848.
Harrison Crow, January 1848.
W.A. Striplin, July, 1848.
Harrison Crow, January, 1849.
R.L. Robertson, January, 1849.
Joseph Savage, January, 1849.
W.F. Caldwell, February, 1849.
Law changed again.
W.H. Spruce, April, 1850.
E.M. Burgess, February, 1851.
D.A. Perryman, August, 1853.
W.T. Wood, August, 1854.
J.C. Burson, August, 1855.
William Ingram, August 1857.
W.A.C. Busbee, August, 1863.
R.L. Robertson, November 1865.
W.H. Cofield, November, 1871.
C.W. Eichelberger, November, 1874.
John Y. Irvin, August, 1877.
Rufus Forester, August, 1884.
J.H. Radney, Assistant Commissioner of Taxes, 1884.
M.P. Pittman, elected August, 1888.
M.P. Stewart, elected August, 1892.

Tax Collectors

Richard Jones, May, 1834.
William Hightower, Sheriff, June, 1835.
Willis Wood, Sheriff, May, 1837.
Sylvanus Walker, Sheriff, May, 1838.
Hugh Harris, elected 1841.

George C. Powell, vice, Hugh Harris resigned in 1842.
W.B. Campbell, 1843.
Elijah Humphries, March, 1844.
William Johns, March, 1852.
Peter Powell, August, 1855.
W.W. Weathers, August, 1857.
W.A.J. Swann, August, 1863.
Warren Armstrong, March, 1865.
John Coston, January 1867.
W. Wood, August, 1868.
C.B. Nichols, November, 1871.
J.H. Davis, February, 1873.
T.J. East, November, 1874.
J.H. Radney, August, 1877.
A.J. Cheeves, March, 1891.
W.A. Radney, August, 1891.
J.M. Kitchens, August, 1892.

NUMBER ELEVEN

Written for The Toiler.

COUNTY TREASURERS

W.H. Cunningham, appointed, 1834.
W.G. Faulkner, December, 1835.
J.W. Stallings, August, 1838.
Joseph Benton, August, 1841.
Isaac Baker, May, 1850.
C.W. Statbane, February, 1853.
W.J. Taylor, August, 1854.
B.J. Hand, August, 1857.
Henry Walls, August, 1863.
B.J. Hand, appointed, November, 1863.
H.H. Huckeba, August, 1865.
F.F. Adrian, November, 1865.
William Colwell, February, 1868.
F. Ricke, November, 1874.
S.E.A. Reaves, August, 1877.
John T. Owens, August, 1880.
M.V. Mullins, August, 1884.
J.M. Bell, August, 1888.
J.H. Barsh, August, 1892.

COUNTY SURVEYORS

Hedgeman Triplett, 1834-8.
Martin H. Wordsworth, 1839-45.
John McPherson, 1840-48.
James McPherson, 1844.
Joseph Curry, January, 1849-54.
F.M. McMurray, December, 1849-57.
R.D. Kennedy, January, 1852-54.
N.N. Ligon, August, 1856.
C.M. Amos, August, 1857-69.
John D. Barron, August, 1858.
John M. Hendricks, August, 1859-60.
W.H. Cofield, August, 1862.
W.M. Perryman, August, 1863.
W.W. Wilson, February, 1868.
Joseph Swint, November, 1874-89-92.
O.H. Perryman, February, 1878.
W.W. Kidd, February, 1881.

W.H. Cofield, December, 1883.
James Walker, August, 1892.

COUNTY SUPERINTENDENTS OF EDUCATION

W.H. Spruce, June, 1856.
W.E. Connelly, May, 1860.
W.H. Spruce, May 1862.
W.A. Striplin, November, 1856.
J.W. Addington, November, 1867.
C.C. Enloe, November, 1868.
J.M.K. Guinn, March, 1871.
C.C. Pittman, October 1879.
W.D. Lovvorn, August, 1888.
G.O. Hill, August, 1892.

REGISTERS IN CHANCERY

Bryon L. Nicks, May, 1844.
W.H. Cunningham, February, 1845.
John Reaves, January, 1849.
W.H. Smith, August, 1851.
R.L. McGonigal, September, 1855.
F.M. Perryman, December, 1858.
Joe Day Barron, August, 1859.
A.S. Reaves, February, 1861.
John Reaves, April, 1866.
J.W. Oliver, October, 1887.
R.A. Parker, January, 1892.
J.W. Stewart, 1893.

COMMISSIONERS

1834--George McKaskle, Willis Wood and James Hanson
1835--William Clemens, James Prothro, James Hathorn and Thomas Blake.
1836--Thomas Blake, William McKnight, Hugh W. Harris and William Mullaly.
1837--Thomas Blake, James Hathorn, William Clemens and James Prothro.
James Hathorn and Thomas Blake resigned. Isaac Baker and Hugh Montgomery appointed.
1838--Richard Young, Andrew T. Ray, B.H. Bazemore and J.T. Wafer, W.G. Falkner, vice Wafer, Resigned.
1840--Richard Young, Ephraim Carpenter, W.G. Falkner and B.H. Bazemore.
1842--B.A. Flinn, W.F. Pritchett, David E. Grisham, Sygmore Moore and John Murphy; vice W.J. Pritchett, Resigned.
1844--John Murphy, E. Ingram, Thomas F. Lundie, and D.E. Grisham.
1846--John Murphy, E. Ingram, T.F. Lundie and James W. Clemmens; vice D.E. Grisham, Resigned
1847--John Murphy, William Owens, J.M. Clemmens, Gideon Riddle and Samuel Carpenter; vice John Murphy, Died
1848--James M. Clemens, Gideon Riddle, William Owens and Freeman Taylor.
1850--E.S. Barber, T.L. Thomason, T.L. Lundie and David V. Crider.
1853--John M. Hendricks, B.J. Hand, W.H. Miller and Harris Stephens.
1854--W.H. Miller, B.J. Hand, William Camp and William Ingram.
1855--Hiram Barron, Charles Foster, Wilson Falkner, and J.F. White.

1857--Hiram Barron, J.F. White, Jeremiah Stephens, and P.G. Trent.
1858--J.F. White, P.G. Trent, J. Stephens and John F. McKey.
1862--J.F. White, W.H. Grogan, Samuel Y. Carlie and J. Day Barron.
1864--D.D. Mitchel, Z.M. Hutchens, J.H. Bell, and R.S.M. Hunter.
1866--J.H. Bell, W.C. Robertson, John W. Noles and John D. Windsor.
1868--J.M. Kitchens, J.B. Cooly, A. Bowen and Samuel McDonald.
1872--W.H. Culpepper, W.H. Osborne, W.D. Lovvorn, T.N. Brown, D.A. Perryman, vice W.D. Lovvorn, Resigned, C.A. Prescott appointed; T.N. Brown, Resigned.
1875--W.P. Jackson, W.S. Mayfield, J.N. Lovvorn, and Enoch Carter.
1877-J.C. Wright, I.T. Weathers, R.A. Arnett, and Charles Davis.
1880--T.T. Holly, J.N. Lipham, W.W. Stitt and J.M. Gay.
1884--J.M. Gay, A.J. Green, W.S. Taylor and H.D. Landers.
1888--H.M. Mickle, J.H. Leftwich, W.G. Preston, and W.M. Moon.
1892--W.J. Barrett, G.W. French, W.J. Cofield and W.R. Sherman.

STATE SENATORS AND REPRESENTATIVES

From 1837 to 1894

Number Twelve

Written for The Toiler.

SENATE

Chambers and Randolph

George Reese, 1840-4   Jefferson Falkner, 1845-6.

Tallapoosa and Randolph

Seborn Gray 1847 to 1850.   John T. Heflin, 1851-2

Randolph

Henry M. Gay, 1853 to 1856   W.T. Wood, 1863-4
R.S. Heflin, 1857 to 1862   Middleton R. Bell, 1865-6

Cleburne and Randolph

H.H. Wise, 1867 to 1871.

Chambers and Randolph

J.J. Robinson, 1872 to 1879   R.S. Pate, 1880-3
N.D. Denson, 1884-7

Birmingham

W.A. Handley, 1888 to 1891.

Chambers and Randolph

H.M. Williamson, 1892-5.

REPRESENTATIVES

Thomas Blake, 1837.
William McKnight, 1838.
F.F. Adrian, 1839.
Jerry Murphy, 1842.
Wyatt Heflin, 1843.
James Allen, 1844.
Wyatt Heflin, 1840-1
Wyatt Heflin and Samuel T. Owens, 1845-6.
William Wood and C.J. Ussery, 1847-8,
C.D. Hudson and R.S. Heflin, 1849-50
John Reaves and R.C. Pool, 1851-2.
John Goodwin and W.P. Newell, 1853-4.
W.H. Smith and R.J. Wood, 1855-6.
W.H. Smith, A.W. Denman and Isaac Weaver, 1857-8.
F.M. Ferrell, F.A. McMurray and Joshua Hightower, 1859-60.
C.J. Ussery, A.W. Denman and James Aiken, 1861-2.
Henry W. Armstrong, M.D. Barron and A.A. West, 1863. Capt. West did not take his seat. Milton D. Barron died during this term and D.A. Perryman was elected to fill the vacancy; he, too refused to take his seat.
J.L. Williams, W.W. Dodson and W.E. Connelly, 1865-6
W.E. Connelly and J.L. Williams, 1867-8.
Jack Wood, 1869-70.
J.H. Davis, 1870-1.
W.D. Lovvorn, 1872-3.
W.D. Heaton, 1874-5.
C.J. Ussery, 1876-7.
J.J. Hearn, 1878-9.
T.E. Head, 1880-1.
F.P. Randall, 1882-3.
C.B. Taylor, 1884-5.
E. Carter, 1886-7.
Samuel Henderson, 1888-9.
W.L. Ayers, 1890-1.
H.H. Whitten, 1892-3.
S.E.A. Reaves, 1894-5.

ORDINANCE SECESSION

1861--H.M. Gay, Senate; R.J. Wood and George Forester, House
1865--R.T. Smith, Constitutional Convention.
1867--J.H. Davis, Constitutional Convention.
1875--B.F. Weathers, Constitutional Convention.

CORONER

The office of Coroner with few exceptions, was filled by appointment for special purposes, but few made bond.
John T. Morrison, 1833.
David E. Grisham, 1841.
S. Carpenter, Jerry Murphy and W. Falkner, 1843.
J.T. Morrison, 1847-50.
Green B. Mullins, 1850.
J.M. Hearn, 1853.
Z. Darden, 1854.
William Owens, 1857.
W.A. J. Swann, 1860.
John Parker, 1863.
J. Bennett and Wiley Mize, 1871.
B.F. Hand, 1889.
Jordan Smith, 1892.

Number Thirteen

Written for The Toiler.

In a former letter you were given a short sketch of Judge Archibald Sawyer's characteristics. And now it will be in order to tell you about the others.

JUDGE ANDREW BURNHAM

Being a very small boy I remember but little about his political or official acts. I remember him as small in statue, crippled in one leg and a practicing physician. He lived on Bear creek, having moved there shortly after his retirement from office. He was very pronounced in his opinions and stood with the people. I remember he once visited my father's to examine what was thought to be poison found in the horse trough mixed with parched meal, and which Dr. Burnham after analyzing pronounced poison. That was about May, 1845, and the second day after James Peeler's dwelling was burned. Father had been employed as counsel for Peeler and had won the suit, and was the only motive that suggested a cause for the burning and poisoning. I recollect Dr. B. was pronounced in that opinion. Sometime after this he was sent for but on account of his leg he was unable to make the trip, and grew worse. Finally it was thought advisable to amputate the leg, and mother assisted in the operation and did the stitching. He never recovered the operation, but gradually lingered until death. J.W. Bradshaw made his coffin; and his remains were tenderly laid in the present City cemetery; and in sleep, awaits the resurrection morning.

JUDGE JOHN D. BOWEN

Judge Bowen was examined and licensed to practice law by Circuit Judges Shorter and Martin in 1842. He was medium in height, spare made and had a red face. He was father-in-law to A.J. Hamilton, commonly called Jack Hamilton, who after moving to Texas attained the reputation of being one of the finest legal lights in that State, and was appointed provisional Governor during the reconstruction days.

JUDGE JEFFERSON FALKNER

Judge Falkner was a lawyer by profession, a Baptist preacher by practice and office-holder by occupation. He represented Randolph and Chambers in the State Senate, was clerk of the County Court for years; and if I remember correctly, represented Elmore in the Constitutional Convention in 1875. Notwithstanding his limited education he made rapid strides to efficiency at the bar and in the pulpit, and stood in the front ranks with his competitors. He was Captain of a cavalry company in the Confederate army, and finding his health failing rapidly he resigned, and on his return home organized a company of Home Guards, and then a battalion, to which he was elected Captain and Colonel. He moved to LaFayette and thence to Montgomery, Elmore and now lives in Montgomery.

There used to be a good joke told on the Judge. It went about this way: There had been a disputed question raised by the summer waggery as to which was the laziest, Jefferson Falkner, Steve Reaves or Hugh Montgomery. They were all legal legs of law. Although the question had been debated and points scored for and against each the question had not been fully determined. One evening in July there sat 8 or 10 summer loafers in the shade of the mulberry trees in front of Walker's Hotel on the northeast corner of the square, and one of the party noticed a dark cloud gathering over the courthouse when he remarked: "Boys, do you see that cloud overhead?" "Well, that cloud will, if I am not disappointed, decide the dispute as to who is the laziest of that trio asleep on the bench." The three were laying on a work bench in the evening's shade of the court-house flat on their backs fast asleep. They all gave heed and consented to the test. In a few minutes big drops of rain began to fall, where upon Judge Falkner got up and went in the courthouse, Steve Reaves turned over on his stomach, but Hugh Montgomery lay and took it all, and was given the verdict.

RANDOLPH
HER COUNTY OFFICIALS

Number Fourteen

Written for The Toiler.

Judge John Reaves

Judge Reaves was a lawyer by profession. He was elected as a Democrat to represent Randolph County in the General Assembly 1851-2; was Clerk of the Circuit Court or Master in Chancery almost continuously from 1847 to his death. He was a member of Wedowee Baptist Church and Clerk of the same from 1847 to his death in 1887. He was one of those Christians who never seemed to doubt the word of God, nor forgot in his public and private acts and dealings with men to be a gentleman and Christian. He was faithful, just and liberal, conservative and reliable; while he was slow to anger, he was quick to resent a wrong, and when a principle was involved he was immoveable. Having been raised in a new county, like Nimrod of old, he "was a mighty hunter." Many a day has the writer spent with him in the sport of hunting and fishing. He moved from Chambers county to Randolph some time about 1843/4, if we remember correctly; and no man ever lived in the county who held and maintained a public trust with more fidelity or integrity than Judge John Reaves.

Judge James W. Guinn

Judge Guinn was born June 11, 1804 in Green County, Tenn. He was the son of John and Rachel Guinn. He studied law and was admitted to practice at the bar in 1828 at Franklin, Macon county, N.C. He married Miss Catharine A. Dodson in 1829. He was elected Solicitor in 1832. He moved to Fish Head Valley, near Chulafinnee, in Randolph County, Alabama, November 19, 1841, and to Wedowee in the fall of 1843. Elected Judge, January 1st, 1846, then moved to Cherokee County, Texas, December 11th, 1858 and to Angelina County, January 29th, 1859. He was elected State Senator from Angelina and Nachadochees Counties in 1866. He was a member of the M.E. Church, loved and respected by all. He was a Douglas Democrat, and opposed secession; had five sons in the Confederate army, all lived to return, but one lost an arm, another captured twice and imprisoned once; the eldest two of whom have since died. While in the Senate at Austin, the State capital of Texas, he was taken sick and died in a few days thereafter, on the 27th day of August, 1866.

Judge Joseph Benton

Judge Benton was a lawyer, moral and conventionally temporate, honest, upright and fair in his dealings, and for many years before his demise a true, faithful and consistant Christian and member of Wedowee Baptist Church. He was one of the oldest or first pioneers in the county and to settle in Wedowee--a bachelor; he hunted and traded with the Indians. He was County Treasurer for many years, and was elected in 1874 County Solicitor. He was a Whig, and was elected the first Probate Judge in May, 1850. The official records during his official term are, perhaps, the neatest, fullest and most reliable of any to be found on file in that office. He was a Bell man and voted against secession. He built the dwelling the writer now lives in on lot 75 when the town was first settled and lived there until his death in August, 1876. The Circuit Court, being in session at the time, was adjourned in honor of his memory.

Judge Joseph Curry

Judge Curry was a farmer, County Surveyor and a bachelor, He was temperate and moral, but did not belong to any Christian denomination. He was a Democrat, stood well and made a good official. He married shortly after his term expired and lived near the northern boundary county line four or five miles southeast from Oakfuskee, where he died.

Judge T. L. Pittman

Judge Pittman was a politician and had served as Clerk in the Probate office with Judge Curry. He was a Democrat and secessionist, extreme and partisan, although capable, prompt, neat and efficient in the discharge of business. It was during war times, and he had many trying difficulties to meet, and necessarily made many enemies personal and political, and the strife engendered during the war forced him to vacate his office and seek a place elsewhere for protection. He moved to Cedartown, Ga. where he lived until a few years since. He joined the Baptist Church, and it is said lived a Christian life for many years before his death.

Judge R. S. Heflin

Judge Heflin, an Indian soldier, lawyer, politician, Representative, State Senator and ex-Congressman, the most noted and popular man, at one time, the county has ever had. A Douglas Democrat, opposed to secession, and later on a Republican in the strictest sense. He was wild and rattling in his younger days, but like Judge Benton and Pittman, reformed and joined the Baptist Church and is now living near Louina in dotage and retirement, where we trust, he will find peace, comforts and companionships to make his latter days his happiest on earth.

Judge W. W. Dodson

Judge Dodson was a farmer; represented this county in the Lower House of the General Assembly in 1865-6 and was Justice of the Peace in Wedowee Beat for many years. He was a Douglas Democrat, opposed to secession and after the war a Republican. He was a pious, orderly and a devoted Christian and belonged to the M.E. Church. He moved from Macon County, N.C. in 1842; to the place where he has since lived, 3½ miles South of Wedowee until his death in 1894.

Judge D. L. Davis

Judge Davis was known and called "Lem" Davis, and was a young man when elected in 1874, full of life, energy, acumen, and a Democrat. He was a man of fine sense and good business qualifications such as are necessary in the make up of a good official, except intemperance and immoral habits. He was kind, sympathetic and generous. Though like most men he had faults; yet you could not help but like Lem. Peace to his many noble deeds, to his big-hearted and kind acts. Although his body is dead and his remains lie in another State, Lem still lives in the memory of this people.

Judge S. E. A. Reaves

Judge Reaves, known and called in boyhood days "Gus" Reaves, is a farmer and mechanic. He was elected County Treasurer in 1877 by the largest majority ever given in the county. He is our present representative. Honest, frank, open and manly in private or public life and dealings, an ex-Confederate Captain, a good and brave soldier, honored and loved by his men. He is a member of the M.E. Church, South and is known and loved for his many Christian virtues and charitable deeds. He was elected Representative in 1894 by the Populist, and is eligible for future honors.

Judge T. J. Thomason

Judge Thomason was a merchant, a member of the Rock Mills Baptist Church, temporate and moral. He was a Democrat, but not a bitter partisan. We know but little of his official capabilities. He owns and runs a good farm in northeast corner of the county and has recently moved his family to Auburn, Ala. He is young and may live to fill some other official position. He is a good, clever man and neighbor and we believe stands very well with his party.

Judge A. J. Weathers

Judge Weathers is a farmer and has made it a success. Moral and temporate, honest, reliable, and everybody likes "Jack." He is a man of good horse sense and fine judgment, but doesn't seem to have any taste for official life and business. He is a Populist and Allianceman, and of course honorable, honest and clever.

Number Fifteen

Written for The Toiler

SHERIFFS

William Hightower

Sheriff Hightower, tradition says, was a bachelor when he came to the county. He was here when the county was first organized and had been for some time previously. He was elected in August, 1833, to the Sheriff's office. He was rough, wild and mischievous, playing tricks on the credulous. Uncle Bill was perhaps as good material as the county had at that time for Sheriff. Tradition further said, he was the original owner of the present site of Wedowee. When we first got acquainted with him he was married and lived on the old McIntosh road about two miles west of Gold Ridge, and with the exception of two or three he lived in Wedowee in 1857-8, his home was at the old home place until his death in 1889 or about that time. He was forty three or four years of age when he came to the county, and in 1880 he was 92; this made him near 100 when he died. When he lived here in Wedowee in 1857, and kept a hotel, we got well acquainted with Aunt Liza, his wife. They had no children. They lived where Sheriff Willoughby now lives. Ira Culbreath had the house built and Uncle John Spence hewed the sills and logs.

Uncle Bill was a terror to evil doers. He had the first Court House built, it was a log cabin, on lot 108 near R.T. West's present store house. He had a jail too, but the hand of man did not fashion it, except the door. This jail may have been as long in construction as Noah's Ark, being an old and very hollow poplar tree, and from the best information known by the writer was on lot number 116, near the foot of the hill east of the present jail and on the bank of Frog Level branch.

While Sheriff, Uncle Bill had to carry a prisoner to another county. He had one guard in a two horse wagon, went into camp on their trip and after supper, the guard wanted to know which one would guard the prisoner in the forepart of the night. Uncle Bill said I'll fix that when bed time comes. The time came after a while and Uncle Bill took the wagon bed off, turned it bottom side up, put the prisoner under it, his and the guard's beds on top---the prisoner was on hand next morning.

Uncle Bill was a good yarn teller. "One time," he said, "I was going to Wetumpka, and as I passed along there was a man clearing up a new ground. It was a pine orchard and the newly made log heaps were general, I said to the man: 'Hello, there, what are you going to do with these pine logs?' "Well, stranger," said the man, "I thought I'd have to burn them to get 'em out of the way." "Well," said Uncle Bill, "what are you going to do with the ashes?" "Nothing," replied the man, "Tut, tut", said Uncle Bill, "pine ashes up in my county are worth a dollar per bushel, and if you will save them, I'll give you 50 cents per bushel and take all you have. I'll be back in a few days and will pay you for them. What do you say?" "Well, I guess" said the man, "I'll have you 500 bushels ready at that price." "All right," said Uncle Bill and drove on. The ash burner soon had one hundred logheaps fired, but not all burned when Uncle Bill got back. "I reckon," said Uncle Bill, "a cyclone had passed through the log heaps, for not a handful of pine ashes were to be seen." The wind, of course, blew them away as fast as burned and Uncle Bill knew it would.

We have told you this, Uncle Bill Hightower yarn., in order for you to get the manner of the man.

Willis Wood

Sheriff Wood was one of the first county Commissioners, elected August, 1833. His family was, probably one of the first to settle in the county. Daniel Phillips entered 80 acres near the old Broughton Church and homesteaded in 1831, but we don't know when he moved his family there. Willis Wood's family was the first we have any information of that settled in South Randolph. It is said, and we are inclined to believe it, Mrs. Fletcher Haynes nee Wood, was the first native born white child in the county. She is 63 years of age. She was the daughter of Willis and Elizabeth Wood. She is not only the first native white, but the oldest citizen inhabitant living in the county. Sheriff Wood lived near the Pate old place when he died. W.R. McGill had a pair of hand cuffs sold at the administrator's sale; we suppose they were bought while Mr. Wood was Sheriff. Sheriff Wood raised a large and respectable family.

Number Sixteen

Written for The Toiler

SHERIFFS

Sylvanus Walker

Sylvanus Walker was elected Sheriff in 1839, and was one of the first settlers. We know but little about him personally.

Robert Caskey

Robert Caskey was elected Sheriff in 1842, but by some means, probably a contest, he did not act until March 1844. Big Sam Carpenter, sometimes called "Pointer" Sam was appointed previously as coroner and acted as Sheriff until Sheriff-elect Caskey qualified. Sheriff Caskey was an early settler and built several houses. The dwelling now occupied by Judge Weathers is his old homestead and he was living there when Sheriff. He seems to have had opposition but from what cause it does not appear. He went West about the time Joe Henry, A.Q. Nix, Jack Hamilton, Walker, Judge Bowen, J.H. Allen and others did.

W.P. Newell

W.P. Newell was elected Sheriff in 1845. He was a farmer and a nice, clever, sober and honorable man and made an excellent and efficient sheriff. He lived 9 or 10 miles north of Wedowee and there is a post office named Newell near his old settlement. He died many years ago, and one of his daughters married ex-sheriff, John V. McKee, and her daughter and his grand-daughter married our present sheriff, Robert Willoughby.

Alman P. Hunter

Alman P. Hunter, was elected sheriff in 1848. He made a good and efficient officer; he was Tax Assessor previously and deputy sheriff subsequently. He was one of those men that made opportunities and obstacles get out of his way if moveable when a friend was involved. He was the father of Bob, Virgil and Bill Hunter. He moved to Beat 8 and died there, after the war, was prudent, cautious, kind and fearless and retained the confidence, love and respect of his friends until his demise.

Joel T. Morrison

Joel T. Morrison was the second son of Rev. William Morrison, a Primitive Baptist preacher and one among the first white families to settle in the northern portion of this county. Joel was a Whig, we believe, and was a deputy sheriff and coroner before elected sheriff in 1850. Joel was a live, big hearted, open handed and all-round good fellow. He had but one fault, that is he was very fond of "tea" and sometimes it got the better of him. He was removed in April, 1852. Wilson Falkner, coroner, acted a short time, when he was restored. Joel was very popular with the masses and his home people stuck closer than a brother by him. He was subsequently Justice of the Peace and township trustee until his physical powers gave way. He died in July, 1884, being in his 74th year.

J. M. Hearn

J.M. Hearn, called "Mouse" Hearn, was elected in August 1853. He had been coroner and deputy sheriff previously. His father, Asa Hearn, was doubtless the first white man, and family to settle in Wedowee. "Mouse" went to Texas, and died in the war.

A. W. Denham

A. W. Denham was elected sheriff in 1854, as a Democrat. He was a farmer and lived near Arbacoochee. Made an excellent sheriff. He made up a company and was elected its captain and went into the Confederate Army, Tennessee division. Is now a citizen of Cleburne county, honored, loved and respected for his many Christian acts and charitable deeds. Is a Baptist and his light shines brightly. As an officer, soldier, neighbor and Christian, he stands well.

John V. McKee

John V. McKee was elected in 1860 as a Democrat. Was raised as a farmer. He built the present business house on north east corner public square now occupied by Guinn Bros., publishers of The Toiler. Was active, energetic and aggressive, honest, honorable and capable, and made a most excellent sheriff. Married ex-sheriff W.P. Newell's daughter. Organized a company and went out at its head as captain. Died during the war.

Larkin Breed

Larkin Breed was elected in 1863 as an anti-war or Union man. Was a farmer, good, easy, clever kind of a man, who was highly respected by his neighbors, but didn't have backbone, manhood and self-reliance and confidence like his predecessor McKee. This weakness got him mixed up badly and generally, and the poor fellow was in the middle of a bad fix. His former friends became his bitterest enemies and his enemies his friends. The fact is, he wanted to stay at home and keep out of war, and with all the political power and machinery in the hands of the war party, he had to cater to that power or go instanter. Party, honor, and profits were not the consideration nor the inducements to hold office---it was to keep out of the army and out of the range of Yankee lead. A man had to have an office and hurrah for Jeff Davis or dig a hole or cross the dead line. Sheriff Breed preferred the former and wisely too.

Lindsey McKee

Lindsey McKee was elected in 1865, as a Union-man. A brother of John V. McKee and lived in Beat 4. He was clever, liberal and a better neighbor did not live in that section of country. Everybody liked Lindsey personally, but being oppressed, stigmatized and persecuted for his political opinions, he became rather partisan and when the surrender came, the other fellows who had had a Divers time woke up in trouble. They didn't ask for mercy, but sought other climes with peaceful surroundings, and got Lind-

sey decided to do so too, and shortly after the war moved to
Minnesota where he still lives.

S. E. Jordan

S.E. Jordan, a Georgian who had been here a few years, was
elected sheriff as a Republican. He meant well, but lacked the
most essential prerequisite necessary in man to make a successful sheriff. He would have made a better commissioner or tax
collector. A successful farmer with taste and judgment and the
best of neighbors. He died, sometime in 187_, near his home 12
miles north of Wedowee.

Jenkins Bennett

Jenkins Bennett was elected in 1871 as a Republican; J.B.
Amos contested his election, but the contest was not tried during
his term. He was a citizen of Wedowee and a good workman. He
now lives within a mile or two of Wedowee and is in his 65th year;
he has the promise, from appearance, of a long lease on life. Made
a good and efficient officer. Takes no interest in politics now.

Robert Merrill

Robert Merrill was elected sheriff as a Democrat in 1874,
but after qualifying held office only about a month and a half.
Bob had every prerequisite nature could give to make an efficient
officer, but it did not suit a miller; grinding corn for toll was
more congenial to him than serving papers and arresting persons.
He lives in Carroll county, Ga. having lived to see a large family grown, married and settled to themselves.

J. B. Amos

J.B. Amos, vice Robert Merrill, resigned, filled the unex-
pired term. Amos was appointed because it was claimed he was
elected in 1871, and that he contested for the office and kept
out by a partisan judge. He made a very good officer at first. By
the latter part of the term, he got mixed and went off on the
"Polly Ann" administration and was badly beaten in 1877. Jim was
a big hearted fellow and as clever as he could be. He moved to
Cleburne county about 1878, and was accidently killed while haul-
ing logs to a saw mill.

W. C. S. Robertson

W.C.S. Robertson was elected sheriff in 1877 on an independent peoples ticket, anti "Polly Ann." He was a Union man and
served in the U.S. Army; voted the Democratic ticket for Seymour
for president. Is 49 years of age, lives in one mile of Wedowee,
appointed and held the post office under Harrison's administration,
made a good and efficient officer. Now a miller, and is eligible
to the Populist promotion, in 1896. A member of the Alhance and
M.E. Church, South.

M. V. Mullins

M.V. Mullins was elected sheriff in 1880 as a Democrat. Was
a confederate soldier, 57 years of age, Baptist, open, frank and
approachable. Made a good and efficient officer. Honest and
clever, said to be a partisan in politics. He was also County
Treasurer and is now Best Register of voters. Stands well in
his church and party, with his people and neighbors, and is a

citizen of Wedowee.

Wilson Ayers

Wilson Ayers was elected in 1884, sheriff as a Democrat, and in 1890 elected Representative as an Allianceman. Has also been elected Justice of the Peace. Wilson is clever, fair and open, a Baptist and a good farmer, 62 years of age and stands well with his neighbors. He made a good, safe and credible sheriff. He lived in Beat 2.

R. H. Ford

R.H. Ford was elected sheriff in 1888 as a Democrat. A member of the Alliance and the M.E. Church, South. He is 39 years of age, active, progressive and aggressive, made an excellent officer, is a Pop and eligible for future political honors. Lives in Wedowee and has a farm.

Robert Willoughby

Robert Willoughby was elected sheriff in 1892 as a Pop, was a Confederate soldier, a good farmer and makes a splendid sheriff. He married ex-sheriff John V. McKee's daughter, is a Baptist, 50 years of age and lives in Wedowee.

Number Seventeen

Written for The Toiler.

CLERKS OF COUNTY COURTS

William Vardeman was the first County Clerk. He was appointed about January 1st, 1833, and removed April, 1834. He may have been a very clever man, but the records are not very creditable as to his efficiency as an officer. Was succeeded by W.H. Cunningham in 1834, and Cunningham by Jefferson Falkner in 1835.

- - - -

W.M. Buchanan succeeded Falkner in 1839. The records during his term are creditable and legible.

- - - -

Charles W. Statham was elected in 1843. Was a Democrat and a bachelor. Married a Miss Martha Kelly, of Calhoun County, in 1844-5. He and his wife, J.W. Guinn and the writer spent the spring and summer at Chamber's Springs in Talladega county. He held the Clerk's office until May 1850. The legislature abolished the county clerk and the court of Orphantage by substituting Probate Judge. He ran as an independent, as a Democrat by J.W. Guinn, and Joseph Benton as a Whig. He came down on the day of the election in favor of Benton which elected, and of course was Benton's clerk during his six years. Was appointed County Treasurer by the Commissioners Court in 1853, and held about one year. Made a good officer. He was honest and sober. His wife was the Rev. Christer Kelley's daughter; everybody knew father Kelly. Statham and family moved to Angelina County, Texas, near Homer, the county seat in 1859, and was elected County Clerk of Angelina County a few years afterwards. He must be in his eightieth year. Mr. and Mrs. Statham live in Lulkin, Texas, feeble and infirm; cared and provided for by their children.

CIRCUIT CLERKS

Jonathan Camp was elected August, 1833, as the first Circuit Clerk. He was an early settler, and lived west of the Big Tallapoosa river, in Fishhead Valley. There are no records in the office to show any of his official acts. He held only about one year.

W.H. Cunningham succeeded Camp in 1834, and held the position until 1848. The records during his occupancy have been mostly destroyed. He bid off the first town lot sold in Wedowee- lot number 13- and built a double log dwelling on it. He afterwards built a hotel on lot 133, subsequently rebuilt by William Owens, and now occupied by L.C. Huckeba. Was a small man and very sensitive. Moved away in 1849. He was a deputy County Clerk of Jefferson Falkner, also County Treasurer a short while. Had a wife when we knew him; stood very well generally, but judging from the records was only ordinarily efficient.

- - - -

W.H. Wood, or "Brister" Wood, as he was generally called, was Clerk from December 6th, 1848 to January 23rd, 1849. He was the son of William Wood, and a brother to Dick, Alfred, Jack and Winston, Mrs. Martha Smith, Mrs. Sarah Knight and Mrs. Mary Pate. "Brister" was a fine man and merchandised for years before the war. He married Miss Josephine L.P. Guinn, May 4th, 1851. Moved to Angelina county, Texas, in January 1860. Mrs. Wood died May 15th, 1863, and was buried at Home cemetery. After the war "Brister" came back and remained until death in 1879 or 1880.

- - - -

John L.C. Danner was appointed and held until 1852. He was a lawyer, well educated, had a firm mind and a business tact. He was of Dutch descent and married Miss Mary Ann Kitchens, sister of our present Tax Collector, J.M. Kitchens. He was a Democrat and through Congressman Dowdle got an appointment in the U.S. Treasury Department at Washington, and when the Jeff Davis government was set up at Montgomery, he resigned and took a position in it, and went with it to Richmond. Some time during the latter part of the war, if we remember correctly, he went North and afterwards returned to Montgomery, and was State Senator, and Supreme Court reporter. He died in 1872.

- - - -

Robert T. Smith was elected in 1852 and held until 1853. He was a man of fine business quality and a Democrat, with a Douglas prefix. He named his eldest son Stephen A. Douglas. A Union man during the war and after was a Republican. Bob was in politics like every other thing he undertook--at head or in front. He was called a partisan, but not a tyrant. While he was quick to resent a wrong, he was easily approached and prompt to forgive. Bob never wrongfully oppressed an enemy, nor would he let others do so if he could prevent it. We have known him to rescue an enemy from his friends and protect him from harm. Was wild and rattling when a boy and full of sport. Married Miss Martha Wood, and after the war was elected State Auditor. He was appointed U.S. Custom House officer at the port of Mobile, moved to Texas and lived for several years. Sometime in '80 he moved back to

Wedowee and merchandised until his death in 1890. He was the son of Jeptha V. Smith, and brother of ex-Governor Smith, now of Birmingham. Was 61 years of age when he died. Mrs. Smith and family are citizens of Wedowee. John Reaves succeeded him and held until 1864.

- - - -

H.H. Wise, an old bachelor, who lived near Arbacoochee, was elected in 1864 as a Union man. He appointed a one arm ex-Confederate as deputy clerk to keep the Confederate tiger and secession leopard quiet. Kept his mouth shut and tongue still, but never lost sight of his friends nor betrayed their confidence. Elected State Senator from Cleburne and Randolph in 1867 to 1871. He was accidently killed at Heflin in 1893 by being thrown from his buggy. Hicks made a good and efficient officer. He was one of those free, open hearted, liberal handed men without a personal enemy; but unfortunately became dissipated and reckless and lost control over his appetite and the temptations of intemperance.

Number Eighteen

Written for The Toiler.

Circuit Clerks

J.H. Davis, Jr., was Circuit Clerk in 1867 and held office about one year. A young man of fine promise, and a Republican. He was Tax Collector in 1873. Married Miss Josie White, an amiable and lovely young lady, and daughter of Dr. W.E. White, of Roanoke. Lives four miles north east of Roanoke, and recently lost his wife, of whom he was devotedly attached, loved and cherished, and will ever remember in sadness and grief. Todd is about 50 years old, and for several years past has taken but little, if any interest in public affairs, preferring home association with wife and children.

- - - -

R.H. Bolt was elected in 1868 as a Republican; in 1874 as a Democrat. Made a most excellent and capable officer. Married Miss Texie Tomlinson, a beautiful and lovely girl. Studied law and grew in popularity until evil communications led him to intemperence. He resigned his office and went to farming; and for several years had a hard struggle trying to cut loose from a habit that had grown to be a second nature; finally by the help of God in whom he trusted, Jesus on whom he believed, the shackles which had fettered his legs, the cords that had bound his hands, the thirst that had parched his lips and the red wine that coveted his eyes were cast out, cut loose and he became a child of God, an heir of heaven and a witness of rightousness unto salvation; and now is a devoted and zealous Baptist. Moved to Mississippi a few years since; is now in his 54th year. He was a member of Company K, 13th Alabama Regiment, made a good soldier; lost his left arm, and was honorably discharged from the Confederate service.

- - - -

John T. Owens was appointed vice, R.H. Bolt, resigned in 1876. He was elected County Treasurer in 1880 as a "Go between" Democracy and Republicanism. Married Miss Alice Prescott, a charming blue-eyed beauty, one of our most successful and prosperous merchants. He is in his 44th year; an organized Grover

Cleveland Democrat; being prominently spoken of as their candidate for probate judge in 1898.

- - - -

O.H. Perryman was elected in 1880. Made a good officer, was county Surveyor. He is a lawyer and editor and published the Wedowee Observer in 1889-90. Has a fine mind, quick perception and wields a trenchant pen, bold, aggressive and sarcastic. He is still young, forty-one, and in the prime of life, and lives one and a half miles southwest from Wedowee where he is now running a saw mill. He is a Republican.

- - - -

J.W. Stewart was elected in 1886 as a Democrat. Made a good officer and is now Register in Chancery. A quiet, peaceable, orderly, Christian gentleman. Owns and runs the Farmers Hotel; a member of the M.E. Church, South; 53 years of age and stands well with the people.

- - - -

B.J. Ford was elected as a Populist in 1892. Is a member of the M.E. Church, South; sober, honest, and virtuous. An efficient officer, a steadfast friend and a zealous allianceman. He is 47 now, was a boy soldier in the late war and is the son of Capt. B.H. Ford, one of Randolph's most respected citizen; has a wife but no children.

- - - -

Number Nineteen

Written for The Toiler.

Tax Assessors

The taxes were assessed and collected by the sheriffs or persons appointed by the Commissioner's Court.

Richard Jones, who lived on the present Robert Birdsong home place, was appointed May 3, 1834. He was the first assessor and collector of taxes for Randolph county. There are no records to show who were tax payers nor the amount collected. It must have been small, as all the other county officers were; and we find one man sometimes holding two and three different offices. Sheriff William Hightower succeeded him in June 1835; Sheriff Willis Wood May 1837. In serial letter number fifteen we inadvertently located Sheriff Willis Wood as living and dying on Corn House creek. It was Fletcher Haynes, who married Sheriff Wood's daughter, that lived and died on Corn House creek. Sheriff Willis Wood lived and died on the LaFayette road south of J.M. Mickle's old home place, and was buried at the Willis Wood cemetery, which is about a half mile south of J.M. Mickle's.

Sylvanus Walker, sheriff, succeeded Wood May 1838. Sheriff Almond P. Hunter in 1839 and 1841. Hugh Harris was elected in August, and in 1842 he was elected collector and the commissioners appointed George C. Powell assessor. Harris resigned and Powell was appointed, assessed and collected the taxes for 1842.

In 1843 assessors were appointed by battalion and regimental districts. John Hannah, 1.--Everybody knew Hannah, and tradition says: Hannah was so elated over the honors conferred he filled up on corn juice and went home to celebrate. A big dinner was prepared and his neighbors invited, but Hannah was too sick to eat, and when he failed to appear the question was asked, "What ails Hannah?"

Hugh Montgomery, 1.--Hugh was a lawyer and it was said, "He was the best common law lawyer practicing at Wedowee's bar." He was a good easy kind of fellow, had no ambition nor pride and was too indolent to succeed in anything, though a man of fine mind and good opportunities.

Thomas Gilland, 3.--He was a good and safe man - a farmer.

R.W. Caskey, 5.--We remember but little about him.

James F. White, 6.--Was a Democrat, a farmer and afterwards county commissioner. He lived in the northeast corner of the county.

Samuel Carpenter, 7.--We don't know which one of the Sams; we had big or painted Sam and little or tanner Sam, but we are inclined to believe it was big Sam as he was handy and ready for anything in that line.

James M. Pittman, 8.--He was a Democrat and farmer; he lived and died in High Shoals Beat; was one of our best citizens and raised a large and interesting family. He was the father of C.C. Pittman, County Superintendent of Education. His brother, Alfonso is still living. I.L., Probate Judge and brother is dead. He was 31 years of age when appointed tax assessor. He was a partisan politically, but a cleverer man could scarcely be found.

Samuel T. Owens, 9.--Was a Democrat; was elected in 1845, with Wyatt Heflin to the Legislature.

J.M. Hornsby, 10.

James Duke, 11.

In 1844 Macajah Goodwin, W.G. Falkner, J.H. Allen and Dr. Andrew Burnham were appointed.

Elijah Humphries was elected April 1895, was 39 years of age, farmer, Democrat, and lived near Newell post office. He stood well and was popular with the poeple.

In 1847 the law was changed, and Harrison Crow, nicknamed "Jude," was elected. He was about 43, full of life, energy and sport, generous, free and open, intemperate, vulgar and profane, dealer in liquors, an incessant smoker and occassionally shuffled cards, ring leader in sham fights and catamounts' devastation of Todd's negroes and calves, which we will tell our readers about in the future.

Number Twenty

Written for The Toiler

Tax Assessors

W.F. Caldwell, a resident of Fish Head Valley, was about 25

years of age then, and had the confidence and endorsement of his people. He was the father of John R. Caldwell, Deputy U.S. Collector, who now resides at Anniston.

- - - -

W.A. Striplin lived in Fish Head Valley when appointed, and was the son of Rev. Ben Striplin. Uncle Ben, as he was usually called, was an indispensable necessity at camp meetings. Father lived at Chulafinnee in 1842, and I remember as if it were yesterday, mother took me with her to camp meetings the stand had been burned down and a new one raised on the same spot, but by some oversight the charcoal and ashes had not been properly cleaned off before services began. It was on Friday when mother and I got there. We took dinner at Dr. John Wesley Hudson's tent, and at the afternoon services we were in attendance. Services had, however, been going on for a day or two previously and were seemingly cold and discouraging; notwithstanding the warm zeal and earnest pleas of the preacher it would have passed for a Quaker meeting. The ministers and tenters could be seen gathered in groups earnestly engaged in conversation. There were all kinds of surmizing as to the cause and as many theories for resuscitating Methodist zeal and activity. Mother was one of those persons who believed that "where there is a will there is generally a way," and as she used to say: "I never cross a bridge until I get to it." I heard her laughingly say to Dr. Hudson: "Just put Uncle Ben Striplin up this evening and you will see your troubles removed and Methodists go to work." Uncle Ben was put up, took his text and in a few minutes warmed up, and with a voice that echoed from hill to hill, said: "What, a thousand souls going to hell for the want of a little straw, brethren?" Suffice it to say, that evening before sun-down, which was Friday, wagons with great loads of straw rolled in, and that night the altar was filled with shouting Methodists and converts, and such clapping of hands, shouting, singing, praying hallelujah, with tears trickling down the cheeks of Uncle Ben as he stood in the pulpit looking down in the altar, the writer hopes never to forget.

- - - -

R.L. Robertson was a mechanic and physician when we first knew him; he was afterwards an M.E. Minister of the gospel. He was then in his 45th year, heavily built, square shouldered, active as a cat and fearless as a lion. He married Miss Susan A. Dodson in 1844, and had born to them Harriett, Mrs. Dr. E. Camp, who died a few years since at Gadsden; John D. who lives now at the homestead one and a half miles of Wedowee; Alice, the wife of Joe Cosper, both of whom are dead; and James F. who lives in Nebraska. Dr. Robertson was a man of fine mind and a successful physician. He made a capable and efficient officer. He was a "Know-nothing" in 1855-6, a strong Union man during the war, and a Republican in 1868, when he was again elected Tax Assessor and held for two or three terms. He was in his 75th year when he died October 1880, and was buried in the Masonic cemetery.

- - - -

Joseph Savage, of Beat 3, Rockdale, was appointed in 1848-9. He was a school teacher, 44 years of age, was honest, sober and moral and well qualified for his duties. He had three sons, Jeff, Shelt and Jesse in Co. K 13th Alabama Regiment. Jesse was undoubtedly the best drilled soldier in Gen. Colquitt's brigade. General Colquitt, when he took command of his brigade at Yorktown,

Va., sent an order to the Captains in each regiment in his brigade to send him the best drilled soldier in their companies. The writer was in command of Co. K., 13th Ala. Regiment, and sent Jesse Savage. Those sent were placed in line and a trial inspection made. On the first all but four were dismissed; on the second two more, on the third trial Jesse stood alone, and received the honor of being the best drilled soldier in the brigade. General Colquitt had him detailed as a sentinel in front of his headquarters. Jesse did not like the idea of being away from his two brothers and neighbor boys, and asked the General to let him go back to his company, which was granted. This characteristic of Jesse was strongly developed in his brothers, which was inherited from their father.

Number 21

Written for The Toiler

Tax Assessors

W.H. Spruce was 46 years of age when elected in 1850. He was a Democrat, teacher, farmer, a member of the M.E. Church. He had a good common school education, made a good officer, and was elected superintendent of education in 1855 or '56, and took a great interest in building and establishing schools and encouraging teachers. He stood well in his church and community. He raised a large and interesting family, but was unfortunate with his sons who are all dead and without posterity. After he lost his favorite son, Johnnie, in the Confederate services, and the oldest, "Spark", had died, he said to the writer in tears of sadness and words of anguish, "I had lived to hope and cherish the one desire of my heart until now to perpetuate and hand down to future ages, time and generation in name of all others to one most dear--Spruce." "But", said he in tones of despondency and desolation, "when I die, and that time you see can't be far off, (he was then suffering with a cancer) and the name Spruce dies. I am the only living male left, and with me it goes, and I shall be forgotten, so also the name of Spruce. I am not dreading death. I feel I am prepared to die and stand in judgment. But how can I reconcile the justice, mercy and love of God in this of all other afflictions to me most tormenting and anguishing?" He died a short time afterwards, December 1879, in his 57th year, after suffering with cancer of the mouth--loved and honored and mourned by all.

Number 22

Written for The Toiler

Tax Assessors

Elias M. Burgess was elected in 1851. He was 39 years of age then, a Democrat, school teacher, farmer and Justice of the Peace, living near Lamar when war was declared. He made up a company of about forty (the writer being one of the number) on July 4th, 1861, at Lamar. There was a big dinner given that day and Miss Cynthia Tomlinson made a nice little speech. E.B. Smith, of Brockville, was present with about forty volunteers on his list; and the two, Burgess and Smith, agreed to unite into one company. They agreed to elect the officers alternately by ballot. Smith was elected Captain; E.M. Burgess 2nd Junior Lieutenant, and on July 12th, 1861, this company left Brockville for Montgomery, where it was mustered into service July 28th. Lieutenant Burgess took a great deal of pride in drill and other duties, and at the Seven Pines battle distinguished himself for bravery, courage and leadership. While the regiment was supporting those engaged, Lieutenant Colonel H. R. Dawson ordered a retreat and was leading the way. Lt.

Burgess saw Col. Dawson's blunder and snatched the regiment colors and rallied all but Dawson back on the breast works. Col. Dawson resigned in short order and nothing but a Junior rank of a second Lieutenancy kept Lieut. Burgess from regimental promotion. On the morning of June 27, 1862, and the second day of the Seven Days fight just as the dawn of twilight cast off the shades of darkness, a brisk breeze kissed the silken folds of the 13th Alabama Regimental colors and she spread her wings in majesty and grandeur in recognition of the will and wishes of the strong arm and brave heart of Col. Sergeant J.W. Stallings, who held her aloft, which chanced to challenge the eye of the Federal sentinel, who in turn sent greetings and salutations on the wings of canister and grape with malice and intent of forethought of her destruction and capture. But there stood four breastworks made of flesh and blood to keep her afloat and defend her liberty; they were the bravest of the brave, Capt. John T. Smith; Lieut. E.M. Burgess; Sergeant J. L. Savage, Co. "K", and Private J.W. Brown, Co. "D". There Capt. Clark, Co. "A", Lieut. Burgess, Co. "K" and Private Thad Pool, Co. "I" crossed the Jordan of life. The writer heard Lieut. Burgess's last farewell to man, saw the spirit of life leaving him before returning to the God who gave it; and as have had promised, saw his body laid to rest within a few feet of where its spirit had left it. He was killed in the road and buried just out and opposite on the bank. God took him as he had expressed a desire to the writer and others he wanted him to do. One Sunday morning in Capt. E.B. Smith's log tent--it was in April, 1862, just before the siege at Yorktown, where we were then in camp--thirteen in number besides Mrs. Lieut. Guinn, the following named persons we remember as a part of those present, Capt. E.B. Smith, Lieut, J.M.K. Guinn, Lieut, A.T. Reaves, Lieut. E.M. Burgess, Corporal Shelt Savage, Rev. Lewis J. Black, Private J.J. Meachum and Thompson Reaves--8 in number, the other five we have forgotten--were passing the time talking about our chances in getting home alive, when the subject came up as to where we had rather be wounded. Thompson Reaves, as well as we remember, started the subject by saying, "I had rather be wounded by having my index finger on my right hand shot off." Then said he, "I would get a discharge and stay at home." John J. Meachum said, "Thomps, I'll take my big toe and that would give me a furlough, and I'll stay if I once get there." (meaning home). Shelt Savage said, "I believe I'd take my left side." Capt. Smith said, "Shelt, I am like you. I want both hands and feet and I'd take my right side." Lieut Reaves said: "Boys, I'll take my foot. Polly is good company and I had rather be with her than anywhere else." Lieut Guinn said, "I'll take my left arm between the wrist and elbow; I could come and go when I pleased." Lieut. Burgess said, (suiting the occasion by placing his finger in the center of his forehead), "I want to be hit right here and where killed be buried." Rev. Lewis J. Black said, "I don't care where I am hit, I only pray God, if I am to be wounded seriously to cause my death, I may be killed so dead that not a muscle of my face, arm, leg or body will move. I pray God that this may be made so as a token and evidence that you all, my wife, father, mother, brother, the members of my church and everybody else, may know that I am a Christian and that I will meet them in heaven." The scriptures say: "The last shall be first." Lewis Black was the first; while laying behind the breastworks, at the battle of Seven Pines, he was struck by a ball in the head. Old soldiers know when a ball hits them, it sounds like a marble hitting a board, this was the case with the one hitting Lewis. Every eye near him was instantly turned toward him; for they all knew and most of them had heard him pray to God that it might be thus--we inquired diligently and critically for we had promised him too, to see if his prayer was answered, and they all testified that not a feature of his person moved that they saw. Lieut. Burgess being next to last selecting, was the next to first killed. On the morning of June 27th, near a cow-trail coming obliquely into the road cutting the space of three or more feet wide through the bank three or four feet high to the level of the road bed, while standing cautioning the boys of the danger in passing it, as the Yankees had one or two pieces of artillery planted to cover it, which had killed Captain Clark and Thad Pool, he was struck with a minnie ball in the forehead just where he had selected and was buried as near the spot as was thought prudent. The last but two and the first but two, Lieut. J.M.K. Guinn was the next. A piece of shell struck his left arm between the wrist and elbow just where he too had selected that fatal Sunday morning. The next was Lieut. A.T. Reaves, shot through the foot as he had selected. Lieuts. Burgess, Guinn and Reaves were shot on the same day--June 27th--the second day of the Seven Day's battle. The next two were Thompson Reaves and John J. Meachum. Reaves had his finger shot off and Meachum his big toe--just as they had selected. The writer was at home on furlough when they came home, when Mrs. Guinn related the circumstances, calling the names of the entire thirteen and with special attention to the six at that time, wounded as desired and selected. In the spring following Capt. Smith and Sergeant Shelt Savage were wounded each in the side, as they had selected. The other five we have forgotten their names. If we knew where Thompson Reaves and Shelt Savage were, for they were alive when last heard from, we would write them; perhaps they would remember the others.

Number Twenty Three

Written for The Toiler

Tax Assessors

August 1853, David A. Perryman, then 27 years of age, and a mail contractor, was elected Tax Assessor. In politics he was ever loyal, open and pronounced in his fidelity to the national nominee; but local and state elections he usually voted for the lesser of two evils. He opposed secession, had no ambition or disposition to shoot or be shot at by the "Yanks" and out-general Herod in keeping out of the war and staying at home, which he certainly did. He voted the Cooperation ticket in 1866, and for Horatio Seymore in 1868; was a Grant man in 1872, and since that time voted the Republican ticket. In state, county and local elections he voted for the man generally. He is one of the most active, industrious, presevering and energetic men in the county; but at the same time, he has never been rightly or justly accused so far as we have heard, of manual hard labor. In fact, he said; "When a boy, I was not able to labor until I was twenty-five; since then I have managed so as not to have to do it." In other words when a boy he was physically incapacitated to labor, and since a man morally indisposed to do so. He has managed to inform himself with the practical workings and requirements of the postal and pension laws and rulings and forms of these departments, from which he had made a good living and educated his children. "All I lack of being a wise man," said he, "is learning it, for I never forget anything I ever learned." This is no doubt theoretically true, for he has a remarkable memory and a never-failing fountain of wit, humor and tenor of sarcasm. He is the encyclopedia of Randolph County and her public men. Judge John T. Heflin who bore the sobriquet "law-library", was another as equally as remarkable for memory. Esq. Perryman came to this county in 1843. He carried the mail for years, and was associated as principal or deputy census taker in 1860, '70, '80, and '90.

He has been Notary Public, Justice of the Peace, County Commissioner of Roads and Revenue, and was elected to the Legislature--vice Milton D. Barron, deceased--in 1863, but refused to take his seat because he feared to trust 200 pounds of Union loyalty to fill a Confederate loyalty seat. He used to be an active Mason. He is now a member of the Primitive (Hardshell) Baptist, and quotes scripture like a theologian student. On one occasion he met Rev. Moses Park, a Christian divine, whose daily theme was the revelation of God's word. And as the reverend and learned divine began to reveal the mysteries and wonders of the treasures of the goodness, mercy and love of God, by quoting text after text to support his church creed, Esq. Perryman, as the opportunity and occasion demanded, dropped in a Primitive text. This at first stimualted Rev. Mose, and he became enthused over the love and mercies of God. Esq. P. quickly quoted one of his Primitive predestinations from before the foundation text. Rev. P. raised his head and looked him in the eye and asked: "Are you a preacher?" "No," answered Esq. P. "Are you not a member of a church?" "Yes," replied Esq. P., "but I am like the negro that had the small pox. It has never marked me."

Esq. Perryman is one of Randolph's best citizens; he is liberal, charitable and neighborly. He is now in his 60th year and is remarkably active and stout for a man of his age. He lives in Rockdale Beat No. 3, where he had made his home for many years.

- - - -

W.T. Wood was elected in 1854, and was at the time 24 years of age. He lived near Chulafinnee, was a Democrat, and made a creditable record. He rasied a company, was elected Captain, and left for the war March 19, 1862. He was elected to the State Senate in 1863 by the Union or anti-war contingent.

- - - -

J.C. Burson, of Burson's beat, formerly Cherokee, but now High Shoals, was elected in 1855. He was one of the leading men in his beat and took a great deal of pride in the discharge of his official duties. He was Justice of the Peace for several years, and stood well with his party and people.

- - - -

William Ingram of Delta beat, was elected in 1857. He was a bachelor, 34 years of age and is now 72 and living in the same community, which is a portion of Clay County. He made a most excellent official, and the Democrat Party, to which he belonged, re-elected him until his political opponents became hysterical and chronic in the extreme. In 1863 when the hardships of the war and men being conscripted and forced out, the sentiments of voters were indifferent as to officers, and turned to partisan and political aspirations and promotions. Mr. Ingram being a secessionest and a war man and that element having been in power and control, was charged with all the cruelties and hardships of the war and the sufferings of poor widows and orphan children. He was defeated by a good majority contrary to his or his opponents expectations. He represented Clay County in the legislature a few years since as an Organize Democrat. He taught school in Wedowee in 1852 or '53. The writer remembers when his father came home one night and said: "Boys, school will open Monday week. We have employed Mr. William Ingram; he is a good teacher, comes well recommended and can teach English grammar to the tenth rule

45

in Smith's grammar"--Prepositions govern the objective case. You need not laugh-that was something almost incredible in those days. We studied spelling and reading--Webster's blue back, Smiley's arithmetic and wrote with Goose quills. Prof. Ingram ruled out paper with his little finger nail and sharpened our pens with his penknife. He married Miss Ada De Freese, an accomplished and refined lady. She was a sister of Mrs. John A. Moore, who lived at Roanoke for some time during the war.

- - - -

W.A.C. Busbee lived in or near Louina when elected in 1863. He was a strong sympathizer with the Union cause. He was a clever good natured fellow. No one else, it seemed, cared to run against Ingram as they expected nothing but defeat. But somehow Mr. Busbee got it into his head he would be elected and he made the people believe it. He said to the writer: "Jim, it is not a hard matter to believe what we want to believe, besides it is a necessity for me now." And before he got through telling us we believed it too. It was not the love of honors or money that made office seekers those days--it was to keep out of the war. The people generally owned homes and everybody was known that needed help, and those who expected to run for office saw and cared for the needy.

- - - -

R.L. Robertson was elected as a Union man in 1865. See serial number 18.

- - - -

W.H. Cofield, a Republican, was elected in 1871. He was 55 then and lived until 1884. He has been County Surveyor and Justice of the Peace, and took the census of his beat in 1880. He was an honorable man and good clever citizen. His education was limited and he wrote an illegible hand. He had a great deal of criticisms and opposition during his term as assessor.

- - - -

C.W. Eichelberger was elected in 1874 as a Democrat. He lived in Bacon Level beat. He was well qualified but careless and negligent in the discharge of his official duties. He was in 1885 connected with the U.S. Revenue Department. He is now living at Roanoke.

- - - -

John Y. Irvin, of High Shoals, was elected in 1877, on an Independent People's ticket. He was 39 then and is said to be living now at or near Columbus, Ga. He was re-elected in 1880 but was shamfully legislated out. He made a good faithful and accomodative assessor, and no man stood higher than John with the honest common people.

- - - -

Rufus Forrester was elected in 1884, but as J.H. Radney, Collector had been appointed tax commissioner, Mr. Forrester never assessed the taxes.

- - - -

M.P. Pittman was elected in 1888, as a Democrat. He made one of the closest and most correct assessments of the tax that had been made in years. In fact, the records show that he took time and patience in preparation and listing the tax payers. The proper assessment of taxes is the most important connected with the county and state finances and it is generally the most careless and imperfect officially performed. Mr. Pittman was 43 years of age when elected. Over confidence in the faithful discharge of duty and unprecedent, undemocratic and outrageous acts of his party, bull-dozing and ballot fraud caused his defeat.

- - - -

M.P. Stewart, a populist, was elected in 1892. He was 37 years of age then, a man that the people esteemed very highly for his many good and moral qualities. He lives in Louina beat. He has been somewhat unfortunate in selecting deputies who have made a creditable official, and is our preeent Assessor. He is very popular and an uncompromising "POP."

Number Twenty Four

Written for The Toiler.

Tax Collectors

As has been previously stated the Tax Assessor and Collectors office were usually held by the same person until 1841.

- - - -

Hugh Harris

Was the first to be elected as Collector. He lived northeast from Wedowee on Little Tallapoosa river. He was one of the first pioneers, a good citizen and clever man. He was re-elected in 1842, but resigned after the Commissioners' court failed to appoint him Assessor.

- - - -

George C. Powell

Having been appointed Assessor previously by the Commissioners was appointed Collector vice Hugh Harris resigned. He lived in what is now known as Roanoke beat. We know but little about him or his official acts.

- - - -

W. B. Campbell

Called Bug Bill Campbell, made his home at Wedowee. He was elected in 1843. If we remember correctly he was son-in-law of Judge John D. Bowen. In 1844 Collector Campbell went west, and it is said abour $1400 of the taxes collected went with him.

- - - -

Elijah Humphries

Was elected in 1844, re-elected and held until 1852. He was a Democrat, honest, sober, and clever. He lived on west side of Big Tallapoosa River and probably in Delta Beat.

William Johns

Was elected in 1852. He was a citizen of Arbacoochee beat, was a cripple and went on crutches. He was open, free, liberal, clever and very popular. He made a good and efficient officer, but unfortunately, he would occasionally drink a little too much. He was elected to succeed himself until 1855. While on his round collecting, in Louina we believe, after closing his day's work, filled up and started for his next day's appointment. Taxes were generally paid in silver and carried in saddle-bags. Uncle Bill made a good collection, and on his way lost his bag of silver, and did not miss it until he stopped to spend the night with a friend. Fortunately, D.A. Perryman was only a short distance behind and found the saddle-bags and carried them to Uncle Bill. He swore off and repented in sack-cloth and ashes, yet, while the people had the utmost confidence in his honesty and integrity they made an example and set a precedent by which there could be no misunderstanding in the future.

- - - -

Peter M. Howle

Of Arbacoochee beat, was elected as a Democrat in 1855. He was 35 years of age then, and now lives on the old Armstrong homeplace south of Arbacoochee. He was a safe, and conservative man, and stands today as one of Cleburn's most honored and respected citizens.

- - - -

W. W. Weathers

W.W. Weathers was elected in 1857 as a Democrat. He was at that time 56 years of age. He made a good and efficient Collector. After being re-elected his own successor two or three times it began to look as though he was there to stay; not only that, but his friends began to say: "You can trot out your best horse, but he won't be in the race at the home stretch." "Can't beat him." It became as aggravating as a sore toe in a dewberry patch to those who wanted a bomb-proof during the war. Just to think the Collector's and Assessor's office filled by two rampant secessionists too old to be conscripted, while two peaceable, home-loving husbands could fill these places and stay at home, were enough to make the situation of the latter desperate. When men become desperate something happens. An ex-Confederate Captain whose loyalty had been proven on the battlefield untarnished or questioned, though not a candidate, was placed at the head of the opposition--"Independent anti-war men's ticket"--it made them hopeful and assured election certain for their entire ticket. Randolph has always had enough patriotism and independence to cut off chronic party office-holders and when that gets too scarce or indifferent as on this occasion, in their desperation will bury selfishness, ambition and party pride and go it blind like they did in 1863.

- - - -

W. A. J. Swann

Of Louina, was elected in 1863. He was a young man of 28 summers, and had returned home with the loss of index and middle fingers of left hand, and its use for life. Capt. Swann volunteered and went out in Capt. Alford C. Wood's company, August 1st, 1861, which belonged to the 14th Alabama Regiment. He was 1st. Lieutenant, and was promoted to Colonel of his regiment. He was a brave and gallant soldier and was loved and respected by his men. After being wounded he resigned and came home and being closely and sympathetically associated with the people with whom he had learned to love from boyhood and aided in bearing and sharing their joys or troubles, he found many of them oppressed and persecuted by a partisan, political and tyranical war administration in county and state. Naturally, his sympathetical words and generous acts went out to aid, cheer and encourage the troubled to patience and fortitude. They were men of thought, principle and unselfishness. They appreciated his brave words and sought to make him their friend and leader and at the same time protect and strengthen him. This is a lesson wise men have learned and successful leaders must have if they stand. A few of the leading men met together and after counselling decided to run him for Tax Collector. This would keep him at home and support him--two very important things, and indispensable to their new leader and their plans and thoughts of conquest. So far as the writer knows, they secured his consent; at least, his friends put his name on their "Independent anti-war" ticket. He was, however, persuaded a few days prior to the election to write a letter saying, "I am no candidate. I have not sought the office." This was not a full surrender to the overture of the enemy. It might mislead the simple, but not those wise and determined men whose only hope for relief and success depended on the election of their ticket. A brave, gallant, maimed Confederate soldier's name at the head of their ticket meant success; otherwise, defeat. Heads of masses met and another letter after consultation was prepared and sent on the day of election to every beat, which in substance said, "Voters, don't be deceived, don't be mislead, Capt. Swann truly says: '"I am no candidate. I have not sought the office,' but his friends, the people, have said he was their choice, their candidate, and he has not said, he would not serve. We promise you that Capt. Swann will accept. We know what we say. We do not want office-seekers nor chronic office holders. You have had enough of that kind of material, and to your sorrow. Let us show we are free men, and dare to vote as we please and not as the bosses say and order. Let those old able-bodied "Warhorses" who have been stabled and pampered and said, "Go boys", have a good recommendation at the ballot box and an opportunity without an excuse to 'go and force peace' and send our boys home to their mothers. Good and true men have been sent to every beat with instructions to 'vote her solid.'" The writer was at home during the election nursing an empty sleeve. He had always voted the Weather's ticket because it was said he had made a good officer, but when a comrade in boyhood and in war equally as competent and certainly as meritorious and deserving was to be endorsed or repudiated by his vote, a second thought never entertained his mind for a moment. Capt. Swann, with the entire independent ticket, was elected. He made a good collector. Capt. Swann has voted the Republican ticket since the war. He is a primitive Baptist. He owns a good farm and runs a successful mercantile and supply business at Swann Hill, eight miles south of Wedowee. He is in his 60th year, and with the exception of a slight paralytic attack, is in remarkably good health and able to control and carry on his business.

Number Twenty Five

Written for The Toiler.

Tax Collectors

In last week's issue in 9 and 10 from first, in speaking of W.A.J. Swann "promoted to Colonel of his regiment", should have been "promoted to Captain of his company".

- - - -

Warren Armstrong

Was elected March, 1865, as a "Union man" - that is what all anti-secession Southern men were called during and at the close of the war. He lived in Fishhead Valley and was one of the most substantial and prominent men in the valley. He was a brother of Bill, Jim and Henry. The latter is living in Clay county now. He was a good, safe and reliable officer and clever man.

- - - -

John Coston

Was a teacher. He moved from Bowdon, Ga., about the close of the war and taught school. He served one term, and a few years afterwards moved to Tennessee and was living when last heard from.

- - - -

William Wood

The son of ex-sheriff, Willis Wood, was elected in 1868 as a Republican. He moved west a few years since. He was clever, accomodating and generally well thought of, but there was some trouble in making his final settlement with the Commissioner's court. He was the Republican "Polly Ann" candidate for probate judge in 1880. As there are a great many readers of The Toiler and others in the county who don't know nor have heard what the "Polly Ann" was , we take it for granted it would be interesting just here to tell them a little about her. Certain prominent anti-prohibition Democrats and Republicans had a boat built and launched on Little Tallapoosa river May 19, 1877, we believe it was, for the purpose of fishing, etc. When launched, a bottle of "red rye" was broken on deck and she was christened "The Polly Ann," and then provisioned with ample and varied supplies necessary for a cruise down the Little and Big Tallapoosa river to Louina. The trip consumed several days, and during the trip it was said, "wet tickets" were agreed upon for county officers for both parties and the tickets selected should be nominated and elected. Two men were selected from each of eight of our thirteen beats, one of whom was to be nominated by the other as chairman of his beat, the other to be committeeman on organization of the county convention. Delegates were to vote by ballot through the chairmen of beat delegations. Each beat was to have ten delegates or votes in the convention; eighty-six and 2/3 would make the nomination by a two-third vote. This assured their man eighty votes when the time arrived to make the nomination. One of the candidates, two weeks before the beat meetings were held said "I'll get 79 votes on first ballot." He got 80, as one delegate from Wedowee beat voted for him not expected, and on the second ballot he was declared nominated. "I'll get 79 votes on first ballot," caused suspicion and before the convention finished its nomination, the writer exposed the scheme and eighty delegates bolted the convention. Gilbert Hurst composed the poetry and Alf Monkus the music and it was named "Polly Ann."

- - - -

C. B. Nichols

A Republican, was elected in November, 1871, and did not collect all the tax for that year. This caused trouble in his and Wood's final settlement; otherwise, it is said, made a very creditable officer. Chris now lives in Clay, and is one of the most popular drummers that handles the "grip." He resigned and J.H. Davis was appointed February, 1873.

- - - -

J. H. Davis

See former letter under heading of Circuit Clerks.

- - - -

T. J. East

Was elected in 1874 as a Democrat. He was merchandising at Louina at the time. He was a member of Captain John T. Smith's company and lost one leg in the war. He made a brave and gallant soldier, belongs to one of the oldest and most respected families in the southern portion of the county. He owns a good farm on Corn House creek. He is living in Roanoke, is a Notary Public and Tax Commissioner. He was nominated by the "Polly Ann" in 1877, and defeated for re-election.

- - - -

J. H. Radney

Was elected on the Independent "Peoples Ticket" in 1877. He made a good Collector during his first term. He was re-elected in 1880 and afterwards appointed Tax Commissioner. He owns a good farm near Roanoke on which he lives. He is a man of good morals, sober habits, liberal and charitable, and member of the M.E. Church, South. The act of the legislature making the Commissioner appointive by the Governor instead of electing by the people and his continued term of office, rendered him very unpopular and no doubt to unjust criticism. The voters of Randolph county are very jealous of their rights, and as a rule, with few exceptions, hold to the one term.

- - - -

A. J. Cheavers

Of Saxon's Beat One, was elected as a Democrat, in 1891. He was 57 years of age then, and from some cause resigned and W.A. Radney appointed in August 1891. He is a very clever man and said to be a good neighbor and citizen.

J. M. Kitchens

Our present Collector is one of the oldest living citizens in the county. He lives in Rockdale beat, where he has lived since boyhood. He has been faithful, energetic, honest and impartial in the discharge of his duties and a better or cleaner record had never been made by a Collector in the county. He is a Republican and voted that ticket since the war, and the Populist ticket in the last county and State elections. He is now in his 65th year, hale, hearty and robust. He was elected and served as County Commissioner in 1868.

Number Twenty Six

Written for The Toiler.

County Commissioners

George McKaskle--One of the two first County Commissioners of Randolph County. He lived in the northern part of the county on Section 21, Township 16, Range 11, and represented all north Randolph while Willis Wood, the other, lived in the Mickle settlement, near the Chambers county line, and represented all south Randolph. There were only two voting places in the county. Their first court was held April 1834, at Triplett, the county seat, now Blake's Ferry, under a mulberry tree, near Triplett's dwelling house, a short distance from the ferry on the west side of the river. We have been unable to find anyone who knew him or what became of him.

Willis Wood--We refer you to serial on Sheriffs.

James Hanson--We find he was appointed by the court on two different occasions as a commissioner, but there is no record evidence he ever qualified or acted.

1835--William Clemens, James Prothro, James Hathorn and Thos. Blake were elected.

William Clemens lived six miles south of here on the place now known as James S. Radney's. He owned a large body of land, several negroes and a big herd of stock cattle. He was said to be a good clever neighbor and an honorable man. We knew his sons, Prosser L., Jesse, James and Ben. He died in June 1840. Ben Clemens, it is said, now lives in Clay county; Prosser died before the war; James and Jesse moved to Louisiana. The old Clemens trail took its name from this family, and was used for driving beef cattle to Georgia.

James Prothro, we believe, first settled near Roanoke, then called High Pine, afterwards moved to Rock Mills, which was called Prothro and McPherson's mill. He was a good citizen and stood well with the people. He died many years ago.

James Hathorn lived near Roanoke, just this side, and had good property. He was a brother of Hugh Hathorn. He resigned and moved west.

Thomas Blake lived 15 miles north. He owned a large body of land, had several negroes and farmed. Uncle Tom was strictly honest and up-right in his dealings. He was re-elected in 1836 and 7, but resigned after his election to the legislature in Aug. 1837. He was Randolph's first member in the House of Representatives. He prided in the euphonous name, "Wool hat boys." He was a Democrat, and we believe a Primitive Baptist in belief, though not a member. He was the grandfather of Stell Blake, Esq. He was born in 1800 and died in 1880. His remains lie in the family cemetery on the hill overlooking his old home. His late widow died Feb. 25th, 1895, and was 89 years of age. She was a noble pioneer mother; and was buried by her husband's side.

RANDOLPH--HER OFFICIALS

Number Twenty Seven

Written for The Toiler, by Capt. J.M.K. Guinn

County Commissioners Continued

1836--Thomas Blake, re-elected; William McKnight, Hugh W. Harris and William Mullaly.

William McKnight, who had just attained his majority and right to vote, being an enthusiastic Democrat, of Big River Beat 5, (now Louina) was elected Commissioner, and in August, 1838, was elected to the Legislature. His boyish ambition and aspiration for office seems to have been fully gratified at the end of his legislative services from what cause does not appear; for the writer finds nothing derogatory in his official acts. I lost sight of him since 1850; can't say for certain, but believe he died in the county.

Hugh W. Harris lived in Henry M. Gay community when elected. He was a brother of Dr. Daniel C. Harris, who now lives near Delta. Hugh moved from the county in 1843 or '44.

William Mullaly was a native of Ireland, 36 years of age when elected. He bid off several town lots at the sale in March 1836, and I suppose made Wedowee his home, but subsequently lived in Lower Fishhead, south of Chulafinnee, originally known as Sawyer's beat 2. He was well-to-do, and stood favorably with the people from the time the writer knew him in 1842 to 1860, since which time he has journeyed over the Jordan of life.

1837--Hugh W. Harris and Thomas Blake succeeded themselves. James Prothro and James Hathorn, who served in 1835, were again elected.

Thomas Blake was not only elected Commissioner at the August election in 1837, but was at the same election and on the same day elected to the lower house of the Legislature. This can be accounted for probably from the following circumstances; Randolph, Chambers, Talladega, and other counties admitted into the State in 1832, did not in all probability properly organize in time to have the census taken in April 1833, and were left out of the reapportionment of Senators and Representatives on the basis of the census. The Constitution of the State made provision for representatives and the basis of representation entitling counties to members of the Senate and Representatives. It also provided for one member from each county, but with provisions that at some future time it should contain a certain number of inhabitants. This provision seems to have been misconstrued or ignored by the General Assembly.

If I remember correctly, one of these counties--Chambers, I believe it was, elected and sent a representative anyhow, but not until the winter session of 1836-7 did the subject come properly before the Legislature, when it was referred to a select committee to investigate and report on the constitutionally of county representation. From some cause, the committee failed to report and the Legislature adjourned without action. However, Governor Clay called a special session in June 1837, in order to make provision for State troops, which had been called on to protect the settlers from the Indians, who were hostile and making preparations for war at this special session, this committee reported each county entitled to one representative, etc.

Having no mail facilities, the people depended largely on "grape-vine" dispatches, which often traveled at the rate of 50 to 75 miles in a day, but were not always credited by the people. So you see the people had heard the news, and in order to be in shape to receive its benefits, elected Thomas Blake, their first representative. And, like our Old Side Baptists usually put it: "In case of failure," a Commissioner. Uncle Tom was, I believe, one of that faith and practice; and, you know they are the best people in the world, relying entirely on God's love and mercy, and not on educated tongues, pride, riches and vain ejaculations.

Blake and Hathorn resigned. Isaac Baker and Hugh Montgomery were appointed. (See serials on County Treasurer and Tax Assessor)

1838--Richard Young, Andrew T. Ray, Blount H. Bazemore and J.T. Wafer were elected.

Richard Young owned and lived at that time at Tripplett's (Blake's) Ferry. Tripplett sold out after the county seat was moved to Wedowee. Richard Young was a good clever man and citizen, and was a brother of Ike Young. The legislature changed the term of office from an annual to a bi-annual. He was re-elected in 1840 and died in the latter part in 1844. Thomas Blake was appointed administrator and at the sale bought the homestead and ferry. His son, John Blake, owned it until his death.

Andrew T. Ray was an early settler and entered land on Section 36, Township 17, Range 10 in 1835. It was in Blake's beat, afterwards Dunston's No. 3. Mr. John R. Ray of Oxford, Ala. is his son. I don't remember to have seen him, unless he was the Ray who visited my father's in Chulafinnee in 1842.

Blount H. Bazemore was about 33 years of age. He lived in Wehadkee, beat 4, now High Shoals. He was re-elected in 1840. His name gave him a noted personality, and he was known all over the county for levity, sport and liberality.

J.T. Wafer was a son-in-law of William Clemens, and established Wafer's now Malone's ferry. He resigned and afterwards moved west. W.G. Falkner was appointed to fill the vacancy. (For Falkner see serial on County Treasury.)

1840--Richard Young, B.H. Bazemore, W.G. Falkner and Ephriam Carpenter.

Ephriam Carpenter was Dutch and came from Germany when a boy. He was a brother of Samuel Carpenter, whose family of children still live here - Bud, Sarah, Frank, Mally, Mary, Ida, Sug and Berta. Eph Carpenter married a Clemens, was a tanner by trade and lived in the house now occupied by Mr. John T. Owen. He moved to Louisiana thence to Texas. It is said, he is now living in Sherman, Texas, in feeble health. He had a beautiful little girl, with black curly hair, named Mattie. She claimed the writer as her sweetheart, and would sing:

"Old Dan Tucker he got drunk,
And fell in the fire and kicked up a chunk;
A red hot coal got in his shoe,
Lord a massa how the ashes flew.

Chorus.

Clear the track for Old Dan Tucker,
You come too late to get your supper."

Number Twenty Eight

Written for The Toiler, by Capt. J.M.K. Guinn

County Commissioners---Continued

A little explanation just here becomes necessary to a better understanding of the divisions of the county at this time:

In 1842 Randolph County was divided into two militia regiments, and those into beats, as follows: Seventy first Regiment: Beats - Able's, 1; Blake's 2; Arbacoochee, 3; Casper's, 4; Lovvorn, 5; Duke's, 6; Owen's, 7; Fish-head, 8; Ninety-first Regiment: Beats - Wesabulga, 1; Roanoke, 2; Bacon Level, 3; Wehadkee, 4; Big River, 5; Wedowee, 6; Flat Rock 7; Rock Mills, 8.

1842-- Benjamin A. Flinn, Wiley J. Pritchett, Davis E. Grisham and Sygmore Moore.

B.A. Flinn lived in Able's beat. He was a Whig and made a dutiful, efficient officer, prompt in attendance, reasonable and just in his opinion and acts. He was a personal friend of father's and shared his confidence. I don't remember having seen him after his term of office expired.

Wiley J. Pritchett was 30 years of age, was a Democrat. He lived in Wehadkee beat, and probably afterwards in Roanoke. He was tax assessor and Justice of the Peace. He moved to what is now known as Clay County and was living when last heard from.

Davis E. Grisham was 38 years of age, and a "Coon" Whig. He lived on the hill north of Wedowee and owned the Che-wastihadgo N 1-2, S 3, 20, R 11 reserved under Creek Treaty of 1832. He sold out to J.W. Guinn in 1843 and moved to Roanoke beat near his old home, located in 1835 on Grave's creek, probably the Bob Birdsong place. He was elected in 1844. He made a good Commissioner and was highly respected. Eventually, he went west. Sygmon Moore was 48 years of age and lived in Lovvorn's beat. When I first got acquainted with him I thought he and Seymore, Bazemore, Latimore, McLemore, Elmore, Fillmore, Gilmore, and Guy Moore, Israel Moore and Lypson Moore were all brothers. It happened, however, that Guy Moore got in court about a wild hog, and during the trial, I learned which was which.

Sygmore Moore, if I remember correctly, was a Charles W. Statham man in the election for Probate Judge in May 1840. Since then I have lost sight of him.

1844--Davis E. Grisham and Wiley J. Pritchett, were elected. Thomas F. Lundie and Edmond Ingram, John Murphy appointed vice W.J. Pritchett resigned.

John Murphy was a Democrat. He lived in Wedowee beat on Wild Cat Creek, at the late residence of Mrs. Mary Camp.

He was an honest faithful officer and re-elected in 1846, and held until his death in 1847. He was an uncle to Esqr. J.P.D. Murphy.

Thomas F. Lundie was a Whig and lived at or near the present Lineville, in Clay county. He was re-elected in 1846 and 1850. In 1853 he was the Whig candidate for State Senate and was defeated by 34 votes by Henry M. Guy, Democrat.

Edmond Ingram was a Democrat. He lived in Fish Head Beat, was 49 years of age, re-elected in 1846, and was living in 1860. (It seems to have been an unwritten law to divide the commissioners with the two parties.)

1846--Davis E. Grisham, Thomas F. Lundie, John Murphy and Edmond Ingram. James M. Clemens was appointed vice Grisham, resigned.

J.M. Clemens was 35 years of age, and a son of William Clemens. He lived at the James Radney place on Corn House creek. He was re-elected in 1848. He went west.

"Big" Sam Carpenter was appointed vice John Murphy deceased. He lived at Wedowee, and was one of those indispensable necessities to the prompt and efficient carrying on of the public business. He was competent, capable, and efficient, always on hand and ready for any emergency. While not an office seeker, yet he did a good business in filling loop holes and vacancies. "Big" Sam was a jack-at-all-trades, professions and callings. A man of good disposition and pleasant manners, and seldom got credit for what he was worth. He went west.

1848--William Owens, James M. Clemens, Gideon Riddle and Freeman Taylor.

William Owens came to Wedowee from Benton county in July, 1842, as a mail contractor. He moved to the place now occupied by Andrew, his son. He kept boarders and worked at the shoemaker trade. Subsequently, he built the Owens Hotel (Huckeba House.)

He was Jailer for years and Coroner one or two terms. He was sober, honest, and upright in his dealings and a good citizen. His two eldest sons, Preston and Henry, died in the Confederate service. Tom, Andrew, Bill and Mrs. Cordelia Griffin are living. Mrs. F.E. Owens, who survived her husband until May 19th, 1894, was a Crook. She had a remarkable memory and a bright intellect. Her biographical, chronological and historical information were faultless and inexhaustable. Up to within a few days of her demise, she related minutely incidents that had occurred when the writer was a small boy fifty years ago. She said sometime previously to the writer, "I am ready, willing and prepared to go when called, only one thing gives me a desire or care to live. You know what that is." The writer answered in the affirmative. Then she continued, "I have asked God for his care and protection when I have been called away, and am persuaded all's well." Husbank, wife and daughter, Yucatan, are sleeping at the City Cemetery.

Gideon Riddle was 47 years of age then, and now 94 and still living, but his hearing is so dull I had to talk through a trumpet to him in 1892 when I last met him. He owned and resided at Oakfuskee, the Sawyer old Ferry on Big Tallapoosa river. He raised a large interesting family and his sons are all good citizens. He makes his home with them.

Freeman Taylor was a South Carolinian, 48 years of age. He lived at the Dick Green place, south of old High Pine Baptist Church. He was a good, safe and well-to-do farmer, a clever man and good neighbor. He died many years since.

Number Twenty Nine

Written for The Toiler, by Capt. J.M.K. Guinn

County Commissioners---Continued

1850---E.S. Barker, T.L. Thomason, David V. Crider and Thomas F. Lundie.

E.S. Barker lived in Louina. He and W.A. Handley carried on a business of merchandise which became insolvent and Barker going out of business. Miss Cattie Barker, a lady of rare beauty and fine literary attainments was his daughter, and W.M. Barker, editor of the Randolph County News, in 1877, and one of the firm of Barker & Hill, merchants at Roanoke, was his son. He died sometime about 1855-6.

Thomas L. Thomason was a Democrat. He lived at Roanoke, afterwards at Rock Mills. He was a big-hearted, wholesoul and jolly comrade; sociable, pleasant and lively. He was popular with "the boys" and occasionally took a hand in horse racing, etc. Aunt Nancy, his better half, was a grand old mother, and a faithful Christian, whose hope was disdained with suffering. They lived with their son, Thom, ex-Probate Judge, T.J. Thomason, at Rock Mills, where they died. John W. Thomason and Nan were their children. John W. Thomason was clever, honest, liberal, sociable, and a faithful member of the Baptist church, whom to know was to love. Judge T.J. Thomason, who now lives in the county needs no commendations by me. You know him. Mrs. G.W. Taylor, an amiable lady, a kind neighbor, a dutiful wife and affectionate mother. Judge T.J. is the only one left.

David G. Grider was 36 years of age; a blacksmith by trade, a Democrat and a M.E. Preacher. He lived at Arbacoochee. He was almost helpless for years before his death. Honored, loved and respected by all and died at Arbacoochee about 1883-4.

1853---John M. Hendricks, B.J. Hand, W.H. Miller and Harris Stephens.

John M. Hendricks was 50 years of age, a Democrat and lived in Bacon Level beat. He was a good, clever, safe and capable man, and very popular and gave strength to his party ticket. Was County Surveyor for several years and made a most excellent and efficient officer. He was noble, generous, kind and true; did the writer an act of kindness and friendship, he then, and now highly appreciates and hopes never to forget. He was living near Texas Court Grounds in Heard County, Georgia, in 1868, and I believe died at the home of his son, Capt. John M. Hendricks near Rock Mills a few years afterwards. Peace to his memory.

Britian J. Hand. (See serial on County Treasurers.)

W.H. Miller was 56 years of age, lived in Flat Rock beat. A Democrat and stood well with his party. He was living in 1860.

Harris Stephens was 47 years of age. Lived in Delta beat, was a Democrat and popular. During the war it was said he was "a bitter partisan and persecutor of Union men." He had previously borne the name of a quiet, pleasant and peaceable neighbor and citizen. He was said to be physically, the best man in the county. Men's surroundings and associations have a great deal to do with their acts. The war times forced every man to be a partisan, and to take sides. There was no neutral ground upon which to stand. Deception didn't deceive, but when attempted it brought two-fold persecution. Willing or unwilling you had to chose one or the other side and abide the consequences. Your own kindred and neighbors became enemies. There were no ties, not that of wife and husband, this cruel war did not separate; nor virtue, it did not insult; nor love, it did not seduce; nor peace, it did not outrage. No saint, sinner, woman, boy or girl could speak above a whisper without fear of proscription. No, not even the poor negro escaped the eagle eyes of war and antiwar persecutions. The lame and aged and Christian ministers had to cry out, like the rabble did that persecuted Christ, or go to prison, the woods or swing by the neck. Don't say you didn't if you were at home, nor that you wouldn't. As good men and women as you dare to be did it. Harris Stephens may have and no doubt did go too far. I, even I, did and said things I would to God I had not; but no man can truly say I persecuted or inflicted suffering on anyone wnatonly.

CORRECTION

In last week's issue two names were incorrectly spelled: "Berta" when it should have been "Barto" Carpenter; "Mattie" should have been "Mallie" Carpenter.

Number Thirty

Written for The Toiler by Capt. J.M.K. Guinn

County Commissioners---Continued

1854---B.J. Hand, W.H. Miller, W.E. Camp and William Ingram.

W.E. Camp was probably related to Jonathan Camp of Delta beat, the first Circuit Clerk of Randolph County. He was 67 years of age, and a Democrat. Probably the father or uncle of William E. Camp, who volunteered in Capt. James Aiken's Company from Arbacoochee beat, and elected Orderly Sergeant and afterwards promoted to a Lieutenant. The Camps were all good citizens & well-to-do farmers.

William Ingram. (See serial on Tax Assessor.)

1855---Hiram Barron, Charles Foster, Wilson Faulkner and James F. White.

Hiram Barron lived in the town of Louina, and was a Baptist minister and Democrat. He was the father of Matthew M., John D., Milton D.[1], and Joe Day Barron. As each of his sons were more or less public characters and associated in the historical and official acts and administration of the county's past, I'll speak of them in their regular order. He was re-elected in 1857. Was honored by the appellation "Father Barron," which in those days

[1]Milton D. Barron was the youngest brother of Hiram Barron according to Stella Weaver Dillahunty as found in family bible records.

meant much. Old fashioned in his ways, positive in his affirmations, energetic and determined in his acts; and when he said a thing he meant it and believed it, and his neighbors respected and sustained him.

Charles Foster lived in Rock Mills beat. Elected as a Democrat; a good electioneerer, popular, energetic and ambitious and made some reputation while Commissioner, but at the expense of his party, or rather the Courthouse contingent. This let his friends suggest and solicit him to offer for the legislature and put the "boss machine" against him which seldom fails. When the convention met and the "Boss Cat" purred, the Foster mice hied to their holes. Thus repudiated, his high sense of honor had been humiliated and the fidelity of his constituencies were questionable, of whom he had a right to expect endorsement. His friends at home were mad and their ambition aroused and his name was announced as "an independent" candidate for representative. The convention had nominated the present ex-Gov. W.H. Smith, ex-Sheriff, A.W. Denman, and Rev. Isaac Weaver. This was in 1857. Foster had not openly and fully declared himself a condidate, but the democrats published that he had--everywhere and on all occasions--and that he was holding back until he saw what his chances were; that if he resigned his Commissionership he might not get in again, and office he must have. They said he knew it would be his last and there was no possible chance for his election to the legislature. T.L. Pittman, a shrewd and coming politician, worked the racket and had men posted to be at every public gathering and the stump speakers, R.S. Heflin and W.H. Smith, to guy and rattle him. "It was considered," they said, "dishonorable and undemocratic to hold one office and run for another." They claimed too, "it showed weakness and want of confidence on his part." Uncle Charlie's pride was too sensitive to be priced with this demagogical goad in the hands of merciless, selfish and tyrannical bosses. He resigned his commission a short time before the election, and no sooner than done, they charged, "he had deserted and gone back on the party, and had sold out to the "Know Nothings and Whigs." They guyed, rattled and shelled the woods and circulated the most rebellious and treasonable "saying and promises" he should have made. They cat-a-combed with crimes his political death and burial. Defeat was bad enough but their venomous and poisoned fangs touched his proud manly heart and stung it to death; for it never recovered. A noble, generous, honest and useful man sacrificed through selfish ambition and partisan strife. God pity the one, and pardon the others. Uncle Charles was a member of Salem anti Missionary or Hardshell Baptist Church, and as far as the writer knew, lived a faithful Christian life until his death in 1894.

Wilson Falkner. (see serial on Sheriff.)

James F. White, lived in Jenkins beat; was 42 years of age and a Democrat. He succeeded himself in 1857-8 and was re-elected in 1862. A clever man, but a bitter partisan. He was dubbed "the Courthouse Cat's Kitten" and lapped milk out of the same dish. Died during or about the close of the war.

1857---Hiram Barron, James F. White, Jeremiah Stephens and P.G. Trent.

Jeremiah Stephens lived in Delta beat, 32 years of age, Democrat and farmer. He was a good, honest and upright man, and commanded the confidence and respect of all classes. He was re-elected in 1858 and was living in 1860.

P.G. Trent lived in Bacon Level beat. A Democrat and a dealer in tobacco. Keen, shrewd and tricky, but pleasant, liberal and hospitable. Re-elected in 1858. Was a member of the Missionary Baptist Church, at Bacon Level. Moved to Tallapoosa county and was last heard from in Talladega county and is still living.

1858---J.F. White, Jeremiah Stephens, P.G. Trent and John F. McKay.

John F. McKay lived in Fox Creek beat; 44 years of age and a Democrat. Plain common farmer, with plenty of good hard horse sense, but knew little about public business. He was still living in 1860.

1862---J.F. White, W.H. Grogan, Samuel Y. Carlisle and Joe Day Barron.

W.H. Grogan lived in Delta beat; was 36 years of age, a secessionist "war man"--tolerably well informed and managed to get an exemption as a school teacher or miller and made himself useful in drawing salt, going to the post office reading soldiers letters, spotting and reporting conscripts and arresting deserters. All of these were considerative in exemptions. "The anti-war" or "Lincolnites" captured all the offices in 1864 and he had to have another consideration attached to his exemptions. He raised a Company of Home Guards and joined Col. Jefferson Falkner Battalion, which was composed of Capt. John Reaves, Capt. B.H. Ford, Capt. O.W. Sheppard, Capt. Joshua Hightower and Capt. W.H. Grogan. He ran for Major but failed to get all of his own Company and none from any of the others and, of course, was defeated. He now lives in Cleburne County, I believe.

Samuel Y. Carlisle lived in Rock Mills beat, was 62 years of age, a Democrat, one of the best men in the county. Had the good will and confidence of his neighbors and the people generally, and retained them until his death.

Joe Day Barron, "Sandy Higgins," was raised in Louina, but at this time lived in Wedowee where he has been since 1857 as editor and publisher of the "Southern Mercury." He was a Breckenridge Democrat and Secessionist. He had formerly been associated with Matthew M. Barron and W.E. Gilbert on the "Louina Eagle." Was Register in Chancery in 1859, and in 1875 wrote the serial letters published in "The Randolph Enterprise," under the nom de plume of "Sandy Higgins." I believe, he published a paper in Clay in 1880 and was Clerk for Secretary of State from 1884 to 1890.

In 1890 he was elected Secretary of State, was re-nominated in 1892 and defeated, but counted in and held until December 1894. Is now editor of the Montgomery "Daily Evening News" which advocates the gold bug or retrograde democracy. He is pleasant, affiable and sociable and a natural born humorist. He was a "minute man" and wore the badge in 1860. It is the only thing, the writer remembers, he never failed to hold fast and maintain, and this might be easily accounted for, since he was constitutionally opposed to being shot at; especially by Yankees. The writer didn't believe then, nor does he believe now, that he would or did stuff ballot boxes, but with bull dog tenacity, he catches, shuts his eyes and sticks. The writer loves him and supported him until honesty and decency forbid, and I believe, would do it again, if sanctified and fumigated of black belt ballot box stuffing, etc.

Correction

Speaking of Probate Judges election in May 1850, I said that Sygmore Moore was a Charles W. Statham man. We had 1840 and "it ought to be 1850" as that was the first election in the state for Probate Judges. We had county judges previously.

Number Thirty One

Written for The Toiler, by Capt. J.M.K. Guinn

County Commissioners---Continued

1864---Dan D. Mitchell, Zachary M. Hutchens, James H. Bell and Robert S.M. Hunter.

D.D. Mitchell lived on Big Tallapoosa river eight miles west and in Wedowee beat. He was a Union man; about 46 years of age; a Douglas Democrat in 1860 but voted the co-operation ticket against secession. He was a well-to-do farmer; had never asked nor sought office until the Alabama legislature and Confederate Congress made it a "bombproof" against conscription. Office, those days, was sought after more earnestly than the kingdon of Heaven. It meant exemption from conscription and liberty to stay at home, with wife and children. It was better than a substitute bought with gold, silver, negroes and lands; the profession of minister, Doctors and school teachers, the occupation of mail carriers, overseers, millers and smithers, the infirmities of the deaf, dumb, blind, halt and maimed; or the diseases of the consumptive, paralytic and lunatic, because behind it was power and renumeration. Yet, not one of those classes escaped persecution. Many had to cross the "Bragg and Sherman line" or play the ground hog act. So, you see, the anti-war, Union men and exempts were in the majority and elected their friends to office.

Zachary M. Hutchens made his home in Roanoke. He was 47 years of age, ran on the Know Nothing ticket for representative with W.H. Burton in 1855 and defeated Ex-Gov.W.H. Smith and R.J. Wood. Voted the co-operation ticket in 1860 and was a Union man when elected. Zach was a live energetic politician and a hard worker. But like most men who make political popularity a hobby, he mixed too freely with "Johnnie Barley Corn," a much more formidable and destructive enemy than Yankees. This was an unfortunate failing, otherwise he was loved and respected by all. He was in his latter days nursed with gentle hands and laid to rest by kind, sympathizing neighbors and mourning relatives in the Roanoke Baptist Church cemetery. His pleasant prominent and personal liberality endeared him to the entire community. M.J. Mickel, Esq., H.M. Mickle and David Manley are three of his friends who watched over and administered to his last wants. A few years after his demise, his widow and children moved to Mississippi.

James H. Bell lived in Arbacoochee beat. He was anti-war and Union man. The Bells were recognized and known far and wide as good, honorable and respectable citizens. James H. Bell was a very prominent character in politics, and a man of means and influence. I believe he died in 1894, at his home near Bell's Mills, in Cleburne County.

R.S.M. Hunter, or "Bob Hunter" as he was generally known and called, lived at Wedowee; was 33 years of age, anti-war and

Union man, a retail whiskey dealer; profane and dissipated in habits; though pleasant, kind and neighborly. An affectionate and loving husband and father. By some means, the writer has forgotten what,he was conscripted,although a county officer. No doubt, however, it was because he boldly and fearlessly, privately and publicly, denounced the County, State and Confederate administration; and gave the county officials uneasiness and apprehensions of personal danger. He was quiet, peaceable and law abiding; yet bold and fearless. Being arrested and paroled by a Brigade Commander; rather than to go into service and take up arms against the cause of the Union, he crossed the line to the Federalist. Some time subsequently he visited his family and was captured; making no effort to resist by violence. (The writer being present.) His capture was caused through the treachery of a masonic friend known to the writer; but, perhaps, not to him. He narrowly escaped being mobbed by soldiers who first arrested him. He owed his escape to bravery, strategy and loyalty to law of three friends, T.N. Berryhill, W.J. Taylor and the writer. They hid him out for a few days and then saw that he was delivered to the civil authorities at Talladega. Here he managed through "a bad case of small pox" to escape and cross the Jordan of proscription in the Union army of security and protection. Mrs. Hunter was a Miss Emily Glover of Heard County, Georgia. She was of a good family and is a noble lady. She now lives 8 miles west of Wedowee at the late home of her husband who died in 1892. Mr. and Mrs. Hunter were neighbors and personal friends of the writer and had been for many years. Bob was ex-sheriff, ex-Tax Assessor. Almond P. Hunter is his eldest son. His remains lie in the Masonic cemetery at Wedowee. Peace to his memory.

1866---W.C. Robertson, John W. Noles, John D. Windsor and James H. Bell.

William C. Robertson was a Bell Whig; voted against secession; an anti-war and Union men when elected; 65 years of age and born in S.C. in 1801. Lived five miles east from Wedowee on the Franklin road. A carpenter by trade, he merchandised and ran a farm. Brother of Dr. R.L. Robertson and father of ex-Sheriff, W.C.S. Robertson of Wedowee, Joseph W. Robertson of High Shoals, Mrs. Agnes Enloe of Langdale, Mrs. Thomas Pollard of Georgia, Mrs. John Tenant of near Wedowee and Bob Robertson of Texas. Was well informed; had high and noble aspirations, a steadfast friend and an open enemy. He had moral and temperate habits and was safe, prudent and conservative, making a good Commissioner---died in 1868.

John W. Noles lived in Lamar beat; 38 years of age; an ordained Baptist minister. Owned a man and ran a farm. A Union man, when elected, and was exempted as miller and preacher and was not in the war. He now lives in Clay county merchandising, said to be well-to-do financially. He was one of those few Baptist ministers who believe, or at least preached, "that unless the Lord gave him a text and put the words into his mouth, he couldn't preach." The writer remembers once, at Wedowee, going to hear him when he said, "Brethren, I don't know what will be my text. The Lord hasn't given me one yet; and unless he does and puts the words into my mouth, I won't preach. It won't be John Noles preaching, but the Lord." (Turning the leaves of the Bible at the time, until finally he stopped and said) "The Lord has given me a text." Rev. J.P. Shaffer was present and after leaving the church in company with Noles and the writer said: "Bro. Noles, you do believe what you preach?" "Yes, Brother

Shaffer, don't you?" "No, Brother Noles, I repudiate that God and that sermon. I worship the true and living, and a different God, to the one that preached that harangue." He has been Moderator of his Association since then, but it is not known whether he is still the mouth piece of God or not. I have heard white women, white and black men preach frequently, but "Lord" only once.

John D. Windsor lived in Louina beat; was 51 years of age; a Union man, and said to be a good clever neighbor and citizen. He was elected township trustee; and I believe Justice of the Peace several times.

Number Thirty Two

Written for The Toiler, by Capt. J.M.K. Guinn

County Commissioners---Continued

1868---J.M. Kitchens, J.B. Cooley, A. Brown and S. McDonald.

James M. Kitchens. (See serial on Tax Collector.)

John B. Cooley, of Almond, Flat Rock beat, was 43 years of age and a Republican. He merchandised and ran a farm; was a pleasant accomodating and useful neighbor, and good citizen. He made an honest effort to advance the interest of the county and her people. He never, so far as the writer remembers suffered his political prejudice to wrongfully lead him to an injustice in his official acts; though, at the time partisan strife ran high; the golden rule not recognizable, but an eye for an eye; a tooth for a tooth, saith-as thou hath sown thou shalt reap. He had a good heart and it bore Christian fruit. He didn't live long after his term of Commissionership expired; honored, loved and mourned by all.

Alanson Bowen was 66 years of age, lived in Wedowee beat, a Republican, and had been a Union man during the war, though a Whig previously. He was a man of fine sense, good intentions, a zealous Christian with temperate moral habits; yet an unconquerable enemy and bitter partisan. Was a deacon in the Wedowee Baptist Church for several years. Refused to hear a secession preacher preach during the war. Mrs. Benjamin P. Dodson and Mrs. H. H. Huckeba are the only two of a large family of children living. He lived several years after his term as Commissioner expired, and as he grew older he became childish and helpless until his death. He had one brother, William C. Bowen, the writer loved as David did Jonathan. Mrs. W.C. Bowen died and was buried at the Masonic Cemetery in 1855-6; he then moved to Pine Bluff, Texas, on west bank of the Sabine river, in 1856-7.

Samuel McDonald lived in Lamar beat; was 56 years of age; a Republican and a farmer. He is still living, I believe, honored and loved by his neighbors.

1872---W.H. Culpepper, W.H. Osborn, W.D. Lovvorn, and T.N. Brown

William H. Culpepper was 59 years of age; lived in Flat Rock beat; a Republican and Union man; a prominent and leading member of the M.E. Church, and still living and reflecting his Christian light, life and character which shines brightly and brilliantly in the constellation of the fixed stars of God's spiritual and temporal kingdon and enjoying the fullness of the promises made, ordained and purposed by God to his children.

William H. Osborn was a resident citizen of Roanoke beat; 58 years of age; a farmer, and a republican in whom there was no guile, hypocracy or deception; honest faithful and reliable in his acts and dealings; prompt and efficient as an officer; dutiful and zealous as a Christian; pleasant, sociable and kind as a neighbor; liberal to the poor and sympathetic for the troubled and afflicted. In December 1892, I believe it was, he bid adieu to this earth and the ties of nature that associated him, you and I together.

William D. Lovvorn lived in Lamar beat; was 41 years of age; a Republican being a miller was exempted from conscription during the war, was, of course, conservative, liberal and accomodating. After the war, he began to accumulate property and loan money on mortgages at a high per cent which it was said: "he invariably collected." He was nominated by the County Republican Convention in 1872, for representative and defeated John W. Thomason as Democrat. His acts, with few exceptions, were conservative. A man of fine thought, big heart, liberal hand and Christian character. Is a zealous Baptist, an uncompromising Republican and a successful money maker. He is living near Bowden, Ga.

Thomas N. Brown lived near Clay county line, in the Ike Young or Dingler settlement, Fox Creek beat. He was a tenderfooted Republican and a good easy, clever kind of fellow; a man of good sense, sound judgment, honest intentions, with little energy. He had a noble, pleasant and amiable wife. She couldn't have been otherwise since she was a sister of John, Dick, George and Bud Hill and Mesdame Moses and Dock Hardy. Tom resigned shortly after his election and was living when last heard from.

David A. Perryman was appointed vice W.D. Lovvorn resigned. (See serials on Tax Assessors.)

C.A. Prescott was appointed in 1873, vice T.N. Brown resigned. He was a Republican; 36 years of age; a miller and farmer and lived in Lamar beat. He was a volunteer conscript and sent to the conscript camp at Talladega, if the writer remembers correctly. Moved to Wedowee in 1876 or 77, and went into the mercantile business where he still continues and has accumulated a good property. He is a deacon in Wedowee Baptist Church. Mrs. C.A. Prescott was a school mate of the writer and a daughter of Jack Morrow. She is one of those unassuming, plain, domestic, Christian mothers, indispensable to the church and community in which she lives.

Number Thirty Three

Written for The Toiler, by Capt. J.M.K. Guinn

County Commissioners---Continued

1875---W.P. Jackson, W.S. Mayfield, J.N. Lovvorn and E. Carter, First Democrat since before the war.

William P. Jackson of Flat Rock beat, was a farmer and member of the M.E. Church South. In politics, he was an extreme partisan Democrat. Being honorable and just in his private dealings, he shared the full confidence and respect of his neighbors. Being selfwilled and self righteous, with implicit and confiding confidence in his party; and believing that by him and others elected the wrongs were to be arighted and the waste places reset with evergreens and roses. He soon realized, however, it was a prodigious undertaking but believed it feasible. And like many other good men whose honesty and ambition are greater than their ability and capacity, imagined an opportunity was the thing needed. His party had preached it, wrote it, talked it, and illustrated it so often and persistently until it was believed and wanted, and perhaps by none more so than Uncle Billy. The Democrats had not been in office since before the war. They said, "Unless we get in and change things everything will soon go to ruin and decay." The leaders hyperbole and stereotype the wrongs and burdens laid on the farmers, until they believed, like the silly, innocent and misguided Democrats believed Grover Cleveland, could and would if elected, correct all wrongs and relieve all wants. Yes, they believed it, voted for it and wanted it. Uncle Billy soon found this Democratic Jordan was too soft to walk on, too deep to wade in and too wide to swim. The task undertaken was hopeless - a thing that had not been anticipated. Having always guarded his word and honor with fidelity, he chafed under restraint and became sullen at defeat, and, at one time, seriously considered tendering his resignation but the opportunity he had coveted so long to retaliate on his enemies, who had piqued him on all occasions, would be lost and his friends and party would feel he had hopelessly deserted them. This was too much for his loyalty and patriotism, and it was said, a "siere facias" had been issued to his party he was willing to be offered as a sacrifice again.

William S. Mayfield lived in Bacon Level beat, was a manufacturer of earthern ware and ran a farm: A Baptist, Mason and Democrat, 45 years of age, and had served as a soldier in the Confederate army. He was pleasant, agreeable and sociable; open, frank and liberal; kind, generous, and hospitable, moral, temperate and conservative, and now is a citizen of Roanoke.

John N. Lovvorn (Free John) was of Lamar beat; a miller and farmer, and a conservative Democrat. Mild, pleasant and unassuming, not disposed to criticism or to meddle with business that didn't concern him. Had few, if any, enemies; a man of good sense and judgment, but no turn, disposition or inclination to wrestle with the public business, or at least, manifested none. Is still living at the same place and is now about 63 years of age.

Enoch Carter, of Saxon beat, was a merchant and farmer; a Baptist, Mason and Democrat; well informed, energetic and progressive. He was elected to the legislature in 1886 and made a very creditable member. He was zealous in the cause of temperance, morality and Christianity. He was ever ready to be present and help the Church and the Sunday School. He died a few years since.

1877---I.T. Weathers, J.C. Wright, R.A. Arnett and Charles Davis, Peoples Ticket.

Isham T. Weathers was a Georgian by birth; came to the county with H.M. Gay about the time of its organization and ran a blacksmith shop; afterwards went back to his home in Georgia and married his present wife, and in 1836 moved to and near his old home in High Shoals beat, and has been a citizen of the county ever since. He was, when elected, 64 years of age, a farmer and had always voted the Democratic ticket; had been Justice of the Peace for several years, but never ran for nor was a candidate for any other office until out on the People's Ticket; he was elected, as were all on the ticket, by a large majority. Uncle Tom is now 82 or 83 years of age, hail and hearty, though not able to get out and about much. He has had the misfortune to lose the sight of one eye. Aunt Sarah, his better half, is still by his side to nurture and console his declining days. Almost sixty years ago, two loving hearts confided their lives, companionship and happiness to each other's care, and today those same hearts with nine loving sons and daughters, are still one in thought, purpose and desire. God grant they may live many years yet, to enjoy the good they have done.

John C. Wright, of Louina beat, was 49 years of age, a farmer, Mason and Baptist. He was well informed and had tact for business for which he seemed to readily fraternize. He was a Democrat, though conservative; good natured, pleasant and easily approached. Had never had any office but Justice of the Peace and did not seek this one. He is still living and retains the good will and confidence of the people, and it is said will be the next Tax Collector of Randolph County. Certainly there is no man in the county today that deserves it more or would fill the position better than John C. Wright. He is as honest as Caesar's wife was virtuous.

Richmond A. Arnett, was from Bacon Level beat; a farmer, and made a good living. He was a member of Roanoke Baptist Church and had always voted the Democratic Ticket. He was 49 years of age and had never asked or run for an office. He loved the dollar and knew its worth and believed the county should have value received for all moneys paid out, extortion and extravagance were abnominations to his sensibilities of right. When he believed he was right, he maintained it, though not wholly indifferent to reason, yet there had to be a better one than he had to change him. He loved justice and practiced economy, not only at home, but in his official acts. Never had there been a time in the history of the county that demanded a better truer or more fearless Commissioner's Court; never was there four better men found; never did a vote cast pay better dividends. If the tax payers and voters in the county knew what the writer does, they would honor Rich Arnett and John C. Wright (Uncle Tom and Charley are physically unable to serve with their votes in 1896).

Rev. Charles Davis, from Hopkins beat, in the 66th year of his age only locally known at the time, proved himself worthy of the support and confidence given.

Number Thirty Four

Written for The Toiler, by Capt. J.M.K. Guinn

County Commissioners---Continued

1880---T.T. Holly, J.N. Lipham, W.W. Stitt and J.M. Gay.

Thomas T. Holly, of near Rock Mills, was a farmer and owned a mill. He was a man of good moral and temperate habits and as clever as he could be; Democratic in politics, open and fair in dealings; liberal and conservative in his official acts. He married a daughter of Jacob Eichelberger and sister of Charlie and George. Uncle Jacob was one of the best informed and most prominent men in the county. The Hollys were all hightoned and well respected. Tom was a brother to Len Holly who now resides at Roanoke. Tom was a special friend of the writer, and it was sad to hear of his demise which occurred a few years since.

Rev. James N. Lipham, of Rockdale beat, preacher and Democrat. His education and business qualities were ordinary, a good, clever and highly respected citizen and neighbor; and, was said to be, very prominent in the councils and ministry of the Primitive Baptist faith and doctrines. He is still living.

William W. Stitt lives in High Shoals beat; a Presbyterian, farmer and Democrat. A good safe and conservative man, and liked by his neighbors. An ex-Confederate soldier and was honorably discharged; though wounded and disabled, had the good fortune to get home alive. Married Col. James Aiken's sister, a nice and lovely lady. He is 63 years of age and still living.

J.M. Gay lived in Flat Rock beat; was 32 years of age and voted the Democratic ticket. Was looked upon as a little extraordinary, erudite and promising young man. Acute, luminous and voluptuous and egotistical and many of his ideas were extravagant and intangible. His perceptions often proved treacherous to his good intentions and obstructed business. It was further said, when obstructed, he was petulent and obstinate. This, you know is common and general with smart ambitious and egotistical young men. Though constitutional, it don't always kill--some hope yet.

1884---A.J. Green, W.V. Taylor, and H.D. Lanier, J.M. Gay, re-elected.

Andrew Jackson Green lived in High Shoals beat; a farmer, Democrat and Baptist. Jack was one of those industrious, hard working farmers who make plenty at home to live on and meant well. A man of good sense and judgment, but limited in education and business qualifications. He stood well with his neighbors and endeavored to discharge his official duties with fidelity and promptness. He still lives.

William V. Taylor, of Roanoke beat, age 46 years, a farmer and Democrat; a man of good judgment, and knows the value of a dollar and has a disposition to keep it or get value received when paid out. Acting on this experience in public affairs made him useful and efficient often in allowing claims. Has a good home and plenty around him and now lives and enjoys it.

H.D. Landers, of Morrison's beat, was a farmer, Baptist and Democrat. Is now merchandising, I believe, and doing very well. His neighbors respect him very highly and speak well of his many Christian virtues.

1888---H.M. Mickle, J.H. Leftwich, W.G. Preston and W.M. Moon.

Hugh M. Mickle, of Roanoke beat; 58 years of age, born and raised within a few miles of where he now lives; Baptist, Mason, Democrat and farmer; standing pre-eminently at the head and in the front rank of Randolph's best and most worthy men. He is the son of James M. Mickle, one of the first bonafide settlers in the southern part of the county in 1832 or 33. He is a brother of M. J. Mickle, Esq., who doubtless, is the oldest living inhabitant in the county today. William Phillips, of Langdale, son of Daniel Phillips, who entered land in 1831, is the oldest living inhabitant, while Mrs. Fletcher Haynes, nee Wood, now in her 63 or 64 year is the first white child born in the county, so far as the writer has been able to learn.

J.H. Leftwich hailed from Fox Creek, an imported school teacher, said to be very well informed, good moral character and well thought of by his neighbors.

W.G. Preston of Halpin's beat, an aged and highly respected farmer, an old citizen and Democrat, honored and loved, sociable and neighborly, conservative and liberal.

W.M. Moon, of Lamar beat, school teacher, well informed, moral and temperate habits. Crippled and uses crutches and stick. Still living and well respected.

1892---W.J. Barrett, George French, W.J. Cofield and W.R. Sharman.

William J. Barrett, of Rock Mills beat, a farmer and Populist; a good and clever man, makes a good and efficient Commissioner; liberal and conservative, manifests zeal and earnestness in the county's welfare, generally acts wisely and judicially. Under special act of the legislature, first term expired in August 1894 and he was re-elected and now serving his second term of two years.

George W. French lives 2 miles north of Wedowee; a Methodist, Populist and farmer. George has a long head; generally digs deep and builds a good foundation, but sometimes the material is not first class and the wall gives and roof leaks and the inmates complain. Robinson, the contractor for the Iron Bridge on the Little Tallapoosa river, said to the writer; "Commissioner French got closer after me than anyone I have ever contracted with; and" said he, "I have a varied experience in the business." He was re-elected in 1894, and is serving his second term of two years.

W.J. Cofield, of Halpins beat, is a merchant, farmer and Populist, a man of good appearance, good morals, good financier, and stands well at home; liberal conservative, reserved and pleasant. His present term as Commissioner expires in August 1896.

William R. Sharman of Bacon Level beat, is a Baptist, Populist and farmer; a good clever, upright man, with good judgment, pleasant unassuming manners, liberal, free and accomodating neighbor; honest, industrious and economical and acts from judgment rather than impulse. He is now, and has been during the greater portion of 1895 in Fla. This creates a vacancy and can only be filled by appointment of the Governor.

RANDOLPH'S STATE SENATORS

Number Thirty Five

Written for The Toiler, by Capt. J.M.K. Guinn

1840---Up to this time, Randolph County had had no representative in the State Senate, but in 1839, the General Assembly made a reapportionment of Senators and Representatives, and Chambers and Randolph counties were made a Senatorial District.

George Reese, of Chambers county was elected. It is not remembered now whether he was a Whig or Democrat. His acts, as a member, seems to indicate he was a honest fearless Independent. He voted to allow the Whigs to illuminate the Capitol in honor of William Henry Harrison's election to the Presidency of the United States, but it was laid on the table, the Democrats having the majority voted with the Whigs to take from the table but it was defeated. He offered a resolution proposing the Whig party of the Senate have the use of the Senate Chamber. Voted for W.R. King, a Democrat for U.S. Senator. Voted against Peyton King's preamble and resolution to unpurge any member who voted other than for his party. In other words, no Representative or Senator is authorized to exercise discretionary power, but is bound to vote for that individual whose political opinion may accord with those of a majority of his constituents. He seems to have stood alone and independently of party when the public good demanded it. His people, at home, endorsed and re-elected him as his own successor. Alabama's Populist U.S. Senator must be a chip from the same stump.

    1845-6. Jefferson Falkner, of Wedowee, Randolph County, was elected. He died in July, 1895, at the home of his youngest son, Hon. Jeff Falkner, Jr. in the city of Montgomery. (See serials on County Judge and Clerk.)

    1847-50---Seborn Gray, of Tallapoosa county was elected Senator from Tallapoosa and Randolph Counties as a Democrat. The re-apportionment in 1845 gave Chambers county, which had rapidly grown to be the largest county in population in the State, one Senator and four Representatives. This accounts for Randolph and Tallapoosa being a Senatorial district. In 1850, Randolph had grown in population and became a senatorial district and with two Representatives in the House.

    1851-2---John T. Heflin, of Wedowee, was elected. He was a son of Wyatt Heflin, brother of Hon. S. and Dr. W.L. Heflin, Mrs. W.P. Poole, Mrs. John Blake and Mrs. H.R. Gay. His father moved from Georgia to Randolph county in 1834 or 1835 and settled on High Pine creek near the present Concord church and cemetery and in Louina beat. Judge Heflin was a boy of fourteen, well advanced in his studies at school when his father moved in the midst of the Indians, and his acute and incentive nature to learn was greatly assisted; for here was a race with life, habits and language that was new and interesting, and his active, energetic and inquiring mind feasted on Indian dialect. Judge Heflin was 31 years of age; a bright and promising young lawyer and a zealous Democrat when elected, who never voted other than for the nominee of his party. This he would do though he refused to speak to him. Was a rabid secessionist and a minute war man. But he, like many others of that sort, some how or other did not go, and those that did, got out some how or other. When they could, they substituted office for war, and served their country like patriots. Grover Cleveland like. In 1836 Judge Heflin, Judge Bob Doughtery and Judge Jefferson Falkner were candidates for Circuit Judge, and again in 1863, Judge Heflin was a candidate for Circuit Judge in 1875 was in the State Constitutional Convention from Talladega County; in 1878, I believe it was, his name was placed before the Democratic State Convention for Supreme Court Judge, but he refused to allow it pressed and it was withdrawn. In 1885 his name was highly commended for United States Supreme Court Judge. No man, not even his political and personal enemies, challenged his ability, but unlike him they refused to rise above personality. Judge Heflin was a strick disciplinarian and dispatched business rapidly when on the bench.

    Judge Heflin had an extraordinary memory. Often quoting book, page, chapter, section and word for word of Supreme Court decision. He was called, in Talladega, "The Walking Library." Lawyers, rather than trouble themselves with hunting up decisions and rulings on cases, when in his presence, invariably referred to him. He knew what the initials stood for in nearly every name of any notoriety in the county. He was a linguist of Indian names, folklore and tradition. As a general thing, men don't realize the value and usefulness of noble men and women in their associations while living, but when they move away or die, and no one to supply their place, they realize and regret their indifference, though lessness and loss. Judge Heflin's attainments as a lawyer, scholar, historian and biographer with his many traits of honesty, fidelity, integrity and liberality, were perhaps, not equaled by any other man in the State. He was irritable, quick to resent an insult or insinuation, so much so, he made enemies unnecessarily and unintentionally. So far as the writer knows, he never sought or made any pretentions to Christianity though he believed and accepted the Bible as the Word of God given by inspiration. He often read it and quoted from it percepts of love, mercy, truth and wisdom. He honored the Christian church, its members and ministers. Believed Jesus was the Christ, the Son of God; Saviour of soul; and when approached by a person living a consistent Christian life on the subject of religion, he reasoned wisely from a wordly standpoint. The writer remembers hearing him say, "I am a Hardshell Baptist in belief." His mother did, and I believe, his father, too held to the teachings and doctrines of the Primitive faith. In manners he was austere, haughty, arrogant and petulant; in conversation jovial, loquacious and entertaining; in passion aggressive, merciless, profane, tyrannical and vindictive; as a friend to the manor born; egotistical in ridicule and criticism characterizing everybody by occupation, habits, form, accident or incident just like the Indian did. He had a redundant command and flow of language, but his delivery was obtuse without effulgency, magnetism or animation. His voice was husky, harsh and acrid. Like Moses, poor in speech, but learned and wise in law and equity; a close tireless student; prodigious thinker; wise counselor and righteous judge; an invective opponent and invariable democrat; no deception, hypocracy nor sevility about him. His whole life seems to have been wrapped up in his profession. An exile to society and sociability. Moved from Wedowee to Jacksonville about 1857 and from there to Talladega in 1878-9. There he met, wooed, won and married Mrs. Frank Bowden, one of the most amiable and esteemed ladies in the State. They had no children, but he educated and associated his step-son, Frank Bowden, Jr., in the practice of law. After Mrs. Heflin's death, he located at Birmingham. In December 1888 his voice was stilled in death--life's work ended; faults forgiven, virtues treasured and now his body lies somnolently beneath a beautiful monument in old Concord's cemetery; where nearby lies father and mother in sleep until the resurrection of the dead, "Jure divino."

Number Thirty Six

Written for The Toiler, by Capt. J.M.K. Guinn

1853-4---Henry M. Gay, of Louina beat, was 41 years of age, a farmer and a stock raiser. When a young man in his twenty-first year, he and Isham T. (Uncle Tom) Weathers migrated from Fayette county, Georgia to Randolph; kept bachelor's hall, ran a blacksmithing business, sold goods and traded with the settlers and Indians. A few years after they both married, and Gay settled what is now known as the "Old Gay Homestead" on the Wedowee and Malone (Wafer) ferry-road.

When the County Democratic Convention met there were several candidates before it for Senator, and after several ballots and withdrawals had been made, a two-thirds vote being necessary to a choice, there was but little hopes and no indications of a break so long as the present candidates were in the race. The convention adjourned for dinner, and Mrs. Elijah Humphries' friends made a proposition to Mrs. Gay's friends. That they would support Mr. Gay for Senator, if they, Gay's friends, would support Humphries for Representative. The proposition was accepted and Gay nominated. Mr. Gay when charged afterwards with the trade, denied all knowledge of it on his part. But it evidently handicapped him and came very near defeating his election; and did defeat Humphries. The writer, a boy of 17, took in the canvass, and remembers the State and County tickets:

For Governor

John A. Winston, D.

A. Q. Nicks, W.

Walker

Earnest

For Congress

James F. Dowdle, D.

Thomas F. Garrett, W.

For State Senator

Henry M. Gay, D.

For Representative

W. P. Newell, D.

Elijah Humphries, D.

John Goodwin, W.

R. G. Roberts, W.

For Sheriff

Wilson Falkner, D.

J. M. Hearn

Hardy Strickland

The canvass was hotly contested and the result in doubt until the last vote was counted and returns all in, and, then, neither party would concede the election nor his defeat. Charges and counter charges were made, and a general fight came very near being precipitated. The law required the coroner to recount the votes within ten days after the election. J.M. Hearn, candidate for sheriff, was coroner, and the Democrats were in a strait. They wanted Goodin defeated, and it was believed if Hearn counted the vote it would be impossible. They kicked, snorted, cowed and cajoled, but all to no purpose, while the Whigs crackled, teased and ridiculed them. Coroner Hearn relieved their fears by allowing each party to have a representative present. When the ballots were counted, Gay's majority 34 and Goodwin's 11. The Democrats elected the rest of their ticket. Gay succeeded himself in 1855. In 1861, he was elected on Co-operation ticket to ordinance Secession Convention.

1857-8---R.S. Heflin, an ex-soldier of the Indian war of 1836, and a promising practicing lawyer, 42 years of age and a citizen of Wedowee, was nominated and elected by the Democrats. Bob previously represented the county in the lower House of the General Assembly in 1849 and 50. He was a fine speaker, and perhaps, the most popular man Randolph county ever had before or since. In 1859-60, 61 and 62, he was his own successor. Was a Stephen A. Douglas Democrat and opposed the war and secession. Gay, the Smiths and Woods, all went with him, but Judge John T. Heflin and other prominent Democrats supported John C. Breckinridge and secession. In 1864 he was arrested for treason to the Confederate States, he and ex-Gov. W.H. Smith having made an alledged treason speech at a public meeting in the Court House a few days previously. He took advantage of a parole and went across the line to the enemy where he remained until Lee's surrender. In August, 1865, he was appointed Probate Judge and held until Judge W.W. Dodson's election in 1868, and in 1869 was elected to Congress as a Republican. He was defeated in 1880 for Probate Judge by T.J. Thomason. Was a candidate in 1884, for representative but defeated by Dr. C. B. Taylor. In 1886 he was nominated by the Republican State Convention for Attorney General although defeated, ran ahead of the ticket. Now, in his 81st year, with mental force abated and eyes dim, providence hath provided him a pension as an Indian soldier of 1836. Twenty-two years ago, his wife died leaving a house full of little children, and he married Miss Mentoria Reaves, daughter of Judge John Reaves, of Wedowee. Mentoria, though a little girl when her mother died, was the stay and dependence of the family; and in the place of a mother, helped to raise and provide for three sets of children of her father, and two sets for Bob, her husband. A woman among women; gentle and kind; motherly and affectionate; domestic and provident; thoughtful and careful; modest and pleasant; hopeful and dutiful and by her humble patient Christian walk and conversation, a few years ago, had the sweet consolation to see her husband, a profane and ungodly man, Baptised into the fellowship of Mt. Pleasant Missionary Baptist Church, the "called and Elect" of God. And now, in his old age and declining days, after a long, honored and eventful life, in the plentitude of love, mercy and goodness of God, in giving him a benevolent Christian companion to cherish and nuture him in peace and love, awaits the summons ere the silver cord be lossed or the golden bowl be broken or the pitcher or the wheel at the cistern to bid her who has been a true helpmate, made his days happy and home pleasant; not forgetting to point out the way of righteousness, peace on earth, and life eternal, in the world to come. He who ere long will by the course of nature have this earthly tabernacle dissolved and and fall asleep in Jesus, to await the sound of Gabriel's trumpet in the morning of the resurrection. "It doth not yet appear what we shall be, but we know we shall be like him ("the Son of Man") in the resurrection of the dead."

Number Thirty Seven

Written for The Toiler, by Capt. J.M.K. Guinn

1863---Capt. W.T. Wood, of Chulafinnee beat, was elected. See serial on Tax Assessor.

1865---Middleton R. Bell, of Chulafinnee beat, was elected. He was a brother of County Commissioner J.H. Bell, 40 years of age and well-to-do farmer; an active, energetic and leading citizen; with union sentiments predominating during the war; since a Republican. He is now living at or near Bell's mills, in Cleburne County.

1867---Hicks H. Wise, of Cleburne County, was elected. See serial on Circuit Clerks.

1872---James J. Robinson, of Chambers County, was elected and was the first Democrat to represent Randolph County in the Senate since ante-bellum days. He had a hard struggle in getting the nomination, but finally pulled through. In 1876, the Democrats were in full possession of the State and every other man wanted office. It was indirectly conceeded at the last Senatorial Convention that Randolph should have the nomination. The bosses and place hunters began to form in clicks and rings and sparring began in earnest as to who should be who. Senator Robinson was a putative candidate, so, also, Col. J.H. Denson of Lafayette. Randolph had hers, too. When the Convention met at Roanoke, Randolph's delegates would not, or at least did not harmonize on any one man. Chambers county had the majority of the delegation, but they too refused to harmonize. There were 38 delegates; 26 were necessary to make the nomination. Chambers had 25, Randolph 13. On the first ballot Robinson 19, Denson 9, Heflin 10. After seven ballots, Heflin's name was withdrawn and Ricke, Ussery and others substituted with a slight variation of the vote. The convention adjourned for dinner and several of the delegates from Chambers expressed themselves perfectly willing to take a good man from Randolph if her delegates would unite. So an agreement was made to vote for all the men whose names had been before the convention seriatim, the man receiving the highest vote should be the candidate and was to be supported without variation-uno animon- until next election. One delegation to the fact that there were only 13 botes from Randolph county. A new ballot showed Dr. W.L. Heflin to be the strongest man from Randolph, but when placed before the Senatorial Convention as Randolph's choice, two of her delegates voted for Denson. After a few ballots without change, Randolph's delegation withdrew to consult. It was agreed to cast one more vote for Heflin, and if no change to withdraw his name and vote for whom they pleased. The vote stood: Robinson 19, Heflin 11, and Denson 8; Heflin's name withdrawn, Robinson 26 and Denson 12. The writer and six others from Randolph voted for Robinson, Judge Davis and five others voted for Denson. Robinson was nominated and re-elected. In 1886 he was a candidate for Probate Judge of Chambers county, but was defeated by Rev. W.C. Bledsoe in the County Convention for the nomination. "Barkis" like, being willing, he became an independent candidate and his solidarity assumed a dark companionship by the change of venue; however, he defeated the Democratic nomination at the election. In 1894, he was nominated by the "Tom Jones Organized" for the legislature and badly beaten by C.H. Cole and J.H. Harris Populists- He is now living and practicing law at Lafayette.

1880---Robert S. Pate, of Randolph, was nominated at Milltown by the Democratic Convention and elected. He was a bright and promising young lawyer in his 38th year and a native born Randolphian. His father, James Pate, moved to the county in the fall of 1834, or spring of 1835, and settled near where Dick Green now lives, south of old High Pine Baptist Church. Bob is a brother of G.G. (Bird) and Thomas F. Pate and Mrs. Dick Green, who are all well-known and highly respected. He married Miss Sue

Scales, sister to Mrs. Mollie Burton and daughter of James Scales. Mrs. Pate is sociable, pleasant and amiable; and, of course, has associated with her a whole-soul big-hearted clever husband, ever standing with open arms and friendly greeting his host of friends. Bob is as honest as the days are long, as free as the water that runs. He is not one of the covetous kind, doesn't want nor wouldn't have more than a living. He is said to be "The best criminal lawyer at Wedowee's bar." Being born, bred and rocked in the cradle of Jeffersonian Democracy, he stands with the honest laboring yeomanry of his country; ready at any and all times to battle for their rights, interest and wants. He, like hundreds and thousands of other true and tried men, was forced to break ranks and leave the Tom Cleveland and Grover Jones Democracy. Self respect, consistency, decency, honesty and respectability; ought, certainly, to justify his course with the people. He stands, today, in the front ranks of Populist simplicity and consistency; and, will, if the vox populi have the good will to say, head and lead them to victory in 1896. Bob was a brave and gallant Confederate soldier; standing at the head of his company led his men and drove back the invading enemy. Bob works well in the lead. Try him.

1884---N.D. Denson, of Lafayette, a very prominent young lawyer and a true and faithful member of Lafayette Baptist Church, succeeded Pate. His moral and temperate habits; Christian character and deportment; acts and walk, won the confidence and secured the endorsement of the people; and in 1892 he was elected Judge of the Fifth Judicial Circuit. He will however have a hard road to travel should he again offer in 1896. It is said "He is building his fences for another term, using Populist timbers." On the other hand his friends say: "He will not offer, owing to his delicate health, but retire and recruit up." Whether this be true or not, it is evidently the only prudent and conversative course for his future; for no man can command the support or confidence of intelligent voters, whose political escutcheon trails in the associations and councils of deception, treachery, extravagance and debauchery at the expense of the dependent poor, suffering and famishing humanity that Clevelandism has seasoned with gall.

Number Thirty Eight

Written for The Toiler, by Capt. J.M.K. Guinn

1888---Hon. William A. Handley, of Roanoke, was nominated by the Democratic Senatorial convention. He was 53 years of age and a retired merchant. Captain Handley was the son of Mr. John R. Handley and brother of Captain, Frank M., Major James M., Dr. John R., Bowden A. Handley and two unmarried sisters. His father was an early settler of the county. The writer remembers seeing him when a small boy. Uncle Jack, as he was sometimes called, invariably attended Circuit Court, County Conventions, Public Speakings and other public occasions at Wedowee, and was an enthusiastic Democrat; always on hand as a delegate from Wesobulga beat. Whether or not he got his choice at the convention he endorsed the nominee; and, as for that, everything else said or done by the convention and his party. It is not remembered now whether Uncle Jack ever ran for any office or not. Yet there was no incident connecting it of notoriety, or the writer would have doubtless remembered it. Mrs. John R. Handley, Captain's mother, the writer never saw to know, but from her general character, she was modest, pleasant, charitable, motherly, domestic, amiable and lovely. There is one incident associated with her name I'll relate which like a diamond in the sky ever so high shines and portrays a noble Christian spirit of humanity living in her heart. It is this - A few years ago there was a negro boy and white man sentenced and started on their way to the chain gang under the care and control of a callous-hearted and cruel wretch who stopped over-night at Uncle Jack's on his way with his prisoners. The night was dark and cold. The wind strong and biting. The ground frozen hard and the next morning covered with snow. On one side of the house there was a veranda and shed room at the end in which the guard slept, the other part of the veranda was open and to one of its post the two prisoners were chained and there they were to remain until morning, tired, wet with sweat, (for they had been forced to travel at the rate of six miles an hour chained to the axle-tree of the guard's buggy) and hungry without anything to eat or sleep upon except the cold hard floor. Mrs. Handley protested and importuned the wretch until he shirked for his own safety and comfort. She gave the prisoners a good and warm supper and some quilts to keep them from suffering and freezing. At 1 o'clock a.m. an Angel touched them and said: "Arise, make haste, get thee northward; thou art free." They arose, the chain parted in the middle and they were not, as though they had wings and flown away. My readers have doubtless heard Capt. Handley tell about his serrated trials in boyhood days which would be redundancy to relate them here. There is, however, a very remarkable character of versatility vested in his life from juvenility to senility. It has followed him like a manes in every pursuit and occupation of life. His sinuated disposition seems to have aided him in his political and financial advancement, upon which, he has established a reputation for popularity and liberality; for on one can truthfully say he is parsimonious, 'though his whole life and aim have been to accumulate money and his success redundantly ambidextrous. His enthusiasm and zeal, if anything, exceeded his father's. He headed his beat delegation and took an active part in the Democratic County Convention before his majority. He headed his beat delegation and took an active collate and wheedle with the delegates to carry his point; if he failed, like Josh Billings, when the cow kicked over the bucket and spilled the milk, he grabbed the bucket and went after another cow. In 1872, the old war horses were all disfranchised; that is, those who had taken up arms or sympathized with the Confederacy. This eliminated all the office-seeking element in the Democratic party. Only here and there, could a man be found eligible. Dr. W.L. Heflin, of Louina, now Roanoke, was tendered the nomination of Congressman from this the third district, but as his brother, Hon. R.S. Heflin was then serving his first term as a Republican and a putative candidate for re-election, Dr. Heflin declined. And without explanation or solicitation the Democratic Convention nominated Captain Bill Handley for Congress, and unexpectedly, elected him by a good majority. By hard work and wily smirking he succeeded in getting some good legislation passed which was credited to his energy and tact. In 1874, the Democratic Congressional Convention met at Opelika where they were several aspirants for the nomination, among them Capt. Handley. The writer was a delegate and scotched on taut pulls. Being editor of "The Randolph Enterprise" published at Wedowee, he published the acts passed and work done in Congress by Captain Handley and distributed it at the Convention. This aided materially in securing his nomination. But unfortunately a disappointed and defeated aspirant through malign treachery and manipulation of ballots in Russell county, defeated Captain Handley at the election, Charles A. Pelham, a Republican, securing the certificate of election. In 1888 he was elected Senator from Randolph and Chambers counties. In 1894, Dr. Jameson-like, he failed to see the Amajuba Hill or pass Laing's Neck, for Judge S.E.A. Reaves, Populist, captured his pickets and spiked his artillery early in the fight. September 9, 1861, he made up a Company, elected Captain and went to Mobile where his command stayed until July 1862. While at Mobile his health became delicate and he came home on furlough unable to do service. When his command was ordered to Tennessee, he went with it, but did not remain longer than the last of July or first of August before he got a certificate of "heart affection" and a discharge from service. The writer got home from Virginia with an empty sleeve, July 29th, 1862, and a few days after Captain Handley was reported home. Captain Handley, like other poor boys, had but few advantages, educationally. Poor boys had only two or three months to go to a school. Spelling, reading, writing and ciphering was all that most school teachers could or professed to teach. "Webster's blue book" was used for spelling and reading, Smiley's arithmetic, goose quills, and red oak hall ink completed his panoply as an advance student. I could read and spell "by heart" half that was in those old blue backs before allowed to see inside of any other book. None but young men and ladies were allowed to "cipher." A teacher that could make a goose quill pen, rule papers with his finger nails, repeat the multiplication table and teach Smith's Grammar to the ten rule-- "Prepositions govern the objective case" was a prodigy. A boy's highest aspirations in those days was to be a clerk in a store or grocery. This, Bill coveted and secured, and, from that time since, has been more or less in the mercantile business, while his versatile turn and tact shows he had bit his talent. He has had many promising outlooks which his adventurous speculations have caused to be downfalls. Perhaps his past experiences will sustain him in his recent prosperity; at least it is to be hoped so.

Captain Handley has many good, genial and neighborly traits of hospitality, liberality, sociability, chivalry and companionship. He has a kind, tender, affectionate and penitent heart, but like the rich young Ruler, he loves money.

1892---H.M. Williams, of Chambers county, was elected to represent Chambers and Randolph. He is a farmer and Populist and a good and true man. So far as the writer knows, he has given general satisfaction and showed up on the right side, salt or no salt. His present term as Senator ends in 1896, and his successor is to be elected in August next.

Number Thirty Nine

Written for The Toiler, by Capt. J.M.K. Guinn

1837---Thomas Blake was the first elected Representative Randolph ever had in the State Legislature. (See serial Nos. 26 and 27 on county commissioners.) But as a matter of information, gathered from a recent publication, I learn the acts of the General Assembly of 1837, which had been thought lost or destroyed during the war, have been found and recovered to the archives of the State Secretary's office. These acts with other important and valuable papers were found filed away in a Masonic lodge, where it is supposed they were carried during the war, for protection and preservation, and since forgotten. (In these serials the writer has had to rely to a great extent on tradition from 1832 to 1838 and for the want of official records and acts passed much valuable and interesting facts in the early days of Randolph county and her officials have escaped notice doubtless.) Uncle Tom died in 1880 in his eightieth year, and Aunt Deliah in 1895, in her eighty-first year.

1838---William McKnight (See serial no. 27 on County Commissioners.)

1839---F.F. Adrine (See serial on County Treasurers.)

1840---Wyatt Heflin of Big River, now Louina beat, was a farmer, 51 years of age and a Democrat. He moved to Randolph county from Fayette county, Georgia, about 1835 or '36. He was well-to-do financially and said to be the largest and best farmer on High Pine creek. He had a fair English education, fine intellectuality and good judgment. He succeeded himself in 1841, but in 1842 Jerry Murphy, Whig, succeeded him in the Legislature, and in 1843 he succeeded Jerry Murphy. In 1844 James H. Allen, Whig, succeeded him. In 1845-6 he and Samuel T. Owens were elected. This was his last term in the Legislature. During his latter days he moved to Louina, near his son, Dr. W.L. Heflin, and there he died. The writer knew but little about his private personality. His general character was good and he and his wife were said to be Primitive (Hardshell) Baptists. Was the father of Hons. Robert S., Judge John T., and Dr. W.L. Heflin; Mrs. William P. Pool, Mrs. John Blake and Mrs. H.R. Gay who lived in this county and state. James Heflin lived in the State of Georgia until 1856, and then moved to Texas. The writer visited his grave at Concord cemetery in 1894. So far as the writer knows and remembers no other father and sons have been honored by the voters of Randolph county as has this one.

1842---Jerry Murphy, a Whig and farmer, 26 years of age, was elected and succeeded Wyatt Heflin, Democrat. Jerry was a hustler, active and energetic, genial and wily. The first time the writer remembers seeing Jerry was during the Polk and Clay campaign in 1844. His defeat in 1843 by Wyatt Heflin and the selection of James H. Allen as the Whig candidate didn't set well on Jerry's ambitious aspirations to make laws. He was on a "tar" and had a big crowd around to help him drink Murphy tips, with Clay mint and Allen sugar, at Jude Crow's fountain of pure homespun corn liquors. It was a public day, an election year and big crowd in town. In those days, men from all over the county came to town. The Democrats had Tom Pollard, a little boy, patting and singing:

> "Shell shell corn
> By the rattle of the horn,
> We'll shear old Clay
> When the weather gets warm."

If the writer remembers correctly Jerry and Allen were defeated in 1845 by Wyatt Heflin and Samuel T. Owens. It is not remembered what became of Jerry Murphy.

1843---Wyatt Heflin turned the tables on Jerry and went back to the Legislature.

1844---James H. Allen, a Whig and school teacher, defeated Wyatt Heflin, Democrat. Allen, when the writer knew him, lived in Wedowee on lot no. 52, east of Mrs. Martha Smith's present home. He taught a ten months school afterwards in the old academy, where Prof. Richey is now teaching. The writer was a pupil and remembers the boys repaired the stick and clay chimney. The boys and girls "ciphering" were allowed to take their chairs and sit outside. While at dinner, someone put a coat of mud on one of the seats, and in retaliation, he put it on the others, and before Prof. Allen got back from dinner the ciphering contingent had daubbed one another. Three or four boys holding and the girls painted. Finally, a fight ensued and nineteen young men and ladies were arraigned before the teacher, with the only alternative, said the rules, "take a whipping or be expelled from school." They all no animo plead guilty and agreed to abide by the rules. The boys sawed wood and waited their time. It was a custom for the pupils to ask a holiday and the teacher had to give it, treat, or be ducked in a mudhole. This, the teachers would not do if there was any way to evade it. Ducking was the last act of his life; however, occasionally it had to be done to dignify the profession, for when once baptised in a mudhole, he invariably perseveres in gifts and holidays. The time grew on apace nigh and the plan and specifications were made ready and the little boys posted. On Tuesday, by chance, one of the little boys learned the school would be out on Thursday instead of Friday. This information was communicated and Wednesday bright and early every little boy and a few large ones were at the school room and barricaded the door and stood inside to keep Prof. Allen out. He wasn't expecting it until Thursday or Friday. He went and unlocked the door, but couldn't open it. The boys left a window open on purpose and through it got in and barricaded the door with benches. Prof. Allen tried for sometime to get the boys to open the door, but they knew their rights and kept him out until "after book" the time to take in, then the door was opened and the professor and the boys had a race; and now had come the opportunity for which the young men had waited since the alternative "take a whipping or be expelled." Whether law or custom, a teacher had to teach his full time to get his pay, and when he was in the school room we dared not to molest him, but if we could barricade the door and keep him out without injury or personal harm, we had a perfect right to so as to get a holiday, make him treat or duck. Charlie Gibbs and one or two others were pert on foot and the professor didn't get far before he was in the arms of as many boys as could get to him and on the broad road that leads the unrepenting and rebellious teacher to the confines of hogdom. He threatened, kicked and pleaded, but it was no use, and he went with the sweet, consoling and inspiring words---"From God all Blessings flow"---choiristers, "the daub maids." He was prepared for the ordinance, one holding his head, two holding on each hand and foot and one standing on top to prevent him from floating. Then the ceremony commenced--"We duck you, thou favored child of misfortune, on the confession of thy confutation in a dishonorable and ill-assumed liberality as a tutor in the name of custon, tradition and practice a---Before the---was finished, "I'll treat, I'll treat, let me up." And he was as good as his word. We had as much candy, raisins, apples and nuts as we could all eat, and that day was given us as a holiday. That was as big and happy time as a boy has ever had. I wish I could be a boy again and live the day over. In 1859, I met Prof. Allen in Homer, Tex. for the last time.

1844---Was a presidential election year. Father lived on the hill north of town in the Davis E. Grisham house. Pa was a Polk man and brother Lee and I were Polk boys and on the boy before the speaking and raising of the Polk flag, and liberty pole, we dyed us a dozen or more flags with poke berries and painted the flagstaff with them too, and had the front yard fence decorated. Whenever a Polk man came along and saw our flags he would raise a yell, wave his hat and hollow "hurrah for Polk and Dallas." The Polk men had their horses decked with poke berries while the Clay men wore coon skin caps with coontails hanging down their backs. Whichever party raised a flag first the other side would raise one higher--it mattered not the cost. The Whigs put up a flag pole near the present southwest corner of the courthouse, and the Democrats caught a coon, killed and buried it under their pole. They had a big time burying that coon. The Whigs then buried an opossum and poke stalk at the foot of their pole. By 1 or 2 o'clock everybody got hilarious and began gathering in great crowds and ere long you might begin to look for fun. For it was certainly to come. A few of us boys use to watch and wait for the fighting to open and when we saw it was propitious, we'd climb up into some china tree that stood in front of Dr. Gibbs and Colwell's drugstore and grocery. Men didn't use pistols, knives nor rocks in those days. We felt perfectly safe with five or six fights going on and two or three hundred men gathered around. If there was a Morrow, Henson or Higginbotham present, and they generally were, you might safely bet your last dollar one or all of them would be in that fight.

1845---Randolph had two members in the House and one in the Senate. Wyatt Heflin and Samuel T. Owens, Democrats, were elected. See Samuel T. Owens in serial on Tax Assessors.

RANDOLPH'S REPRESENTATIVES

Number Forty

Written for The Toiler, by Capt. J.M.K. Guinn

1847-8---William Wood and Calvin J. Ussery

William Wood was an early settler coming to the county probably in 1833-4, and settled on Corn House creek near its mouth. He owned and settled the place where Mr. James A. Knight now lives on the old Wafer ferry road. He was a farmer and stock raiser, a plain old fashioned homespun round about jeans coat, wool hat Democrat; with temperate habits, an honest and upright life; unimpeachable veracity; good sense and sound judgment. It was said: He wore a round home made coat, jeans or homespun pants, wool hat, home tanned and made shoes to the Legislature. He owned and and cultivated a large farm and had good property both real and personal besides a large herd stock of cattle. If he was a member of any church I never heard of it. He was the father of R.J., W.H., A.C., Jack and Winston Wood; Mrs. Mary, wife of G.G. Pate; Mrs. Sarah, wife of J.A. Knight; and Mrs. Martha, wife of R.T. Smith. His daughters are all living, but his sons are all dead. Taking the family as a whole just as they each arrived to manhood and womanhood, perhaps not another could be found with more or brighter promise for their future. Their paternal tutorage was faultless, with perhaps, one exception, Christianity.

Calvin J. Ussery, of Bacon Level, a potter, 32 years of age, Baptist and Whig was elected. He was said to be the best still hunting campaigner in the county. His education was very poor and limited although he was extraordinarily successful in his business and creditable as an energetic hard worker and a successful legislator. He had plenty of nature's wit and mother's will. He could not make a stump speech but was a good reasoner, good talker and a good judge of human nature, which made him a successful "campaign logger."

A log campaign meant to visit every house and see every voter in the county. This Calvin J. Ussery did and assured his success. Was sociable, clever, honest and fearless; extreme, fanatical and incorrigible. He was, however, defeated in 1855 for County Commissioner. The Democrats ran J.F. White, Hiram

Barron, Wilson Falkner and Charles Foster, the Whigs ran C.J. Ussery, D.V. Crider and John McCollough, the Know Nothings ran Dr. R. Robertson, E.B. Smith and James Cole, and Independent Z. Darden. Ussery's defeat was about one hundred majority. He was a strong secessionist in 1861, and was elected to the Legislature with Col. James Aiken and ex-sheriff A.W. Denman. After the war he voted with the Democrats, and in 1876, was again elected to the Legislature. He had indomitable energy and self-reliance and carried on a good mercantile, grist and saw mill and wool carding at High Shoals which accumulated to him a good property. He was a zealous Missionary Baptist and his official acts were pure, clean and untarnished. He died leaving an honorable and cherished character, good works and noble deeds to live after him.

 1849-50---C.D. Hudson and R.S. Heflin.

  Cicero D. Hudson lived in Bacon Level beat. A potter and afterwards studied and practiced law; a Democrat and Deacon in a Baptist church. During the latter part of the war, he openly avowed his sympathies with the Union cause and alligned himself with the Republicans. When Col. Hudson first began the practice of law he was the butt of the Bar, but that only stimulated him to more efficiency, for he soon stood head and shoulders above some of his critics. He was a close student, hard worker and faithful and wise counsellor. He was full of tricks and you had to watch and be careful or he would catch you napping, especially if he had a bad cause to defend. For all that, he was reasonable and liberal and easily approached. If he professed friendship you could depend on him, for he would not go back on you. He was noble, generous, tactable and when you once sounded him, you could but love and admire his fidelity and fealty. Unfortunately, with a heart full of Christian charity, mercy and liberality, his intemperate habits gathered in clouds of dissipation and hid his good qualities from those that need light and cheer. "If out of the abundance of the heart the mouth speaketh," certainly out of a Christian heart noble, generous and charitable deeds abound. I am persuaded these many Christian traits - with a confession of faith and burial in Baptism were none other than a foundation no other man can lay that is laid, which is Jesus Christ. Though it may not seem to have been gold, silver or precious stones, it may have been wood, hay or stubble and burn up and his works suffered loss, but he himself shall be saved; yet so as by fire." "By grace through faith you are saved, and that not of yourselves, it is the gift of God." God is able to save. It is through his goodness, mercy and love we are saved. Who knoweth the will and depth of God's love, mercy and power? If man can forgive wrongs, and who is it that doesn't, why not a loving, merciful God? His transgressions were moral disobedience. Christ had redeemed him from a spiritual death.

 R.S. Heflin, see serial No. 36.

Number Forty One

Written for The Toiler, by Capt. J.M.K. Guinn

 1851-2---John Reaves and R.C. Pool.

  Judge John Reaves. (See serials on Clerk and County Judge.)

  Robert C. Pool lived on High Pine Creek, south of Concord Church, in Roanoke beat, or near the line. He came to Randolph County when there were only a few families anywhere near. It must have been in 1831 or 32, from the best information gathered. He was 53 years of age when elected, a farmer, a stock raiser and a Democrat. He was a brother of the late William P. Pool, who lived on the Roanoke and Louina public road. Pole, Thad and Polk were three of his sons. Napoleon and Polk are living in Texas. Thasseus was a member of Capt. John F. Smith's company "I" 13th Alabama Volunteers and was killed June 27th, 1862 at Mechaniesville, Va. just about good daylight. The writer saw him sitting, leaning his back against the bank of the road. It was said: "He was shot through the thigh and bled to death." Uncle Bob was one of the Trustees of Roanoke Academy incorporated by the Legislature in 1844. He made plenty of everything and lived well; was a plain old-time farmer, full of life and activity. He died many years ago.

1853-4---William P. Newell and John Goodin

William P. Newell. (See serial on Sheriff.)

John Goodin was a Whig, farmer, land speculator and negro trader. He was 47 years of age when elected. He had no education; could neither read nor write, except his name, yet his callidity (?) seemed boundless. With ready wit, tireless tongue and an inexhaustible fund of ancedotes, which he told in a fluent flexible and humerous style, without any rapidness; he higgled them out by the wholesale on all public occasions.

1849---The Democrats defeated him for the legislature, and again in 1851, but the last time by a small majority vote. When the full returns were in and the result known, on the night following the election, I heard Goodin tell father he was a "Standing candidate," and would run again in 1853. "And" said he, "in every election thereafter until I am elected." In 1853, the Whigs ran Thomas F. Lundie, for the State Senate, John Goodin and R.G. Roberts for the Legislature. Neither Lundie nor Goodin could make a stump speech, but Uncle Roberts, the bell maker and Methodist class leader, could talk and reason very well. Neither could Gay, Democratic candidate for Senator, nor Newell nor Humphries, candidates for the Legislature, make a speech; but the Democrats had Bob Heflin, whose voice was fluent, flexible and stentorious, with fascinating spontainety; Ex-Governor W.H. Smith and Judge John T. Heflin, who were all in the vigor of manhood. John Goodin dreaded Bob Heflin, for he was a fanatic on smutty yarns and anecdotes. He told one on Goodin in the campaign of 1851 that Goodin, with all his ready wit and chicanery, couldn't appease. It was like Banquo's ghost--it wouldn't go down.

Goodin had dark skin, black hair and eyes, and was one of the first pioneers of the county, being here before and at the time of the Creek treaty in March, 1832. Land speculators, stock owners and herders, old bachelors and young sports, many absconding criminals and horse thieves, were the advance guard. Pony Clubs were organized, justifying their acts under the claim of protecting property owners; but, like all outlaw organizations which are ruled by self-interest, self-will and conquest, many wrongs were chargeable to its door, and it became so tyrannical, aggresive and unbearable, another organization was formed and Christized (?) into existance, styling themselves "regulators." It, too, was a hotch potch of cow-thieves and land grabbers, whose main object and purpose was to keep honest bona fide settlers from coming in and taking up the choice reservation and other tracts of land. The above explanation will enable my readers to understand why Bob's anecdote trenched and touched so closely on

Goodin's past life and at the same time, made it impossible to be treated with silence or rebutted by answering. (It is not wished to convey the idea that Goodin was a bad man, or worse than others.) Bob Heflin said: "One day as Goodin was riding along two Indians met him in the road, and one of them recognized him as one of the Pony Club, who had recently whipped one of their clan, and they said to him, "Light, you are one of the Pony Club that whipped one of our clan, and we are a-going to whip you." Goodin protested his innocence and denied being in any way connected or sympathizing with the Club." "But", said the Indian, "A itsee hatkee," (all white men whip Indians.) Goodin realizing that a charge so broad as to embrace "all white men" left him only one plea that could touch the sympathy of an Indian's heart. He thought quick and fast. It was his only alternative. It seemed feasible and he took courage and said: "K'ok shi (good) dakoe (friends or comrades) ma (why) luk i a (this) te-k win-te (is unexpected) hom (to me) yat-ton-ne (today). Hom (my) tsita (mother) ton (is thy) an (own) shi-i-nan (flesh) kiah-kwin (and blood). Ha (I) tanka (am) hatkee tsau na (the little man or son of) seme-hechee (hide it away) waukau t sauna (little woman or daughter of) tuston nogee (brave warrior) harno-o-na-wi-la-po-na (holder of the paths) ton (of thy) na dowe si (enemy) wompi (white) hatkee (man)". "U-u-g-h", said the Indians, and at the same time ran his hand down Goodin's back and, pulling it out, said "No Indian here--Negro, by God."

This was a stunner and Goodin felt it keenly, but he was the last man to succumb or be driven from his ambitious desire to go to the Legislature. His acute cunning and ready wit soon decided him that strategy was the better part of valor, and he made his preparations for the campaign of 1853. The campaign opened at Chulafinne; the writer was present. The Democrats had built a brush arbor in the grove west from the town, and preparations were made for a big crowd. Goodin had a big crowd around listening to his anecdotes an hour before speaking was to commence. When the time came the announcement was made, as Judge John T. Heflin took the stand to speak, Goodin called on in a loud voice, "All who want Goodin whiskey follow me," and about nine-tenths of the crowd followed Goodin more than a hundred yards away to a wagon with a keg of good corn whiskey. They were all placed in line and the whiskey dealt out in a small tin cup. He managed to keep them, too. I don't think more than thirty or forty heard the speaking. He had arrangements made for each beat. Sometimes it would be a barrel of cider or a wagon load of ginger cakes. He played his hand well and spiked the enemy's big guns. He was elected, defeating Elijah Humpries eleven votes. I heard T.L. Pittman saying: "We were confident of Humphries' election on Saturday before. That six votes by the Stephens at Delta, who were Goodin men, had been as they (Democrats) thought, assured for Humphries. "But" said he, "John Goodin had heard or suspicioned we had been working on them, and, I have learned, went Sunday night to see them and secured their support; for he knew as well as we did if he lost those six votes he was defeated."

Goodin was happy and so also his friends on learning he was elected. He was a red-hot secessionist during the war. After Bell's defeat for President the Whig party died.

He went to Texas after the war and bought him a home and while moving his family he took sick and died on the road.

Number Forty Two

Written for The Toiler, by Capt. J.M.K. Guinn

1855---W.H. Smith and R.J. Wood

Ex-Gov. William H. Smith was a lawyer, about 30 years of age; a Democrat, and lived at Wedowee. He was re-elected in 1857. In 1866 he was Judge of the Circuit Court. In 1868 he was elected Governor of Alabama. In 1870 he was a candidate for re-election as Governor and was defeated by Robert Lindsay, Democrat. Before the war, he was a Douglas Democrat, and, I believe, an elector on the Douglass ticket for President. When the election was held for secession or co-operation, he voted for the latter. In the winter of 1862 he and Hon. R.S. Heflin made speeches in the court house at Wedowee criticising the Confederate States administration at Richmond, Va., which were said to be treasonable by Judge T.L. Pittman and others, who, it is supposed, so notified the authorities at Montgomery; for in a few days thereafter, Major Vandiver, of Montgomery, with a company of cavalry, came to Wedowee, and learned his arrest had been ordered and a company of soldiers were at Wedowee. Fortunately for him he was not at Wedowee when Major Vandiver arrived. When the State and Confederate Governments ordered free speech suppressed at the insistance of a cowardly political partisan, the cause for which brave men had taken up arms to protect and defend, was lost; and from that day hence, officers resigned and privates deserted the flat. This was the beginning of the end of liberty, and free speech in Alabama, and from that day on justice was outraged, liberty strangled and no mercy shown, and the Confederacy's cause of repelling subjugation and defense of person and property was doomed.

He, of course, without any ceremony or delay, made haste to cross the "dead line." He remained there during the war as a private citizen, though his elder brother, David, was a Captain, and his younger brother, Dallas, a Lieutenant in the First Alabama regiment U.S. Army, which was composed almost entirely of his own neighbors, friends and county men. Since that time, he has affiliated with the Republican party.

Gov. Smith, was a son of Jeptha V. Smith, and brother of David D., Robert T., Charles A., John O.D., James M., Andrew J., and Dallas Smith; Mrs. Dr. Daniel C. Harris, and Mrs. Ayers. His father moved to the Talbert May Mills, afterwards owned by Green Harper, Brown and McPherson, and now known as the Rock Mills. He stayed there a year and then moved to Wedowee in 1836 or '37 and lived in a house not far from W.N. Clifton's present home place, west. He was appointed in 1837 or '38, as well as I now remember, one of the county "Building Commission" to locate and direct the public buildings. About 1844 or '45 he moved to Rockdale and built a mill on Piney Woods creek, near Jeptha Post Office, which takes his name. His father was so pronounced a "Unionist" he had to leave home during the war to save his life and died during his exile in Mississippi.

The Smiths like the Heflins and Woods, have been prominently connected with the political and public administration of Randolph County almost since its organization to within a few years back. These three families usually directed and dictated the policy and conventions of the Democratic party, to which they all belonged up to 1860. They have been divided, somewhat, eversince until now there are but two of their leading men living, and in their senility their "shibboleth" hath departed. Ex-Gov. Smith was in his ninth or tenth year when his father moved there. Like other boys in his day and surroundings, who were in a new and wild county, did not have the advantage of a collegiate education. He is self made, and stands today as one of the safest barristers and most forcible and magnetic pleaders at the bar and before the jury in the State of Alabama. He has had three sons, all lawyers. His eldest, David D., who, in life, stood on the highest and last round of the ladder of professional fame, was stricken down in death; and, perhaps, the most promising young lawyer the State of Alabama has ever had the honor to claim. The writer knew him from infancy to manhood and though unlike any other boy, did not recognize the hidden jewel of professional fame until its bright and effulgent rays were treasured in the vault of endless time. His father knowing by experience the value of good practical education took care to see his son had the advantages of an English education. He sent him to Chattanooga, Tenn. one or two years and then secured him a position in the Supreme Court contingent at Montgomery, where he remained, perhaps, for two years and in the meantime, had him under his own tutorage. From boyhood to manhood, the writer can't now call to mind or locate one instance in which David ever engaged in a game of marbles or ball, or took part in a dance or social. I don't say he did not, but if he did, I can't call it to memory. Yet he was pleasant, jovial and hilarious at all times. This may seem incredible, nevertheless, it is true. Sit tibi terra levis. John Anthony Winston is the second son of Governor Smith. He did not get the advantages nor preparation of a first-class school tutorage his brother David did, nor the benefit of the Supreme Court hearings sine-qua-non-an indispensable addition to a professional young man. However, he had the best a country teacher could give and he has forged to the front until he has few superiors in formulating and preparation which secures almost invariably success in complicated suits. He is associated with his father at Birmingham. William H., Jr., is destined to make his mark of a high calling. He has every indication associated which mature years will develop into ripeness and perfection.

Governor Smith is now about 70 years old, with mental and physical force still active. Neither he, nor any of his father's family, so far as I know, have ever made any pretension religiously. His habits and morals have always been temperate and conservative. He is sociable and pleasant in companionship; upright and honorable in dealings; egotistical and self-reliant in opinions; faithful and true in friendship; aggressive and forcible in argument; inflexible, magnetic, magnificient and versatile in debate. There is no vanity or aristocratic show about him. He is plain, pleasant and easily approached by common country folk, of whom he has always shared their confidence and support and defended their rights. Mrs. Smith was of poor, but honest and virtuous parentage. She was a Wortham, and a native born citizen of Randolph. She is one of the most pleasant, and amiable lady neighbors I have ever lived by, and a true and devoted Christian. They moved to Birmingham 12 or 15 years ago.

Richard J. Wood was a farmer, in his 31st year of age; a Democrat and lived in Louina Beat. He was one of those plain, honest temperate, country raised, country educated and country trained boys, raised in old farmer style of economy, who were usually bountifully fed and worked hard. Nature endowed him with several of her most rare and choice gifts and he husbanded them carefully all through life. He had fine thought, business tact, equanimity, energy, acumen and avidivity. Perhaps, there never has been a man living in the county that had his pecularities. His mind, thought, foresight, judgment, reason, comparison, designation, discernment and perception, with force, effort, energy, efficiency, and tenacity were associated in all his undertakings, which made success phenomena. He established a tannery one mile north of Wedowee and ran on a process by which leather could be tanned in 30 days. He made shoes and mail bags for the Confederate Government, and bought during the time near one hundred bales of cotton and stored it in different localities. For the want of protection, a large part of this cotton was burned by robbers and cut-throats, but he sold what was left at 40 or 50 cents per pound at the close of the war. He then located and opened the Wood Copper Mines, for which, it was said, he was offered fifty thousand dollars. For the want of means to develop it, he sold four out of ten shares at $5,000 each and invested in machinery, after which he was forced into litigation and lost all.

Being brought up and taught to believe all men claiming respectability were honorable, honest and truthful and should be treated as such, in dealings, politics and other associations, he entered public life with a conscience innocent and void of offense; integrity as pure as rectified gold and honor as spotless as snow. Deception had never entered his heart, wrong had never disturbed his sweet repose in sleep, believing, confiding and trusting implicitly in the integrity of man as the noblest handiwork of an all-wise God. Although thrice seduced by subtility as were Adam and Eve, his faith was predicated and rooted in paternal tutorage, that only through honesty and industry could success in life be attained. It is the innocent that is wronged, the honest that is swindled, the believer that is deceived. With these characteristics, I have traced Dick Wood (for that is what everybody called him) from youth to manhood, senility and death. Bearing these in mind, it can easily be seen why his success in business was like the incoming and outgoing tide. He believed honesty, honor, integrity, fidelity, liberality, industry and peace were the beneficiaries of perfection and a reward of righteousness in death. Whatever his sacrifice, trials, troubles and suffering cost him to maintain them, no one can know. What reward God shall grant him, none can know now. For the Word sayeth: "He that lives under the law shall be condemned by the law." The rich young Ruler who had kept the law said: "What lacketh I yet?" By this question it seems he recognized something else was needed. While the writer has known of Dick Wood for fifty years, the last fifteen or twenty years he was not intimately associated with him and I don't know whether he ever made any profession, religiously, or not, but he does know and can testify that Dick had every attribute of a child of God in his life's walk and dealings with men.

In 1861, he was one of the delegates elected to the convention that passed the ordinance of secession. Henry M. Gay, Richard J. Wood and George Forester were elected on the co-operation ticket. They stood almost alone in the convention and were finally prevailed on to vote for the ordinance. This, though he had voted for Douglass and opposed secession, destroyed his political promotion ever afterwards. After the war, he affiliated with the Republican party. He was appointed post-master at Heflin during Harrison's administration. He married a lady near Franklin, Ga., and during her lifetime he lived happy, content and prosperous life. But after his second marriage, peace, contentment and prosperity took wings and soared on the chilly winds of adversity, hardship and discontent. His last days spent on earth were with his first wife's relatives and friends, where his happiest hours were once enjoyed. And let us hope these latter days were happy and pleasant in simplicity, loneliness of thought and rememberances of a dutiful, affectionate and lovely companion, who then, somnolently awaited his coming. His noble, generous, manly personality so pleasantly associated with us in earthly ties of humanity, bade adieu, fare thee well, fare thee well forever., July 25th, 1895, and now rest by the side of one he loved and cherished in life, mourned in absence and sleeps by in death.

Number Forty Three

Written for The Toiler, by Capt. J.M.K. Guinn

1857-8---W.H. Smith, A.W. Denman and Isaac Weaver

Hon. Abner W. Denman. (See serial on Sheriff.)

Rev. Isaac Weaver was a Missionary Baptist Minister of the Gospel, aged 26, and lived in Louina beat. He was a zealous Democrat and highly respected by his neighbors and loved by his church. His private and public life was spotless so far as the writer knew. He had three sons, Rev. G.F., O.B., and Henry Weaver, all of whom were good citizens and clever men. Rev. Isaac Weaver died during the war.

1859-60---F.M. Ferrell, F.A. McMurray and Joshua Hightower.

Hon. F.M. Ferrell lived near Lineville now Clay county. He was a very prominent man and highly respected by his community. After the election of John Goodin, (Whig), the Democrats locally selected their candidates in order to strengthen their ranks, and as a matter of course nominated and elected some men they were ashamed of afterwards, but it had become traditional with the party and its success, and every beat had a good man it wanted honored. It was stimulating and exhilarating to the cross-road ambitious Statesman. The writer was living in Texas at this time and knows nothing derogatory to the official acts of the three representatives; he remembers no criticism.

Hon. Franklin A. McMurray lived near Louina, was a farmer 50 years of age, and a Democrat. He came to Randolph county just before or after the Indian war in 1836, in which he served as a soldier, and now draws a pension from the United States. He is a brother of F.M. McMurray, County Surveyor from 1849 to 1857. Uncle Frank is the father of F.M. McMurray, who married a Gay and grandfather of W.H. McMurray, merchant at Wedowee. He has always been an active, energetic farmer and had accumulated a good property. He was appointed by the Confederate Government as war Tax Assessor. He is a man of good sense, sound judgment and well informed; kind, generous and charitable; pleasant sociable and entertaining. He is still living at the old homestead, and is now in his 87th year, with remarkable tenacity, energy and agility, honored and respected by all, and votes the Populist ticket.

Joshua Hightower was a farmer, an extreme Democrat, an old settler, 45 years of age, and lived in Jenkins beat. He was a brother of William Hightower, Randolph's first Sheriff. Mrs. Hightower was said to be an exceptionally good lady, and their son, William M., was a good, clever boy and a member of Co. K, 13th

Alabama regiment, and still living. Hon. Joshua Hightower was a Breckenridge Democrat and voted for secession. He made up a company of Home Guards and was its Captain. He was arrogant, selfish and egotistical, and said to be tyrantical and oppressive during the latter part of the war, persecuting men and women who differed with him politically, or in anyway showed or expressed their sympathy for the Union cause. It was said, and from personal knowledge, it is believed that Captain Hightower was in command of the squad of men who were detailed by Captain Robinson, commander of the post at Wedowee, to carry Bone Trent and Dock King to Talladega conscript camps, which they never reached nor were seen alive afterwards, but were said to have been found by Capt. E.B. Smith sometime afterwards in a pit several feet deep, partially filled with water, at Gold Ridge gold mines. The next day following Captain Smith's find, the whole community turned out to recover their bodies; but on reaching the pit, they found it had been filled during the previous night with logs and brush, which had evidently been done by the parties commiting the crime. This, with other circumstances connected, intimidated those who were gathered there and they went home without any further effort, believing their own lives would be in jeopardy. It has been said also that he was one of the men who shot and killed Capt. E.B. Smith at his home in 1865. The writer was in Texas at the time, but was told this by a man unimpeachable, though dead now. It was also told the writer, but by whom it is not now remembered, that three of these men went to the Indian Territory, and the Indian's split P's tongue, cut off L's ears and jobbed out H's eyes. Whether guilty or not as charged the writer does not know personally, but the circumstances point very strongly against him. In the first place, he left Wedowee with Trent and King as prisoners. Secondly, the pit was accessible for him to reach that night. Thirdly, Captain Smith's testimony would have been very strong against him. Fourthly, he left the county as soon as there appeared to be a probability of investigation. Fifthly, if guilty, he would naturally do something justifying the punishment said to have been inflicted by the Indians.

This was the last Democratic member elected to the Legislature from Randolph county until 1874.

1861-2---Alabama had passed the ordinance of secession and seceded from the Union. C.J. Ussery, A.W. Denman and Capt. James Aiken were elected. All secessionists.

Captain Aiken was a lawyer, 31 years of age, but previously a pedagogue. He was associated with ex-Gov. W.H. Smith at Wedowee, in the practice of law, and when the war broke out he raised a company and was elected Captain. Dr. H.C. Ghent, Dr. Wiley M. Kemp, and Algernon Sidney Reaves were respectively elected lieutenants. (They are all living today.) Captains Aiken, E.B. Smith and M.D. Robinson and companies left on July 12, 1861. Capt. John T. Smith left July 4th, and all belonged to the 13th Alabama regiment. Captain Aiken was promoted Colonel in the Spring of 1863, and went through the war, surrendering as commander of his regiment with Gen. R.E. Lee, April 9th, 1865. He was a brave and faithful soldier; an upright and honorable man; an humble, faithful and trusting Christian whose integrity, character and virtue were unimpeachable; modest, plain and every day the same pleasant, kind and courteous commander, without vanity, pride or self-conceit. And, although he votes the "organized" ticket, those who know him have a higher estimate placed on his past life than to believe he would sacrifice it to accept an election by the Tom Jones process--the orthodox of "organized"

Democrary. Colonel Aiken is in no sense an office-seeker or hunter, although one of the brightest legal lights at the Alabama Bar. He has held but one official position since the war--that of Circuit Judge of his district. Why it is that men of his known legal, mental and moral qualities are relegated to private life, and less meritorious ones promoted, can only be reconciled by the emergencies and necessities for party proscription, venality and corruption. Since the war, he married a most amiable and charming domestic lady who lived at Lineville. They have an interesting and promising family of children and live at Gadsden.

Number Forty Four

Written for The Toiler, by Capt. J.M.K. Guinn

1863---Henry W. Armstrong, Milton D. Barron, Augustus A. West and David A. Perryman.

Henry W. Armstrong lived at Chulafinnee beat. He was a farmer, 44 years of age, anti-war Democrat but after the war a Republican. He was a good, substantial, well-to-do farmer, with fine mental and moral attributes; an active, energetic, progressive and aggressive politician. He was largely and well-connected by men with influence and means. He is still living and resides in Clay county, not far from Delta, honored and loved and respected by his neighbors.

M.D. Barron lived below Louina, on Big Tallapoosa river. He was a farmer, 45 years of age, anti-war Democrat and a son of Rev. Hiram Barron. The writer had only a slight acquaintance with him. He died during his term as a member of the Legislature.

Capt. A.A. West was at the time of his election a Captain in the 31st regiment; 27 years of age and a farmer. He made up a company and went out March 31, 1862. He had been a Douglass Democrat and opposed secession. After the conscription act and the political persecution began, his sympathies grew stronger for the Union, and after his election to the Legislature he resigned and came home, but from some cause failed to take his seat as a member. His brother, Eph, was a Captain in the United States army and his entire family sympathized with the Union cause. He was a plain, honest and hard-working farmer before the war; had no ambition or aspiration to seek or hold office. He moved to Kansas probably in 1871, where he has since lived, with the exception of five or six months spent at Wedowee with his son, R.T. West, during the spring of 1895. He married a Miss Bornby, daughter of Mrs. Isaac Baker, Now Mrs. Griffin, who still is living and went west with her son-in-law.

Gus was a neighbor boy, and had pride and ambition enough to let no one do more or better work at log-rollings, house raisings and corn-shuckings. Everybody liked him for his many noble qualities and when he visited his old home and old friends last year, it was one of the most pleasant greetings common to men of mature age. That happy boyhood friendship, confidence and attachment that grows stronger and closer, as has manhood grown older and wiser, took new life, new energy and full possession of its once undisputed territory, and the memory of blissful boyish congenial love permeated the sympathy and cemented the ties that had lain somnolently, though not dead, set aside though not discarded, supplanted though not disinherited, separated though not divorced for twenty-odd years. While we cannot be boys and playmates again, thank God we can enjoy in meditation and thoughts of rememberance those once happy and pleasant days over again. How good and pleasant it is to be permitted to banish trouble, trials and affliction with an hour of sweet meditation of those past happy moments. Oh, God, how merciful, kind and thoughtful Thou hast been to allow a day, a year or a life-time to be lived in one short hour time of meditation, that we might forget sorrow and sadness. Is not this a taste of heavenly life? Is it not a reward of Christian charity and hope promised in the suffering, crucified, and resurrected Savior? "God is love" and those attachments associated in childhood and boyhood are attributes of God. Separation, old age, poverty, affliction, persecution, trials, troubles, height nor depth can separate, annul, set aside, overcome nor supplant these sweet remembrances of the past. O, were it possible that we could live as in childhood our latter days. For of such is the Kingdom of Heaven and redemption of the lost.

David A. Perryman was elected to fill the vacancy of West or Barron, I don't remember which, but he too refused to qualify or take his seat. (See serial on Tax Assessor.)

1865-6---W.W. Dodson, J.L. Williams and W.E. Connelly.

Judge Wallace Washington Dodson. (See serial on Probate Judge.)

Judge James L. Williams formerly lived at Louina but when elected lived at Lineville. He was a Douglas Democrat and anti-war Union man. He merchandised at Lineville for several years subsequently and was elected Probate Judge of Clay county. He was of fine appearance and had the reputation of being very popular with the masses. His official acts were said to be highly creditable. He died several years ago.

W.E. Connelly. (See serial on Circuit Court Clerk.)

The Legislature reduced Randolph's representation from three to two, and called a Constitutional Convention for 1867.

1867---W.E. Connelly and J.L. Williams were elected.

1869-70---The Legislature in 1867-8, cut off township 17 to Cleburne county, and range 9 to Clay. This reduced Randolph's members from 2 to 1, under the new Constitution.

Jack Wood was a farmer, in his 39th year, and lived in Louina beat. He was a Douglass Democrat and opposed secession and the war. He was the son of William Wood and married Miss Ann Anderson, daughter of Lewis Anderson. Ann's mother was a Glover, and sister to Mrs. Emily Hunter. I used to think, when we went to school together, Ann was the prettiest girl I ever saw. There were others who thought so, too, if one is to judge by the beaux she had. Bob Smith, Jack Wood and others were smitten and be-sieged her hand and heart, but Jack proved to be the winner. He moved to Kansas about 1871 and is said to have died there several years since.

1871---Dr. Joseph H. Davis, of Roanoke, was elected as a Democrat. George Forester, of Louina beat, a Republican was his opponent and given the certificate of election. Davis contested and was seated. Forrester held the certificate on a technicality and only took his seat at the urgent, solicitation of his party. He, however, like an honorable man, such as he is and always was, made no fight and the contest on his part went by default.

Dr. Davis was elected to the Constitutional Convention of 1867, as a Republican. He was exempted during the war, as a practicing physician, but was so pronounced a Unionist he had to leave "the home of the brave and the land of the free" of Dixie in 1864. In 1868 he was a Seymore Democrat. He was a skillful physician, well informed, keen, shrewd and a cunning politician. He was high tempered, self-willed and egotistical, yet at the same time, kind, liberal and true to his friends. He was a close and warm friend; a bitter and aggressive enemy. He was a member of the M.E. Church, South. He was superstitious and would not go close by a graveyard after night. He had a heart disease, and told the writer he expected to drop off suddenly, which he did, August 25, 1878. While he differed with many of his neighbors politically and some times personally, yet they all honored and respected him and turned out en masse to pay their last earthly respects to his remains. His second wife was a Miss Mary Gillespie, a modest, pleasant and refined lady; a dutiful wife and affectionate mother. Mrs. Davis now lives at LaFayette, Ala., where the writer recently visited her at home and was delighted to find she retained a remarkable degree of her many former charms of beauty and vivacity. She showed the writer a life-size picture of Dr. J.H. Davis. It is a perfect life likeness, so much so you are almost constrained to greet it as if living.

Number Forty Five

Written for The Toiler, by Capt. J.M.K. Guinn

1872-3---Hon. W.H. Lovvorn. (See serial No. 32)

1874-5---Hon. William D. Heaton lived in Saxon's beat. He was a farmer, Democrat, Mason and Baptist. Several years previous he and brother merchandised at Gold Ridge. He was a very clever man and stood well in Shiloh Baptist Church, of which he was a member. His education was limited, but his energy, good judgment and business tact secured to him a good property. He was passionate, excitable and easily deceived and led astray, but when cool and deliberate would correct mistakes and right wrongs. His selection as a candidate was on account of locality, the writer making the suggestion. He married a daughter of S.W. Hearn, known as Whit Hearn, who was at that time, said to be the wealthiest man in Randolph county. He visited Texas several years afterwards and on his return home was taken sick and died shortly after. Mrs. Heaton still lives on the old homestead.

1876-7---Hon. C.J. Ussery. (See serial No. 40)

1878-9---Hon. Jason J. Hearn lived at Rock Mills beat, a farmer, Polly Ann Democrat and a member of the Primitive Baptist Church. He was said to be a very clever neighbor, a good citizen and a worthy member of his church. He was scarcely known outside of his beat until defeated in the Polly Ann convention by A.C. Saxon, in 1877 for Tax Assessor. He is still living.

1880-1---Hon. Thomas E. Head lived in High Shoals beat. Was a farmer, democrat and about 50 years of age. Tom was a first rate, good and clever citizen and neighbor. His death was very sudden and thought to have been voluntarily and of his own free will. Was an old citizen and universally loved and respected for his quiet, peaceable and neighborly traits. It is one of those unaccountable mysteries which probably will never be known by the public.

1882-3---Hon. F.P. Randall, a citizen of Rock Mills, and at the time superintendent of the Wehadkee Mfg. Company, was elected. Capt. Randall's business qualities, keen perception, fine intelligence, Christian character, temperate habits and good morals demanded his selection and election as a necessity for relief from railroad bond indebtedness. Many of his personal and political opponents voted for him on account of his availability and confidence in his integrity and interest in the public good. He was known to be a conservative, energetic and zealous in his private business, and though he had time and again refused to accept a nomination, backed by strong solicitation, he was prevailed on to run and was elected, but he failed to appreciate the confidence universally bestowed and reposed and left his post and official duties to attend his private matters at home. This showed, on his part, he had no aspirations or ambition for office or official duties, while on the part of the people was disappointment and loss of confidence. While Captain Randall is a zealous partisan politically, office is repugnant to his sensibilities and he seems to loathe the thought of its charm and honors. Why, I don't know, for he is public spirited and a strong advocate for good government and wholesome laws. He came from Kentucky to this county since the war and for many years has been the Superintendent or President of the Wehadkee Cotton Mills at Rock Mills. He has been recognized as the most zealous and active leading democrat in Rock Mills beat for years; and, today, is the most prominent Administration Democrat in the county. I have been told that he is a Clark man. If there is in existance today such a thing as an organized Democratic party, to be consistent, it must be that part which recognized the present State and National Administration. The Johnson men may hold to the traditional Democratic principles of free coinage of gold and silver, but they are not in the true sense of party parlance Democrats, but seceders. And like the Jeffersonians and Populists will patch up a compromise and vote once more together and then organize a new party. They have two precedents, (and a Democrat will see his soul for precedent) the Douglas and Breckenridge, Kolb and Jones. The writer is not a prophet nor the son of a prophet, but mark his prediction--if Johnson is nominated, A.T. Goodwyn will be the next governor of Alabama, if Clark is nominated, whether elected or not, he will be the governor of Alabama, for he will certainly get the certificate and there is no law by which his seat can be contested. A wayfaring man though a fool need not err therein. It is as plain as open and shut that 90 per cent of the administration Democrats will never vote for a free silverite. Turn your eye to the National Administration at Washington and then the administration Democrats in the Kentucky General Assembly. That ought to convince any sane mind the silverites are looked upon as Populists; the only difference is as to whether the vote shall be first class or counted.

1884-5---Hon. C.B. Taylor, of Rock Mills, was a Democrat, Primitive Baptist minister and a practicing physician. He was egotistical, or self-willed and pharisaical. Was said to be neighborly, friendly and sociable. A prominent minister and a fluent speaker, but being a Mason his usefulness in the pastorate was not extensively sought or desired by the brotherhood. He died years ago.

1886-7---Hon. Enoch Carter. (See serial on County Commissioners.)

1888-9---Hon. Samuel Henderson of Roanoke, was a young lawyer, member of Roanoke Baptist Church and a Democrat. He came from Talladega several years ago, and was the son of Rev. Samuel Henderson, who was known and prominently associated with the leading Baptist ministers throughout the South. Judge John Henderson honored by Randolphians as Circuit Judge, was his uncle. Sam is a fine lawyer and a fluent speaker. Unfortunately for Sam, whose physical, mental and Christian sensibilities are fully developed, there is a serious and questionable characteristic connected with his daily life that degrades and demoralizes his would-be championship; i.e., he is an old "bach." The fact is, he is an arrant coward through fear and intimidation of a broomstick in the hands of laughing, sparkling eyes, ruby cherry cheeks, coquetish smiling face, birnanous caressing arms of maiden, mine or portly buxom widowhood. Let me implore you, Sammy, ere 1896 shall chronicle the golden moments and fleeting days of leap year and pass into endless time, to shave off that buttermilk strainer, iron out those crab apple wrinkles, rope that stage breath and imprison your bachelor timidity in the heart affectionate of wifedom.

1890-1---Hon. Wilson L. Ayers. (See serial on Sheriffs.)

1892-3---Hon. H.H. Whitten, lived in Roanoke beat, is a farmer, Populist and allianceman, good morals and temperate habits, and active, energetic worker and a successful farmer. He came to the county ten or fifteen years ago and the writer only knows of him since the election. He supported and maintained the principals of the Populist party which was in the minority and unable to pass any acts of reform or repeal class or unjust laws, as were desired by the masses of the people.

1894-5---Hon, S.E.A. Reaves. (See serial on Probate Judges.)

Number Forty Six

Written for The Toiler, by Capt. J.M.K. Guinn

RANDOLPH'S REPRESENTATIVES
STATE SECESSION CONVENTION

1861---H.M. Gay, R.J. Wood and G. Forester

Hon. Henry M. Gay. (See serial No. 36.)

Hon. Richard J. Wood. (See serial No. 42.)

Hon. George Forester lived north of Louina on Big Tallapoosa river. He was a farmer, 41 years of age, and a Co-operationist, previously a Douglas Democrat. Rev. Charles P. Cission, of Jenkin's beat, and Dr. W.E. White, of Roanoke, were Forester's and Wood's competitors. Gay's opponent has slipped me. However, a young lawyer, of Wedowee, by the name of J.J. Hill, canvassed the county for secession, and John O.D. Smith, now of Opelika, but then a tender bud of law at Wedowee, canvassed for co-operation. The campaign was opened by Hill at Dunston's court ground. John Goodin, Dunston and some others swore Smith should not speak, but when assured free speech would be had if it took a secession vote to get it, they changed their tactics. The crowd seemed to be almost unanimously with them up to this time, but Smith, with his comrade by his side, soon won the friendship of two-thirds of the crowd. Hill and Goodin looked disappointed

and mortified, and, no doubt, felt it. They tried to play the
intimidating act at Chulafinne, but it was no go. Smith told them
if they did not want to cooperate the next best thing they could
do was to practice what they preached, and "secede." The boys
caught on and gave Smith a rousing boost, but Hill and company
cold comfort. George Forester was then and is now one of Randolph's best and purest men. He loved his State and people and for
them he was willing to sacrifice personal and private opinions
for their public good. When he, Wood and Gay took their seats in
the Convention at Montgomery, they were greeted as brothers not
only by former Democratic comrades but by Whigs also. Party lines
were obliterated; State rights, Southern valor and self-government called on their patriotism and for unity. Division in vote
would be like cowardice of soldiers in front of the enemy. It
would be treason to desert the State and give support and encouragement to the enemy. Cooperation must come through State sisterhood and unity of interest. This was impossible or probable without unity, power and respectability. Both Whigs and Democrats
had united their strength at the ballot box and sent almost a
solid delegation in favor of seceding. A few cooperationists
could accomplish nothing good for their cause, but bring division
and ridicule on themselves, and destroy the confidence and unity
of the Body. These and many other stronger and pointed reasons
were brought to bear on them to vote for the ordinance of secession which they finally did. He was the Republican candidate
for the Legislature in 1871, and was given the certificate of
election, but believing Dr. J.H. Davis, had been fairly elected
and the certificate given him through a technicality caused by
throwing out Burson's beat, the returns not being properly certified too, he refused to take his certificate or seat until persuaded to do so by his personal friends, when Davis contested,
he did not defend it, but let it go by default. He has always
stood well with the people and but few public men have had a
stronger hold on the confidence of their neighbors then he. He
is now in his 76th year of age enjoying life, quiet and happiness surrounded by relatives and friends.

CONSTITUTIONAL CONVENTION

1865---R.T. Smith, see serial on Circuit Court Clerk

1867---Dr. J.H. Davis, See serial No. 45.

1875---Capt. Benjamin F. Weathers, Roanoke, was nominated
May 28, 1875 by the Democrats of Randolph and elected in August
following. He was 37 years of age and had been raised on a farm
though at the time engaged in merchandising. He was the oldest
son of I.T. and Sarah Weathers and brother of our present Probate
Judge, A.J. Weathers. He was a condidate for Probate Judge in
1877, and defeated in the convention by James C. Sherman, he
bolted and announced himself an independent candidate, but before
the election withdrew and supported Judge S.E.A. Reaves and
accepted a clerkship. In 1894 he took sides with the wet ticket
in Roanoke's city election which it is claimed, makes his promotion questionable and improbable in the near future. Captain
Weathers volunteered in Capt. Boss White's company and was promoted from Lieutenant to a Captain and was a brave and gallant
soldier in the field. He is one of that class of men known by
their open-handed liberality who makes his visitors pleasant while
showing his hospitality and companionship. He is now cashier of
Roanoke Bank and holds the confidence of those with whom he is
associated. He married a Miss Jennie Mickle, daughter of William
and Mary Mickle, among the first and best people of the county.

Jennie was one of the most bewitching, fascinating and charming young ladies in all lower Randolph and is as munificent and charitable as the Captain, full of life, energy and vivacity, a zealous member of the M.E. Church, South, a pleasant and sociable companion and a most excellant and kind neighbor.

This closes the historical sketches of the county officers of Randolph County from January 1, 1833 to January 1, 1896. There are some typographical and other corrections which I wish to make, but can't do so until I have the opportunity to visit Wedowee.

It is more than probable someone in person or through a friend feels an unjust or an unjust construction has been placed upon them would, if afforded an opportunity, furnish the proper correction. The writer would take as a favor, as he intends sometime in the future to publish it in book form.

It is the purpose of the writer to resume these serials in August or September, the subject of which will be the Captains and other Confederate Soldiers; Editors and Publishers of Randolph's Newspapers; the most noted characters of the County before the war: J.W. Bradshaw, Benjamin Bolt, Eph. Higginbotham, the Hensons, Marrows, Aggie Rose, Merchants and Lawyers; Cattamounts and Todd's negroes; the Talladega mad boy and his conviction; Jim Snively shoal diving; a sack of salt; A.B.C. Guason, the Toiler; Domino (Jesse Haywood) and negro dogs; Tom Hearn and old Napper; the Hotel keep and wild hog, etc. etc. It might be possible, you know, that my host of friends might take up the idea to run and elect me to some office, and in order to remove all encumbrances and have an open way before me to accept. I have cancelled all contracts until after the election and am now engaged in fishing for luck.

Formerly the municiple complex of Roanoke (City Hall, Jail and Fire Department), this building now houses the Headhunters Beauty Salon. c. 1885.

RANDOLPH COUNTY

BY

WILLIAM WALLACE SCREWS

From

The Montgomery Advertiser

March 1, 1898

RANDOLPH COUNTY

Mr. Screws' letter on Randolph County

Editorial Correspondence of the Montgomery Advertiser

Roanoke, Alabama-March 1

The change in appearance of Roanoke twenty years ago, as compared with the present day, is very great to the visitor who has not been here during the intervening time. The business then was transacted in two or three stores and the population all told would scarcely number more then 300 souls. Now there is a population in the neighborhood of 2,000 people and business houses whose trade is equal to that done in the largest cities of Alabama.

Randolph's Emporium

Roanoke is beyond question the emporium of Randolph County. Settlements by white people were not made in this part of the State as early as in the Southern and Western portions. The Indians were here in great numbers by reason of treaty and otherwise when they had vacated other portion of the State. An act of the Legislature approved December 18, 1832, established the county of Randolph. It was named for the distinguished but eccentric Virginian, John Randolph. The land embraced in the act was included in the last session.

Indian Names

As a general thing, the Creeks clung to the streams and swamps and alluvial lands lying on them, and thus many of the creeks bear Indian names. Sometimes a stream was named from a town near it, and at others the stream gave its name to the town. The Tallapoosa River, which runs the full length of this county means "cat town" and the river undoubtedly received its name from a town somewhere on its banks, the locality of which is not now known. Wedowee, the seat of justice, is said to mean "falling water," and derives its name from the creek near by, which, in much of its course, tumbles over high falls which would make its name quite appropriate.

Roanoke takes its name from the old Carolina or Virginia town of the same name, but that name is an Algonquin Indian word, meaning a shell, such as wampum was made of.

Twelve miles west of Roanoke is Louina, which gets its name from an old Indian Woman who lived at the site of the present village. She was the widow of one of the subchiefs and very wealthy. It is said by old residents that when old Louina set out for the west she had one pony loaded with silver dollars, and it is a tradition among old residents that the Indians declared that there was a valuable silver mine just above the village, but if so, its locality is yet hidden. Other Indian names of streams are:

Hoote Archee, now called Corn House Creek; Kitchomadogga, from Ketchoputake, literally "maise pounding block," meaning the mortar in which they pounded their corn.

Weoka, "sounding water," and Wehadkee "white water" are two other creeks with appropriate Indian names. High Pine Creek was called Chulehalwe, meaning the same as Wesobulga means "many sassafratrees," or bushes. Thus did the aborigines leave all time record of their language in the streams and towns where they made their homes.

A Political Incident

There are no stirring incidents in early or later days connected with Randolph county. Its ways have always been those of pleasantness, barring occasional personal troubles and the severing of relations between a large part of the population in 1861. In this correspondence there has been an international ignoring of current political matters, but some past events in this county are somewhat anamalous and worthy of note for historical purposes. The majority of voters of the county up to the secession period were Democrats, but many were intense Union men. This class supported Douglas for President and when the trouble between the North and South arose many of them adhered to the Union side. Ex-Governor W.H. Smith, W.T. Wood and Robert S. Heflin, were men of influence. They had large followings, and they bitterly opposed secession. Numbers of them left the county and entered the Union lines where they remained until the conflict ended. At least one full company of men joined the Federal Army from the county, while there were hundreds of Union sympathizers who remained at home.

When matters began to readjust themselves after the war closed there was a large Republican vote cast by white men in Randolph county. This was somewhat surprising for as a rule the white people of the State were opposed to the Republican Party from tradition, from principle and expecially because of the kind of legislature enacted by Congress for the purpose of controlling the Southern States. The white Republican vote is still large in the county - very nearly one half. It is cast by men who are good citizens, and who enjoy the confidence of their friends and neighbors. The bitterness of the past had disappeared and while there is hot contention at the polls there is peace and good will between the political opponents.

Wedowee since 1836 has been the county site. It is about fifteen miles north of Roanoke. In 1839 the name was changed to McDonald, but a year or so afterwards it resumed and has ever since retained its Indian nomenclature. The first courts in the county were held at what is now called Blake's Ferry, then Triplett's or Young's, ten miles west of Wedowee.

There has been but little growth at Wedowee. It boasts a fine school and a court house that will bear comparison with any in the State. Its coast was $21,000. It is 74X96 feet, has eight well-proportioned and arranged rooms for offices on the lower floor with wide hall and two fire proof vaults. There are five rooms, besides the large court room upstairs and a spacious gallery capable of holding a large crowd. The tower is 120 feet high and contains a fine tower clock. The roof is of slate and the entire building is regarded as fire proof. The county has lost more than one court house by fire and the authorities have acted wisely in seeking to avoid such disaster in the future. Court houses should be built to last for a century and not for a day only. Commissioners who on the score of economy accept cheap John affairs are derelict in duty and doing a positive injury to those whose interests they are sworn to protect.

Gold and Copper Mines

There has always been more or less gold mining interest in this county. The distance from railroad and the cost of handling machinery has kept down what would have proven to be a profitable industry. The Pinetuckey gold mine twelve miles north of Wedowee has recently put in modern machinery and much work is being done. It is operated by the Fair Milling and Mining Company.

The W.L. Ayers mine is a curiosity. It is situated on the old Arbacoochee Copper land just on the line between Randolph and Cleburne counties. The vein is about the shape and size of a large hogs head, one lying on top of the other. There is a hollow space in each roll about three inches in diameter. About a mile and a half west of Wedowee, D. and A.D. Smith have just opened up a rich mine. The assay made at Denver, Colorado, shows $27 per ton. On this same land about seven miles southwest is Bradford mine which (torn---) recently purchased by (torn---) Montgomery parties are also interested in this property. Aug. is at present prospecting on this land and as the representative of capitalists has purchased several pieces of property.

There is a fine Kaolin property between the Little and Big Tallapoosa Rivers belonging to Birmingham parties on which they have expended about $80,000. This Keolin has been made into fire-proof brick tested in Boston Furnaces and stand the test.

The Wood Copper mines are close on to the line of Randolph and Cleburne counties and are now being worked.

The population of Randolph county in 1870 was 12,006. In 1890 it was 17,219, of which 13,984 were white and 3,235 colored. Nearly all the colored people are in three beats, only scattering ones being found in other portions of the county.

First Settlement of Roanoke

Although Randolph county was formed in 1832 it was not until 1835 that there was a vestige of inhabitation, where is now the thriving town of Roanoke. In the latter year James Furlong built a small store house for the trade of the people who were scattered for miles around the place. The site of the present town was owned by James and Hugh Hathorn who possessed many negroes. They erected a blacksmith shop where such work was done by negro smiths as the neighborhood needed. Hugh died and was buried here. His brother, James, sold his lands and moved to Mississippi. Wall Wood located here in 1834 and James and W.D. Mickle in 1835. Many of their descendants are now honored citizens of the community.

The father of Dr. Will Heflin settled about seven miles of here in 1836. He was the progenitor of the Heflin family, members of which have been conspicious in the legal, political and medical history of Alabama.

Isham T. Weathers, father of Capt. B.F. Weathers, of this place, settled first at Louina where he conducted a store and traded with the Indians in 1834. The Indians were not hostile and soon afterwards joined their kindred in the western reservations. Mr. Weathers had a remarkable life in many particulars. He died here March 10, 1897, and his wife October 10, 1897. They reared twelve children, all of whom survived them. In October,

1896, there was a family reunion at which all of their children were present. In addition, grandchildren and great-grandchildren to the number of 88 were present, while forty three were absent. From the day of the marriage of these two worthy people, until they were laid away to rest, only two of their family died, and they were infant grandchildren. This is a remarkable record of unbroken family relations.

Almond United Methodist Church. Established in 1845. Courtesy Laurene Wilson Caldwell of Montgomery, Alabama.

PROBATE NOTICES FROM
THE AMERICAN EAGLE

10 July 1856

D.V. Crider, Adm. of Estate of William Armstrong, deceased, late of Randolph Co. will sell at public auction to the highest bidder corn, bacon, horses, etc. from the Estate.

W.H. Spruce and B.J. Hand, Execs. of Estate of James H. Rouse will sale personal property of the Estate, such as dry, furniture, stock, kitchen furniture, etc.

L.H.W. Guinn, Adm. of Estate of Shedrick Kelly, deceased, will sell land in the Estate adjoining the property of William Gladney in Randolph Co. on the third Monday in July.

10 January 1856

W.V. Thomaston was married to Miss Catharine Darnall on Sunday the 6th by Rev. B. Goss, all of Randolph Co.

Mrs. M.R. Porter, consort of Dr. C.C. Porter, died in Jacksonville on the 26th at her home. She was a member of the Presbyterian Church.

A.W. Denman, Sheriff & ex officio Adm. of Estate of Elijah Y. Linch, late of Randolph Co., filed an obligation in writing declaring the Estate insolvent.

7 February 1856

Jacob and Rhoda, two slaves from the Estate of the late Stephen Nixon will be sold Feb. 22nd on the premises in Randolph County.

James M. Mickle, Adm. of the Estate of A.B. Dabney, filed accounts and vouchers for final settlement.

14 February 1856

J.P. Barnett was married to Miss M.H. Riddle on the 5th of February by Rev. J.C. Beverly, all of Randolph County.

G.B. Davis, the second son of J.B. and E.H. Davis, died in Hempstead County, Ark. on Sept. 19, aged 2 years 7 months and 9 days.

21 February 1856

N.B. Garrett, 35, died Jan. 1st at his residence at Hicory Flat, Chambers County. He was born in Fayette County, Ga. In 1821 where he lived until 10 years old when he moved with his father to Troup County, Ga. He lived at that place until emigrating to Alabama in 1850. He joined the Baptist Church in Antioch Church, Troup Co., being baptized by Rev. Jesse Moon. He was buried on Jan. 2nd with Masonic honors.

28 February 1856

100

Spencer Wilson, Guardian of the Estate of Martha A. Bassett, W.H. Bassett, James Bassett and John Bassett, minor heirs of Richard Bassett, deceased, filed accounts and vouchers for final settlement with William H. and Martha A. Bassett and annual settlements with James and John Bassett.

13 March 1856

Spencer Wilson was married to Miss C.A. Wilkerson on Sunday the 9th by Dr. R.L. Robertson, all of Randolph County.

20 March 1856

E. Strickland was married to Miss Mary E. Leverett on the 13th by Rev. J.C. Beverly, all of Randolph County.

Notice was given to John Baker, a non-resident heir and devisee of Elizabeth Sadler, late of Randolph County, to appear in Court and answer the petition of J.B. Mapp, Adm. of the Estate. It was necessary to sell the real estate for equal distribution to the heirs.

27 March 1856

John Eve Verdery, 6 years 10 months 24 days, died in Cedar Town, Ga. on the 6th. He was the youngest son of Mr. and Mrs. A.N. Verdery.

3 April 1856

J. Truman Shepard, 7 years 5 months, died in Warren, Alabama on March 29th, 1856.

10 April 1856

Joseph Darnall, 74 years old, died in Roanoke on the 7th. Was a member of the Missionary Baptist Church. Was survived by his wife and children.

1 May 1856

James Posey, Guardian of Mary Ann Clark, James Clark and Marion Clark, minor children of William M. Clark, deceased, filed accounts and vouchers for final settlement with Mary Ann Clark and annual settlement for the other wards.

Virginia Harriett Young, only child of William and Elizabeth Young, was born Nov. 24, 1853 and died April 11, 1856 after an illness of a few days.

8 May 1856

ELECTION NOTICE

An election will be held in the several Townships in Randolph County, Alabama, on the 2nd Monday in May next for three School Trustees in each Township in said county, at the following mentioned places and the following named persons are appointed managers of said election, in the respective Townships, to-wit:

T.17, R.9, at Warren; Nelson Higginbotham, Hardy Strickland and Cary Caldwell managers and Robert Whitfield returning officer.

T.18, R.9, at Delta; William R. McClintock, William Mullalley and Prior Reaves managers, and William Ingram returning officer.

T. 19, R. 9, at Isaac Young's; Waller Owens, Uriah C. Spragberry and Isaac Young managers, and J.E. Whitfield returning officer.

T.20, R.9, at Wesabulga; Burton Walker, John Orr and David Billingsley managers, and John C. Johnson returning officer.

T.21, R,9, at James H. Smith's; W.W.Weathers, G.W. Billingley and William Jordan managers, and Irvin Woodruff returning officer.

T.22, R.9, at James McCosby's; John Coleman, William Wood and James McCosby managers, and David N. Hearn returning officer.

T.17, R.10, at Andrew McCullar's; William Camp and Moses Wright managers, Abner Vice returning officer.

T.18, R.10, at John A. White's; Harris Stephens, L.N. Daniel and John A. White managers, and Jonathan Garrett returning officer.

T.19, R.10, at William Gladney's; Wilson Falkner, Hugh Marrow and William Gladney managers, and Pucket Higginbotham returning officer.

T.20, R.10, at John Blake's; John Taylor, William Cosper and John Blake managers, and Spencer Morris returning officer.

T.21, R.10, at George W. Key's; William Dinglar, A.P. Hunter and George W. Key managers and Levi Wilkinson returning officer.

T.22, R.10, at Louina; John Culpepper, Henry L. Wood and James Person managers and William Welch returning officer.

T.17,R.11, at M.G. Howles; David V. Crider, William Howle and William Hight managers, and J.H. Roberts returning officer.

T.18, R.10, at Presley Humphries; James M. Putnam, John F. Freeman, and J. Knopp, managers, and Richard E. Braden returning officer.

T.19, R.11, at Francis M. Perryman's; Daniel C. Harris, John G. White and F.M. Perryman, managers, and David D. Smith returning officer.

T.20, R.11, at Wedowee; Jeremiah W. Stallings, I.M. Hightower and Thomas N. Berryhill managers, and C.F. Clifton returning officer.

T.21, R.11, at William R. Nunn's; Peter Green, Ephraim Parker and William R. Nunn managers, and James Molton returning officer.

T.22, R.11, at Concord Meeting-House; W.L. Heflin, John McVey and Peter Mitchel managers, J.J. Chuning returning officer.

T.17, R.12, at Allen Jinkens'; Thomas Collier, Caswell Kite and Daniel C. McSwain managers, and Allen Jinkens returning officer.

T.18, R.12, at James Saxon's; John Harris, Thomas D. Treadway and Joel H. Cosper managers, and James Saxon returning officer.

T.19, R.12, at E.M. Burgess'; James W. Burdon, James S. Pearson and Henry Rampey managers, and E.M. Burgess returning officer.

T.20, R.12, at Joshua Spear's; William C. Robertson, A. Bowen and John C. Carlisle managers, P. T. Okeit returning officer.

T.21, R.12, at Roanoke; P.H. Taylor, Seaborn Spradling and James Scales managers, T.L. Pittman returning officer.

T.22, R.12 at Garrett Wilder's; P. Haynes, E. Longshore and Garrett Wilder managers, J.M. Lane returning officer.

T.19, R.13, at W.F. Bailey's; Samuel McKey, Lindsey Harcrow and Tarpley Hester managers, and W.F. Bailey returning officer.

T.20, R.13, at Isaac Burson's; John C. Blair, Hugh Freeman and J.D. Heard managers, and J.J. Burson returning officer.

T.21, R.13, at Charles Foster's; John McPhearson, William R. Duke and Charles Foster managers, and Isham B. Lee returning officer.

T.22, R.13 at Bacon Level; Calvin J. Ussery, Joseph Rushton and Benjamin Reaves managers, and Thomas Gladney returning officer.

Managers and officers will take due notice, and make return of said elections to my office according to law. Given under my hand, this 24th day of April, 1856. Joseph Benton, Judge of Probate.

15 May 1856

John R. Ragan, infant son of R.G. and M.A. Ragan, died in Benton County on the 13th.

John Stroud, 70 years old, died at the residence of his son on the 2nd, 8 miles west of Wedowee of dropsy of the chest. Was a member of the M.E. Church. Survived by an aged wife, one son and two daughters.

Tribute of Respect to James H. Rouse who died on the 7th instant, by Sawyer Lodge No. 93. Was a member of the Primitive Baptist Church and is survived by his wife and other relatives. Signed by John Reaves, J.A. Moore, J.W. Guinn, Committee, D.A. Perryman, W.M. and W.H. Spruce, Secretary.

29 May 1856

James W. Guinn, Guardian of the Estate of Roxilla Dempsey, filed accounts and vouchers for final settlement with said ward.

Rhoda W. Noel, Executrix and George W. Noel Executor of Estate of Richman Noel, deceased, notified all persons with claims to present them.

Jeremiah Shepherd, Guardian of Estates of Mary A. Spears, wife of Thomas Martin, William R. Spears, James R. Spears, Amanda Spears, Nancy Spears and Daniel Spears, minor heirs of Daniel J. Spears, filed accounts and vouchers for final settlement with Mary A. Martin, late Mary A. Spears and annual settlement with all the other wards.

Richard J. Wood, Adm. of Estate of Sanford Hudson, filed petition setting forth that a Military Bounty Land Warrant No. 57479 was issued May 9, 1849, war of 1812, and he prayed for sale of the Land Warrant for the purpose of paying debts of the Estate.

David A. Perryman, Guardian of the Estates of Matilda C. McDaniel, formerly M.C. Haywood, Cyntha M.A. Haywood, Sarah A. Haywood and William A. Haywood, filed accounts and vouchers for final settlement with Matilda C. McDaniel and annual settlements on the other wards.

Citation was given to Elizabeth and John Birdsong and to John W. Freeman, non-residents and heirs and devises of Jacob Freeman, late of Troup County, Ga., who are all of full age, to appear in the Court House of Randolph County to answer the petition of Calvin J. Ussery, Adm. Ussery prayed for order of sale of the property for equal distribution among the heirs: Ezekiel, Jacob, Martha J., Sophia D. and Emma Freeman who are all represented to be minors and the only heirs of said Jacob Freeman.

12 June 1856

Jane F. Garrett, Executrix of Last Will & Testament of Nathan Garrett, deceased, late Guardian of the Estate of Marcus L. Garrett, an infant son of J.B. Garrett, deceased, filed accounts and vouchers for final settlement.

William L. Preston was married to Miss Mary Ann Williams, on the 25th ult. by H. Baird, Esq., all of Benton County.

William Armstrong, 70 years, died at his residence in Randolph County on the 3rd inst. He was a native of South Carolina, and emigrated and settled where he died while he was still young. He was a kind husband and parent and an indulgent master. Anderson (S.C.) Gazette please copy.

Calvin J. Ussery, Adm. of Estate of Jacob Freeman, deceased late of Troup County, Ga. to sell land at public auction at the Court House in Wedowee on December 25th.

The American Eagle was published in Wedowee, Alabama on Thursdays. W.H. Burton, Proprietor.
* * * * * * * *

Southwestern Bapt. 12/13/1855, Macon Co., AL.

Henry Stephens, 14, died at the residence of his father, Overton Stephens, in Milner, Randolph Co. on the 2nd after a short illness.

John H. Hand, 38, died at his residence near Wedowee Oct. 9th. He is survived by his wife and a large family. Member of the Bapt. Ch.

Southwestern Bapt. 2/18/1852.

Catherine Ashcraft, 64, wife of Thomas Ashcraft, died of dropsy Sept. 16th at his home in Randolph Co. She was the daughter of the Rev. Ephraim Abel and was born 5/28/1787 in Orange Co., Va. She married first William Stigler on 12/24/1805 and was baptized by her father in 1806. Her husband died in 1813 and was survived by 3 children. She married Mr. Ashcraft 3/15/1815.

PROBATE NOTICES FROM
THE RANDOLPH ENTERPRISE

11 December 1874

J.M.K. Guinn, Administrator for Estate of James Emby set January 5, 1875 as date for final settlement.

18 December 1874

David L. Davis officiated at the marriage of Charlie Jackson and Miss Katie Dobson on Tuesday last at the residence of B.J. Dobson.

1 January 1875

Mrs. James Holaway died December 23rd from dropsy.

Our new neighbors, James B. Amos, Dr. Hood, P. Rieke the county treasurer, Dr. J.H. Davis, Sr. and Dr. Gauntt will move to town. R.S. Heflin and Mr. Connelly will move out.

E.W. Kerr died on the 26th of December.

Judge D.L. Davis released a listing of all the marriage licenses issued between November 10th and December 25th, 1874.

GROOM	BRIDE
W.L. Long	N.M. Ables
John R. Brooks	A. Austin
Thomas J. Evans	Belle Smith
J.C. Birch	A.J. Eubanks
T.M. Phillips	D.S. Sherriar
John Knop	F.D. Wright
A.J. Preston	C. McCollough
W.B. Meacham	S.E. Ussery
R.F. Meacham	D.J. Ussery
E. Oneal (colored)	P. Pool (colored)
J. Houston (colored)	M. Oneal (colored)
J.W. Overton	N. Smith
A.C. Cantrell	S.F. Stubbs
William P. Norward	S.J. Mathews
C.A. Jackson	C.T.G. Dobson
W.A..Dean	S.A. Hucuba
J.H. Embry	F.H. M'Kilroy
D. Jones (colored)	M.J.F. Pinkard (colored)
W. McKinzie	E. Childers
J.D. Hawkins	Sarah F. Phillips
B.G. Harmon	A.C. Austin

C.J. May	M.N. Bowen
J.L. Bradley	M.N. Moon
L.C. Hutchens	M.A. Greene
L.L. White	M.J. Taylor
J. Hammons (colored)	A. White (colored)
John Sheppard	Juda Whitten
M.P. McMurray	H.E. Swan
E.H. Horten	Mary E. Stewart
R.T. Hodges	R.A. Fredwell
J.B. Brown	L. Hay
B. Turner (colored)	H. Davis (colored)
H.G. McCord	M.A. Littleton
B. Hodnett (colored)	Melia Wadkins (colored)
T. Bassett	A. Mays
T.J. Camp	M.A. Musick
M.D. Haynes	G. Edwards
P. Nixon (colored)	Manda Hurd (colored)
W.A. Yates	Vinie McCarley
W. McQuerter	S. Mize
B.J. Ford	Ella McPherson
W.C. Fowler	F.E. McQuerter
J.M. Fincher	N.A. Greene
W. Burns (colored)	Isabell Phillips (colored)
W.H. Wright	S.E. Ward

8 January 1875

John Shepherd and Miss Zuda Whitten were married Dec. 22, 1874 at the residence of Jacob Havens by P.G. Trent, all of Randolph County.

Mr. T.C. Henry and Miss Mollie Bradshaw, both of Randolph Co. were married at the residence of F.M. Bradshaw on Dec. 24, 1874, by P.G. Trent.

22 January 1875

Following is a list of Jurors during the Spring Term, 1875 the Circuit Court of Randolph County. Judge D.L. Davis.

GRAND JURORS

A.C. Saxon	J.F.M. Key	T.E. Disharoon
J.J. Moore	W.A. Pittman	C.J. Ussery
S.E.A. Reaves	J.M.K. Guinn	W.N. Harris
M.V. Mullins	J.H. Radney	E.H. Disharoon
J.C. Sherman	W.J. Taylor	J.C. Newell
J.W. Thomason	J.H. Keeble	William McCarter

PETIT JURORS

A.J. Cheeves	Joseph Norred	B.W. Mayfield
T.M. Humphries	J.T. White	J.M. Saunders
William Lovless	W.N. Watson	E.S. Burnes
G.O. Thomas	W.R. Cole	W.R. Avery
F.M. Earnest	M.A. Johnson	William Knight
T.D. Holpin	J.F. Bolt	W.A. Radney
Thomas Bassett	H.L. Fuller	V.A.P. Hunter
F.A. Adamson	T.F. Pate	H.M. Mickel
Samuel Fossett	J.M. Askew	W.N. Ellis
R.M. Foster	E.D. Andrews	C.H. Cole

19 February 1875

Francis E. Gilbert, Admx. of Estate of Hiram Barron, filed accounts and vouchers for final settlement of the Estate.

Letters of Administration were granted to J.S. Veal and T.R. Veal on the Estate of J.M. Veal, deceased by the Hon. D.I. Davis on Feb. 3, 1875.

J.M.K. Guinn, Adm. of Estate of James O. Stoned, deceased, filed statements, accounts, vouchers and evidences for final settlement of his administration.

E.B. Stephens, Adm. of Estate of Soloman and Sarah Stephens, deceased, filed statements, accounts, vouchers and evidences for final settlement of his administration.

W.S. Rice and R.O. Gray, Adms. of Estate of Mansfield Gray, deceased, filed for order of sale of certain described land for the purpose of paying debts. Probate Court of 12/31/1874.

Letters of Administration were granted to J.M. Sanders on Dec. 19, 1874 on the Estate of R.H. Willingham, deceased. He requested all claims against the Estate to be filed with him.

5 March 1875

Mrs. Issabella Reaves died Feb. 18, 1875 near New Harmony Church, Chambers County, after a lingering illness of consumption. She is survived by a family of children and many relations in Randolph County.

2 April 1875.

Mrs. Emily Reaves, wife of E.W. Reaves and sister of the wife of Capt. Guinn of Wedowee, died at her residence in Roanoke on the 29th. The message was given to the paper by Capt. B.F. Weathers and Bud Davis.

Rev. N.W. Moore, who served as Baptist minister, committed suicide at his residence near Lamar, Randolph County on the 29th. He cut his throat from ear to ear with a razor.

In Chancery Court. Alsey Stephens, et al vs. John C. Greene, et al. William Ivey for the Complainant moved for an order of publication as to the Defendants, Elizabeth A. Willingham and Cash Willingham, heirs of Martha A. Parker, deceased; the heirs of Eda A. Parker, deceased; the wife of William Parker; Samuel

J.Y. Carlile, Francis A. Carlile, Margaret B. Hill and William her husband; and Lucy J. Carlile, wife of W. Carlile, deceased. They were ordered to appear before the Register in 60 days to answer to a Bill of Complaint.

A.L. Braden was married to Miss Emily A. Warren by W.L. Ayers, Esq. on the 29th, all of Randolph County.

9 April 1875

Caroline Keeble, wife of John Keeble, died in Bacon Level, Randolph Co. on March 23, 1875 of pneumonia, aged 25 years 1 month and 6 days. She is survived by her husband, mother, brothers and sisters. Member of the Baptist Church.

30 April 1875

Mrs. I.W. Holloway died last week at her home on Big Tallapoosa.

James F. Campbell, about 65, an old and respected citizen dropped while driving a wagon last week and never spoke another word. He died that night after being removed to his residence. He is survived by his wife and children.

17 December 1875

Mrs. Sarah A. Heflin, relict of the Hon. Wyatt Heflin was born 11/19/1795, married 12/31/1811 and died 1/7/1869, aged 74 years. She was buried beneath the weeping willows she had planted with her own hands. She had 11 children. The oldest son, Wiley, died as an infant from croup. Another son, James W. Heflin, died in 1842. Another son died in the Battle of Chickamauga.

Mrs. Sarah Mitchell was born in March 1844, married Stephen Mitchell and died in 1872. She joined the Methodist Church in 1871.

The above home was built by members of the Handley family in the Louina Community in the mid-1800s. Courtesy of the Birmingham Public Library.

TAX SALES

Taken from the Feb. 12, 1875 issue of the Randolph Enterprise. Full property description can be determined by examining the copy on file in the Department of Archives and History in Montgomery.

On March 1, 1875 the property belonging to the following named persons was to be sold at public auction to the highest bidder from the Court House in Wedowee.

BEAT I   Township 18, Range 12

W.H. Butler, Sr.	Pickens Butler	Whit Butler, Jr.
J.W. Branon	W.A. Breed	R.N. Breed
Joseph Buchanan	B.O. Branon	T.M. Calhoun
W.H. Cofield	W.H. Cofield,	J.C. Coats
J.W. Dawkins	agt for Pullin	William Hightower
J.C. Hayes	A. Hooten	H. Johnson
William McKee	James Rice	Aaron Rice
Moses Rice	J.L. Rice	George Rice
S.J. Rigby	Thomas Roseman	John Stillwell
William Traylor	W.M. Williams	T.M. Williams
F.M. Moats	_____ Mitchell	N.W. Moore

BEAT II   Township 18, Range 13

Walter Bell	Thomas Blake	James Blake
R.E. Braden	Nancy Braden	James Burden
E.L. Buchanan	J.G. Craft	A. Coley
Joseph Curry	P.A. Childers	W.L. Camp
E.A. Drewery	J.W. Dodd	Andrew Dodd
J.S. Daroughty	Miles Fowler	J.J. Gray
W.R. Hand	J.L. Hill	T.C. Haines
Joseph Harper	S.E. Jordan	Soloman Johnson
T.F. Johns	J.B. Johns	William Jordan
E.G. Kidd	A.J. Knowles	Thomas Kirklin
W.H. Kemp	W.F. Knox	John Kee
Milton O. Lee	H.D. Landers	H.R. Loveless
W.P. Morrison	T.J. Morrison	W.E. Morrison
W.E. Murphey	Jeff Miller	R.G. Neal
Miss Harriet Nolen	Samuel N. Pate	William R. Pearce
W.H. Riddle	A.J. Roberts	Gideon Riddle
G. Riddle, agt.	James Stewart	L.G. Shockley
for Spence	J.F. Stephens	George Shaw
Thomas Strong	P.T. Umphries	N.R. White
John A. White	E.M. White	Arch Waters
J.D. Ward	R.P. Wood	

BEAT III   Township 19, Range 10

J.G. Adamson	Able Amos	Willis Brewer
Daniel Butler	Isham Bolt	M.J. Ball
J.D. Barrow	William Butler	James Butler
J.M. Bell	J.D. Ball	A.C. Ball's heirs
Jackson Boyed	E.D. Bearden	Clark Butler
James Cofield	George Crawley	D.M. Craft
Mrs. M.A. Crocket	W.S. Enterkin	H.P. Ethridge
S.B. Fowler	Dempsy Fowler	G.W. French
Unicey French	G.W. Gregg	John Hollaway
John Hunter	Matilda Hughbanks	Miss Francis Hill
G.M. Hurst	A.D. Hightower	Raulaughy Hand

109

Harriette Harris	S.B. Jordan	Lewis Kelley
William Kidd	Mrs. Louisa Kitchens	J.M. Kitchens
Caroline Loveless	James Linley	T.A. Lipham
T.M. Linley	Jessee Levins	Harriet Lovens
Reuben Mise	Mrs. Louisa Mise	J.F. McCruless
J.A. McCruless	E.M. Morgan	J.F. Morgan
Hiram McClung	J.W. Morris	James Nunn (col'd)
D.A. Perryman	D.A. Perryman for	
John Reaves, Sr.	Cintha Perryman Est.	Elbert Pate
Mrs. Rhoda Ragan	Cyrus Stewart	John Strong
Lee Smith	J.M. Smith	Rial Smith
Mrs. Nancy Smith	John Sellers	Elizabeth Saterwhite
Benjamin Sumberlin	Martha Stewart	F.M. Thrasher
Mrs. C.H. Thomas	Charles Taylor	William Wright
Mrs. B.M. White	Mrs. Mary Watson	John Wortham
T.N. Wortham	A.M. Wortham	J. Willoughby
J.W. Watwood	J.F. White	Elic Williamson
Vincent Walls	J.N. Williams	J.W. Young
J.F. Young	William Yarbrough	W.D. Lovvorn
H.N. Hand	Mary A. Taylor	James Wright
T.H. Young		

BEAT IV   Township 19, Range 4

S.H. Bowen	P.G. Branan	Daniel Butler
Mrs. Mary Connell	E. Cofield	James Crouch, Sr.
Raichell Eason	Samantha French	Joshua Green
N.B. Green	Josiah Green	James Garner
J.B. Gore	A.J. Knowles	John Lovvorn, Sr.
J.W. Lancaster	J.J. Nichols	Alexander Owens
Jacob Overton	C.A. Prescoat	J.M. Smith, agt
Mary C. Sears	W.H. Spears	for J. Smith
J.A. Smith	J.D.W. Strain	J.T. Smith
J.M. Saxon	C.W. Tenant	Washington Traylor
W.B. Traylor	John Traylor, Sr.	Benjamin Veal
S.S. Wilson	William Wilson	

BEAT V   Township 20, Range 13

J.M. Boggs	D.S. Barnes	Caroline Brown
J.C. Barton	T.V. Barret	Robert Benifield
William Barrett	John A. Bowen	B.H. Bigham
W.D. Balldin	Francis E. Bryant	J.C. Burson, Jr.
E. Barton	J.C. Burson, Sr.	J.W. Blair
J.P. Braziel	F.M. Braziel	William Barton
Elizabeth Crow	Martha Cockrell	Mrs. E. Caplin
Mrs. A.M. Dale	A.M. Dale	Mrs. Mary Davis
Mrs. Francis Davis	J.A. Daniel	D.S. Downs
Chesley Davis	W.B. Enloe	W.N. Edwards
Miss Sarah Forbus	Eli Freeman	H.C. Freeman
J.J. Freeman	E.J. Freeman	J.N. Fincher
Frank Foster	Sarah M. Gordan	A.H. Green
J.W. Green	A.J. Green	Knatty Gore
J.T. Grisham	R.M. Grisham	J.A.T. Hendon
C.W. Hunt	Hugh Harralson	Gilbert Hunt
H. Hester	H.E. Hester	G.R. Hester
Matthew M. Hester	J. Holder	J. Hester
B.F. Head	Allen Hester	Benton Johnson
J.W. Kent	Stephen Liles	Mrs. Sarah Lipp
Miss Ann M. Lipp	Miss E.J. Lipp	S.L. Lewis
Mrs. M.E. Leverett	N.L. Langley	Mrs. Susan Moses
William Music	Rauley Moon	B.W. Mayfield BATTLE
A.B. Mayfield	D.M. Mayfield	J.F. Matthews

W.A. Moses	Lydia Mecham estate	Mrs. N.S. Neely
Mrs. Caroline Noles	Amanda Pike	Elizabeth Pressnell
J.F. Pittman	W.A. Pittman	Joshua M. Pittman
J.W. Prestridge	Henry Rodgers	Mrs. Mary Rodgers
J.W. Robertson	Mahala Ray	J.H. Ray
Paralee Spears	J.M. Spears	J.T. Stitt
Robert Stitt, agt. for A.E. Pittman	W.F. Smith	Mrs. Jane Shellnut
	H.M. Shellnut	Mrs. Mary Spears
Mrs. Nancy L. Spears	W. Stitt	Robert Stitt
J.T. Stitt	William Stephens	Mrs. Sarah E. Scipper
Calip Stone	L. Talley	C.J. Ussery
F.F. Ussery	Barbary Vowell	Thomas Vaughn
Mrs. E. Vaughn	Jarrett Veal	Willis Wood
J.T. Weathers	Thomas Weathers	B.F. Walker
F.W. Walker	S. Walker	Thomas Waldrep
B.F. Wilson	Charles Wilson	Milton Webb
J.M. Woodson	J.M. Weaver	Robert Young
Samuel Young		

BEAT VI   Township 20, Range 11

A.H. Avery	W.R. Avery	John Avery
Levi Arnold	James Abbott	E.R. Almon
John J. Burrow	E.A. Brown	G.N. Bryan
E.R. Burnes	Mrs. Sarah Bell	V.T. Bonner
J. Bennett	M.B. Bradley	T.D. Baker
F.F. Busby	W. Burrer	S.T. Bass
R.H. Bolt	R.A. Colwell	John Carlile
C.F. Clifton	W.N. Clifton	J.T. Clifton
W.J. Clark	Lydia Clark	Martha Chafin
J.W. Cumming	W.E. Connelly	S. Carter
S.D. Carter	Clifton & Swan	Cathorine Dickson
W.W. Dobson, Sr.	W.W. Dobson, Jr.	Greenberry Edwards
T.J. Edmondson	G.A. Fetner	J.T. Fincher
Lemuel Grimes	T. Gibbs	T.P. Green
Nathan Gann	Mrs. M. Hudson	F.T. Hudson
C.D. Hudson	John Holloway	Joseph Hughey
Sally Henson	J.C. Henderson	J.R. Hood
E.B. Higginbotham	D.C. Harris	Bryant Ingraham
W.I.P. Jeter	Thomas Joiner	M.W. Mashburn and T.B. Mashburn
Polly Moore	J.A. Meacham	
F.J. & N.B. Mitchell	Charlotte Mitchell	J.A. Moon
J.P.D. Murphey	J.C. Mitchell	Mrs. Sarah Mitchell
J.M. McLeroay	Mitchell McManus	Simon Morgan
W.A. Nunnelly	A.D. Owens	J.J. Pool
S.N. Posey	Moses Prothrow	S.D. Parker
Floyed Phillips	Percilla Rodgers	A.W. Roundtree
J.D. Robertson	J.S. Radney	E.G. Richard, agt. for Bachelor
R.W. Richards	Mrs. S.A. Robertson	
Mrs. E.C. Robertson	John Reaves	I.N. Stewart
C.A. Smith	R.T. Smith	W.H. Smith
D.B. Smith & Co.	J.M. Sykes	A.J. Spence
W.R. Spruce	W.B. Smith	Mrs. Rebeca Slaton
L.C. Thornton	T.H. Thornton	Irvin Turner
Peter Turner	Peter Taylor	William Traylor
E.P. Waldrup, Adm.	Mrs. Lucinea West	Stephen West (col.)
Ivin West (col.)	W.(?) F. Whaley	Elizabeth Wallis
Marth Ann Weldon	Alexander Waldrep	T.P. Wier
A.J. Wright	Peter T. Yates	Asa Young
Mrs. Mary Yarbrough		

BEAT VII   Township 20, Range 10

E.A. Burch	J.C. Burch	B.A. Baker
G.W. Burress	Permelia Burson	George W. Bruce
W.J. Barrow	Y.J.A. Bartlett	P.B.M. Burrow
J.G. Burrow	T.N. Brown	James Brown
Wiley Bean	D.M. Bean	W.C. Brazwell
J.F. Brazwell	L.B. Burch	Nathaniel Bradford
John Bradford	John Blake	W.H. Cockrell
J.H. Creel	Mrs. Mary Colins	T.M. Cockrell
Jonathan Cockrell	Mrs. Permelia Conner	Miss Caroline Creel
L.E. Cofield	W.S. Cofield	Joshua Collier
Charles Davis	J.N. Daniel	N.M. Daniel
William Dothard	F.M. Dingler	Z.R. East
J.W. Freeman	B.E. Farrow	H.B. Ferrill
Mrs. Nancy Giles	D.S. Gregg	M.M. Gregg
John Gravett	James Gann	John Garrett
Samuel Gladney	T.M. Hayes	B.W. Hayes
B.F. Hayes	F.M. Hunt	Elias Hallis
Levi Hendricks	William Inghram	W.T. Knight
Thomas Kirk	James Lashley	Daniel Lambert
G.B. Knight	Miss J.A. Kimbell	Mrs. S.B. Kitley
M.V. Mellins	James McComic	Elijah McComic
Mrs. Nancy Meadows	J.T. Maning	James McCullers
J.J. Moore	J.C. Messer	W.H. McCallom
H.T. Mitchell	Miss Nancy McCain	Gilbert McInish
Spencer Morris	R.D. Orr	G.H. Preston
A. Poore	W. Polk	George Peterman
Rachell Robertson	J.H. Robertson	J.M. Robertson
J.L. Rice	O.T. Stephens	H.H. Stephens
D.L. Stephens	Mrs. Mary Stephens	E.A. Smith
Jordan Smith	C.M. Smith	Mrs. M. Smith
P.M. Smith	H.C. Stidman	D.C. Sharp
W.A. Taylor	John Taylor	L.B. Teague
Thomas Thompson	Pearcy Taylor	G.W. Waite
John Walker	W. Yates	James J. Yates
William James Yates	A.A. Young	

BEAT VIII   Township 21, Range 10

John Brown	Thomas Bassett	G. W. Beard
Elizabeth Barrow	John J. Culpepper	W.W. Culpepper
H.C. Camp	S.W. Chiles	J.T.L. Cummings
Jane Conaway	J.A.J. Clarady	Malinda Dannelly
J.O. Davis	Henry Fisher	Joseph S. Fetner
William A. Fetner	H.L. Fuller	William & J.A.M. Gay
Elbert Griffin	V.A.P. Hunter	D.N. Hearn
C.C. Hearn, Adm'r	James Hamilton	W.T. Jackson
James Kidd	Sarah Ann Kirk	W.J. Kirk
W.H.P. Knowles	D.W. Linch	John Motley
James Muncus	J.E. McGill	William McGill
Mrs. M.A. Malone	J.H. Mooty	N.W. McClain
D.B. McClain	J.M. Pearson	W.S. Rice
Hardy Robertson	C.W. Robertson	M.H. Radney
James W. Swan	Jno. Swan	Charles Swan
J.H. Stewart	S.A. Seymour	R.W. Tidwell
J.H. Tidwell	W. Weathers	B. Wilkinson
James Watson	J.H. Worthy	W.A. Welch
May L. Wilder	J. Wilkinson	L.E. West, Agt.

BEAT IX   Township 21, Range 11

J.C. Auston	S.M. Adamson	W.C. Adamson
Larkin Auston	Elic Birdsong	W.T. Capehart
George Austin	J.M. Carson	William Cummins
L.B. Austin	Brice Dollar	Jno. H. Dial
F. Adamson	Giles Dewberry	T.J. East
B. & T.J. East	E. Fielder	Guler Fuller
George Forrester	Hiram Gipson	Mrs. Francis Gilbert
Miss M.A. Gay	R.R. Gay	Julia Gay
H.R. Gay	E. Gay	W.J. George
Happy George	Peter Green	John Heflin
M.L. Horton	Isiah Hawkins	Lizan Houston
S.T. Hunter	John Horton	F.M. Handley
Joseph Johnson	Barny Jeter	Z. Johns
Frederic Kent	Rhoda Kee	J.B. Kee
W.E. Knight	W. Knight & Co.	W. Lawson
Amos Liles	A.J. Langley	M.E. Langley
M.P. McMurry & Co.	W.F. McMurry	F.A. McMurry
D.A. Melton	A.T. McCombs	J.T. McCarley
J.A. Noell	Benjamin Nelson	Timothy Orr
M.E.R. Parish	T.M. Phillips	Tyler Phillips
George Pool	Smith & Baily	N.B. Swan
W.H. Stewart	Mrs. S.W. Stewart	J.F.N. Stephens
B.A. Treadwell	Wade Taylor	Jane M. Ward
Lucy Wood	W.H. Wood	W.W. Windsor
Daniel White	O.B. Weaver	Garrett Wilder

BEAT X   Township 21, Range 12

A.P. Allen, Sr.	J.M. Askew	L.L. Buckaleu
J.C. Bailey	J.H. Bailey	W.H. Burton
W.R.V. Brown	W.O. Brown	Mrs. N.E. Brown
A.J. Brown	Abnor Brown	Mrs. E.A. Burgess
James Beverly	S.F. Colwell	J.S. Cummings
A.B. Cogswell	Allen Cook	R.H. Duke
W.A. Dean, Sr.	E.H. Disharoon	T.H. Dunn
A.E. Dabney	Elizabeth Embry	Simeon Edwards
Benjamin East, Adm'r	Benjamin East	Jesse Fausett
Ford & Stephens	Isaac Goggins	S.B. Gaston
F.M. Gay	I.G. Hill	C.C. Hodges
J.M. Hodges	Thomas Hodges	Bennett Hodges
L.J. Hall	G.W. Hill	Caroline Holder
J.Y. Irvine	J.B. Jackson	W.L. Johnson
Nancy Johnson	W.T. Kirby	D.J. Marable
Peter Mitchell	Jury Mickle	S.B. McCarden
W.P. Norred	D.R. Nixon	W.H. Osborn
Moses Parks	G.G. Pate	T.F. Pate
N.B. Pool	M.A. Pool	C.C. Pittman
Mrs. Paseline Peck	W.H. Pool	Francis Parker
A.P. Robertson	Mrs. M.A. Robertson	Y.A. Roberts
Henry Riley	George T. Robertson	Luke Robinson
W.J. Stallings	Thomas Stenford	W.F. Stubbs
W.J. Tomlin	J.M. Ward	W.L. Ward
D.G. Waldrop		

BEAT XI   Township 21, Range 13

E.D. Andrews	J.G. Adamson	S.H. Adamson
W.J.N. Arm	Mrs. S.E. Benfield	Mrs. Sarah Brun
R.D. Bennett	N.C. Bennett	Mrs. L.M. Bennett
G.W. Burgess	R.J. Breed	Wiley Burk
William Burk	J.S. Burk	J.H. Boyed

E.M. Boyed	F.M. Boyed	Mrs. P.F. Burgess
Samantha Cumbie	J.M. Chatam	Martin Duke
Sarilda Edge	N.T. Foster	W.H. Foster
F.F. Folsom	P.A. Formby	Elizabeth Foster
Charles Foster	W.H. Gamble	N.B.S. Green
Wyatt Harper	William Harper	Green B. Harper
G.B. Hendon	W.N. Hendon	T.E. Head
J.J. Hearn	B.H. Hearn	Richard Head
Mrs. M. Hughes	Louisa King	Z. Landers
J.B. Lee	Edward Lewis	Jane Mathews
J.P. Muldrew	James McCaffrey	J.C. Newell
Sarah Pittman	J.R. Phillips	J.F. Pike
William Pike	E. Prater	W.F. Pike
W.A. Pike	King Prather	J.T. Pollard
B.J. Reed	J.J. Robertson	Rock Mills Mfg. Co.
Barnett Smith	S.S. Smith	Mrs. Ann Swint
W.R. Sherman	W.N. Shelnut	T.L. Thomason
Mrs.J. E. Towler	H.M. White	Mrs. Nancy Woodson
J.H. Young	W.J. Young	E.M. Yates

BEAT XII   Township 20, Range 13

R.A. Arnett	Jesse Arnett	J.T. Arnett
Henry Aldridge	J.F. Abner	J.F. Burgess
J.N. Burden	J.W. Bonner	F.M. Beard
Joseph Breed	B.F. Caswell	C.F. Crowder
D.G. Crowder	H.E. Cumbie	W.Z. Crowder
Eichelberger & Holly	E.E. Guantt	Luther Guantt
J.C. Guantt	T. Gladney	Noah Gladney
T.E. Gamble	L.F. Hall	T.C. Holly
M.V. Hudson	J.T. Hudson	William Henry
J.J. Hary	N.T. Johnson	J.H. Keeble, Jr.
T.S. Keeble	A.M. Knight	H. Lane
C.A. Lane	Jesse Lane	J.S. Meacham
R.B. Mitchem	J.M. McDonough	B.F. McDonough
J.E. McCosh	William McCarter	J.M. McDonald
King Prather	Murk Ray	Martha Rushton
Jno. Robertson	Kinian Rowe	Jno. Siminton
J.P. Shepard	Jerimiah Shepard	J.C. Strickland
H.A. Strickland	Elbert Suddoth	R.J.A. Tharp
Martin Tarver	H. Tarver	Jno. Tarver
Noah Turner	Trent & Suddoth	P.G. Trent
M.J. Ussery	H.W. Vinson	Willis Weathers

SUPPLEMENT

Sarah E. Taylor	J.M. Thornton	Hanah Kirbey
Joseph Swint	John White	Iverson & Co.
T.D. Rowe	Thomas Simpson	S.A. Arington
S.S. Walker	Westly Young	____ Addington
William Colwell	Robert Merrill	Merrill & Traylor
J.B. Merrill &	D.C. Harris	John T. Heflin
R. Merrill	O.H. Perryman	C.C. Enloe
L.W. Hunly	____ Taylor	D.A. Wood
J.M. Towles	W.W. Cardwell	Mary Sikes
J.J. Camp	James Terrill	Bernettie Allen
Maj. A. Marion	W.P. Pool	T.D. Crouch
W.C. McGahee	John N. Gibbs	Van. Morris
J.A. Hurley	M.C. Camp	S.S. Waller
William Barritt	Adline Brown	Thomas Stephens
John Lehanan	Jesse Weathers	John Robinson
Shadrick Crouch	W.Y. Norman	W.H. Abbott
David Gaston	J.C. Wright	J.C. Milton
G.W. Burden		

REGISTER OF DEATHS
RANDOLPH COUNTY, ALABAMA

The information provided in this ledger is as follows: name of deceased, date of death, place of birth, age at death, sex, color, marital status, occupation, cause of death, place of death, place of burial, and the last space was for the name of the physician, mid-wife or head of family. (From the Dept. of Archives & History)

JAMES H. KEEBLE, 1/25/1886, Tenn, 61 years, male, white, married, farmer, cystitis, died and buried in Raldolph Co., Dr. P.G. Trent, M.D.
Infant, 1/1/1886, Beat 11 Randolph Co., 1 yr 3 mo, female, white, Bum, died and buried in Randolph Co., Dr. P.G. Trent
FANNIE WARE, 1/6/1886, Ga., 38, female, white, married, Pelvic peritonitis, Randolph Co., Dr. E. T. Gauntt
Infant, 1/30/1886, Randolph Co. Beat 6, 2 yr., male, black, pneumonia, Randolph Co., Dr. E.T. Gauntt
JAMES T. TAYLOR, 2/16/1886, Beat 1 Randolph Co., 5 yr., male, white, Intussuseption of bowel, Randolph Co., J.D. Duke, M.D.
AMELIA GRAY, 2/11/1886, Beat 9 Randolph Co., female, white, married, Uterine hemmorhage, Beat 9, Buried Forrester's Chapel in Beat 9, J.D. Liles, M.D.
JAMES McLEMORE, 2/3/1886, Randolph Co., 23 yr. 3 mo., male, black, single, farmer, pneumonia, beat 6, buried at Flatwood Church beat 6, E.T. Gaunt, M.D.
THOMAS SHERRER, 2/23/1886, Ga., 51, male, white, single, farmer, pneumonia & paralysis, Beat 10, Buried at Broughton Church, James H. Radney, M.D.
NOAH CASWELL, 2/22/1886, Ga., 32 yrs., male, white, married, farmer, pneumonia, Beat 12, Buried in Ga., P.G. Trent, M.D.
ROBERT B. MEACHAM, 2/25/1886, Ga., 80 yrs., male, white, married, Minister, Pleuro-pneumonia, Beat 11, Buried in Beat 14, P.G. Trent, M.D.
Infant, 2/19/1886, Randolph Co. Beat 10, ¼ day, female, black,for want of attention, Beat 10, W.E. White, M.D.
MONROE BRADSHAW, 2/25/1886, Ga. 60, male, white, married, farmer, heart disease, Beat 12, P.G. Trent, M.D.
J.K. HOLLIS, 2/5/1886, Carolina, 96, male, white, widow, farmer, old age, Beat 10, Mount Pisga, W.H. Pool, M.D.
JOHN W. HENDERSON, 2/2/1886, Beat 6 Randolph Co., 1 yr. 11 mo. 20 days, male, black, whooping cough, Beat 6, Wedowee, Leah Carter (col.) M. wife
MORRIS CRIM, 3/7/1886, Ga., 22 yr., male, black, married, farmer, pneumonia, Beat 6, Dr. E.T. Gauntt
MATTIE JONES, 3/14/1886, Beat 6 Randolph Co., 1 mo. 10 days, female black, bold hives, Beat 6, Leah Stephens, m. wife.
HENRY JOHNSON, 3/7/1886, Beat 10 Randolph Co., 23 yrs., male, black, married, farmer, pneumonia, Beat 10, H.B. Disharoon, M.D.
JOHN T. TURNER, 3/15/1886, Chambers Co., AL, 4 yr., male, black, burns, Beat 12, P.G. Trent, M.D.
POLLY MICKLE, 3/16/1886, Ga., 60 yr. 11 mo. 29 days, female, white, widow, Ulcer of stomach. Beat 10, Old High Pine, H.B. Disharoon, M.D.
MATTIE LOVERN, 3/16/1886, 25 yrs., female, white, married, Bright's disease of kidney, Beat 4, Poplar Springs Beat 1, J.D. and A.W. Duke, M.D.
MARY ANN MOTES, 3/20/1886, Beat 10 Randolph Co., 14, female, white, single, pneumonia and whooping cough, Beat 1, Shilow, J.D. and A.W. Duke, M.D.
MRS. BURSON, 3/10/1886, female, white, married, Chronic Bronchitis,

Beat 5, Big Spring, J.D. and A.W. Duke, M.D.
Infant, 4/28/1886, Beat 1,Randolph Co., female, black, 1 yr., Buried in Camp Ground, Beat 1, J.D. and A.W. Duke, M.D.
Infant, 4/21/1886, 7 mos., Beat 6 Randolph Co., female, black, Pneumonia, Beat 6, Wedowee, E.T. Gauntt, M.D.
JAMES LOVERN, 4/10/1886, Morgan Co., Ga., 77 yrs., male, white, married, farmer, Brain Concussion, Beat 4, Providence, J.D. and A.W. Duke, M.D.
Infant, 4/4/1886, Beat 8 Randolph Co., 6 mo., female, black, Suffocation by bedclothing, Beat 9, Liberty Church, W.L. Heflin, M.D.
JOHN R. BENNETT, 4/8/1886, 39 yr. 8 mos. 29 days, male, white, married, Epilepsy, Beat 11, Dr. P.G. Trent, born in Ga.
JOHN JOHNS, 4/11/1886, Cleburne Co., Ala., 26 yrs., male, white, married, farmer, Typhoid Fever, Beat 1, Shilow, J.D. and A.W. Duke, M.D.
ADELINE BROOKS, 4/6/1886, unknown, 84 yrs., female, black, married, old age, Beat 6, E.T. Gauntt, M.D.
Infant, 4/15/1886, Beat 3, 3 days, male, white, unknown, Union Hill Church, J.D. Liles, M.D.
LUCY TUCKER, 5/11/1886, unknown, 100 yrs., female, black, widow, old age, Beat 10, W.E. White, M.D.
Infant, Beat 13,Randolph Co., 3 days, male, white, unknown, Mt. Prospect Beat 13, J.D. Liles, M.D., death date 4/18/1886
Infant, 1 yr. 1 mo. 5/1/1886, male, white, Diptheria, Beat 4, W.R. Allen, M.D.
BARTHOLOMEW WILKINSON, 5/11/1886, 47 yrs., male, white, married, farmer, Valvular disease of heart, Beat 8, William Moncus Grave Yard, Beat 8, J.D. Liles, M.D.
NORA GRIZZLE, 5/6/1886, Clay Co., AL, 3 yrs. 11 mos. 6 days, female, white, Meningitis, Beat 7, Wesolulga, Clay Co. Beat 4, C.A. Jordan, M.D.
ISABELLA BURNS, 5/8/1886, Beat 9 Randolph Co., 30 yrs., female, black, married, Paralysis, Beat 6, Beat 9, Wyatt Heflin, M.D.
TEULA ANGELS, 5/3/1886, Beat 6 Randolph Co., 17 yrs. 2 mos., female, black, single, Pneumonia, Beat 6, M.M. McManus, M.D.
WILLIAM H. BENAFIELD, 5/17/1886, Henry Co., Ga., 57 yrs., male, white, married, farmer, Paralysis, Beat 5, Pleasant Hill Beat 6, Henry Walls, M.D.
MARTHA M. WILLINGHAM, 5/19/1886, Canada, 43 yrs. 8 mos. 26 days, female, white, married, Cancer of breast, Beat 6, Greens Chapel, W. Heflin, M.D.
Infant, 5/28/1886, 2 yrs., female, white, Dysentery, Camp Ground, J.D. and A.W. Duke, M.D.
Infant, 5/29/1886, Ala., 3 mos., female, white, Cholera Inf., Beat 11, Salem Church, S.J. Davis, M.D.
MARTINIE MATHEWS, 5/8/1886, Ala., 23 yrs., female, white, married, Phthisis Pulmonatis, Beat 12, P.G. Trent, M.D.
EDDIE BAILEY, 6/26/1886, Beat 10 Randolph Co., 3 yrs. 4 mos. 8 days, male, white, Dysentery, Beat 10, Zions Rest, L.L. White, M.D.
MRS. SPENCE, 6/6/1886, Ga. 83, female, white, old age, Beat 6, E.T. Gauntt, M.D.
FED USSERY, 6/26/1886, S.C., 84 yrs., male, black, married, laborer, Typhoid Fever, Beat 12, P.G. Trent, M.D.
MARY PINKARD, 6/27/1886, Tallapoosa Co., 19 yrs. 4 mos. 5 days, female, black, single, drowned, Beat 6, Wedowee, Ann Pinkard (mother).
Infant, 6/11/1886, Randolph Co., 2 mos., male, black, Pneumonia, Beat 12, P.G. Trent, M.D.
NANCY JACKSON, 6/29/1886, Greenville Ga., 58 yrs. 5 mos. 13 days, female, white, married, Opium poisoning, Beat 10, Mrs. Elliott's Grave Yard, H.B. Disharoon, M.D.
Infant, 6/8/1886, Beat 12 Randolph Co., 1 mo., male, black, Pneumonia, Beat 12, P.G. Trent, M.D.

Infant, 6/18/1886, Beat 10, 2 yrs. 6 mos, female, white, Dysentery, Zions Rest, L.L. White, M.D.
WALTER BAILEY, 6/15/1886, Randolph Co., 4 yrs., male, white, Dysentery, Beat 10, S.J. Davis, M.D.
JAMES BROOKS, 6/10/1886, Randolph Co., 4 mo. 1 day, male, black, Dysentery, Beat 12, S.J. Davis, M.D.
SALLIE LOU PATE, 7/21/1886, Raldolph Co., 4 yr., female, white, Dysentery, Beat 10, Roanoke, L.L. White, M.D.
ANNIE MORA WHITE, 7/1/1886, Randolph Co., 4 yr., female, white, Dysentery, Beat 10, Roanoke, L.L. White, M.D.
Infant, 7/15/1886, male, white, Dysentery, Beat 10, High Pine Ch., L.L. White, M.D.
MANLEY BARRON FAUSETT, 7/3/1886, Randolph Co., 1 yr. 7 mos. 9 days, male, white, Dysentery, Beat 10, Roanoke, Ala., H.B. Disharoon, M.D.
IKE YOUNG, 7/17/1886, Henry Co., Ga., 60 yrs., male, white, single, farmer, Dysentery, Beat 5, Big Spring Church, L.L. White, M.D.
Infant, 7/17/1886, Randolph Co., 2 mos., male, mulatto, Cholera Infantum, Beat 8, Mrs. Elliott's Graveyard, Inmon Busby, grandfather.
Infant, 7/10/1886, Randolph Co., 1 yr. 14 days, male, white, Cholera Inf., Beat 8, M.D. Liles, M.D.
Infant, 7/5/1886, Randolph Co., 1 mo. 1 day, female, white, unknown, Beat 9, M.D. Liles, M.D.
JAMES JOHNS, 7/24/1886, not given, 60 yrs., male, white, married, farmer, Chronic diarrhoea, beat 1, Camp ground, J.D. and A.W. Duke, M.D.
Infant, 7/26/1886, Beat 11 Randolph Co., 1 yr. 1 mo., female, black, Remittent fever, Beat 12, P.G. Trent, M.D.
WILLIAM P. JACKSON, 7/5/1886, Ga. 66 yrs. 8 mos. 6 days, male, white, widow, farmer, Chronic alcoholism, Beat 10, Mrs. Elliott's Graveyard, H.B. Disharoon, M.D.
LUCINDA TURNER, 7/20/1886, N.C., 80 yrs., female, white, widow, Valvular diseased heart, Beat 12, P.G. Trent, M.D.
BUD KNIGHT, 7/20/1886, Chambers Co., Ala., 25 yrs., male, white, single, farmer, Coxalgia, Beat 9, M.D. Liles, M.D.
WILLIAM BURNS, 7/22/1886, Randolph Co., 36 yrs. male, mulatto, widow, laborer, drowning, Beat 9, M.D. Liles, M.D.
MARTHA MONGHAM, 7/12/1886, Henry Co., Ga., 55 yrs., female, white, widow, Dysentery, Beat 5, Big Spring Church, L.L. White, M.D.
WILLIE INNIS CHEWNING, 7/5/1886, Roanoke, AL, 1 yr. 6 mos, 23 days, female, white, Dysentery, Beat 9, Milltown, Chambers Co., Drs. L.L. White, H.G. Disharoon, and Gay.
GERTRUDE DUKE, 7/24/1886, Brockville Beat 1, 2 yr. 2 mos., female, white, Dysentery, Beat 1, Camp-ground, J.D. and A.W. Duke, M.D.
COLUMBUS COLE, 7/18/1886, Brockville Beat 1, 1 yr. 6 mos., female, white, Dysentery, Beat 1, Camp-ground, J.D. and A.W. Duke, M.D.
LENNIE LOVERN, 8/26/1886, Bowden, Ga., 2 yrs. 2 mos., female, white, Dysentery, Beat 1, Bowden, Ga., J.D. and A.W. Duke, M.D.
JOSHUA TURNER, 8/2/1886, Randolph Co., 12 yrs., male, black, single, Accidental gun shot, Beat 10, W.H. Pool, M.D.
GREEN HOOPER, 8/5/1886, Randolph Co., 19 yrs., male, white, married, laborer, Remittent Fever, Beat 11, P.G. Trent, M.D.
FANNIE YATES, 8/30/1886, Rock Mills, AL, 18 yrs., female, white, married, typhoid fever, Beat 11, Beat 12, S.J. Davis, M.D.
Infant, 8/5/1886, Randolph Co., 1 yr., male, white, Dysentery, Beat 12, P.G. Trent, M.D.
WILLIAM L. BENNETTE, 8/19/1886, Randolph Co., 9 mos., male, white, Meningitis, Beat 12, S.J. Davis, M.D.
Infant, 8/9/1886, Randolph Co., 2 mos., male, white, Cholera Inf., Beat 12, Bacon Level, P.G. Trent, M.D.
JOHN CARTER, 9/26/1886, Randolph Co., 3 yrs., male, black, Pneumonia, Beat 6, Wedowee, E.T. Gauntt, M.D.
Infant, 9/21/1886, Randolph Co., 11 mos., male, white, unknown,

Beat 1, Camp ground, Mr. Lowery, grandfather
FANNIE HARDNETT, 9/28/1886, Randolph Co., 3 yrs. 6 mos., female, black, Pneumonia, Beat 6, E.T. Gauntt, M.D.
SARAH TOMBLIN, 9/12/1886, 50 yrs., female, white, married, Gastric affection, Beat 10, Roanoke, AL, W.H. Pool, M.D.
ZILPHEY MORROW, 9/18/1886, Lamar, AL, 12 yrs. 3 mos. 21 days, female, white, Typhoid Fever, Beat 4, Prospect Church, U.R. Allen,
Mrs. FERRELL, 9/23/1886, Heard Co., Ga., 73 yrs., female, white, widowed, Chronic Pneumonia, Beat 1, Camp Ground, A.W. Duke, M.D.
ELLA McCREA, 9/10/1886, Alabama, 34 yrs. 1 mo. 1 day, female, white, single, Phthisis Pulmonalis, Beat 11, P.G. Trent, M.D.
CORA WHITE, 9/2/1886, Griffin, GA, 33 yrs. female, white, married, Chronic Bronchitis, Beat 1, Camp Ground, A.W. & J.D. Duke, M.D.
SOPHIA BUCKHANNAN, 9/18/1886, Georgia, 45 yrs., female, black, married, Dysentery, Beat 6, E.T. Gauntt, M.D.
RUTH AWBRY, 9/18/1886, Roanoke, AL, 10 mos., female, white, Dysentery, Beat 10, Roanoke, W.E. White, M.D.
HASSY CALHOUN, 9/6/1886, 35 yrs., female, white, Dysentery, Beat 1, Campground, A.W. and J.D. Duke, M.D.
CASSIE TRUETT, 9/2/1886, Randolph Co., 1 yr. 10 days, Dysentery, Beat 10, W.E. White, M.D.
JAMES BOYKIN, Beat 6 Randolph Co., 4 yrs., male, black, Dysentery, Beat 6, E.T. Gauntt, M.D., Date of death 9/22/1886
SARAH SMITH, 10/29/1886, Ala., 51 yrs., 2 mos. 17 days, female, white, widowed, Phthisis Pulmonalis, Beat 11, Beat 12, P.G. Trent
SEABORN S. BROWN,10/13/1886, DeCalb Co., Ga., 50 yrs., male, white, married, Chronic Diarrhoea, Beat 1, Shilo, A.W. & J.D. Duke,M.D.
ROBERT PINKARD, 10/23/1886, Beat 6 Randolph Co., 14 yrs., male, black, Abscess of brain, Beat 6, E.T. Gauntt, M.D.
WILLIAM E. KNIGHT, 10/4/1886, S.C., 67 yrs., male, white, married, farmer, Chronic Gastritis, Beat 9, J.D. Liles, M.D.
RACHEL BRAND, 10/6/1886, Randolph Co., 1 yr. 1 mo., female, white, Dysentery, Beat 12, Bacon Level, P.G. Trent, M.D.
WILLIAM POPE, 10/31/1886, Randolph Co., 4 mos. 18 days, male, white, Pneumonia, Beat 10, Near Rock Mills, S.J. Davis, M.D.
MATTIE DAVIS, 10/12/1886, Randolph Co., 12 yrs. 3 mos. 9 days, female, white, Remittent fever, Beat 10, High Pine Grave Yard, W.H. Pool and H.B. Disharoon, M.D.
WILLIAM D. STEWART, 10/30/1886, 33 yrs. 3 mos. 17 days, male, white, married,Merchant, Remittant fever, Beat 11, Heard Co., Ga., R.G. Trent, M.D.
MARY FLETCHER BRADSHAW, 10/6/1886, Randolph Co., 1 yr. 1 mo. female, white, Whooping Cough, Beat 12, Bacon Level, AL, P.G. Trent, M.D.
WILLIAM H. SWAN, 10/23/1886, Randolph Co., 20 yrs., male, white, single, Typhoid fever, Beat 9, J.D. Liles, M.D., merchant.
ALPH PITMAN, 10/13/1886, Randolph Co., 26 yrs., male, black, single, Typhoid fever, Beat 11, Near Rock Mills, L.L. White, M.D.
LILLEY TRUETT, 11/3/1886, Beat 1 Randolph Co., 9 yrs., female, white, Pseudo-membranous croup, Camp grounds, A.W. Duke, M.D.
SUSAN E. McCARLEY, 11/18/1886, Beat 4, 7 yrs., female, white, Laryngitis, Providence Beat 4, A.W. Duke, M.D.
MARION PEARCE McMURRAY, 11/2/1886, Beat 9, 34 yrs., male, white, married, Merchant, Typhoid fever, Concord Church, J.D. Liles,M.D.
RILEY SMITH 11/6/1886, Beat 4, 30 yrs., male, white, married, farmer, Abscess of lung, Providence Beat 4, A.W. and J.D. Duke, M.D.
JOHN CRISWELL, 11/7/1886, Alabama, 36 yrs., male, white, married, farmer, Remittent fever, Bacon Level Beat 12, P.G. Trent, M.D.
LADORA WOOD, 11/27/1886, 22 yrs. female, black, single, Typhoid fever, Beat 9, J.D. Liles, M.D.
W.M. BARNETT, 11/10/1886, Randolph Co., 56 yrs., female, white, married, Gastritis, Beat 5, L.L. White, M.D.
DENIA HANKS, 11/5/1886, Georgia, 18 yrs., female, white, single, Dropsey, Beat 11, Wehadka, P.G. Trent, M.D.

MILTON J. USSERY, SR., 12/2/1886, 68 yrs., male, white, married, farmer, Broncho-pneumonia, Beat 12, Bacon Level, P.G. Trent, M.D.
ROBERT LEE BOYD, 12/26/1886, Randolph Co., Beat 1, 3 mos., male, white, Gastritis, Beat 1, Camp Ground, J.C. Brock, M.D.
LUCINDA BOLT, 12/14/1886, Beat 3 Randolph Co., 18 yrs., female, white, single, Typhoid fever, Union Church, M. McManus, M.D.
DOLLIE NOLES, 12/27/1886, Beat 1 Randolph Co., 12 yrs., female, white, Typhoid fever, Shilo Church Beat 1, A.W. & J.D. Dukes,M.D.
LIZZIE HENDERSON,12/4/1886, Randolph Co., 35 yrs., female, white, married, Phthisis Pulmonalis, Beat 4, Liberty Grave yard, J.C.A. Henderson, Head of Family
NEWTON M. MASHBURN, 12/27/1886, Beat 6 Randolph Co., 2 yrs. 6 mos. 20 days, male, white, Cholera Infantum, Wild Cat Church Beat 6, M.W. Mashburn, Head of Family
SIMPSEY PIKE, 1/26/1887, Georgia, 54 yrs., male, white, married, farmer, Double Pneumonia, Beat 11, P.G. Trent, M.D.
MARY MOODY, 1/8/1887, Georgia, 68 yrs. 2 mos, female, black, married, Beat 10, W.E. White, M.D.
HOMER B. HIGGINBOTHAM, 2/15/1887, Alabama, 1 mo. 6 days, male, white, Inflamation, Beat 3, Levons Graveyard, M.C. Nelson, M.D.
MOLLEY TRAMMEL, 2/15/1887, Alabama, 38 yrs., female, black, married, Beat 3, Near J.M. Smith's Mill, Feraby Crawley, Mid-wife
SARAH AIKINS, 2/27/1887, Georgia, 76 yrs., female, white, widowed, Chronic Diarrhoea, Beat 7, Gladney Grave Yard, J.D. Liles, M.D.
FRANK GASTON, 2/16/1887, Alabama, 27 yrs. 11 mos., male, white, single, Congested base of brain, Beat 10, Broughtons Church, H.B. Disharoon, M.D.
LUCINDA BELL, 2/22/1887, Georgia, 43 yrs. 6 mos., female, black, married, Cardiac dropsy, Beat 10, H.B. Disharoon, M.D.
ETHEL PITTS, 3/22/1886, Georgia, 8 yrs., female, white, Pneumonia, Beat 12, P.G. Trent, M.D.
____ HUCKEBY, 3/31/1886, 24 yrs., female, white, single, Pneumonia, Beat 5, Pleasant Hill Church, William Weathers, M.D.
WILLIAM H.E. RAMPY, 3/13/1887, Bell Co., TX, 10 mos. 3 days, white Cholera Morbus, Beat 4, Liberty GA Church, M.M. McManus, M.D.
LUCIUS C. WHITTEN, 3/4/1887, Randolph Co., 1 yr. 8 mos., male, white, Cholera Morbus, Beat 4, Zion Church, M.M. McManus, M.D.
LUCINDA D. MATHEWS, 3/24/1887, Alabama, 31 yrs., female, white, married, Dropsy, Beat 2, Union Church, A.W. Duke, M.D.
CARRIE E. YARBROUGH, 3/26/1887, Alabama, 1 yr. 4 mos. 12 days, female, white, Dysentery, Beat 12, P.G. Trent, M.D.
MATTIE BOWDEN, 3/2/1887, Georgia, 22 yrs., female, white, single, Operative in factory, Measles, Beat 12, Salem Church, P.G. Trent
EDMOND TRUETT, 4/15/1887, Georgia, 60 yrs. male, white, married, farming, Gangrene lungs, Beat 1, Campground, A.W. & J.D. Duke,M.D.
DOCIA MICKLE, 4/13/1887, 25 yrs., female, black, married, Typhoid Fever, Heard Co., Ga., State Line Church, Ga., S.J. Davis and E.H. McClendon, M.D.
T.V. BARRETT, 4/2/1887, 60 yrs., male, white, married, heart dis., Beat 11, Paron Church, Ga., S.J. Davis and E.H. McClendon
MARY POOL, 4/12/1887, Alabama, 7 days, female, white, Beat 3, M.C. Nelson, mid-wife
ELLA NOLES, 4/20/1887, Alabama, 3 yrs., female, white, Pneumonia, Beat 4, Providence Church, A.W. and J.D. Duke, M.D.
NANCY WRIGHT, 4/4/1887, Georgia, 25 yrs., female, white, widowed, Housekeeping, Measles, beat 11, Wehadkee, P.G. Trent, M.D.
LULA COLLISTA CAMP, 4/8/1887, Alabama, 10 mos., female, white, Infl. pneumonia, Beat 8, C.A. Jordan, M.D.
RACHEL PINKSTON, 4/18/1887, 68 yrs., female, white, widowed, Measles, Beat 11, Wehadkee Church, S.J. Davis, M.D.
JOHN HENRY CARSON, 4/2/1887, 26 yrs. 4 mos. 23 days, male, white, single, farmer, Pneumonia, Beat 6, Forrester's Chapel, beat 9, John M. Carson, Head of Family

NANCY OGLETREE, 4/8/1887, 16 yrs. female, white, single, measles, Beat 11, Wehadkee, S.J. Davis, M.D.
JOHN DUKE, 4/30/1887, Ala., 12 yrs., male, black, measles, Beat 11, Wehadkee, S.J. Davis, M.D.
LUCINDIE HENDRICKS, 4/3/1887, Ga., 10 yrs. 7 mos. 24 days, female, white, measles, Beat 11, Wehadkee, P.G. Trent, M.D.
FLORIDA GARRETT, 5/22/1887, Ala., 2 yrs. 2 mos., female, black, dysentery, Beat 11, Beat 12, P.G. Trent, M.D.
JIMMIE KEEBLE, 5/29/1887, Ala., 1 yr. 4 mos., male, white, dysentery, Beat 12, Wehadkee Church, beat 11, P.G. Trent, M.D.
T.J. PHILLIPS., 5/24/1887, Ga. 60, female, white, widow, dysentery, Beat 9, Concord Church, J.D. Liles, M.D.
JOHN STEPHENS, 5/31/1887, Ala., 6 yrs. male, black, dysentery, Beat 6, Pine Flat, William P. Long, Col. informant
JAMES L. POAGUE, 5/22/1887, Ga., 7 yrs., male, white, dysentery, Beat 5, Lebanon, L.L. White, M.D.
ISAAC G. HARPER, 5/4/1887, Ala., 2 mos. 18 days, male, white, pertussis (whooping cough) and measles, beat 12, Wehadkee Church, beat 11, P.G. Trent, M.D.
S.O. PRATHER, 5/24/1887, Ga., 18 yrs., male, white, single, measles, Beat 11, Wehadkee Church, P.G. Trent, M.D.
THOMAS A. CRUTCHFIELD, 5/2/1887, 60 yrs., male, white, married, blacksmith, cardiac dropsy, beat 9, Liberty Church, W.L. Heflin, M.D.
WILLIAM C. WHORTON, 5/9/1887, Ala., 45 yrs. 6 mos. 1 day, male, white, single, lawyer, homicide, beat 6, Masonic Cem., E.T. Gauntt, M.D.
ALEM ANDERS, 5/3/1887, 69 yrs., male, white, married, farmer, Hodgkins disease, beat 4, Bear Creek Church, J.D. & A.W. Duke
NANCY BRAIDY, 5/3/1887, Ga., 46 yrs. female, white, farmer, typhoid pneumonia, beat 2, Union Church., Dr. M.M. McManus
WARREN HESTER, 5/16/1887, male, white, typhoid fever, Beat 5, Dr. E.H. McClendon
GROVER PITTS, 6/2/1884, Ala., 9 mos. male, white, dysentery, Beat 12, Wehadkee Church, Beat 11, P.G. Trent, M.D.
Infant of J. & T. PITMAN, Ala., 8 mos., male, white, Beat 5, family graveyard at Tom Weathers', William Weathers, M.D.
AMANDA HILL, 6/20/1887, Ala., 28 yrs. female, black, married, Carbuncle, Beat 3, Near J.M. Smith's, Feraby Crawley, mid-wife.
J.W. LANCASTER, 6/9/1887, N.C., 76 years, male, white, married, farmer, typhoid fever, Beat 4, Jordan's graveyard, Beat 2, Dr. M.M. McManus.

Infant of MARION & LUCY BROWN, 6/20/1887, Ala., 1 yr. 6 mos., female, white, meningitis, Beat 10, Broughton's Church, Dr. H.B Disharoon.
LEOSIER DINGLER, 6/18/1887, Ala., 7 yrs., male, white, intestinal invagination, Beat 7, J.D. Liles, M.D.
E.L. GREEN, 6/19/1887, Ala., 30 yrs., male, white, married, farmer, consumption, beat 4, Providence Church, Dr. M.M. McManus.
RICHARD HEAD, 6/4/1887, S.C., 85 yrs. 4 mos. 14 days, male, white, widowed, senility, Beat 11, Salem Beat 12, P.G. Trent, M.D.
MARIAH McPHERSON, 6/25/1887, Ala., 43 yrs., female, white, single, dysentery, Beat 10, Dr. W.E. White.
MARY E. OVERTON, 6/20/1887, Ga., 43 yrs. 8 mos. 8 days, female, white, married, dysentery, Beat 6, Masonic Cemetery, Wm. Heflin M.D.
MAUD STEPHENS, 6/2/1887, Ala. 5 yrs. 4 mos., female, black, dysentery, Beat 6, Pine Flat, William P. Long, col.
CORA R. PITTS, 6/9/1887, Ga., 7 yrs. 9 mos. 16 days, female, white, dysentery, Beat 11, Wehadkee, Dr. P.G. Trent.
FLORENCE PITTS, 6/2/1887, Ala., 5 yrs. 10 mos., 23 days, female, white, dysentery, beat 11, Wehadkee, Dr. P.G. Trent

FRANKLIN N. GRAY, 6/2/1887, Ala., 5 yrs. 9 mos. 17 days, male, white, Beat 9, Massedonia, Dr. Wm. Heflin.
GRACIE JOHNSON, 6/5/1887, Ala., 2 yrs., female, black, dysentery, Beat 6, Pine Flat, Leah Stephens, mid-wife.
AUGUSTA A. JOHNSON, 6/3/1887, Ala., 2 yrs., female, black, dysentery, Beat 6, Pine Flat, William P. Long, col.
RUFUS F. OLIVER, 6/23/1887, Ala. 2 yrs. 10 mos., male, black, dysentery, Beat 6, Pine Flat, Leah Stephens, mid-wife.
IRVIN JOHNSON, 6/11/1887, Ala., 2 yrs., male, white, dysentery, Beat 1, Camp Ground, A.W. Duke.
LULA BELLE BAILEY, 6/18/1887, Ala., 1 yr. 3mos., 1 day, female, white, dysentery, Beat 10, Dr. L.L. White
WALTER PIKE, 6/17/1887, Ala., 1 yr. 10 mos., male, white, dysentery, Beat 11, Dr. P.G. Trent
CORA USSERY, 7/15/1887, Ala., 21 days, female, white, cyanosis, Beat 12, Bacon Level, Dr. P.G. Trent
Infant of JOHN & REBECCA FULLER, 7/22/1887, Ala., 4 yrs. female, white, cerebraspinal meningitis, Beat 8, J.D. Liles, M.D.
MARY GASTON, 7/17/1887, Ga., 56 yrs., female, white, married, dropsy, Beat 10, Dr. W.E. White.
Infant of JOE & SARAH HADLEY, 7/19/1887, Ala., 1 yr., 4 mos. 17 days, male, white, dysentery, Beat 3, Dr. Wm. Heflin
AMANDA BURROW, 7/18/1887, Ga., 58 yrs., female, white, married, Heart disease, Beat 7, Mt. Prospect Church., Dr. J.D. Liles
SALEMA HERNDON, 7/3/1887, Ala. 7 mos. 16 days, female, white, Abscess of brain, Beat 6, Masonic Cem., Dr. Heflin
GEORGE HOUSTON, 7/18/1887, Ala., 13 yrs. 1 mo., male, black, consumption, Beat 9, Mt. Olley Church, Dr. H.B. Disharoon
JAMES LIPHAM, 7/30/1887, Ala., 77 yrs., male, white, married, farmer, old age, Beat 4, on homestead, Ibbervilla Bowen, midwife.
SUSIE USSERY, 7/9/1887, Ala., 1 yr. 5 mos. 21 days, female, white, Tabes Mesentinca, Beat 11, Bacon Level, Beat 12, Dr. P.G. Trent
JIMMIE WYATT, 7/17/1887, Ala., 10 yrs., male, black, malarial fev., Beat 1, Camp ground, Drs., J.D. and A.W. Duke
BAMA A. BENNETT, 8/7/1887, Ala., 10 mos. 22 days, female, white, Pertussis, Beat 11, Rockmills, Dr. P.G. Trent
CORDELIA EAST, 8/10/1887, Ala., 27 yrs., female, white, married, Puerperal fever, Beat 10, High Pine graveyard, Dr. W.H. Pool
HEZEKIAH HOMAN, 8/20/1887, Ala., 3 yrs. 10 mos. 1 day, male, white, remittent fever, Beat 11, Salem Beat 12, Dr. P.G. Trent
JAMES C. HOMAN, JR., 8/20/1887, Ala. 1 yr. 3 mos. 13 days, male, white, remittent fever, Beat 11, Salem Beat 12, Dr. P.G. Trent
EDMON SWINT, 8/18/1887, Ala. 26 yrs., male, white, single, teacher, dysentery, Beat 1, Campground, A.W. and J. D. Duke, M.D.
DORA USSERY, 8/9/1887, Ala., 1 yr. 6 mos., female, white, dysentery, Beat 12, Bacon Level, Dr. P.G. Trent.
MARY LILES, 8/3/1887, S.C., 69 yrs., female, white, widow, Intermittent fever, Beat 9, Chambers Co., Beat 3, Dr. J.D. Liles
EMMA ELLIOTT, 8/8/1887, Ala., 25 yrs., female, white, married, Puerperal Eclampsia, Beat 9, Liberty Church, Dr. J.D. Liles
R.J. BUTTS, 8/12/1887, Ga., 74 yrs., male, white, widow, Gastritis, Beat 3, Union Church, Dr. Wyatt Heflin
REBECCA CASPER, 8/9/1887, Ala., 55 yrs. female, white, widow, Congested stomach, Beat 1, Campground, A.W. and J.D. Duke, M.D.
HENRY CLINE, 8/28/1887, Tenn., 68 yrs., male, white, widow, farmer, Dropsy, Beat 4, Liberty Grove, Dr. M.M. McManus
JIMMIE DURHAM, 8/16/1887, Ga., 8 yrs., male, white, inflamed bowels, Beat 1, Carrol Co., Ga. Pleasant Grove, A.W. & J.D. Duke
WILLIAM HILL, 8/4/1887, R.I., 69 yrs. 4 mos. 27 days, male, white, married, machinist, Ascites, Beat 11, Rock Mills, Dr. P.G. Trent
ELIZABETH KENNEDY, 8/14/1887, S.C., 74 yrs 2 mos 12 days, female, white, widow, Phthisis Pulmonalis, Beat 11, Rock Mills, Dr. P.G. Trent.

MARY ANN MICKLE, 8/30/1887, Ga., 78 yrs., female, white, widow, typhoid fever, beat 10, Broughton Church, Dr. H.B. Disharoon
JOHN CAPEHART, 8/30/1887, Ala., 7 yrs. 6 mos., male, white, typhoid fever, Beat 10, Forrester's Chapel, H.B. Disharoon, M.D.
LEVI IDSON, 9/30/1887, Ga., 80 yrs., male, white, married, farmer, Paralysis and Gastritis, Beat 4, Beat 1, Dr. A.W. Duke
MOLLIE TATUM, 9/16/1887, Ga., 30 yrs., female, black, married, Remittent Fever, Beat 11, Liberty Church, Dr. P.G. Trent
THOMAS KNIGHT, 9/12/1887, Ala., 16 yrs., male, white, single, farmer, Pneumonia, Beat 11, Liberty Church, Dr. J.D. Liles
THOMAS L. HARRIS, 9/24/1887, Ga., 65 yrs., male, white, married, Ascites, Beat 11, Rock Mills, Dr. P.G. Trent
FRANK T. MANLEY, 9/12/1887, Ala., 28 yrs., male, white, single, merchant, typhoid fever, Beat 10, Roanoke, Dr. H.B. Disharoon.
Infant of SANDERS MARTIN, 9/18/1887, Ala., 1 day, female, white, unknown, Beat 7, Flat Rock Church, Dr. J.D. Liles.
Infant of WILLIAM BARROW, 9/10/1887, Ala., 10 days, female, white, unknown, Beat 13, Liberty Church, Dr. J.D. Liles.
Infant of FRANK FOLDSOM, 10/28/1887, Ala., 1 yr. 2 mos., female, Remittent fever, Beat 11, Dr. P.G. Trent
JOHN REAVES, 10/9/1887, Ga., 78 yrs, 5 mos 12 days, male, white, widowed, Register in Chancery, Softening of brain and cord, Beat 6, Wedowee, Ala., Dr. William Heflin
SALLIE FREEMAN, 10/12/1887, Ga., 3 yrs., female, black, Remittent Fever, Beat 11, Ga., Dr. P.G. Trent
KATIE CARTER, 10/19/1887, Ga., 60 yrs., female, white, married, Morphine habit in the main, Beat 11, Rock Mills, Dr. P.G. Trent
STEPHEN NOLAND, 10/15/1887, SC, 82 yrs., male, white, married, farmer, Unknown, Beat 7, Mt. Prospect Church, Dr. J.D. Liles
JOHN BARNES, 10/29/1887, SC, 62 yrs, male, white, widow, Potter, Hepatic dropsy, Beat 12, Bacon Level, Dr.P.G. Trent
JONES BENNETT, 11/8/1887, SC, 69 yrs., 2 mos. 26 days, white, male, farmer, Ascites, Beat 11, Rock Mills, Dr. P.G. Trent
DAVID SEERS, 11/9/1887, Ala., 35 yrs, male, white, married, farmer, typhoid pneumonia, Beat 4, Providence, Dr. A.W. Duke
HENRY GIBSON, 11/4/1887, Ala., 17 yr. 5 mos. 24 days, Typhoid Pneumonia, male, white, laborer, Beat 6, Mt. Prospect Church, Dr. Wyatt Heflin
CARABEL LEWIS, 11/3/1887, Ala., 1 yr. 3 mos. 1 day, female, white, diarrhoea, Beat 11, Wehadkee, Dr. P.G. Trent
CLARISA JANE HENRY, 12/20/1887, Ala., 35 yrs., female, white, single, Phthisis, Beat 12, Bacon Level, Dr. P.G. Trent
MARY MANLY, 12/17/1887, SC, 67 yrs. 10 mos. 27 days, female, white, widow, Cancer of stomach, Beat 10, Baptist Church at Roanoke, Dr. H.B. Disharoon
J. WILLIAM BLAIR, 12/30/1887, Ga., 49 yrs., male, white, married, farmer, Scrofula, Beat 13, Christiana Church, Dr. M.D. Liles
HUSTON HALPIN, 12/10/1887, Ala., 12 yrs., male, white, Alcoholic Poisoning, Beat 13, Westlys Chapel, Dr. J.D. Liles
MARY NELSON, 12/15/1887, Ga., 12 yrs., female, white, Diptheria, Beat 3, Hopewell Church, Dr. J.D. Liles
ALSIA M. RICE, 12/20/1887, Ala., 11 mos. 17 days, female, white, unknown, Beat 2, Liberty, Beat 1, S.E. Norton, mid-wife.
SALLIE WILLIS, 12/24/1887, Ala., 32 yrs. 3 mos. 10 days, female, white, married, consumption, Beat 5, Big Spring Church, Dr. L.L. White.
G.W. BRUMBLAW, 12/10/1887, Ala. 41 yrs, 2 mos. 5 days, female, white, married, consumption, Beat 10, near Handley, P.O., Dr. L.L. White
The year 1888 was not included in the records.
MRS. SUSAN WOOD, 1/27/1889, Ga. 20 yrs., female, white, married, housewife, Pneumonia, beat 12, Christian Church, Dr. C.B. Taylor.
WADE D. SMITH, 1/30/1889, Chambers Co., 19 yrs. 10 mos. 25 days,

male, black, single, farmer, Pneumonia, Beat 12, Chambers Co. Beat 1, Dr. P.G. Trent and Son.
ROSA LEWIS, 1/27/1889, Ga., 1 yr. 5 mos. 26 days, female, white, Pneumonia, Beat 11, Ga., Dr. P.G. Trent & Son.
MRS. HENSON, 2/3/1889, 45 yrs., female, white, Measles, Beat 4, Dr. J.D. Duke.
LUCINDA BARTON, 2/7/1889, Ga., 60 yrs., female, white, married, housewife, Angina Pectoris, Beat 11, Dr. C.B. Taylor
LULA BELLE CHILDS, 2/15/1889, Beat 12, 5 mos. 15 days, female, black, Pneumonia, Beat 12, Drs. P.G. Trent & Son.
ROBERT PARKS, 3/10/1889, Ala., 23 yrs., male, black, single, farmer, Consumption, Beat 12, Salem, Dr. P.G. Trent & Son
KISSIE HAMMONS, 3/6/1889, Ala., 22 yrs., female, black, single, laborer, Extra Uterine Pregnancy, Beat 12, Dr. P.G. Trent & Son
FANNIE USSERY, 3/28/1889, not given, 28 yrs., female, white, single, laborer, Consumption, Beat 12, Bacon Level, Dr. P.G. Trent
MRS. SINGLETON, 3/18/1889, Selma, Ala., 65 yrs., female, white, married, Apoplexy, Beat 1, Drs. A.W. & J.D. Dukes
NATHAN SMITH, 3/26/1889, 76 yrs., male, white, married, farmer, Hydrothorax, Beat 4, Dr. A.W. Duke
WILLIAM COFIELD, 3/12/1889, 25 yrs., Beat 4, male, white, married, farmer, Blood poisoning from pistol wound, Beat 4, Beat 1, Dr. J.D. Duke
LEANDER FOSTER, 3/29/1889, Beat 11, 18 yrs., male, white, single, laborer, Cerebral Abscess, Beat 11, Wehadkee, Dr. S.J. Davis
LUCINDA UPCHURCH, 4/21/1889, SC, 81 yrs. 6 mos., 13 days, female, white, married, Cancer of head & face, Rock Mills, Rock Mills Cemetery, Dr. P.G. Trent & Son
ISAAC J. YARBROUGH, 4/11/1889, Rock Mills, 3 yrs. 2 mos. 1 day, male, white, Inflamation of stomach, Beat 11, Wehadkee, Dr. C.B. Taylor
JAMES SHARMAN, JR., 5/14/1889, Beat 12, 1 mo. 14 days, male, white, Pneumonia, Beat 12, Dr. C.B. Taylor
EADY M. BAGGS, 5/29/1889, N.C.,66 yrs. 5 mos.21 days, female, white, married, Paralysis, Beat 12, Rock Mills Cemetery, Dr. P.G. Trent & Son
_____ STAPLER, 5/29/1889, Beat 1, 25 days, male, white, unknown, Beat 1, Bethlehem, Robert Stapler, head of family.
ANNA GREEN, 6/15/1889, Beat 12, 2 mos., female, black, Infantile convulsions, Beat 12, Bacon Level, Dr. P.G. Trent & Son
EMMA OWENS, 6/26/1889, Beat 12, 7 mos. 4 days, female, black, pneumonia, Beat 12, Bacon Level, Dr. P.G. Trent & Son.
MARY ANN MARTIN, 6/16/1889, 70 yrs., female, white, single, Rupture of abscess with diarrhoea, Beat 1, Shiloh, Dr. J.D. Duke.
MATTIE HARTON, 6/30/1889, Ala., 3 yrs., female, white, Dysentery, Beat 8, Forrester's Chapel, Dr. S.J. Gray.
ALBERT SMITH, 6/30/1889, Ala., 3 days, male, white, Inanition, Beat 13, Mt. Moriah Cem., Dr. A.R. Stephens
CORNELIA A. MOON, 6/3/1889, Ala., 37 yrs., female, white, married, Consumption, Beat 10, Roanoke Baptist Church, Dr. H.B. Disharoon.
WALTER POOL, 7/4/1889, Ala., 10 mos., male, white, Dysentery, Beat 10, Dr. W.H. Pool.
EMMA WHITE, 7/14/1889, Ala., 2 yrs. 1 mo., female, black, Infantile convulsions, Beat 12, Bacon Level, Dr. P.G. Trent & Son.
SUSAN M. HOLLIS, 7/1/1889, Ala., 39 yrs. 6 mos. 11 days, female, white, married, Pyenia, Beat 11, Wehadkee, Dr. C.B. Taylor
L.J. JOHNS, 7/8/1889, Ala., 18 mos., male, white, Dysentery, Beat 1, Rock Springs Cleburne Co., Dr. S.P. Hopgood
ROBERT A. WHITE, 8/20/1889, Ala., 3 mos. 3 days, male, white, Gastro Enteritis, Beat 11, Rock Mills Cem., Dr. P.G. Trent & Son
GRECIE McPHERSON, 8/21/1889, Ala. 4 yrs., female, black, Pneumonia, Beat 4, Bethel Church, Dr. J.D. Duke
LARKIN TRALOR, 8/15/1889, Ala. 50 yrs., female, white, married,

Congestion of brain, Beat 4, Dr. J.D. Duke
BETTY GREEN, 8/6/1889, Ga., 68, female, white, widow, Congestion of brain & bowels, Beat 4, Providence Church, A.W. Duke, M.D.
GLEN ADDIE GREEN, 8/4/1889, Ala., 1 yr. 9 mos. 28 days, female, white, Dysentery Perotinitis, Beat 4, Providence Baptist Ch., R.M. Lovorn, M.D.
BETHANIA LIPHAM, 8/21/1889, Ga., 18 yrs., female, white, single, Congested chill, Beat 9, Valley Grove Church, Dr. unknown.
JAMES A. HENDERSON, 8/19/1889, Ga., 55 yrs., male, white, married, Consumption, Beat 10, Union Hill Church, Dr. unknown.
LAURA CASTLEBERRY, 9/5/1889, Ala., 16 yrs., female, black, married, farmer, Puerperal Peritonitis, Beat 6, Wedowee, Dr. G.W. Taylor
ROYER KNIGHT, 9/6/1889, Ala., 1 yr. 1 mo., male, white, Cholera Infantum, Beat 11, Dr. P.G. Trent & Son.
MARY ANN A. BLANTS, 9/5/1889, Tenn., 91 yrs. 6 mos. 2 days, female, white, widow, Senility, Rock Mills, Old Harmony Cem. in Ga., Dr. P.G. Trent & Son
JAMES KEEBLE, 9/25/1889, Ala., 8 mos. 14 days, male, white, Hepatitis, Beat 12, Beat 11 Wehadkee, Dr. P.G. Trent & Son.
ALFRED KELLEY, 9/19/1889, Ala., 60 yrs., male, black, single, servant, Beat 6, Wedowee, C.W. Taylor, M.D.
BETTIE HULL, 9/25/1889, Ala., 25 yrs., female, white, married, Remittent fever, Beat 6, Beat 3, Dr. E.T. Gauntt
JOHN G. NOLES, 9/30/1889, Ala., 44 yrs., male, white, married, Mail Carrier, Typhoid pneumonia, Beat 4, Dr. J.D. Duke
REBECCA DIXON, 9/10/1889, Ala., 65 yrs., female, white, widow, Paralysis, Beat 1, Camp ground Cem., J.D. Duke, M.D.
NATHAN DANIEL, 9/25/1889, Ala., 8 yrs., male, white, Intususception, Beat 4, Dr. J.D. Duke
JANIE PARKS, 10/2/1889, Ala., 12 yrs., female, black, single, Phthisis Pulmonalis, Beat 12, Salem, Dr. P.G. Trent & Son
GROVER HOLLEY, 10/24/1889, Ala., 1 yr. 6 mos. 3 days, male, white, single, Gastro Enteritis, Beat 11, Beat 12, Dr. P.G. Trent & Son
A.E. ABERNETHY, 10/16/1889, 73 yrs., female, white, widow, Cancer, Beat 6, Wesobulga, AL., Dr. C.W. Taylor
LEATHA C. BRADLEY, 10/10/1889, Ala., 27 yr. 3 mos., female, white, married, farmer, Ascites, Beat 6, Mt. Pleasant Ch., Dr. C.W. Taylor.
LEMUEL GRIMES, 11/26/1889, Ga., 80 yrs., male, black, married, farmer, Strangulated hernia, Beat 6, Wedowee, Dr. E.T. Gauntt
NANCY YOUNG, 12/13/1889, 70 yrs., female, white, married, Pericarditis, Beat 1, A.W. Duke, M.D.
FANNIE PARMER, 12/15/1889, Ala., 25 yrs. female, white, male, chronic diarrhoea, Beat 4, Dr. A.W. Duke
EMMA MORRIS, 3/10/1890, Ala., 36 yrs. 2 mos. 13 days, female, black, married, Pneumonia, Wehadkee Church, Dr. L.L. White
THORNTON WELCH, 3/24/1890, Va., 60 yrs, male, black, married, farmer, Ascites, Beat 7, Blake's Ferry Cem., Dr. J.T. Manning
SALLIE ORR, 4/1/1890, Ga., 32 yrs. 5 mos. 3 days, female, white, married, housewife, Influenza with Pneumonia, Beat 10, Liberty Church, J.D. Liles, M.D.
REBECCA BRADSHAW, 4/19/1890, SC, 77 yrs. 11 mos., female, white, married, housewife, Dropsy & Heart disease, Beat 6, Wedowee, Dr. C.W. Taylor
SHERMAN PARRISH, 5/28/1890, Ga., 80 yrs., male, white, pneumonia, Beat 9, Concord Church Cem., Dr. W.L. Heflin
ROBERT TRAYLOR, 5/28/1890, 9 mos., male, white, Dysentery, Beat 4, Dr. J.A. Gibson, born in Ala.
THOMAS STEPHENS, 5/27/1890, Ala., 2 yrs., male, white, Dysentery, Beat 4, Dr. J.A. Gibson
BETSY FOWLER, 5/17/1890, Ga., 54 yrs., female, white, farmer, Cancer, Beat 8, Antioch Church Cem., Dr. S.J. Gay
JAMES T. OWENS, 5/28/1890, Ga., 40 yrs., male, white, farmer, Scro-

fula, Beat 10, Rock Springs Church, Dr. W.L. Heflin
NANCY JONES, 5/4/1890, Ga., 60 yrs., female, black, Laborer, Ascitis & heart disease, Beat 6, Wedowee, C.W. Taylor, M.D.
CORDELIA THOMPSON, 5/25/1890, Ala., 25 yrs., female, white, Housewife, Unknown, Beat 4, Lamar, Dr. J.B. Gibson
SARAH HENDON, 5/21/1890, SC, 85 yrs. 11 mos. 7 days, female, white, widow, Valvoular disease of heart, Beat 11, Wehadkee Church Cem. Dr. P.G. Trent and Son
JAMES RICE, 6/9/1890, Ala., 18 yrs., male, white, single, farmer, Inflamed brain, Beat 1, Dr. J.D. Duke
BURREL WALLACE, 6/21/1890, Ala., 34 yrs., male, white, single, female, Stenosis Pylonie orifice of stomach, Beat 6, Greens Chapel Cem., Dr. W.L. Helfin
RACHIEL L. BENNETT, 6/15/1890, Ala., 21 yrs., female, white, single, Operator in cotton mill, Remittent fever, Beat 11, Rock Mills Cem., Dr. P.G. Trent & Son
ELLA SHIRD, 6/22/1890, Ala., 14 yrs., female, white, School girl, Dysentery, Beat 4, Beat 1, Dr. J.D. Duke
CLAUDIE SHIRD, 6/19/1890, 7 yrs., female, white, School girl, Dysentery, Beat 4, Beat 1, Dr. J. D. Duke
ALICE PRESCOTT, 6/24/1890, Ala., 9 yrs. 7 mos., white, single, School girl, Dysentery, Beat 4, Beat 1, Dr. J.D. Duke
WALTER SHIRD, 6/25/1890, Ala., 5 yrs., male, white, Dysentery, Beat 4, Beat 1, Dr. J.D. Duke
LEOLA STEVENS, 6/27/1890, Ala., 15 mos., female, white, Beat 4, Beat 4, Mrs. C.J. C. Stevens, informant
A.M. REEVES, 6/22/1890, Ala. 29, male, white, married, farmer, Homocide, Beat 3, Liberty Grove Church Cem., C.W. Taylor, M.D.
CLARA PIKE, 7/23/1890, Ala., 2 mos. 29 days, female, white, Bold Hives, Beat 3, Pleasant Hill Church, S.J. Ashcraft
BRADFORD HINTON, 7/28/1890, Ala., 3 mos., male, white, Membranous Croup, Beat 6, Dr. W.T. Gauntt
ANNA M. DUKE, 7/12/1890, Ala., 1 yr. 5 mos. 27 days, female, white, Hepatitis, Beat 11, Wehadka Church, Dr. P.G. Trent & Son
JANE FINDLEY, 7/15/1890, Ala. 48 yrs., female, black, married, Consumption, Beat 10, C.M. Mickle
SARAH ANN WORTHAM, 7/31/1890, Ga., 72 yrs., female, white, single, Chronic Bronchitis, Beat 6, Rock Dale, C.W. Taylor, M.D.
S.B. GIBSON, 8/5/1890, Ala., 40 yrs., male, white, married, farmer, Consumption, Beat 9, Concord Church Cem., Dr. W.H. Pool
EUGENIA CLEPTON, 8/13/1890, Ala. 20 yrs., female, white, single, Uremic Convulsions, Beat 6, Wedowee, C.W. Taylor, M.D.
BERNICE TAYLOR, 8/11/1890, Ala., 11 mos., female, white, Cholera Infantum, Beat 10, Roanoke, J.D. Leslis
NANNIE HEAD, 8/7/1890, Ala., 2 mos. 26 days, female, white, Dysentery, Beat 6, Beat 5, Dr. L.L. White
HILLIARD DUNN, 8/25/1890, Ala. 27 yrs., male, black, married, farmer, Poison, Beat 12, Dr. P.G. Trent & Son
ROBERT T. SMITH, 8/8/1890, Ga., 61 yrs., mlae, white, married, merchant, Beat 6, Beat 9, Dr. C.W. Taylor
JAMES EIDSON, 8/30/1890, Ga., 40 yrs., male, white, married, farmer, Bright's disease, Lineville, Dr. J.T. Manning
JAMES B. STEVENSON, 9/6/1890, Tenn., 68 yrs. 9 mos. 19 days, male, married clergyman, Hepatitis, Roanoke, Dr. J.D. Liles
KELLA ROBERTSON, 8/6/1890, Ga., 19 yrs., female, white, married, Peritonitis, A.W. Duke and J.D. Duke, M.D.
FANNIE DUKE, 9/13/1890, Ga., 23 yrs. 4 mos. 13 days, female, white, Bronchitis, Beat 5, Friendship Church Cem., Dr. L.L. White
PINK BURGES, 9/14/1890, Ala., 35 yrs., male, white, single, Beat 4, Dr. J.A. Gibson

The Ledger skips to 1893   P.E. Dean, Health Officer

Mrs. N.E. KELLY, 11/23/1893, 46 yrs, female, white, widow, house-keeper, Pneumonia, Beat 2, Union Church Cem., Dr. W.H. Mitchell
JOHN R. WRIGHT, 12/9/1893, 53 yrs. 9 mos. 28 days, male, white, married, farmer, Scrofulas Tumor, Beat 3, Union Ch, Dr. W.H. Mitchell.
MENDY NELSON WAGGONER, 12/23/1893, 71 yrs. 6 mos. 10 days, female, white, widow, house-keeping, LaGrippe, Beat 14, Antioch Church Cemetery, Dr. W.H. Mitchell
MARY GOODSON, 12/30/1893, Ala., 43 yrs. 2 days, female, white, married, house-keeping, Consumption, Beat 14, Antioch Church Cemetery, Dr. W.H. Mitchell
Infant of JACK & EMILY ANN TIDWELL, 12/6/1893, Ala., 1 mos. 20 days, male, white, Convulsions, Beat 8, Almond, Dr. S.J. Gay
DOCIA A.T. DISHAROON, 12/22/1893, Ala., 58 yrs. 8 mos. 10 days, female, white, widow, house-keeping, Pneumonia, Roanoke, Beat 10, Baptist Cem. in Roanoke, Dr. P.E. Dean
SIDNEY McCULLOUGH, 1/1/1894, Ala., 26 yrs. male, white, married, farmer, Pneumonia, Beat 9, Forrester's Chapel, Dr. Overby
DAVID JONES, 1/4/1894, Ga., 75 yrs., male, black, married, farmer, LaGrippe, Beat 6, Wedowee, Dr. E.T. Gauntt
Infant of W. & M. TRAYLOR, 1/6/1894, Ala.,.white, Still birth, Beat 6, Dr. G.W. Traylor
MYRTLE HOLLOWAY, 1/6/1894, Ala., 3 yrs. 18 days, female, white, unknown, Beat 1, Campground Cem., Dr. A.W. Duke
WILLIAM COLWELL, 1/24/1894, Ala., 52 yrs., male, white, married, Merchant, Paralysis, Wedowee, Wedowee Cemetery, Dr. E.T. Gauntt
JIMMIE CHAPPELL, 1/26/1894, Ala. 11 yrs., male, black, single, Farmer, LaGrippe, Beat 6, Dr. E.T. Gauntt
CROSBY COFIELD, 1/21/1894, Ga., 65 yrs. 3 mos., male, white, married, farmer, Pneumonia, Beat 14, Poplar Springs, Dr. J.D. Duke
WILLIAM H. COFIELD, 1/14/1894, Ga., 78 yrs. 5 mos., male, white, married, farmer, Pneumonia, Beat 1, Poplar Springs, Dr. Duke
GEORGE DOROUGH, 1/13/1894, 38 yrs., male, white, married, farmer, Pneumonia, Beat 1, Camp Ground Cemetery, Dr. J.D. Duke
LOU PATE, 1/14/1894, 33 yrs., female, black, married, house-keeping, LaGrippe, Beat 6, Dr. J.C. Swann
WALLACE WASHINGTON DOBSON, 1/12/1894, N.C., 83 yrs. 11 mos. 2 days, male, white, married, Farmer LaGrippe, Beat 7, Mt. Pisgah Cem. Dr. J.C. Swann
WILLIAM ELMA REAVES, 1/30/1894, Ala., 3 mos. 28 days, male, white, Capillary Bronchitis, Beat 2, Union Church, Dr. W.H. Mitchell
DURA WILLIAMSON, 1/21/1894, Ala., 3 mos. 10 days, female, white, single, LaGrippe, Beat 2, Valley Grove Cem., Dr. W.H. Mitchell
MARTHA JANE REAVES, 1/15/1894, Ala., 24 yrs., female, white, single, house-keeping, LaGrippe, Beat 2, Union Church, W.H. Mitchell
JENNIE BIBLES (Bibbs?), 1/18/1894, Ga., 18 yrs., female, white, single, house-keeping, Typho-Malarial fever, Beat 2, Pinetucky Church Cem., Dr. W.H. Mitchell
HENRY DIXON, 1/9/1894, Ga., 17 yrs., male, white, single, farmer, LaGrippe, Beat 2, Union Church Cem., Dr. W.H. Mitchell
FLETCHER W. HAYNES, 1/9/1894, 78 yrs., male, white, married, Farmer, Paralysis of bowels, Beat 9, High Pine Church Cem., Dr. W.G. Floyd
ELIZA M. ADCOCK, Jan. 1984, Ala., 61 yrs., female, white, married, house-keeping, LaGrippe, Beat 5, Friendship, Goodwin Adcock, head of family
ANNIE ELOISE MANN, 1/5/1894, Ala., 3 mos. 3 days, female, white, single, infant, LaGrippe, Beat 10, Roanoke, Roanoke Leader
MASSIE CLARK, 1/2/1894, female, white, widow, house-keeping, Pneumonia, Beat 6, Rock Springs Church
OMI STONE CLARDY, 1/2/1894, Randolph Co., 25 yrs., female, white, married, house-keeping, Puerperal convulsions-instrumental delivery, Beat 8, Flat Rock Cem., Dr. S.J. Gay

KING JOINER, 1/20/1894, Randolph Co., 15 yrs., male, black, single, Farmer, Pneumonia, Beat 6, Dr. S.J. Gay
____JOHNSON, 23 yrs., black, married, house wife, Puerperal Eclampsia, Beat 9
CYRUS WILSON STEWARD, 2/20/1894, Mecklingburg Co., N.C., 92 yrs. 20 days, male, white, widow, Farmer, Shock, Beat 3, Dr. W.H. Mitchell
R. HENSON, 2/10/1894, male, black, Farmer, Broncho-pneumonia, Pinetucky Gold Mines
Infant of G.N. TRAYLOR, 2/11/1894, Randolph Co., 8 mos., female, white, Pneumonia, Beat 4, Dr. A.W. Duke
GEORGE TRAYLOR, 2/4/1894, 76 yrs., male, white, married, Farmer, Pneumonia, Beat 4, Dr. A.W. Duke
A.F. McKENZIE, 2/13/1894, male, white, Farmer, Buried Blake's Cem. Cleburne Co., Ala. From Randolph Leader
2/5/1894, MARY TRAYLOR, 70 yrs., female, white, married, Housekeeping, Pneumonia, Beat 4, Beat 1, Dr. A.W. Duke
Infant of TEA & TOUCH SMITH, Randolph Co., 1 yr., female, white, Convulsions, Beat 4, Providence Church, Dr. Geo. W. Traylor
WATSON WILKERSON, 3/2/1894, Ga., 40 yrs., male, black, married, Farmer, Gastro-Enteretis, Beat 10, Georgia, Dr. P.G. Trent & Son
J.W. STEEN, 3/14/1894, Ga., 42 yrs., male, white, married, Farmer, Dilatation of heart, Beat 14, Union Ch. Cem., Dr. J.W. Martin
W.E. McKAY, 3/25/1894, N.C., 33 yrs., male, white, married, Post Master, Phthisis Pulmonalis, Beat 7, Wedowee, Dr. J.C. Swann
Infant of T.M. HORNSBY, 3/9/1894, Beat 6, female, white, Strangulation, Beat 6, Pleasant hill, Octavia Radney, mid-wife
Infant of LARKIN WATERS, 3/23/1894, Beat 3, 15 days, male, white, Umbilical hemmorhage, Beat 2, Dr. W.H. Mitchell
ARTHUR GRUBBS HOLDER, 3/9/1894, Beat 10, 1 yr. 4 mos. male, white, Meningitis, Beat 10, Roanoke, Dr. W.G. Floyd
Infant of JAMES SELLERS, 3/21/1894, Beat 2, male, white, still birth, Beat 2, R.E.S. Lindley, mid-wife
Infant of RICHARD BATTLE, 3/8/1894, Beat 8, 8 mos., female, black, Abscess of larynx, Beat 8, Dr. J.M. Welch
Infant of MOSES LAY, 3/25/1894, Beat 1, female, black, Still birth, Beat 1, Dr. A.W. Duke
ELSIE HESTER, 4/11/1894, 70 yrs., female, white, single, Chronic bronchitis, Beat 5, Dr. G.W. Traylor
THOMAS A. LIPHAM, 4/9/1894, Ga., 65 yrs. 5 mos. 26 days, male, white, married, Miller, Septicaemia, Beat 2, Valley Grove Cem., H.L. Lipham
CHARLES EDWARD PIKE, 4/5/1894, Ala., 4 yrs., male, white, Dysentery, Beat 11, Family burial ground, Dr. S.J. Davis
MANDY CARPENTER, 4/17/1894, Ala., 55 yrs., female, white, married House-keeping, Gastritis, Beat 2, Valley Grove, Dr. W.H. Mitchell
JASON LEE, 4/17/1894, Ala., 24 yrs., male, white, farmer, Typhoid Fever, Beat 3, Union Chapel Cem., Dr. P.E. Dean
Mrs. LINDLEY, 4/19/1894, Convulsions, Beat 3, Dr. P.E. Dean
POLK LEE, 4/23/1894, 60 yrs., male, white, married, Farmer, Beat 3 Union Church Cem., W.H. Mitchell, M.D.
CORNELIA MADDEN, 4/27/1894, Randolph Co., 25 yrs., female, black, single, Dropsy, Beat 4, Dr. R.M. Lovvorn
LUCY J. WOOD, 4/24/1894, 66 yrs., female, white, widow, Housekeeping, Rheumatism & neurasthma, Beat 8, Dr. J.M. Welch
WESLEY VINSON, 4/8/1894, Randolph Co., 65 yrs., male, white, married, Farmer, Diabetes, Beat 10, Broughton's Cem., Dr. Disharoon
DAVY PHELPS, 4/28/1894, 60 yrs., male, white, married, Farmer, Congested lungs, Beat 10, Lanes Chapel, Dr. W.H. Pool
AMBURS PITTMAN, 5/2/1894, Randolph Co., 45 yrs., male, black, married, Farmer, Dropsy, Beat 4, Mt. Carmel Cem., Dr. G.W. Taylor
Infant of JERRY & BETTIE HUCKEBY, 5/8/1894, Randolph Co., 1 yr. 7 mos., male, white, Pneumonia Beat 1, Dr. Traylor

FANNIE DeLAMAR, 5/6/1894, Randolph Co., 11 mos. 7 days, female, white, Entero Colitis, Beat 2, Walls Burial Ground. Dr. P.E. Dean.
FRANCES E. OWENS, 5/19/1894, 73 yrs. 3 mos. 13 days, female, white widow, House-keeping, Phthisis Pulmonalis, Beat 6, Wedowee, Dr. J.C. Swann
LYDIA CLARK, 5/23/1894, Ga., 88 yrs. 3 mos. 5 days, female, white, House-keeping, Dysentery, Beat 6, Wedowee, Dr. E.T. Gauntt
MARTHA HARRIS, 5/22/1894, SC, 84 yrs., female, white, House-keeping, Paralysis, Beat 6, Family Cemetery in Beat 8, John W. Perry, Sr., head of family.
____ WHALEY, 5/23/1894, Randolph Co., 5 yrs., male, white, Dysentery, Beat 6, Wedowee, Cem., Dr. J.C. Swann
R. ALONZO BRADESHAW, 5/25/1894, Ga., 38 yrs., male, white, married, Chronic Diarrhoea, Beat 12, Bacon Level, Dr. P.G. Trent
LORENZO COCKRELL, 5/3/1894, Randolph Co., 7 yrs., male, white, Gastritis, Beat 7, Mt. Prospect Church, Dr. J.D. Liles
JAMES KENNIE WHITE, 5/2/1894, Randolph Co., 9 mos. 22 days, male, white, Dysentery, Beat 11, Rock Mills, Ala., Dr. W.W. Bonner
JOEL SCOTT DAUGHERTY, 5/13/1894, Upson Co., Ga. 66 yrs. 1 mos. 27 days, male, white, female, Indigestion & Toopidity of Liver, Beat 2, Corinth Church, Dr. W.H. Mitchell
SUSAN M. NORTON, 5/12/1894, NC, 74 yrs. 4 days, female, white, widow, House-keeping, Heart failure, Beat 2, Smyrna, Young Norton, informant
DAVID E. HARPER, 6/14/1894, Randolph Co., 23 yrs. 8 mos. 25 days, male, white, married, Morphine poisoning-Suicide, Beat 11, Wehadkee Cemetery, Dr. W.W. Bonner
Mrs. BARTON, 6/10/1894, Randolph Co., 40 yrs. female, white, married, housewife, Tuberclosis, Beat 5, Dr. E.T. Gauntt
Mrs. A. WINDSOR, 6/9/1894, Ala., 40 yrs. female, white, married, Housewife, Cardian Dropsy, Beat 9, S.J. Gay, M.D.
RUTHY BROWN, 6/1/1894, Randolph Co., 19 yrs. 10 mos. 18 days, female, white, married, Housewife, Pneumonia, Beat 10, Broughton Church Cem., ____ Brown, Head of family
LEW CAMP, 6/5/1894, Carroll Co., Ga., 4 days, female, white, Diarrhoea, Beat 14, Midway Cem. Carroll Co., Ga., Dr. A.W. Duke
CORDELIA TRAYLOR, 6/30/1894, 80 yrs., female, white, married, Housewife, Senility, Beat 4, Zion Cem., Dr. G.W. Traylor
JOHN STEWART, 6/11/1894, Randolph Co., 38 yrs., male, white, married, Farmer, Bilious Colic, Beat 3, Union Ch., Dr. W.H. Mitchell
MARTHA ESTES, 6/21/1894, 65 yrs., female, black, widow, Laborer, Remittent Fever, Beat 12, Ga., Dr. P.G. Trent and Son
JESSIE MARSHALL, 6/28/1894, Ala., 50 yrs., male, black, widow, Laborer, Abscess of liver, Roanoke, Dr. W.G. Floyd
FRANCES KELLIE, 7/1/1894, Randolph Co., 27 yrs., female, black, married, Farmer, Tuberculous, Beat 10, Liberty Cemetery, Lucinda Wright, col.
MARTHA HOUSTON, 6/28/1894, Ala., 23 yrs., female, mulatto, married, Housewife, Puerperal Fever, Beat 9, Mount Olive, Drs. Heflin & Heflin
JANE AUSTIN, 6/12/1894, DeKalb Co., Ga., 52 yrs., female, white, single, Farmer, Hepatitis & Gastritis, Beat 9, Drs. Heflin and Heflin
____ TARVER, 60 yrs., male, white, married, Farmer, Rock Springs
NANCY COFIELD, 6/9/1894, Newell, AL, 8 mos. 1 day, Female, White, Single, Inf. Phthisis, Beat 14, Harmonc Ch., W.H. Mitchell, MD
CYNTHIA E. KNIGHT, 7/23/1894, Randolph Co., 23 yrs., female, white, married, Operative, Leacorythaemia, Beat 11, Rock Mills Cem., Dr. J.D. Liles
ELIN YEARTY, 7/21/1894, Ga., 70 yrs., male, white, married, Peddlar, Paralysis, Beat 9, Forrester's Chapel, Co. Health Officer
MORGAN CALHOUN, 8/21/1894, SC, 83 yrs., male, white, married, Far-

mer, General Debility, Beat 1, Beat 1, Dr. A.W. Duke
T.C. GREEN, 8/6/1894, Randolph Co., 18 yrs., male, white, Farmer, Peritonitis, Bt. 4, Beat 4, Dr. J.D. Duke
JOHN WILLIAMS, 8/7/1894, 50 yrs., male, black, married, Farmer, Dropsy, Beat 4, Mt. Corinth Ch., Dr. G.W. Traylor
JAMES H. WARD, 8/17/1894, Chambers Co., Ala., 54 yrs. 2 mos. 10 days, male, white, widow, Farmer, Typhoid Fever, Beat 11, Fredonia Cem. in Chambers Co., Dr. L.L. White
Infant of WILLIAM JOHNSON, 8/28/1894, Beat 11, male, white, single, Thrush and Worms, Beat 11, Wehadkee, Dr. W.W. Bonner
Infant of ALEXANDER JONES, 8/28/1894, Beat 10, 1 mos., male, black, single, Gastro-Enteritis, Beat 10, Dr. P.G. Trent & Son
Infant of JOHN COSPER, 8/11/1894, Beat 7, 4 days, male, white, Single, Beat 7, Mt. Prospect Ch. Cem., Dr. M.D. Liles
HENDERSON GATES, 8/6/1894, Chambers Co., AL, 27 yrs., male, black, married, Brakeman, Stab in neck, right common caritid cut, City of Roanoke, Roanoke, AL, Dr. Heflin & Heflin
SAMANTHA BUTLER, 8/27/1894, Ala., 63 yrs. 7 mos. 4 days, female, white, married, House-wife, Dropsy, Beat 14, Beat 14, Dr. George W. Traylor
GEORGE OAKS, 8/4/1894, Ala., 19 yrs., male, white, single, Farmer, Typhoid Fever, Beat 9, Dr. S.J. Gay
MARY TERRELL, 8/20/1894, Ala., 19 yrs., female, black, married, Housewife, Typhoid Fever, Beat 9, Mt. Olive Church, Drs. Heflin and Heflin
HEWLAND PRESTON, 8/12/1894, 70 yrs., male, white, married, Farmer, Heart failure, Beat 13, Mt.. Moriah Ch. Cem., Dr. P.E. Dean
ALAXANDER BARSH, 8/8/1894, Ala., 45 yrs., male, black, married, Farmer, Congestion of Brain, Beat 6, Wedowee, Dr. E.T. Gauntt
Infant of W.T. LOVELESS, 8/2/1894, Beat 3, 7 mos., male, white, single, Dysentery, Beat 3, Dunson's Chapel, Dr. W.H. Mitchell
Infant of WELDEN HESTER, Sept. 1894, Beat 6, 2 mos. 15 days, female, white, single, Beat 6, Zion Ch. Cem., Dr. G.W. Traylor
Infant of W.H. BAIN, 9/24/1894, Beat 4, 12 days, male, white, single, Pneumonia, Beat 4, Dr. G.W. Traylor
JIMMIE CROUCH, 9/2/1894, Beat 4, 8 days, female, white, single, Gastro-Enteritis, Beat 4, Providence Ch. Cem., Dr. M.M. McManus
CHARLES BAILEY, 9/5/1894, Beat 5, 26 yrs., male, white, married, Farmer, Typhoid Fever, Beat 5, Haywood Cem., Dr. G.W. Traylor
Infant of G.W. FRENCH, 9/4/1894, Beat 6, 8 mos, female, white, single, Dysentery, Beat 6, Beat 6, Dr. J.C. Swann
NELLIE LUCILLE CATO, 9/6/1894, Newell, AL, 22 days, female, white, single, Gastro-Enteritis, Beat 2, Rock Springs Ch., W.H. Mitchell
Infant of CHARLES BRIT, 9/22/1894, Clack, AL, 3 days, male, white, single, Premature birth, Beat 2, Dunson's Chapel, Dr. W.H.Mitchell
MARY COFIELD, 9/24/1849, Ala., 34 yrs., female, white, married, Housewife, Phthisis, Beat 2, Harmony Ch., Cem., Dr. W.H. Mitchell
Infant of K.L. CLEGG, 9/8/1894, Ala., 4 days, male, white, single, Ictirus Neonatorum, Beat 8, Beat 8, Dr. J.M. Welch
MATTIE HAYWOOD, 9/9/1894, Randolph Co. 20 yrs., female, black, single, Whore, Criminal abortion, Beat 9, Beat 6, Dr. E.T. Gauntt
EARNEST ROY, 9/6/1894, Opelika, AL, 12 yrs., male, white, single, School-boy, Hydraphobia, Beat 10, Roanoke, AL, Drs. Heflin
Infant of COL. BURNS. 9/10/1894, Beat 6, 10 mo., female, black, single, Pneumonia, Beat 6, Beat 6, Dr. E.T. Gauntt
MARY EICHELBURGER, 9/16/1894, Ala., 45 yrs., female, black, married, Laborer, Beat 6, Beat 6, Jim Mathis, col.
Infant of JAMES & LOVIE NEWELL, Beat 7, 4 mos., female, white, single, Beat 13, Unknown, Dr. M.D. Liles
EMMA TRENE EICHELBURGER, 9/24/1894, Ackworth, Ga., 33 yrs. 10 mos., 18 days, female, white, married, Housewife, Prostration from Hyperemises, Roanoke, AL, Roanoke, Dr. P.G. Trent & Son
WARREN SMITH, 9/16/1894, LaGrange, GA, 26 yrs., male, mulatto,

Single, Farmer, Typhoid Fever, Beat 10, Roanoke, Dr. Heflin & Heflin

MORGAN KIRK, 10/17/1894, Ala., 15 yrs. 4 mos., male, white, single, farmer, Acute Articular Rheumatism, Beat 8, Elliott's Graveyard, Dr. S.J. Gay

PINEY BRIT, 10/2/1894, 33 yrs., female, white, married, Housekeeping, Cardiac Dropsy, Beat 2, Beat 2, Dr. W.H. Mitchell

Daughter of JESSIE WEATHERS, 10/7/1894, 1 yr. 3 mos., female, white, Chronic Catarrah, Beat 5, High Shoals, Dr. L.L. White

Son of James Stitt, 10/19/1894, Ala., 1 yr. 4 mos., male, white, single, Pneumonia, Beat 5, Paren Ch., Dr. L.L. White

LUCINDA NIX, 10/11/1894, 70 yrs., female, white, widow, Housekeeping, Endometritis, Beat 6, Dr. E.T. Gauntt

ABARILLA BOWEN, 10/20/1894, Ga., 68 yrs., female, white, widow, Midwife, Carcinoma Uteri, Beat 4, Dr. G.W. Traylor

NANCY CADENHEAD, 10/29/1894, Merriweather Co., Ga., 65 yrs. 5 mos. female, white, widow, House-Keeping, Consumption of throat, Beat 10, Lane's Cemetery, T.H. Bonner

RICHMAND CONNELLY, 10/11/1894, Ga., 65 yrs., male, black, single, Farmer, Beat 6, Beat 6, Jim Mathews, col.

Infant of WILL & ETTA WOOD, 10/22/1894, Rock Mills, AL, 1 yr. 2 mos. 10 days, male, white, Pneumonia, Beat 11, Lebanon Church Cem., Dr. L.L. White

SUSIE BROOKS, 10/12/1894, Chambers Co., AL, 30 yrs., female, mulatto, married, Cook, Pthisis Pulmonalis, Roanoke, Roanoke, Drs. Heflin & Heflin

CORA BROOKS, 10/28/1894, Mill Town, AL, 29 yrs., female, black, married, Cook, Septecaemia, Roanoke, Dr. Heflin & Heflin

Infant of WILLIAM & M.P. CREEL, 10/21/1894, Randolph Co. Beat 1, 1 mo. 6 days, male, white, Inflamed bowels, Beat 7, Camp Ground Cem., Dr. J. Davis Duke

LOSSIE BAILEY, 11/7/1894, Ala., female, white, married, Housewife, Puerperal Peritonitis, Beat 3, Valley Grove Cem., Dr. W.H. Mitchell.

Infant of D.R. PEARSON, 11/4/1894, Randolph Co., 11 mos. 5 days, female, white, Articular Rheumatism, Beat 8, Dr. J.M. Welch

FANNIE KIRBY, 11/14/1894, 46 yrs. 3 mos., female, white, married, Housewife, Cardiac Dropsy, Beat 5, Dr. G.W. Traylor

JERRY ROBINSON 11/14/1894, Ala., 45 yrs., male, mulatto, married, Farmer, Cardiac Dropsy, Beat 6, Pine Flat Cem., Dr. P.E. Dean

CARRIE STRONG, 11/27/1894, Ala., 1 yr. 6 mos., female, black, Remittent fever, Beat 10, Beat 12, Dr. P.G. Trent & Son

COMER PARISH, 11/15/1894, Ala., 2 yr., male, white Tubercular Menengitis, Roanoke, Dr. Helfin & Heflin

JOHN NICKSON, 11/9/1894, Ala., 16 yrs., male, mulatto, single, Typhoid Pneumonia, Beat 9

RHODA RAGAN, 11/27/1894, Ga., 86 yrs. 8 mos., female, white, widow, Housewife, Cardiac Dropsy, Beat 14, Antioch Ch., Dr. W.H. Mitchell

Infant of J.H. DANIEL, 12/30/1894, Randolph Co., 5 mos., female, white, widow, housewife, Cardiac Dropsy, Beat 14, Antioch Ch. Cem., Dr. W.H. Mitchell

Infant of J.H. DANIEL, 12/30/1894, Randolph Co., 5 mos., female, white, Smothered, Beat 4, Dr. G.W. Traylor

LESSIE KEEBLE, 12/28/1894, Randolph Co., 16 yrs. 8 mos. 10 days, female, white, single, Consumption, Beat 11, Roanoke Cem., Dr. L.L. White

HENRY NORRED, 12/29/1894, Randolph Co., 18 yrs. 4 mos. 21 days, male, white, single, Farmer, Typhoid Fever, Beat 11, Lebanon Cem., Dr. L.L. White

WILLIAM TRAYLOR, 12/9/1894, Ala., 60 yrs., male, white, married, Farmer, Secondary Traumatic Meningitis, Beat 6, Wedowee Cem., Dr. J.C. Swann

FANNIE HEARON 12/16/1894, Ala., 26 yrs., female, white, widow,

Septicaemia, Beat 14, Harmony Cem., Dr. G.W. Traylor
MONROE HADLEY, 12/29/1894, 19 yrs., male, white, single, Farmer, Typhoid Fever, Beat 3, Dr. G.W. Traylor
Infant of DORA JOHNSON, 12/10/1894, Ala., 1 yr. 9 mos., female, white, Catarrhal Meningitis, Beat 10, Green's Ch. Cem. in Beat 6, Dr. M.D. Liles
ANTHONY GOTIER, 12/5/1894, Ala., 20 yrs., male, black, single, Laborer, Epistaxis, Beat 9, Dr. S.J. Gay
Infant of GEORGE WATSON, 12/20/1894, Ala., 3 mos., female, white, Double Pneumonia, Beat 9, Forrester's Chapel Cem., Dr. S.J.Gay
CAROLINE McLEMORE, 12/10/1894, 50 yrs., female, black, married, Typhoid Fever, Beat 9, Dr. S.J. Gay
MARY CARSON, 12/12/1894, Marion Co., Ga., 75 yrs., female, white, widow, Midwife, Senility, Beat 9, Forrester's Chapel Cem., Dr. D. Allen
ALMA R. SHIPP, 12/26/1894, Ala., 9 yrs., female, white, School girl, Drowning, Beat 9, Rock Springs Cem., Dr. C. Allen
ELIZA JANE WHALEY, 12/27/1894, NC, 65 yrs., female, white, married, Housewife, Cardiac Failure, Beat 7, Dr. P.E. Dean
WILLIAM DOBBS, 12/6/1894, Chambers Co., Ala., 40 yrs. 5 mos., male, black, married, Farmer, Cardian Hypertrophy, Beat 10, Roanoke, Dr. H.B. Disharoon
MANDY KNOT, 12/26/1894, Ga., 67 yrs. 7 mos, female, white, widow, Housewife, Pneumonia, Beat 14, Cool Springs Cem., James Knot, head of house
J.H. CARD, 12/20/1894, 40 yrs., male, white, married, Dentist, Homicide with pistol, Roanoke, Dr. P.E. Dean
Daughter of R. LIPHAM, Dec., 1894, Randolph Co., 7 yrs., female, white, Cholera Morbus, Beat 3, Dr. M.D. Liles
WILEY HENDERSON, 12/26/1894, 65 yrs., male, white, single, Farmer, Beat 10, County Health Officer
ELISABETH YEARTA, 9/1/1894, Ga., 65 yrs., female, white, widow, Housewife, Consumption, Beat 9, Forrester's Chapel Cem., County Health Officer
1/11/1895, BETSY FULLER, 81 yrs., female, white, widow, Housewife, Paralysis, Beat 10, Dr. W.H. Pool
POLLIE ANN BAILEY, 1/5/1895, Beat 5, 66 yrs., Female, white, widow, Housewife, Beat 5, Union Hill Cem., Randolph Toiler
EDWARD MEADOWS, 1/4/1895, Ga., 49 yrs., male, white, married, farmer, Typhoid Fever, Beat 1, Harmony Cem., Dr. R.M. Lovvorn
Infant of NAN & B. RAMPEY, 1/12/1895, Beat 4, 1 day, male, white, Premature birth, Beat 4, Dr. G.W. Traylor
HARRIET HARRIS, 1/24/1895, 65 yrs., female, white, widow, Pneumonia, Beat 2, Valley Grove Cem., Dr. W.H. Mitchell
LARKIN WATERS, 1/28/1895, Milner, AL, 26 yrs., male, white, married, Farmer, Pneumonia, Beat 2, Valley Grove Cem., H.W. Mitchell, M.D.
ROBERT CANADA, Feb. 1895, Beat 6, 4 mos, male, white, Croup, Beat 6, Green's Chapel Cem., Dr. P.E. Dean
Infant of ROBERT & EMMA STRONG, 2/20/1895, Beat 6, male, black, Croup, Beat 6, Allen' grave yard, Elisabeth Overton, informant
WILEY LEE, 2/1/1895, 19 yrs., male, white, single, Farmer, Typhoid Fever, Beat 3, Dr. G.W. Traylor
Infant of R.B. TRENT, 2/16/1895, Beat 4, 3 mos, female, white, Beat 4, Dr. G.W. Traylor
Infant, of HENRY FRANKLIN, 2/4/1895, Beat 2, 1 day, male, black, Beat 2, Agnes Sears,informant
DOVEY MASHBURN, 2/16/1895, Calhoun Co., AL, 16 yrs., female, white, married, Housewife, Obstruction of bowels, Beat 1, Loss Creek Cem. in Cleburn Co., Dr. J.D. Duke
LAURA YATES 2/22/1895, Randolph Co., aged 22, female, white, married, housewife, Consumption, Beat 1, Camp Ground Cem., Dr. A.W. Duke

ELBERT DAVIS, 2/27/1895, Randolph Co., 22 yrs., male, white, single, Typhoid Fever, Beat 11, Roanoke Cem., Dr. A.W. Duke
JEFFERSON WRIGHT, 2/23/1895, Randolph Co., 7 days, male, white, Pneumonia, Beat 6, Valley Grove Ch., Dr. M.M. McManus
Mrs. ELISABETH SMITH, 3/8/1895, Ga., 54 yrs., female, white, widow, Heart Disease-smoking, Beat 10, Ga., Dr. P.G. Trent & Son
RUBE SHEELY, 3/5/1895, Randolph Co., 2 yrs., male, black, Spasmodic Croup, Beat 10, Ga., Dr. P.G. Trent & Son
MITTIE JACKSON, 3/12/1895, Ala., 30 yrs., female, black, married, Housewife, Phetisis, Beat 12, Beat 12, Dr. P.G. Trent
JOSIE E. DAVIS, 3/29/1895, Randolph Co., 47 yrs., female, white, married, Housewife, Typhoid Fever, Beat 11, Roanoke Cem., Dr. L.L. White
ROBERT A. McCARLEY, 3/25/1895, 79 yrs., male, white, married, Farmer, Vertigo with spinal irritation, Beat 1, Camp Ground Cem., Dr. A.W. Duke
MARY ANN FULLER, 3/15/1895, SC, 80 yrs., female, white, widow, Paralysis & Phethisis, Beat 11, Mt. Gillead Cem., Dr. M.D. Liles
JOHN C. MONCUS, 3/9/1895, Ala., 45 yrs, male, white, married, Farmer, Pneumonia, Beat 8, Malm's Graveyard, Dr. S.J. Gay
FERABY SEARS, 3/31/1895, Ga., 38 yrs., female, black, married, Housewife, Ascites, Beat 6, Dr. Gauntt
HENRY CRAWFORD, Mch. 1895, Whaley, AL, 8 mos. 6 days, male, white, Beat 9, Rock Springs Cem., County Health Officer
ELLIOTT DEAN, 3/7/1895, 15 yrs. 5 mos. 7 days, male, white, single, Gun shot wound (Accid.), Beat 6, Mt. Pisgah Cem., Dr. P.E. Dean
Infant of J.D. & ELLA BRITT, 3/6/1895, Mecaville, AL, 3 days, female, white, Beat 2, Dr. W.H. Mitchell
MALINDA JANE HILL, 3/2/1895, Ga., 70 yrs., female, white, married, House-keeping, Pneumonia, Beat 3, Idemea, Dr. W.H. Mitchell
MARIE YATES, 3/8/1895, 21 yrs., female, white, married, Housewife, Consumption, Beat 4, Providence Church, Dr. G.W. Traylor

LIST OF MIDWIVES IN LEDGER

Beat 1, Graham	No names	
Beat 2	Mrs. M.C. Nelson	
	S.E. Nelson	
	- Mrs. F.H. Young	
Beat 3, Rockdale	R.E.S. Lindley	Newell and Milen, AL
	Feraby A. Crowley, col.	Wedowee, Rockdale
	Franky Falkner	Dingler, AL
	Lydia Stephens	Newell, AL
Beat 4, Lamar	Mrs. Sarah R. Dalrymple	
	Mrs. Lydia Stephens	Lamar, AL
	Lydia Lancaster, col.	
	L.C. Moore	
	Mrs. Mary Parrish	
Beat 5, High Shoals	Pollie Edmondson	Omaha, AL
	Peggie Greathouse, col.	High Shoals, AL
Beat 6	Mrs. Octavia Radney	Corn House, AL
	Mrs. Mary A. Roundtree	
	Mrs. Hanah Furgerson	Wedowee, AL
	Phylis Byrd, col.	"
	Puss Harris, col.	"
	Margaret Shepherd, col.	"
	Sylvia Banks, col.	Gay, AL

	_____ McLemore, col.	Gay, AL
	Mrs. M.J. Taylor	Wedowee, AL
	_____ Foster, col.	"
	Fannie Heard, col.	Gay, AL

Beat 7, Fox Creek

Beat 8, Flat Rock

Beat 9, Louina   Alsey Phillips, col.   Forrester's Chapel
                    Susan Trammell, col.   "
                    Jane Melton, col.   "

Beat 10, Roanoke   Lucinda Wright, col.   Roanoke
                    Mahala Wright, col.   "
                    Mrs. S.H. Bailey, white "

Beat 11, Rock Mills Mrs. Mary Hicks   Rock Mills, AL

Beat 12, Bacon Level

REGISTER OF DEATHS CONTINUED

Infant of BARBARA CULPEPPER, 4/2/1895, Randolph Co., 12 days, female, white, Inacition, Beat 8, Beat 8, Dr. J.M. Welch
ERNEST WOOD, 4/16/1895, Randolph Co. 4 mos., male, white, single, Bronchitis, Beat 8, Pleasant Hill Cem., Dr. J.M. Welch
WILLIAM WILKERSON, 4/1/1895, 60 yrs. 8 mos. 23 days, male, white, married, Farmer, Apoplexy, Beat 8, Almand Cem., Dr. S.J. Gay
Infant of HATTIE SEYMOUR, 4/1/1895, Randolph Co., female, mulatto, Accidental smothering, beat 6, Wedowee Cem., Co. Health Officer
Infant of MALLIE MICKEL, 4/27/1895, Randolph Co., 2 mos, 2 days, female, black, Accidental Smothering, Beat 6, Walls Grave yard, County Health Officer.
EZEKIAL KING, 80 yrs., male, white, married, Farmer, Dropsy, beat 4, Antioch Church Cem., Dr. W.H. Mitchell
HARDY HORTON, Apr. 1895, Ala., 34 yrs. 6 mos., male, white, married, Farmer, Phthisis Pulmonalis, Beat 9, Forrester's Chapel Cem., Co. Health Officer.
ELLA HANNAH, 4/11/1895, 26 yrs., female, white, married, Housewife Accidental burn, Beat 4, Providence Cem., Dr. G.W. Traylor
Infant of WILLIE RAMPEY, 4/23/1895, Ala., 1 mo. 27 days, female, white, Whooping cough, Beat 4, Providence Cem., Dr. G.W. Traylor
GEORGIA L. MADDEN, 4/25/1895, 18 yrs., female, black, single, Haemoptysis & epistaxis, Beat 4, Dr. G.W. Traylor
MARTHA SHARP 4/5/1895, SC, 81 yrs., female, white, widow, Housewife, Chronic Interstitial , Roanoke, Roanoke Cem., Dr. P.E.Dean
WILLIAM O. DRAKE, April 1895, Randolph Co., male, white, single, Merchant, Suicide with pistol, Roanoke, Roanoke Cem., County Health Officer
JOSEPH SCALES, April 1895, Randolph Co., 30 yrs., male, mulatto, single, Minister of Gospel, Phthisis Pulmonalis, Beat 10, Broughton's Chapel Cem., Alexander Scales, informant
SIMON D. BRADY, 4/6/1895, Ireland, 60 yrs., male, white, married, Farmer, Pneumonia, Beat 2, Union Ch. Cem., Dr. W.H. Mitchell
MARY AMOS, 4/9/1895, Randolph Co., 47 yrs., female, white, married, Housewife, Menopause & hemaptosis, Roanoke, Roanoke Cem., Dr. Heflin & Heflin
LOUELLA COFIELD, 4/17/1895, Chambers Co., 1 yr. 9 mos, female, black, Gastro Enteritis, Roanoke, Roanoke Cem., Dr. P.G. Trent
GUSSIE SEARS, 4/2/1895, Ala., 5 yrs., male, black, Phthisis Pulmonalis, Beat 6, Shake Rag Cem., Dr. P.E. Dean
JANE JORDAN, 5/26/1895. Ala.. 45 yrs., female, black, married,

Housewife, Phthisis Pulmonalis, Beat 1, Butler Grave yard, Dr. W.H. Mitchell
Mrs. MATHEWS, 5/19/1895, 82 yrs., female, white, widow, Housewife, Pneumonia, Beat 3, Dr. J.C. Swann
RHODA L. CREED, 5/23/1895, Carroll Co., Ga., 64 yrs. 3 mos., female, white, married, Beat 3, Valley Grove Cem., J.B. Creed, head of family
Infant of WASH TRAYLOR, 5/16/1895, Ala., 1 yr., male, white, Beat 6, Liddie Lancaster, col., mid-wife
ROBERT SEARS, 5/26/1895, 49 yrs., male, black, widow, Farmer, Phthisis Pulmonalis, Beat 6, Shake Rag Ch. Cem., Dr. W.H.Mitchell
NANCY DUNSON, 5/19/1895, Ga., 56 yrs., female, black, married, Housewife, Heart Failure, Beat 6, Poor House Cem., Jeff Dunson, head of family
RILEY EAST, 5/30/1895, Randolph Co., 16 yrs., male, white, Farmer, Typhoid Fever, Beat 7, Christianna, Dr. M.D. Liles
SARAH A. TAYLOR, 5/26/1895, Ala., 67 yrs., female, white, married, Farmer, Apoplexy, Beat 8, Pleasant Hill Cem., Dr. Welch
D.F. WADSWORTH, 5/31/1895, Ga., 73 yrs., male, white, married, Farmer, Tuberculosis, Roanoke, Roanoke, Dr. P.G. Trent & Son
PEGGY GREATHOUSE, 5/2/1895, female, black, widow, Mid-wife, Typhoid Fever, Beat 11, Wehadkee Church, Dr. L.L. White
Mrs. JAMES A. CROUCH, 6/27/1895, Ga., 41 yrs., female, white, married, Housewife, Uterine hemorrhage, Beat 12, Dr. P.G. Trent & Son
ALEXANDER M. KNIGHT, 6/28/1895, Ga., 73 yrs., male, white, Farmer, Cardiac Dropsy, Beat 12, Dr. P.G. Trent & Son
SHELLY CARROLL, 6/5/1895, Clay Co., AL, 8 yrs. 2 mos. 4 days, male, white, Accidentally killed by cart, Roanoke, Roanoke Cem., Dr. L.L. White
CICERO PATTERSON, 6/1/1895, male, white, married, Farmer, Consumption, Beat 14, Harmony Ch. Cem., Dr. W.H. Mitchell
NANCY A. JOHNSON, 6/28/1895, Ga., 50 yrs., female, white, widow, Farmer, Tuberculosis, Beat 2, Dunson's Chapel, Dr. W.H. Mitchell
Infant of JOHN SIMS, 6/28/1895, Randolph Co., 1/24 day, male, white, Beat 2, Friendship Cem., Dr. W.H. Mitchell
PRISSIE STEVENS, 6/7/1895, 81 yrs., female, white, widow, Housewife, Apoplexy, Beat 8, Pleasant Hill Cem., Dr. S.J. Gay
LUCINDA BENNEFIELD, 7/16/1895, 83 yrs., female, white, widow, Housewife, Dislocated hip, Beat 5, Dr. L.L. White
WILLIE NAPIER, July 1895, Wedowee, 5 mos., female, white, Capillary Bronchitis, Beat 6, Wedowee Cem., Dr. J.C. Swann
WILLIAM P. POOL, 7/28/1895, SC, 78 yrs. 10 mos 20 days, male, white, Married, Farmer, Peritonitis, Beat 10, High Pine Cem., Dr. W.H. Pool
MALLIE McCULLOUGH, 7/30/1895, Ala., 23 yrs., female, white, widow, housewife, Septicaemia, Beat 10, Broughton's Ch., Heflin & Heflin, M.D.
LULA BELL WHITLOCK, 7/9/1895, Ala., 24 yrs., female, white, married, Housekeeping, Cholera Morbus, Beat 11, Rock Hill, AL, Dr. E.H. McLendon
SEWELL SIMS, 8/21/1895, Carroll Co., Ga., 2 yrs., male, white, Cholera Infantum, Beat 1, Camp Ground Cem., Dr. J.D. Duke
MARY SIMPSON, 8/30/1895, 66 yrs., female, white, married, Housewife, Dropsy, Beat 4, Providence Cem., Dr. G.W. Traylor
NANCY C. SMITH, 8/15/1895, Jackson Co., Ga., 92 yrs. 8 mos. 12 days, female, white, widow, Housekeeping, Cholera Morbus, Beat 3, Smith's Grave Yard, A.J. Smith, head of family
J.W. BRADSHAW, 8/7/1895, SC, 93 yrs. 2 mos. 23 days, male, white, widow, Carpenter, Heart failure, Beat 6, Wedowee Cem., Dr. W.H. Mitchell
WILLIAM CHARLIE HEAD, 8/30/1895, Ala., 2 yrs., male, black, Beat 6, Mt. Pleasant Cem., George Head, head of family

TOLBERT MAY, 8/22/1895, Ga., 84 yrs., male, white, widow, farmer, Gravel, Beat 6, Beat 6, Dr. W.T. Gauntt
Infant of WILLIAM AND SARAH BYRD, 8/18/1895, Ala., 5 days, male, black, single, Premature birth, Beat 6, McBurnett's Grave Yard, Phyllis Byrd, mid-wife
SOLOMON McLEMORE, Aug. 1895, Ala., male, Mulatto, married, Farmer, Indigestion, Beat 6, County Health Officer
JAMES AIKIN STITT, 8/31/1895, Ala, 5 yrs. 4 mos, male, white, Tuberculosis, Beat 6, Paran Church, Dr. P.G.Trent
SALLIE KENEDY, 8/3/1895, Ga., 58 yrs., male, white, married, house-wife, Typhoid Fever, Roanoke, Roanoke Cem., Heflin & Heflin, M.D.
MARTHA FERRILL, 8/11/1895, TN, 40 yrs., female, black, married, Housewife, Perintonitis, Beat 10, Beat 9, Dr. Heflin & Heflin
PETE TRAYLOR, 8/14/1895, Ala., 20 yrs., male, white, single, Farmer, Cardiac Dropsy, Beat 14, Pine Hill Cem., Dr. G.W. Traylor
FRANK EASON, 8/19/1895, Carroll Co., Ga., 34 yrs, male, white, widow, Inflamation of bowels, Beat 2, Dr. J.M. Harrison
WILLIE STEWART, 8/28/1895, Ala., 2 yrs. 3 mos. 10 days, male, white, Dysentery, Beat 2, Dr. J.M. Harrison
OTTO HALL, 9/21/1895, Chulafinne, AL, 2 yrs., male, white, Bronchitis, Beat 1, Beat 1, Dr. J.D. Duke
Infant of STEVEN HALE, 9/22/1895, Ala., 2 days, male, white, single, Cholera Infantum, Beat 1, Beat 1, Dr. A.W. Duke
ISAAC GRAY, 9/14/1895, Ga., 54 yrs., male, white, married, Farmer, Chronic Bronchitis, Beat 2, Beat 2, Dr. J.M. Harrison
FRANK COPELAND, 9/29/1895, Carroll Co., Ga., 42 yrs., male, white, married, Farmer, Convulsions, Beat 2, Beat 2, Dr. J.M. Harrison
BIRD LINEVILLE, 9/16/1895, Ala., 23 yrs., male, white, married, Farmer, Typhoid Fever, Beat 2, Union Church Cem., Dr. J.D. Liles
Infant of G.W. LIPP, 9/12/1895, Ala., 6 mos. 5 days, male, white, Inflamation of bowels, Beat 5, Pike Grave Yard, Dr. L.L. White
SUSAN JANE HEAD, 9/14/1895, Ala., 26 yrs., female, black, married, Housewife, Ascitis, Beat 6, Mt. Pleasant Ch., George Head, head of family
MALLIE PATRICK, 9/22/1895, Ga., 5 yrs. female, white, Tramatism, Beat 6, Wedowee, Dr. J.C. Swann
HENRY BOWEN, 9/10/1895, Ala., 23 yrs., male, white, married, Farmer, Cardiac dropsy, Beat 6, Rock Springs Church, Dr. P.E. Dean
WILLIAM GIBSON, 9/1/1895, Ga., 58 yrs., male, white, married, Farmer Cardiac dropsy, Beat 6, Beat 6, County Health Officer
MARY FRANCES FORRESTER, 9/25/1895, 73 yrs., female, white, married, Housewife, Pneumonia, Beat 9, Forrester's Chapel, Dr. S. J. Gay
WAIF WILDER, Sept. 1895, Ala., 23 yrs., male, white, married, Farmer, Typhoid Fever, Beat 9, Drs. Heflin & Heflin
CARRIE MICKLE, 9/2/1895, Ala., 27 yrs., female, black, married, Housewife, Peritonitis, Beat 10, Drs. Heflin & Heflin
JEFFERSON DUNSON, 9/27/1895, Ga., 58 yrs., male, black, married, Farmer, Cardiac failure, Beat 6, Perryman's Graveyard, County Health Officer.
A.J. HOLMES, 10/2/1895, Ga. 26 yrs., male, white, married, Farmer, Typhoid Fever, Beat 2, Valley Grove Cem., Dr. J.C. Swann
ADA DISHAROON, 10/20/1895, Ala., 23 yrs., female, white, single, Phthisis Pulmonalis, Beat 2, Randolph Toiler, informant
Infant of JAMES ADAMS, 10/25/1895, Ala., 1 yr. 6 mos. male, white, Pneumonia, Beat 3, Providence Church Cem., Dr. G.W. Traylor
LOU TAYLOR, 10/26/1895, Ala., 28 yrs., male, black, single, Farmer, Typhoid Fever, Beat 5, near Stroud, AL, Dr. L.L. White
LINDA MOFFETT, 10/20/1895, Walton Co., Ga., 84 yrs., female, black, married, Housewife, Paralysis, Beat 6, McBride's Graveyard, William Sheppard, col.
ALLEN PATE, 10/ 8/1895, male, black, widow, Gambler, Pistol wound

(Homicide), Beat 6, McBurnett's Graveyard, The Randolph Toiler
IRENE CUMMINS, 10/9/1895, Putnam Co., Ga., 84 yrs. 6 mos., female white, widow, Housewife, Senility, Beat 9, Concord Cem., Thomas Cummins, informant
CORDIE HARDY, 10/25/1895, Ala., 19 yrs., female, white, single, Saleswoman, Peritinitis, Roanoke, Roanoke, Dr. P.G. Trent & Son
NANCY JANE BURGESS, 10/26/1895, Monroe Co., Ga., 55 yrs., female, white, married, Housewife, Heart failure, Beat 11, Lane's Chapel, Dr. L.L. White
HAL MITCHELL, 11/25/1895, Ala., 42 yrs., male, white, married, Laborer, Tertiary Syphilis, Beat 2, Dr. W.H. Mitchell
MARTHA SHELNUTT, 11/18/1895, 54 yrs. 1 mo. 25 days, female, white, Married, Housewife, Beat 5, The Randolph Toiler, informant
BEN ALLEN, 11/7/1895, Chambers Co., AL, 59 yrs., male, black, married, Laborer, Cardiac dropsy, Beat 6, Dr. P.E. Dean
SHADRICK PORTHRO, 11/1/1895, Randolph Co., male, black, married, Laborer, Influenza, Beat 6, Shake Rag Ch. Cem., Dr. W.H. Mitchell
JACKSON MITCHELL, Nov., 1895, Randolph Co., male, white, Farmer, Hepatic Abscess, Beat 7
ANDERSON CLEMMONS, 11/3/1895, Ala. 64 yrs., male, white, married, Farmer, Trauma, Beat 9, Fredonia, AL, Dr. W.H. Mitchell
LILLIE MICKLE, 11/13/1895, Roanoke, 1 yr. 2 mos. 15 days, female, white, single, Gastro-Enteritis, Roanoke, Roanoke Cem., Dr. P. G. Trent & Son
JAMES CUMMINGS, 12/21/1895, Ala., 8 yrs., male, white, Typhoid Fever, Beat 3, Dr. J.D. Liles
Infant of J.P. GORE, 12/5/1895, AL, 5 mos., male, white, Deformity, Beat 5, Dr. G.W. Traylor
MARTHA EDMONDSON, 12/1/1895, AL, 65 yrs., female, white, married, Housewife, General Anasarca, Beat 6, Oslin's Chapel, Dr. J.C. Swann
Infant of Dr. F.G. THOMASON, 12/26/1895, Ala., 2 days, female, white, Incomplete Closure for Ovale, Beat 6, Wedowee Cemetery, Dr. W.H. Mitchell
SARAH BAGGETT, 12/8/1895, Ala., 48 yrs., female, white, widow, Housewife, Hanging (Suicide), Beat 11, Lebanon Cem., Dr. L.L. White
JANE GASTON, 12/14/1895, Va., 76 yrs., female, black, widow, Housewife, Paralysis, Beat 3, Rock Dale Cem., Dr. W.H. Mitchell
ELMIRA HILL, 12/11/1895, R.I., 77 yrs., female, white, widowed, Paralysis, Roanoke, Rock Mills, AL, Dr. W.H. Pool
MARTHA WILLINGHAM, 12/7/1895, AL, 24 yrs., female, white, married, Housewife, Phthisis Pulmonalis, Beat 10, High Pine Cem., Drs. Heflin & Heflin
CILLA CUMMINGS, 1/5/1896, AL, 22 yrs., female, white, married, Housewife, Typhoid Fever, Beat 3, Pleasant Hill Cem. Dr. M.D. Liles and J.C. Swann
Infant of MANUEL BAILEY, 1/8/1896, AL, 9 days, female, black, Trismus Nascentium, Beat 6, Wall's Graveyard, Dr. P.E. Dean
Infant of BURK HARDNET, 1/25/1896, AL, 25 days, male, black, Croup, Beat 9, McLemore's Graveyard, Becky Trimble, col, Inf.
SARAH THURSTON, 1/30/1896, Troup Co., Ga., 45 yrs., female, mulatto, married, Housewife, Tuberculosis, Beat 6, Pleasant Grove, Becky Trimble, col., Informant
NANCY TRIMBLE, 1/5/1896, Ala., 13 yrs. 7 mos. 9 days, female, black, Farmer, Burnt in dwelling, Beat 6, Pleasant Grove, Becky Trimble, Informant
VIOLET TRIMBLE, 1/5/1896, Ala., 6 yrs. 7 mos. 19 days, female, black, Burnt in dwelling, Beat 6,Pleasant Grove, B. Trimble.
LAMA TRIMBLE, 1/5/1896, Ala., 5 yrs. 6 mos. 9 days, male, black, Burnt in dwelling, Beat 6, Pleasant Grove, Becky Trimble, Inf.
ELLA TRIMBLE, 1/5/1896, Ala., 2 yrs. 4 mos. 27 days, female, black, burnt in dwelling, Beat 6, Pleasant Grove, Becky Trimble, Inf.

JANE YARNELL, 1/7/1896, AL, 55 yrs., female, black, married, Washerwoman, Pneumonia, Roanoke, Roanoke, Dr. P.G. Trent & Son
CLARINDIA MICKLE, 1/14/1896, NC, 79 yrs. 4 mos. 14 days, female, white, single, Pneumonia, Roanoke, Roanoke Baptist Cem., Dr. H.B. Disharoon
ENOCH BARTON, 1/2/1896, 78 yrs., male, white, married, Uraenica, Beat 11, Rock Mills, Dr. P.G. Trent & Son
Son of OCIE WRIGHT, 1/19/1896, AL, 2 yrs., male, white, Measles & Pneumonia, Beat 9, Forrester's Chapel, Dr. S.J. Gay
JEFF LANGLEY, 1/15/1896, 48 yrs, male, white, married, Farmer, Measles & Pneumonia, Beat 9, Forrester's Chapel, Dr. S.J. Gay
WILLIAM HESTER, 1/23/1896, AL, 3 yrs., male, white, Measles & Pneumonia, Beat 8, Forrester's Chapel, Dr. S. J. Gay
FANNIE HARRINGTON, 1/31/1896, AL, 3 yrs. 6 mos., female, white, Membranous Croup, Beat 4, Biven Cem., Dr. G.W. Traylor
EMMA PATILLO, Jan. 1896, Ga., 35 yrs., female, black, married, Housewife, Measles-Pneumonia, Beat 9, Mount Olive, County Health Officer
GEORGE SHELL, 2/3/1896, 35 yrs., male, black, single, Farmer, Pneumonia, Beat 1, Beat 1, Dr. J. D. Duke
Infant of TOM LINVILLE, 2/21/1896, 6 days, male, white, Dr. J.M. Harrison
PERRY BAILY, 2/6/1896, AL, 2 mos, male, white, Pneumonia, Beat 2, Micaville, Dr. J.M. Harrison
Mrs. BROOKS, 2/22/1896, 76 yrs., female, white, widowed, Housewife, Beat 4, Dr. G.W. Traylor
KATIE EARNEST, 2/29/1896, Clark Co., GA, 77 yrs. 3 mos. 2 days, female, white, Senility, Beat 6, Green's Chapel, Mrs. J.M. Barsh informant
JANE MITCHELL, 2/6/1896, GA, 70 yrs., female, white, married, Farmer, Gen. debility, Beat 6, Oslin's Chapel, Drs. Gauntt and Mitchell
SARAH CULBERTSON, 2/16/1896, GA, 23 yrs., female, black, single, Measles complicated with Cholera, Beat 6, Pine Flat Cem., County Health Officer
CLAUDIA BASS, 2/3/1896, AL, 1 yr. 3 mos. 6 days, female, white, Measles complicated with Pneumonia, Beat 6, Mt. Pisgah, Dr. P. E. Dean
Infant of JAMES POSEY, 2/9/1896, AL, 8 days, male, white, Croup, Beat 6, Walls Cem., County Health Officer
RHODA HEFLIN, Feb. 1896, AL, 14 yrs., female, black, Phthisis Pulmonalis, Beat 10, Beat 10, Heflin & Heflin
RICHARD GREEN, 2/4/1896, Troup Co., GA, 72 yrs., male, white, Farmer, Chronic Nephritis, Beat 10, Old High Pine Cem., Heflin & Heflin
WILLIAM WRIGHT, 2/29/1896, 60 yrs., male, black, married, Farmer, Right Strangulated Hernia, Beat 10, Mount Olive, Heflin & Heflin
EARNEST COLE, 2/26/1896, Chambers Co., AL, 20 yrs., male, white, single, Farmer, Measles complicated with Pneumonia, Beat 10, Bethel Cem., Dr. H.B. Disharoon
JUDSON FEARS, 2/17/1896, 67 yrs., male, black, married, Farmer, Euraemic Poison, Beat 10, Dr. W.H. Pool
TINEY PEAK, 2/27/1896, 72 yrs, female, white, widow, Nervous Prostration, Beat 10, Roanoke Cem., Dr. W.H. Pool
MAURICE BAILEY, 2/17/1896, male, white, married, Farmer, Phthisis Pulmonalis, Beat 12, Wehadkee Ch. Cem., Dr. W.W. Bonner
HARVEY MOSELY, 3/28/1896, 30 yrs., male, black, single, Hack driver, Accidental Gun-shot Wound, Beat 3, Alexander City, AL, Dr. J.C. Swann
Infant of JACK DOSTER, 3/15/1896, 2 yrs., male, white, Pneumonia, Beat 4, Dr. G.W. Traylor
LULA WILLIAMS, 3/6/1896, 21 yrs., female, black, single, Cardiac Dropsy, Beat 4, Mt. Corinth Cem., Dr. G.W. Traylor

____ SMITH, 3/10/1896, SC, 80 yrs., female, white, widowed, Paralysis, Beat 4, Bear Creek Cem., Dr. G.W. Traylor
OLA WOOD, 3/18/1896, AL, 19 yrs. 6 mos. 21 days, female, white, married, Farmer, Dysentery, Beat 5, Rocky Branch Cem., E.M. Beck
NANCY E. BENNEFIELD, 3/24/1896, Heard Co., GA, 64 yrs., female, white, widow, Infl. of bowels, Beat 5, Bennefield Cemetery, Dr. L.L. White
MARTHA S. VEAL, 3/1/1896, Chambers Co., AL, 57 yrs., female, white, married, Cardiac Dropsy, Beat 5, High Shoals Ch., Dr. L.L.White
CYNTHIA ELLIOTT, 3/19/1896, AL, 74 yrs., female, white, single, Cardiac Dropsy, Beat 8, Elliott's Cem., Dr. J.M. Welch
ETHER MOON, 3/10/1896, AL, 6 mos. 22 days, female, white, Inf. Meningitis, Beat 10, Dr. P.G. Trent & Son
NANCY FINCHER, 3/29/1896, 65 yrs., female, white, single, Apoplexy, Beat 10, Roanoke Cem., Dr. W.G. Floyd
ALICE WILLINGHAM, 4/9/1896, AL, 22 yrs., female, white, single, Typhoid Fever, Beat 6, Green's Chapel, Dr. P.E. Dean
SARAH JANE WILLINGHAM, 4/26/1896, AL, 43 yrs., female, white, married, Housewife, Angina Pectoris, Beat 6, Green's Chapel, Dr. W.H. Mitchell
MOLLIE STEPHENS, 4/1/1896, Ga., 42 yrs.. female, white, married, Farmer, Neurasthemia, Beat 8, Pleasant Hill Cem., Dr. J.M. Welch
WILLIAM H. WELCH, 4/10/1896, 75 yrs. 2 mos. 10 days, male, white, married, Farmer, Insanity, Beat 8, Elliott Cem., Dr. J.M. Welch
MARION GEORGE, JR., 4/9/1896, AL, 2 days, male, white, Asphyxia, Beat 9, Beat 9, Heflin & Heflin
TILMAN TAYLOR, 4/5/1896, 82 yrs., male, white, married, Farmer, Cystitis, Beat 10, Lebanon, Dr. L.L. White
Infant of Dr. W.S. TRENT, 4/22/1896, AL, ½ day, female, white, Premature Birth, Roanoke, Dr. P.G. Trent & Son
EMA NAIL WASHINGTON, 5/27/1896, AL, 14 mos. 2 days, female, white, Cholera, Beat 5, Haywood Cem., Dr. E.M. Beck
DOLPH SMITH, 5/30/1896, AL, 9 yrs., male, black, Farmer, Cerebro Spinal Meningitis, Beat 6, McBride's Cem., Dr. P.E. Dean
MATHEWS PORTHRO, 5/28/1896, AL, male, black, married, Farmer, Phthisis Pulmonalis, Beat 6, Wedowee, Dr. W.T. Gauntt
LAURA BINDER, 5/27/1896, 50 yrs., female, black, single, Farmer, Cardiac failure, Beat 6, McBride's Cem., Dr. W.H. Mitchell
VIDA STONE, 5/23/1896, AL, 1 yr. 3 mos., female, white, Dysentery, Beat 8, Flat Rock Cem., Dr. J.M. Welch
BARNEY C. SWANN, May 1896, AL, 14 yrs., male, white, Farmer, Killed by mule, Beat 9, Broughton's Graveyard, The Randolph Toiler,Inf.
BETTIE WHATLEY, 5/20/1896, AL, 65 yrs., female, black, married, Farmer, Cardiac Dropsy, Beat 10, High Shoals, Dr. L.L. White
SABE SCALES, 5/31/1896, 70 yrs., male, black, married, Farmer, Apoplexia, Beat 10, Broughton's Graveyard, Dr. P.E. Dean
PINKIE PORTHRO, 5/31/1896, AL, 1 yr., female, black, Beat 10, Broughton Graveyard, County Health Officer
MARTHA OLIVER, 5/2/1896, Clay Co., AL, 38 yrs., female, black, married, Nephritis, Roanoke, Roanoke Col. Cem., Dr. H.B. Disharoon
Infant of LOU COTTLE, 5/12/1896, AL, 1 yr. 1 mos., male, black, Dysentery, Roanoke, Roanoke, Wyatt H. Pool, M.D.
THOMAS N. GLADNEY, 5/24/1896, 77 yrs. 10 mos., male, white, married, Farmer, Dysentery, Roanoke, Bacon Level, Dr. W.G. Floyd
E.M. NOLES, 6/6/1896, male, white, married, Farmer, Beat 1
E.B. CALHOUN, 6/8/1896, female, white, single, Beat 1
Infant of JAMES BRAZZELL, 6/8/1896, male, white, Beat 2
LENARD HOLLOWAY, 6/20/1896, Carroll Co., GA, male, white, Dysentery, Beat 2, Jordan Cem., Dr. J.M. Harrison
NEWTON HIGGINS, 6/16/1896, GA, 22 yrs., male, white, single, Farmer, Typhoid Fever, Beat 3, Union Hill Cem., Dr. J.M. Harrison
Infant of DELLA GRANT, June 1896, 3 mos. 9 days, male, white, In-

anition, Beat 3, Beat 3, H. Furgurson, Mid-wife
RAS MADDEN, 6/27/1896, 60 yrs., male, black, married, Farmer,
  Apoplexy, Beat 4, Lovvorn's Mill, Dr. G.W. Traylor
LEVI HURLEY, 6/13/1896, 80 yrs., male, white, married, Farmer,
  Senility, Beat 6, Dr. W.H. Mitchell
J.L. TRAYLOR, 6/19/1896, Ala., 26 yrs., male, white, married,
  Deputy Sheriff, Continued fever, Beat 6, Masonic Cem. in Wedowee
  Dr. J.C. Swann
LUCINDA MORGAN, 6/24/1896, AL, 50 yrs., female, black, married,
  Phthisis Pulmonalis, Beat 1, Beat 1, Dr. J.D. Duke
YOUNG DeKALB LILES, 6/24/1896, AL, 1 yr. 2 mos., male, white, Dy-
  sentery, Beat 7, Gladney's Graveyard, M.D. Liles, M.D.
AMANDA TAYLOR, 6/24/1896, GA, 48 yrs., female, white, married,
  housewife, Phthisis Pulmonalis, Beat 13, Liberty Church, Dr.
  M.D. Liles
STEPHEN C. MITCHELL, 6/16/1896, Fulton Co., Ga., 52 yrs. 3 mos.,
  male, white, married, Farmer, Carcinoma of stomach, Beat 10,
  Concord Church, Dr. H.B. Disharoon
MARION SHIFLETT, 6/7/1896, AL, 2 mos. 10 days, male, white, Chol-
  era Inf., Beat 5, Rock Mills Cem., E.M. Beck, informant
ISHAM THORNTON, 6/28/1896, Morgan Co., GA., 78 yrs. 4 mos. 3 days,
  male, white, married, Mechanic, Gastritis, Roanoke, Roanoke
  Cem., Dr. H.B. Disharoon
MAUDY BAILEY, 6/25/1896, AL, 14 yrs., female, black, Typhoid Fev.,
  Beat 9, Stonewall J..Gay, M.D.
LULA WHATLEY, 7/1/1896, AL, 26 yrs., female, black, married, House-
  wife, Phthisis Pulmonalis, Beat 6, Green's Ch., M.E. Bradley,
  informant
M.R.J. HIGGINS, 7/20/1896, GA, 15 yrs., female, white, single,
  Typhoid fever, Beat 3, Valley Grove, J.C. Higgins, informant
Infant of T.J. LOVVORN, 7/28/1896, AL, 14 days, male, white, Pneu-
  monia, Beat 4, Dr. G.W. Traylor
MARTHA RAYBURN, 7/14/1896, GA, 40 yrs., female, black, married,
  Farmer, Phthisis Pulmonalis, Beat 4, Mount Common Col. Cem.,
  Dr. M.M. McManus
JOHN HULL, 7/15/1896, AL, 1 yr. 4 mos., male, white, Pneumonia,
  Beat 6, Mt. Pleasant, Dr. E.T. Gauntt
POLLY GOODWIN, 7/24/1896, AL, 2 yrs., female, mulatto, Tonsilitis,
  Beat 6, Dr. W.H. Mitchell
SOLOMON McLEMORE, 7/5/1896, 40 male, black, married, Farmer, He-
  patic colic, Beat 6, Pine Flat, Charley McLemore, informant
FRANK JOINER, 7/23/1896, AL, 47 yrs., male, black, married, Far-
  mer, Typhoid fever, Beat 6, Dr. W.H. Mitchell
LULA WATLEY, 7/15/1896, 28 yrs., mlae, black, married, Farmer,
  Oedaema Lungs, Beat 5, E.M. Beck, informant
Infant of ANDREW SHELLNUTT, 7/28/1896, AL, 1 yr. 6 mos., female,
  white, Meningitis, Beat 5, Dr. G.W. Traylor
WILLIAM R. POOL, 7/16/1896, 47 yrs. 11 mos., male, white, single,
  Farmer, Gastritis, Beat 10, High Pine Cem., Dr. W.H. Pool
Infant of THOMAS McGILL, 7/13/1896, AL, 3 mos., female, white,
  Gastro Intestionsl Catarrh, Pleasant Hill, Pleasant Hill Cem.,
  Dr. S.J. Gay
Infant of M.W. WOOD, 7/15/1896, 1 mo. 15 days, male, white, Ileo-
  Colitis, Beat 8, Pleasant Hill Cem., Dr. J.M. Welch
Infant of K.L. KLEGG, 7/19/1896, AL, 6 mos., 5 days, male, white,
  Ileo-Colitis, Beat 8, Pleasant Hill Cem., Dr. J.M. Welch
ISAAC DUKE, 8/19/1896, Heard Co., GA, 18 yrs., male, white, single,
  Farmer, Remittent fever, Beat 1, Shilo Church. Dr. J.D..Duke
JOHN HIGGINS, 8/12/1896, GA, 16 yrs., male, white, Farmer, Typhoid
  Fever, Beat 3, Valley Grove Cem., Dr. W.H. Mitchell
PUSS SMITH, 8/30/1896, female, mulatto, married, Housewife, Beat
  3, Dr. W.H. Mitchell
B.F. HIGGINS, 8/29/1896, GA, 9 yrs., male, white, Farmer, Typhoid

Fever, Beat 3, Valley Grove Cem., J.C. Higgins, head of family
M. E. HIGGINS, 8/28/1896, SC, 46 yrs., female, white, married, Housewife, Typhoid Fever, Beat 3, Valley Grove, Cem., J.C. Higgins, head of family.
Infant of JOHN McCARLEY, 8/22/1896, AL, 1 mo. 2 days, male, white, Pneumonia, Beat 4, Providence Cem., Dr. G.W. Traylor
Infant of HENRY LOWERY, Aug., 1896, AL, 1/3 day, male, white, Beat 4, Dr. G.W. Traylor
Infant of BARD COLWELL, 8/13/1896, AL, 1 day, female, white, Beat 5, Octavia Radney, Mid-wife
ELVIRA MAYS, 8/9/1896, AL, 62 yrs., female, mulatto, widow, Farmer, Cardiac Dropsy, Beat 6, Green's Ch., Dr. P.E. Dean
Infant of RENA HALLAWAY, 8/3/1896,,AL, 26 days, female, black, Inanition, Beat 6, McBride's Graveyard, , Lucy Hallaway, head of family
HERBERT RADNEY, 8/23/1896, AL, 3 yrs., male, white, Membranous Croup, Beat 8, Pleasant Hill Cem., Dr. S.J. Gay
MINERVA BOWLING, Aug. 1896, 65 yrs., female, black, widow, Midwife, Beat 9, Gat's Graveyard, W.J. George, informant
SUSAN MATHEWS, 8/31/1896, AL, 22 yrs., female, white, married, Housewife, Typhoid Fever, Beat 11, Roanoke, Dr. J.D. Liles
MAGGIE RUSSELL, 8/16/1896, AL, 8 yrs., female, white, Pneumonia, Beat 12, Bacon Level, Dr. P.G. Trent & Son
MINNIE ALBRIGHT, 8/17/1896, GA, 14 yrs., female, white, Remittent Fever, Beat 12, Bacon Level, Dr. P.G. Trent & Son
Infant of MARION RICE, 9/12/1896, AL, 10 mos., male, white, Infl. of brain, Beat 1, Beat 4, Dr. A.W. Duke
MATTIE COFIELD, 9/17/1896, AL, 16 yrs., female, white, single, Remittent Fever, Beat 1, Troup Co., GA, Dr. J.D. Duke
WYATT CAMP, 9/24/1896, AL, 4 mos., male, white, Whooping cough, Beat 2, Dr. J.M. Harrison
SMILEY M. LIPHAM, 9/15/1896, AL, 6 mos, male, white, Whooping cough, Beat 2, Dr. J.M. Harrison
LIZZIE STARNES, 9/15/1896, AL, 22 yrs., female, white, single, Typhoid Fever, Beat 3, Valley Grove Cem., Dr. W.H. Mitchell
FRANK HIGGINS, Sept. 1896, GA, 8 yrs., male, white, Farmer, Typhoid Fever, Beat 3, Valley Grove Cem., Dr. J.D. Duke
JULIUS LAWLEY, 9/16/1896, AL, 14 mos. 12 days, male, white, Cholera Infantum, Beat 5, Friendship Cem., Dr. E.M. Beck, informant
GOODWIN ADCOCK, 9/1/1896, GA, 75 yrs., male, white, widow, Farmer, Cardiac Dropsy, Beat 5, Friendship Cem., Dr. E.M. Beck
MATHEW COLWELL, 9/15/1896, AL, 58 yrs., male, white, married, Farmer, Apoplexia, Beat 5, Friendship Cem., Tobe Colwell, informant
INMAN BUSBEE, 9/5/1896, 78 yrs., male, white, widow, Farmer, Cardiac dropsy, Beat 8, Elliott's Graveyard, Dr. J.M. Welch
Infant of ADA ZACHARY, 9/9/1896, 8 yrs., male, black, Phaemia, Beat 8, Cemyline (?) Church, Dr. S.J. Gay
SAMUEL PRICE, 9/2/1896, AL, 8 yrs., male, white, Membranous Croup, Beat 9, Forrester's Chapel, Dr. S.J. Gay
THOMAS S. STITT, Sept. 1896, 58 yrs., male, white, married, Farmer, Traumatic Erysipelas, Beat 10, Wehadkee, Heflin & Heflin,MD
STELLA SATTERWHITE, 9/27/1896, West Point, GA, 6 yrs., female, white, Farmer, Membranous Croup, Roanoke, Roanoke, Dr. H.B. Disharoon
AMANDA ESTERS, 9/12/1896, AL, 23 yrs., female, black, married, Housewife, Childbed fever, Beat 12, Beat 12, Dr. P.G. Trent & Son
TOM BLAKE, 9/19/1896, 40 yrs., male, black, married, Farmer, Remittent Fever, Beat 12, Canaan in Chambers Co., Dr. P.G. Trent
RICHARD BEARDEN, 10/25/1896, GA, 72 yrs., male, white, married, Farmer, Paralysis, Beat 2, Dr. J.M. Harrison
BILLIE YARBROUGH, 10/2/1896, 96 yrs., male, white, widow, Farmer, Cardiac Dropsy, Beat 4, Providence Cem., Dr. G.W. Traylor

WILLIAM SUDDUTH, 10/10/1896, 86 yrs., male, white, married, Farmer, Typhoid Fever, Beat 10, Lebanon Ch., Dr. L.L. White
CANDY SUDDUTH, 10/11/1896, AL, 30 yrs., female, white, single, Phthisis Pulmonalis, Beat 10, Lebanon Ch., Dr. L.L. White
LAURA HOUSTON, 11/28/1896, AL, 30 yrs, female, black, married, Housewife, Pneumonia, Beat 9, Mt. Olive Ch., Drs. Heflin & Heflin
WILLIE WHATLEY 11/16/1896, AL, 6 yrs., male, white, Dropsy, Beat 5, Dr. L.L. White
ETTA KIRBY, 11/23/1896, AL, 3 yrs., female, white, Catarrh & Bowels, Beat 11, Rock Mills Cem., Dr. L.L. White
ELDON STRICKLAND, 11/17/1896, AL, 28 yrs., male, white, married, Farmer, Catarrh Fever, Beat 6, Oslin's Chapel, Dr. W.H. Mitchell
MATHEW MOAT, 12/10/1896, 68 yrs.,male, white, married, Farmer, Typhoid Fever, Beat 3, Valley Grove, Dr. M.D. Liles
JEREMIAH HILL, 12/21/1896, AL, 18 yrs. 6 mos., male, white, Farmer, Typhoid Fever, Beat 3, Valley Grove, John Hill, head of family
JOE RODGERS, 12/6/1896, 44 yrs., male, white, married, Farmer, Gun shot wound (Homocide), Beat 4, Dr. G.W. Traylor
JOHN HEAD, 12/24/1896, AL, 24 yrs., male, white, single, Farmer, Convulsions, Beat 5, Hilobahatchee, Dr. L.L. White
BELLE FOSTER, 12/25/1896, AL, 21 yrs, female, white, single, Typhoid Fever, Beat 5, Pike Graveyard, Dr. L.L. White
SOPHIA WILLINGHAM, 12/27/1896, 58 yrs., female, white, married, Housewife, Pneumonia, Beat 6, Green's Chapel, Dr. P.E. Dean
MARTHA HORTON, 12/9/1896, Guinett Co., GA, 70 yrs., female, white, single, LaGrippe, Beat 6, Rock Springs, S.P. Horton, head of family
WILSON THOMASON, 12/27/1896, AL, 9 yrs., male, black, Pneumonia, Beat 10, High Pine Cem., Dr. H.B. Disharoon
LUCY THOMASON, 12/31/1896, AL, 6 yrs., female, black, Accidental poisoning, Beat 10, High Pine Church Cem., Dr. H.B. Disharoon
CATHERINE GREGG, 12/19/1896, SC, 74 yrs., female, white, Treaher, Cardiac Dropsy, Beat 10, Rock Springs, County Health Officer
EMMA WRIGHT, 12/17/1896, 15 yrs., female, white, single, Hemmorhage, Beat 10, High Pine Cem., Dr. W.H. Pool
ANGELINE TREADWELL, 12/20/1896, 55 yrs., female, white, single, Pneumonia, Beat 8, Dr. W.H. Pool
SALLIE C. STEPHENSON, 1/15/1897, Huntsville, AL, 66 yrs. 9 mos., female, white, widow, Housekeeping, Bronchitis, Roanoke, Roanoke, Dr. M.D. Liles
SAMUEL FANCELL, 1/23/1897, Columbia, GA, 79 yrs. 2 mos. 8 days, male, white, married, Farmer, Cerebral Hemmorhage, Roanoke, Roanoke, Drs. Heflin & Heflin
ZACHARIAH J. WRIGHT, 1/1/1897, GA, 70 yrs. 6 mos, 27 days, male, white, married, Farmer, Heart failure, Roanoke, Roanoke, Dr. P.G. Trent & Son
NANCY HANDLEY, 1/14/1897, GA, 8r yrs. 11 mos., female, white, widow, Heart Failure, Beat 7, Flat Rock Ch., Dr. M.D. Liles
ISHMAN WEATHERS, 3/10/1897, N.C., 85 yrs. 4 mos. 9 days, male, white, married, Farmer, Paralysis of bladder, Roanoke, Roanoke Cem., J.D. Weathers, informant

RANDOLPH COUNTY
MEDICAL DIRECTORY
1894

PHYSICIAN	OFFICIAL POSITION	BEAT	POST OFFICE ADDRESS
J.D. Duke, M.D.		1	Graham
A.W. Duke		1	Graham
W.H. Mitchell	A.H.O. Bt. 2,3,14	3	Newell
George W. Traylor	A.H.O. Bt. 4,5,1	4	Lamar
J.C. Swann	Vice Pres. Medical Society and Member Board Censors A.H.O. Beat 6	66	Wedowee
		66	Wedowee
E.T. Gauntt		66	Wedowee
P.E. Dean	Member Board of Censors, County Health Officer	66	Wedowee
J.B. Hunter		6	Talbut
M.D. Liles		7	Ophelia
C.A. Jordan		7	Ophelia
S.J. Gay	A.H.O. Beat 8 and Member Board of Censors	8	Almond
James Clegg		8	Almond
J.M. Welch		8	Truet
___ Overby	A.H.O.	9	Louina
H.T. Heflin		10	Roanoke
P.J. Trent, Jr.		10	Roanoke
H.B. Disharoon	Pres. County Medical Society	10	Roanoke
J.D. Liles	Member Board Censors	10	Roanoke
W.H. Pool		10	Roanoke
W.G. Floyd	A.H.O. Beats 10,11,12	10	Roanoke
L.L. White		10	Roanoke
S.J. Davis		11	Rock Mills
E.H. McLendon		11	Rock Mills
J.L. Vineyard		11	Rock Mills
W.H. Bonner		11	Rock Mills
P.G. Trent, Sr.	Pres., Board Censors	10	Roanoke
W.L. Heflin		10	Roanoke

ALABAMA STATE GAZETTEER
&
BUSINESS DIRECTORY
1887 - 1888
Randolph County

ALMOND. A county post office 15 miles southwest of Wedowee, the seat of justice and 20 from Buffalo, its nearest railroad point, via which it is about 85 miles to Montgomery. Bank at LaFayette. Population 50. Mail tri-weekly. W.A.J. Hester, Postmaster.

Clardy, J.A.J., grist mill and ginner
Clegg, B.F., blacksmith
Clegg, James, physician
Cotney, A.W., justice
Culpepper, Rev. W.H. (Methodist)
Hodge, H.P., general store and blacksmith
Hodge, J.M., general store and justice
Hodge, Rev. J.M., (Baptist)
Hunter, W.A.J., postmaster
Liles, J.R., lumber manufacturer
Liles, J.T., blacksmith
McGill, W.R., flour and grist mill and ginner
Perry, Rev., J.R., (Methodist)
Perry, Rev. W.W. (Methodist)
Stephen, S.S., flour and grist mill
Waller, S.A., shoemaker
Wilson, G.T., wagon maker

BLAKE'S FERRY. A village, 12 miles west of Wedowee, the county seat, and 30 from Oxford, the banking and shipping point. Population 250. Mail tri-weekly, W.A. Baker, Postmaster.

Baker, W.A., postmaster
Bell, W.C. and A.S., flour mill
Blake, W.H., physician
Blake and Giles, flour mill and cotton gin
Burroughs, W.J., blacksmith
Devaughan, W.F., general store
McCrary, N.E. and Son, general store
Mitchell, U.D., cotton gin
Orr, John, flour mill and cotton gin
Smith, C.A., flour mill and cotton gin

CHRISTIANA. A farmer's postoffice, 12 miles northwest of Wedowee, the county seat, and 25 from Oxford, the banking and shipping point. Mail tri-weekly. Mattie M. Preston, Postmaster

Cofield, W.J., general store
East, Joe, millwright
Foster, F.M., wagonmaker
Foster, G.B., wagonmaker
Hamton, Rev., C.J., physician
Newell, W.P., teacher
Preston, Rev., A.G.
Preston, Mattie M., postmaster

DINGLER. A farmer's postoffice, 15 miles west of Wedowee, the county seat. Mail semi-weekly. J.T. Dingler, Postmaster.

Ashcraft, Thornton, saw mill and cotton gin

Burrows, J.W., general store
Cockerell, T.M., wagonmaker and blacksmith
Dingler, F.M., grocer
Dingler, J.T., wagonmaker
Giles, Butler, flour mill and cotton gin
Hadnett, B., flour mill
Knight, Monroe, blacksmith
Leftwich, Joseph, flour mill and cotton gin
Yates, W.M., blacksmith
Young, Isaac, flour mill and cotton gin

GAY. A rural postoffice 5 miles south of Wedowee, the county seat. Ship to West Point, Ga. Population 15. Mail by special supply. J.C. Murphy, Postmaster.

Murphy, J.C., cotton gin, flour and saw mill and general store
Phillips, Samuel, blacksmith
Smith, C.A., cotton gin and saw mills

GRAHAM. A small settlement, 16 miles northwest of Wedowee, the county seat. Ship to Waco, Ga. Population 100. Mail, semi-weekly. John T. Hayton, Postmaster

Brown, J.A. justice
Cole, J.R., shoemaker
Cole and Casper, blacksmiths and wagonmakers
Daniel, T.Y., general store
Duke, A.W. and J.D., physicians
Hard and Co., saw mill
Harrod and Co., saw mill
Hayton, John T., general store
Johnson, D.T., constable
Simas, W.A., tanner
Swint, Joseph, teacher
Walker, W.H., wagonmaker
Widner and Hearn, grocers

HANDLEY. Simply a rural office, 8 miles southeast of Wedowee, the county seat. Mail tri-weekly.

HAYWOOD. Only one store, 6½ miles east of Wedowee, the county seat. Mail, weekly.

Bailey, N.G., shoemaker
Bailey, P.G., general store and flour mill
Canady, J.T., justice
Robinson, N.B., blacksmith
Rollins, J.A., miller

HIGH SHOALS. A country postoffice, 13 miles southeast of Wedowee the seat of justice and 22 north of Buffalo, the shipping point by mail. Population 50. Mail tri-week.y J.R. Ussery, Postmaster.

Parker, P.W., general store
Ussery, J.R., postmaster
Ussery, M.F., flour, saw and woolen mill
Ussery, W.H., tanner
Weathers, William, general store.

LAMAR. A small settlement, 10 miles northeast of Wedowee Court House. Ship to Waco, Ga. Population 35. Mail semi-weekly. A.J. Noler, Jr., Postmaster

Boone, H.C., saloon
Daniel, J.S., general store
Grant, P.J., flour mill
Johnson, B.D., general store
Johnson, Mrs. B.D., general store
Laron, M.D., general store
Noler, A.J., Jr., general store
Sears, D.P., flour mill

LEVEL ROAD. A village, 10 miles south of Wedowee, the county seat. Ship to Buffalo. Bank at LaFayette. Population 400. Mail tri-weekly. Nicholas J. George, postmaster

George, N.J., general store
Gray, E.O., cotton gin
Key, W.W., blacksmith
Nicholas, George J., general store (Note name as written above.)
Parker, S.D., grist mill
Stewart, W.L., general store
Swan, W.A.J., general store

LOUINA. A small village, on the Tallapoosa River. 15 miles south of Wedowee, the county seat and 14 from Buffalo, the nearest shipping point. Population 100. Mail, tri-weekly. W.L. Heflin, Postmaster

Gibson, Hiram, justice
Handly, F.M., general store
Heflin, J.L,, general store
Heflin, W.L., physician and flour mill
Kent, A.J., general store
Liles, J.D., physician
Orr, T., carriage and wagonmaker
Orr, W.J., carriage and wagonmaker

MILNER. A store and postoffice, 10 miles north of Wedowee, the county seat, and 18 south of Heflin, the shipping point. Population 8. Mail daily. J.G. Halpin, Postmaster

Halpin, J.F., general store
Lials, M.D., physician (Should be Liles)
Smith, J.M., flour mill and gin
Tipham, T.N., flour mill and gin

OMAHA. A milling point, 12 miles east of Wedowee, the county seat and 24 from Carrollton, Ga., the shipping point. Mail tri-weekly. E.E. Ballard, Postmaster

Green, A.J., grist mill and gin
Green, Thomas, grist mill and gin
Gill, L.E., saw and grist mill
Hester, H.E., grist mill and gin
Moore, Henry, saw mill and gin.

ROANOKE. A village, five miles south of Wedowee, the seat of justice, and 25 from West Point, Ga., the shipping station. Roanoke has a weekly newspaper. Population 350. Mail daily. M.J. Mickle, Postmaster.

Amos, A.J., grist mill and blacksmith
Amos & Davis, blacksmiths
Arnett, J.T., grist mill
Barron, J.F., boots and shoes

Barron, Mrs. J.F., milliner
Davis, A.J., physician
Dishasoon, H.B., physician   (should be Disharoon)
Ford, B.H., tanner
Hill, Hardy and Co., general store
Manly and Handly, general store
Mickle, E.P., general store
Mickle, M.J., justice
Pate, T.F., grist mill
Pearson, W., barber
Rowland, R.G., furniture
Taylor, J.L.B. and Co., general store
Waller, Amos F., grist mill and lumber manufacturer
White, W.A., dentist
White, W.E., physician
White and Awbrey, general store

ROCKDALE. Simply a rural postoffice, 6 miles northwest of Wedowee Court House. Ship by Heflin, and bank at Talladega. Population 15. Mail, daily. E.M. Perryman, Postmaster.

Ashcraft, R.C.A., flour mill
Bell, J.M., boot and shoemaker
Crumley, G.W., boot and shoemaker
Edmonds, I.M., boot and shoemaker
Gibbs, W.C., flour mill
Kidd, J.M., carriage and wagonmaker
Kitchen, _____, flour mill
Perryman, D.A., justice
Perryman, E.M., postmaster
Poole, J.J., constable
Poole, J.J. and W.C., carriage and wagonmaker and blacksmith
Smith, J.M., flour mill
Wright, J.R., justice

ROCKMILLS. A small village, within 2 miles of the Georgia line and 20 southeast of Wedowee, the county seat and 24 from West Point, Ga., the shipping and banking point. Population, 400. Mail, daily. Mrs. F.C. Andrews, Postmaster.

Allison, William, general store
Andrews, Mrs. F.C., millinery and drugs
Arnott, J.F., flour mill
Atkinson, N.L., flour mill
Baker, C.A., general store
Baker, C.N., justice
Bowden, W.D., lumber manufacturer
Boyd, F.M., pottery
Bradshaw, Mrs. C., flour mill
Breed, R.J., boot and shoemaker
Darden, W.C., flour mill
Davis, S.J., physician
Harper and Wyatt, general store
Heally, T.T., lumber manufacturer
Hearn, J.J., justice and boot and shoemaker
Hunter, J.D., boot and shoemaker
Lawrence, S.C., fruit agent
McClendon, E.H., physician
Pittman, W.W., general store
Randall, F.P., flour mill
Sharman, J.C. and W.R., flour mill and cotton gin
Stevens, M.S., lawyer
Stevens, Mrs. W., flour and grist mill

Taylor, C.B., physician and justice
Taylor, W.M. and Co., notaries, justices and express agents
Trent, P.G., Jr., physician
Turner, J.C., blacksmith
Wehadka Mfg. Co., cotton and grist mill

SEWELL. A rural postoffice, 12 miles northeast of Wedowee the county seat. Mail semi-weekly.

WEDOWEE. County seat situated 40 miles east of Talladega, and about the same distance north of Buffalo. Ship to Heflin, 30 miles distant. Bank at Anniston. Population 278. Mail, daily. John T. Owens, Postmaster.

Colwell, William, general store
Dobson, W.W., general store and grist mill
Gaunt, E.T., physician
Gibbs, William, druggist
Gibbs, W.C., grist mill and cotton gin
Heflin, Wyatt, physician
Huckaba, H.H. and Co., general store
Morgan, R.M., justice
Owens, Mrs. F.E., hotel
Owens, John T., drugs, grocery and sewing machines
Pate, R.S., lawyer
Prescott, C.A. and Sons, general store
Smith, R.L. and Co., general store
Smith, and Smith, lawyers
Taylor, Peter, blacksmith
Wedowee Observer, O.H. Perryman, publisher

WEHADKEE. A farmers postoffice, 7 miles southeast of Wedowee, the county seat. Ship by LaGrange, Ga. Mail, tri-weekly. A.J. Pittman, Postmaster and general store.

WILDWOOD. Only a discontinued rural office. Mail to Stone Hill.

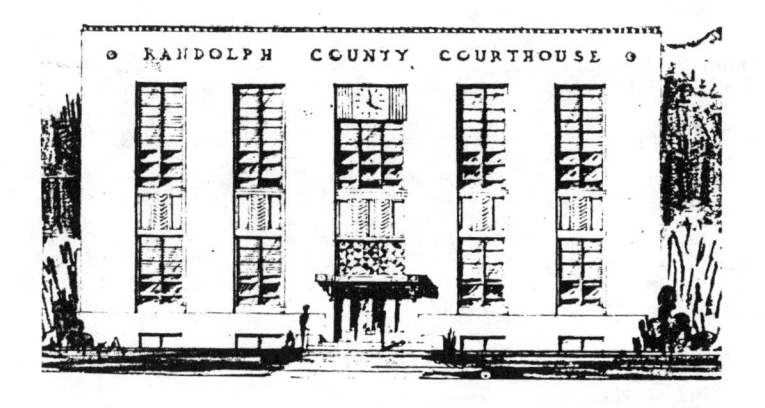

Randolph County Courthouse. Courtesy of the Birmingham Public Library. Undated article. 1940/41.

PROBATE NOTICES FROM
THE JACKSONVILLE REPUBLICAN

There being no newspapers in Randolph County at this time, many of the probate notices were placed in The Jacksonville Republican in Benton (now Calhoun) County.

24 February 1841

Sylvanus Walker, Sheriff, will sell from the Court House door in the town of McDonald (now Wedowee) all the interest claimed in lost 110,111 and 48 of Jefferson Faulkner in order to satisfy an execution in favor of Moore Bazemore.

In order to satisfy executions - one in favor of Ware and Co. for the use of Marcus A. Mills, another in favor of Robert Benton and another in favor of Thomas Smith, Sylvanus Walker, Sheriff of Randolph Co. will sell to the highest bidder from the door of the Court House in McDonald all the interest of Jefferson Faulkner in certain named property.

3 March 1841

Sylvanus Walker, Sheriff by J.T. Morrison, Deputy Sheriff, by virtue of 2 Fi.Fas., one in favor of James A. Williams and one from the Circuit Court for costs, certain property of Thomas Ables will be sold at the Court House door in McDonald to satisfy claims.

All the interests claimed by Matthewson Putnam in property located in Sec. 6 Township 17 Range 11E will be sold by the Sheriff to satisfy a Fi. Fa. of Terry Riddle.

Certain named property belonging to Carter Wells will be sold at the Court House door to satisfy an execution in favor of John A. Hunter.

Eli C. Joiner and Samuel H. Likes are copartners in the practice of law. Office on the northeast corner of the public square in the Town of McDonald, Randolph County.

10 March 1841

Certain lots in the possession of Zachariah Reynolds are to be sold to satisfy an execution in favor of T. and W. Dothard.

Taken up and posted by Fielding Beecher, one sorrel horse, one white hind foot (the right), white in the forehead and small white spot on his nose. Appraised to $65 before William Ford and James Allen. William M. Buchanan, Clerk.

Advertisement. Seaborn Williams, Attorney at Law, McDonald.

14 April 1841

ADMINISTRATOR'S NOTICE. Letters of Administration on the Estate of Laughlin McIntosh, deceased, have been granted to Elija Muckelroy who requested all claims against the estate to be submitted in the time prescribed by law.

Certain named lots belonging to Matisin Putman will be sold at the Court House door in McDonald to satisfy an execution in favor of J.T. Neely.

Property belonging to Michael Dowdy will be auctioned to the highest bidder from the Court House to satisfy an execution in favor of James F. White.

Deed of Trust. Samuel _____ (paper torn), trustee of Jefferson Falkener, will sell for cash at the Court House door in McDonald, Bartlett, a negro man about 45, _____, 35, Dorcas, a girl about ___teen years and Mary, a girl eighteen years.

13 April 1842

Sylvanus Walker by R. Caskey, Deputy Sheriff, will sell land of Cager Miller, listed as property of Cager Miller & Co., to satisfy executions in favor of Ledger Horton and Co. and Sanford Greenwood and Co.

20 April 1842

At an execution of the Morgan County Sheriff, land belonging to F.F. Adarine will be sold from the Court House door in McDonald to satisfy an execution of the Bank of the State of Alabama at Decatur. The land lies in Benton, Randolph and Talladega Counties as certified by Thomas and John Goodin, Andrew Turnipseed and C.A. Green. (About 30 pieces of land were listed.)

1 June 1842

Named property belonging to Jesse Johnson will be sold by the sheriff by his Deputy Sheriff, J.T. Morrison, to satisfy an execution of John Lattemore.

J.T. Morrison will sell at public auction from the Court House door in McDonald certain property belonging to Gabriel Ingram to satisfy an execution of James Greer.

Named property of James W. Allen will be sold at public outcry to satisfy executions from the Circuit and County Courts.

The Sheriff of Randolph County will sell certain property of Samuel Carpenter to satisfy an execution of Ira Culbreath, and a second one in favor of A. Finley.

In order to satisfy sundry judgments, property of George McKaskell will be sold, with proceeds going to William Crompton, Joseph C. Beard, John H. Porter, Francis Derrett, Henry Amarine and James Dowdy.

8 January 1842

Orphans Court of May 10, 1842. William W. Wood v. Prosser L. Clements and Thomas B. Wafer, Administrators of Estate of William Clements. Action to compel Clements and Wafer, to make title to land at the mouth of Crooked Creek. William M. Buchanan, Register.

17 August 1842

Coroner's Sale. By virtue of fi. fa. of Circuit Court property of Robert Livrett will be sold at McDonald Court House to satisfy execution in favor of the Branch of Bank of State of Alabama in Montgomery.

28 September 1842

The co-partnership between Jefferson Falkner, Joseph Benton and Francis M. Perryman in the practice of law is this day dissolved. Jefferson Falkner and the undersigned will continue their joint services. Joseph Benton. 9/15/1842.

12 October 1842

Letters of Administration were granted to Absalom Castles on the Estate of Henry Castles, deceased, on 10/4/1842. He made a call for claims within the time limits of the law.

14 June 1843

A sale will be made at public outcry in McDonald of property of Daniel Hopkins to satisfy executions in favor of S.J. Dukes, Robert Black, Ira Culbreath and J.B. Willingham.

Property of Howard M. and Simeon Putman will be sold from the Court House door to satisfy executions of John B. Armstrong, and Daniel Barnwell.

Certain property belonging to N. Hanners will be sold at public auction from the Court House door in McDonald to satisfy an execution in favor of William Price.

All the interest in certain land belonging to John D. Bowen to be sold at the Court House door to settle a claim by R.R. Singleton, Daniel Hopkins, James Howlin and John S. Taylor.

Property of Jiles J. Adams to be sold at public auction to satisfy 2 fi. fas. in favor of Charles Philips.

William Parker's interest in certain land to be sold to satisfy execution in favor of Bowen and Williams for use of Jacob Peeler.

Property of James S. Porter to be sold to satisfy execution in favor of John Miller, and one in favor of Martin and Foster.

One sorrel mare has been taken up by David E. Gresham, about 8 or 9 years old, 14 hands high, one hind foot white, blaze in face, some collar marks, appraised at $30.

Taken up by Albert McBurnett who lives on little Tallapoosa, 4 miles from McDonald, one sorrel horse about 7 or 8 years old, 13 or 14 hands high.

9 August 1843

Frances Ray, Administratrix of the Estate of A.T. Ray, deceased, has set the first Monday in November as the date for final settlement of the Estate in McDonald. John D. Bowen, Jr. Co. Clk.

13 September 1843

Property of Henry H. Porter will be sold at public auction

to the highest bidder from the Court House door to satisfy fi.fa. of E.L. Woodward.

20 September 1843

Absalom Cassells, Administrator of the Estate of Henry Cassels, deceased, made application for sale of property both real & personal for equal distribution to be heirs of the Estate.

11 October 1843

Letters of Administration were granted to James Burden on the Estate of Stephen Treadwell, deceased, on Aug. 21th. A call was made for settlement of all claims against the estate.

7 February 1844

Letters of Administration were granted to Henry W. Armstrong on the Estate of James Smith, deceased. He made a call for claims against the Estate.

Joseph C. Baird and Andrew N. Baird, Administrators of the Estate of Matthew Marable, filed accounts current and vouchers for final settlement. Charles W. Statham, County Clerk.

14 February 1844

Letters of Administration were granted to Samuel Carpenter, Sheriff, on the goods, chattels, rights and credits of John Dobson, deceased on 2/1/1844, and made a call for claims against the Estate and all bills to be paid.

6 March 1844

BANKRUPTCY SALE. On March 18th next in Wedowee, a large lot of notes, accounts, bonds, judgments, etc. to be surrendered in bankruptcy by Francis M. Perryman, Wiley Martin McClendon, Euclidus Longshore, James Akens, Zechariah Holloway, William Williams, Samuel B. McClure, Samuel S. McQuorter, Samuel Wells, Levi R. Lawler, Alvis Q. Nicks and Joel T. Morrison.

10 April 1844

Ketrel F. Daniel of Fish Head Valley has taken up a bright bay mare, 3 white feet, small spot on forehead and snip on the nose, full 15 hands high, appraised to $30.

8 May 1844

William H. Cunningham has taken up a bright bay mare, 4 years, all feet white, few saddle marks on back, appraised to $70.

22 May 1844

Taken up by Washington Billingsley, one sorrel horse, 4 years old, small star on forehead, no brands, appraised to $30.

5 June 1844

Taken up and posted by Francis M. Perryman, one brown filly, 2 years, 13 hands, some white hairs on forehead. Appraised to $20.

17 July 1844

Taken up by Prosser L. Clements, one bay mare, 8 yrs., no marks or brands, appraised at $35.

19 November 1845

Circuit Court of Randolph County to sell lots 24 and 33 in the town of Arbacoochy, property of Isaac Payne, to satisfy execution of John Huey. William P. Newell, Sheriff.

Letters of Administration were granted to Elkanah Wilkinson on Estate of Shadrach Wilkinson, deceased, on 10/22/1845.

25 February 1846

All interest of Lawson C. McKee in named property to be sold in Wedowee for Samuel Carpenter, Sheriff and Administrator of Estate of John Dobson, deceased. William Falkner, Coroner.

4 March 1846

Shadrick Kite has taken up a black mare pony inclined to be a little rone about the head and neck, 15 or 16 years old, rooch main and swab tail. Appraised at $6.

11 March 1846

Mary Thompson was qualified on February 29th in Orphans Court as Executor of the Last Will & Testament of Parish Thompson, dec. She requested claims on the Estate to be filed in time limits of the law.

WEDOWEE HOTEL. William Owens informs the public that he has taken charge of the Wedowee Hotel where he will be prepared to entertain travelers at exceedingly low prices, etc.

29 April 1846

Letters of Administration were granted to Oliver W. Cox on the Estate of John P.C. Pettit, late of Randolph Co. on April 8.

William Reeves has taken up a gray horse 6 or 7 years, 4' 9" or 10", no brands, appraised at $20.

William P. Newell, Administrator of Estate of John Dobson, deceased, has declared the estate insolvent.

16 September 1846

Letters of Administration were granted to William P. Newell, Sheriff, on the Estate of Hugh Harcrow, deceased, on 7/23/46. He made a call for claims against the estate.

Letters of Administration were granted to William P. Newell on the Estate of Jacob Peeler on August 19th.

Lambird Linville, administrator of Estate of Worly Linville, deceased, stated Worly died intestate and the land cannot be divided equally among his heirs and that Daniel B. and William Linville (both of full age and reside in Kentucky); Elizabeth Jackson, late Elizabeth Linville; Elender Cassels, late Elender Linville; both of full age and residents of Georgia; Rebecca Philips, late Rebecca Linville, wife of Wilkins Philips, of full age and residing in Miss. It is ordered that notice be issued to Merriam Linville and Mark Cassels to appear in Court in October.

By virtue of fi. fa. of Circuit Court levied on property of Jonathan McCollum, said property to be sold to satisfy execution of Hurst, Cox & Co.

One negro woman about 26 years, to be sold as property of William Fannin in a case in favor of A. Adcock, Guardian etc.

One-fourth part of a certain gold mill on Crooked Creek, known as the Gold Mill of Williams, Walkers, Likins and Hammonds and levied on as property of William Williams to be sold to settle execution in favor of D.M. Connaly and in favor of J.T. Henry.

Property of Charles Wood to be sold in Randolph County to settle execution in favor of Joel King, Exec., etc.

28 October 1846

Sarah Miller, widow of Eli Miller, deceased, gives notice she will make application for her dower in December 1846.

James McPherson, James Prothro, James Hathorn, David E. Gresham and John Harrist v. Byers, Phonick & Co. for the use of Charles W. Statham. In Chancery Court 9/16/46. Complaintant by his solicitor, James W. Guinn, moved for order of publication as to Henry J. Byers, of age 21 and residing in Panada Co., Ms. for him to answer, plead or demur within 60 days. William H. Cunningham, Register

25 November 1846

William P. Newell, Administrator of Estate of Hugh Harcrow, deceased, named the following heirs: Children: James, Mary and David Harcrow; Rachael Johnson, wife of Peter; Peggy Gilbert, wife of Simon, all of Randolph County and of lawful age; Samuel and Hugh Harcrow, residents of Georgia and Jane Harcrow, residence unknown, all of legal age.

Thomas B. Wafer and P.L. Clements, Administrators of Estate of William Clements, deceased, name the following heirs: Joseph Harkins, for wife; Ephraim Carpenter for wife, James M. Clements, Benjamin A. Clements; Jesse M. Clements; James Smith for wife; Thomas B. Wafer for wife; William Cosper for wife; John Pinckard for wife; John M. Dorris for wife; Winfred Clements, widow of William Clements. All of full age and residents of Chambers and Randolph Counties with the exception of John M. Dorris, resident of Georgia. Hearing set for December Term.

7 December 1847

Property of the Estate of Lewis Freeland to be sold at the Court House door at public auction on December 31, 1847.

18 April 1848

Tax Collector's Sale. Land on Guss Creek adjoining lands of Robert L. Levritt and William Henry, owner unknown, to be sold for taxes for 1847 on June 26th. Elijah Humphries, T.C.

Lands on Chulafinne Creek adjoining coal lands and lands of

John Campbell and M.H. Wadsworth, owner of lands unknown.

Land to be sold adjoining lands of T.A. Cantrell and Joshua Spears, deceased, owner unknown.

Lands located on the waters of Guss Creek adjoining public lands and lands of M.J. Ussery, owner of said land unknown.

Randolph County Sheriff Sales - Property of Joel Falkner to be sold at public auction to satisfy an execution in favor of the Branch Bank of Alabama in Montgomery.

Property of Jefferson Falkner to be sold from the Court House door to satisfy execution in favor of Richard Nolen.

Property belonging to John L. Burk to be sold at public auction to satisfy an execution in favor of William Hightower.

Mary E. Vance, daughter of Marcus D. and Matilda Ann Vance, died of pneumonia on March 27th near Greensport, aged 24.

8 May 1849

Randolph Sheriff's Sale. Property of William Hightower located in Wedowee to be sold by A.P. Hunter, Sheriff.

James M. Mickle, Executor of Last Will & Testament of William Fannin, deceased, petitioned the Court for permission to sell land in the Estate for equal distribution to the heirs which include children and grand-children of Fannin as follows: William M. Fannin and John M. Fannin of Randolph County; E. Kimbel, wife of Peter Kimbel of Newton County, GA; Sara Hopkins, wife of Daniel of Arkansas; Nancy Brown, wife of Christopher Brown of Herd County, GA; Mary McGowan, wife of Mr. McGowan, she of Randolph County and his residence unknown; James C. Fannin of Lawrence Co. Miss; Joseph P. Fannin of Troup Co., GA, all over 21 years of age and the following grandchildren, to wit: Sarah Darden, wife of George Darden, daughter of Annis House, formerly Annis Fannin; and also Nancy, Amanda and Emeline House under age 21 years and residents of Texas for whom Charles W. Statham is appointed guardian. Notice hereby given the case will be heard in June.

15 May 1849.

Orphans' Court of Randolph County. Almond P. Hunter, Sheriff and administrator of the Estate of John Murphy, declared the Estate insolvent.

19 June 1849

Property in Arbachooche belonging to M.M. Beget (?) to be sold by A.P. Hunter, Sheriff, to satisfy an execution in favor of James E. Alexander.

27 November 1849

Frederick Ross, administrator of the Estate of Andrew Burnham, deceased, declared the estate of his intestate to be insolvent.

24 September 1850

Isaac William, Administrator of the Estate of John S. Hays,

filed accounts current and vouchers for final settlement.

Almond P. Hunter, Administrator of the Estate of John Murphy deceased, filed accounts current and vouchers for final settlement.

21 January 1851

Andrew J. Hall, Administrator of the Estate of Thomas Moon, deceased, filed notice for all persons interested in the Estate to appear in Court on the third Monday in January.

Amos Willingham filed a Petition to Compel Worley D. Linville, Administrator of Estate of Worley Linville, to convey land to him which Worley had given him bond to before he died.

Frederick Ross, Administrator of the Estate of Andrew Burnham, deceased, posted his notice for settlement of all outstanding claims against the Estate.

Property belonging to John S. Heard to be sold at public auction from the Court House door to settle claim in favor of H. and O. Warren. This property consists of one negro girl, by name of Charity, 8 or 9 years old.

Property of Gorden (?) and McKee to be sold by the Sheriff, J.T. Morrison, in settlement of an execution in favor of Mariland Risley & Co.

Joel T. Morrison, guardian, will sell certain named real estate belonging to the children and heirs at law of Sturdy Garrendeed.

1 April 1851

Robert S. Wood, by his attorney Hugh Montgomery filed a Petition to Compel William Wood, administrator of James M. Twilley, deceased, to convey title to certain property to him.

William C. Kennedy, Administrator of the Estate of John W. Striplin, deceased, filed accounts current and vouchers for annual settlement.

9 March 1852

Andrew J. Hall, Administrator of the Estate of Thomas Moon, deceased, filed accounts current and vouchers for final settlement.

27 April 1852

David V. Crider, Administrator of Estate of John R. Armstrong, deceased, requested all claims against the estate to be presented in the time limits of the law.

Joel T. Morrison, Sheriff, will sell certain property of J. C. Maberry to satisfy an execution in favor of James W. Guinn.

Samuel B. Landrum, Constable, will sell to the highest bidder a negro boy, John Henry, about 8 yrs., levied on as property of Peachy Bledsoe to satisfy an execution in favor of George W. Key for the use of J.J. Jackson.

18 May 1852

    Joel T. Morrison, Sheriff, will auction to the highest bidder certain property of Hansell Hunt to satisfy a fi.fa. in favor of Benjamin Hunt, assignee.

1 June 1852

    Letters of Administration were granted to Henry H. Gazaway on the Estate of Jesse Gazaway, deceased. He made a call for the settlement of all claims against the estate.

3 August 1852.

    Joel T. Morrison, by his Deputy, Wilson Falkner, will sell at public auction certain property levied on belonging to Angus McDonald to satisfy a fi. fa. in favor of William Buchanan

28 September 1852

    Sheriff's Sale. Certain property of William Cormack will be sold to the highest bidder from the Court House door to satisfy a fi. fa. from the Circuit Court in favor of Edmond Salter, and also property of William Hightower in favor of the Branch of the Bank of the State of Alabama in Montgomery against William Hightower and others.

9 November 1852

    J.T. Morrison, Sheriff, by virtue of two Venditioni Exponas from Randolph Circuit Court to auction property of J.M. Hearn to satisfy 2 exponas in favor of Thomas Stricklin, one for the use of James Price and the other for the use of J.H. Baven. Also to be sold is property of James Bell to satisfy an execution in favor of James W. Guinn.

16 November 1852

    Joel T. Morrison to sell certain property of Jethro Baker to satisfy a fi. fa. in favor of John H. Edmondson for the use of John T. Heflin.

    J.T. Morrison to sell property of David P. Perryman to satisfy an execution in favor of Thomas T. Lunday.

1850 MORTALITY SCHEDULE
RANDOLPH COUNTY

NAME	AGE	SEX	COL.	FREE/ SLAVE	BORN	MONTH DIED	CAUSE OF DEATH	DAYS SICK
Martha Thomason	11	F	W	F	Ala.	Apr.	Bil. fever	32
Augustus Hunter	4	M	W	F	Ala.	Feb.	Bold hives	5
Elizabeth Park	9	F	W	F	Ga.	Aug.	Chills	10
Moses Park	9/12	M	W	F	Ala.	Oct.	Chills	7
Augustus Griffin	2/12	M	W	F	Ala.	Sept.	Unknown	21
Burrell Bales Married, Farmer	75	M	W	F	SC	Aug.	Unknown	365
Mary Ware Widowed	75	F	W	F	SC	July	Unknown	21
Jack	3/12	M	B	S	Ala.	Dec.	Unknown	1
Elijah Nunn Married	72	M	W	F	SC	June	Liver compl.	365
Ann	55	F	B	S	Ga.	Apr.	Colick	3
Thomas J. Bowers	13	M	W	F	Ga.	Jan.	Calculas	13
William McNeal Married	75	M	W	F	Ga.	May	Diarrhoea	17
William Laning	1/12	M	W	F	Ala.	Sept.	Unknown	1
Hudson Garner	3	M	W	F	Ala.	Sept.	Unknown	3
Benjamin Flinn	3	M	W	F	Ala.	July	Unknown	
Thomas S. Crider	4/12	M	W	F	Ala.	Apr.	Pneumonia	14
Nancy Knight	65	F	W	F	NC	June	Unknown	150
James W. McClure	2/12	M	W	F	Ala.	Nov.	Fever	30
Jacob J. Greene	9/12	M	W	F	Ala.	Aug.	Diarrhoea	42
Sopha Phillips Married	36	F	W	F	Ga.	Aug.	P. Fever	14
Temperance Abele Married	30	F	W	F	Tenn.	Sept.	Childbed	1
Sarah Snow Widowed	95	F	W	F	Va.	Nov.	Unknown	30
J.M. Coghren	1/12	M	W	F	Ala.	Mch.	Croup	3
- - -McCullars	1d	M	W	F	Ala.	Mch.	Unknown	1
- - -McCullars	1d	M	W	F	Ala.	Mch.	Unknown	1
Rebecca Riddle Married	35	F	W	F	SC	May	Scrofula	3mos.
Nancy Shockly	24	F	W	F	TN	Sept.	Fever	7
Jonathan Jones Married	35	M	W	F	GA	Mch.	Diarrhoea	14
Elizabeth McDonald Married	79	F	W	F	SC	Apr.	Dropsy	20

Elizabeth Ivins Married	47	F	W	F	GA	Feb.	Inflamation	1
William Stewart	1	M	W	F	Ala.	Aug.	Unknown	10
Ann Rogers	12	F	W	F	NC	June	Inflamation	21
---Osborn	6/12	M	W	F	Ala.	Dec.	Unknown	6
Benjamin Otwell	1	M	W	F	Ala.	Aug.	Croup	3
John McElroy	1	M	W	F	Ala.	Aug.	Unknown	7
Thomas Moore Farmer	69	M	W	F	GA	Apr.	Consumption	365
George W. Jones	3	M	W	F	GA	Nov.	Burn	2
Ransom Knowles	1	M	W	F	Ala.	Dec.	Pneumonia	11
Nancy Cumming Married	45	F	W	F	NC	Apr.	Pneumonia	10
William West	6/12	M	W	F	Ala.	Dec.	Pulmonary Aff.	30
Sally	4	F	B	S	Ala.	Dec.	Poison	160
Mary McConnell	9	F	W	F	GA	May	Pleursy	40
Isaiah Herren Married, Farmer	60	M	W	F	SC	Sept.	Consumption	200
N.A. Coffee	3/12	M	W	F	Ala.	Sept.	Croup	7
Mary Spears	19	F	W	F	GA	Sept.	Consumption	34
Catharine Ashcraft	63	F	W	F	VA	Sept.	Dropsy	300
Elizabeth Lee Married	52	F	W	F	SC	Oct.	Bronchitis	120
B.S. Todd	8/12	M	W	F	Ala.	Nov.	Hives	8
James Laintait Married, Farmer	60	M	W	F	VA	Feb.	Consumption	38
Margarett J. Farris	7	F	W	F	Ala.	Jan.	Fever	14
Matilda Long	1	F	W	F	Ala.	Dec.	Croup	5
Mary A. Carter	3/12	F	W	F	Ala.	July	Diarrhoea	7
Mary	5	F	B	S	GA	Nov.	Brain fever	21
Mary Hammonds Married	35	F	W	F	GA	June	Dropsy	30
Mary E. Young	3	F	W	F	Ala.	June	Burn	1
Lettitia Huff Married	45	F	W	F	SC	Dec.	Consumption	300
Henry Wood	1/12	M	W	F	Ala.	Nov.	Unknown	20
Alfred	8/12	M	B	S	Ala.	May	Croup	3
Lucinda Gilleland	12	F	W	F	Ala.	June	Pleurisy	1
William German Married, Farmer	70	M	W	F	SC	Jan.	Pleurisy	7
Elizabeth Striplin Married	55	F	W	F	SC	July	Cancer	250
John H. Lance Married, Blacksmith	32	M	W	F	SC	Jan.	Pleurisy	3

David A. Perryman, Ass't Marshall
F.M. Perryman, Ass't Marshall

RANDOLPH COUNTY
POSTOFFICES AND POSTMASTERS

This information was obtained from Alabama Postal History, compiled by J.H. Scruggs, Jr. and is used with the permission of the Department of Archives and Manuscripts in Birmingham Public Library.

1845

POSTOFFICES	POSTMASTERS
Arbacoochee	John Gooden to 3d September
Beaver Dam	William McKnight
Chulafinnee	Charles Rodahan
Eastville	George H. Cosper to 31st March and James
Lamar	Langston Coffee G. Cosper
Oakfusky	Archibald Sawyer
Roanoke	Wm. McClendon
Wedowee	Ira P. Culbreath
Weehadkee	Frederick W. Chandler

1851

Arbacoochee	James E. Alexander
Chulafinnee	E.P. Reeves
Eastville	J.G. Cosper
High Pine	S.A. McCash
Lamar	Elias B. Burgess
Lee's Ridge	James H. Lee
Louina	E.S. Barber
Molino	Sygmore Moore
Roanoke	W.M. McClendon
Rockdale	John G. White
Rock Mills	George Findley
Weedowee	John Reaves
Weehadkee	P.G. Trent
Wesobulga	James McArthur, 3 Q
	J.H. Edmonson, 1 Q
Winston	Allen Jenkins

1855

Almond	A.P. Hunter
Arbaconnehee	David Creamer
Chulatinner	Hardy Strickland
Eastville	J.G. Cosper
Ingram	J.C. Mitchell
Lamar	J.S. Pearson
Louina	E.S. Barber
Mellow Valley	W.H. Miller
Milner	Israel Putnam
Oakinhy	S.W. Riddle
Roanoke	Z.M. Hutchins
Rock Mills	N.B. Garrett
Wedowee	J.H. Rouse, 2 Q
	John O. D. Smith, 1 Q
	L.H.W. Guinn, 1 Q
Weehadkee	P.G. Trent, 3 Q
	Jacob Eichelberger, 1 Q
Wesobulga	Little Harris
Winston	Allen Jenkins

1859

Postoffices in Randolph County, Alabama.

Almond	Arbacoochee	Buchanon
County Line	Delta	Eastville
Fish Head	Gold Ridge	Haywood
Hebron	Ingram	Lamar
Louina	Mellow Valley	Milner
Molino	Oakfusky	Roanoke
Rockdale	Rock Mills	Warren
Weedowee	Wehadkee	Wesobulga
Winston		

PLANS UNDER WAY TO REPLACE BURNED COURTHOUSE

These pictures show the courthouse in smoldering ruins the morning of Aug. 24. The top view is a look through the front entrance down the hallway. The back stairs can be seen still standing. The white spots in the lower right corner of the right arch are flames. Sunlight streams in from above. The picture at the right shows the hollow top story and the tower where the clock once was.

Judge Maddox Brittain and the county commissioners are losing no time making plans for a new courthouse. Meanwhile the various county workers are trying to get accustomed to their new locations here and there in Wedowee.

Contractors are said to have been in Wedowee this week making estimates, and heads of the various departments have been asked to outline their needs in office space.

Plans, of course, cannot be definite at this time, Judge Brittain explained, but tentatively they call for using some of the old walls for the new structure, extending the new building toward the front, cutting down somewhat on the space for the court room, and adding several offices, thus accounting for an increase of about 25% in office space.

Courtesy of the Birmingham Public Library.

PROBATE NOTICES FROM
THE RANDOLPH TOILER

17 October 1895

Eucatan Owens, sister of J.T. and A.J. Owens died at the residence of A.J. on the 12th, aged 47 years. Her mother died only a few months ago.

Brother Guy Orr died at the home of his parents in Chambers County on Sept. 16th from typhoid fever. Was a member of the Baptist Church in Liberty.

31 October 1895

Mrs. Elizabeth Avery, 86, died on the 15th near Stroud in Chambers County. Joined the Primitive Baptist Church over 60 years ago.

A little child of John Morgan died last Friday and was buried Saturday at Levin's graveyard near Rockdale.

Dave Perryman of Heflin and Miss Kate Robertson of Oxford were married on Thursday of last week.

Ella Catherine Bartlett and Ethridge Jackson Garrison of Jackson, Ill. are to be married on Nov. 6th at the residence of her parents in Lineville, AL.

Mrs. George Burgess died last Saturday from dropsy of the heart near Rock Mills.

21 November 1895

Eva Johnson, wife of Billie Johnson, died a few days ago. She is survived by her husband and two little boys.

28 November 1895

Anderson Clemens of Fredonia, Chambers County, was found in a dying condition on the road near one of the several farms he owns on Corn House creek in Randolph County. It appears his horse ran away from the bruises on his body. He died Tuesday night. He was a brother-in-law of Robert Gay.

26 December 1895

Mrs. William Hill of Napoleon has died.

2 January 1896

Hoyt W. Enloe of Randolph County was married to Miss Ellen A. Mooty at the residence of the bride's father at Viola, GA on Dec. 29, 1895 by the Rev. A.S. Brannon.

Mr. T.J. Shelnutt, son of J.T. Shelnutt, and Miss A.M. Barton, daughter of J.C. Barton, were married in Peace, AL on Dec. 31, 1895 at the residence of T.P. Bailey by Rev. T.A. Camp.

16 January 1896

O.C. Waller was married to Miss M.O. Truitt at the residence of Mr. W.W. Dobson in Wedowee on Jan. 12th by P.D. Murphy, Esq.

Mr. O.B. Laney was married to Miss M.J. Pollard in Haywood last Thursday, January 9th, by the Rev. T.A. Camp.

23 January 1896

Mitchell Burns was married to Miss Ada Bradley on January 16th at the residence of the bride's father, 3 miles east of Wedowee by the Hon. A.J. Weathers

C.E. Seegar and Sudie Weathers were married on the 8th in Wehadkee.

Mr. A.H. Head was married to Miss Abbe Graham on the 12th by the Rev. I.N. Daniel in Wehadkee

6 February 1896

James Cummings who lived about 7 miles from town in the fork of the river, died of Typhoid Fever on Jan. 10th. Prior to his death his little son and a married daughter had died, and on Tuesday last, his son, Bailey, died of the same disease. Five others in the family had the disease but are now convalescent according to Mr. Swann who called to see them.

13 February 1896

Letters of Administration were granted to H.A. Tompkins on the Estate of Fred Rieke, deceased, by the Hon. A.J. Weathers, Judge of Probate Court. He requested all claims against the estate to be presented in the time allowed by law.

John Terrell filed notice to make final proof of claim to Homestead entry No. 25,166. His witnesses were Jesse Roe of Peavy,AL., John Houston, Irvin Pratt and Wash Terrell of Level Road, AL.

20 February 1896

Susan Evans, about 60 years, living alone 3 miles southwest of Wedowee, was most brutally murdered. Her body was found Monday by Anderson Moon, (col.) who reported the matter. Suspicion at once pointed to Ike and Len Clifton, two young brothers whose habitation is down on Corn House Creek, they having been heard to make threats against the old woman at different times.

27 February 1896

James Creed, about 60, was married to Mrs. M.E. Waters, about 50, in Graball on the 15th at the residence of his son, Sam Creed, by Esq. Bole.

5 March 1896

Susie Neal, wife of William Neal, and mother of Mrs. R.H. Ford of Wedowee, died at home in High Shoals, Sunday, March 1, after a long illness of heart disease, about 50 yrs. Was a Baptist.

13 March 1896

    H.W. Cofield was married to Miss Amsie Foster last Sunday by the Rev. T.M. Linley at Christiana.

27 March 1896

    Mrs. M.L. Wood, wife of Milton Wood, died at home near Potash on the 18th. She was a member of the Rocky Branch Church.

12 February 1897

    Joycey Anjaline Calhoun, daughter of Joe and Eliza Dennis, was born in Harris Co., GA on Dec. 19, 1839 and died Feb. 2, 1897 near Lamar, AL, aged 57 years, 1 month 13 days. Her father died Dec. 3, 1883 and her mother is still living and is 81 years old. She joined the M.E. Church South at age 15 and married Craven Jenkins Whitten 4/2/1857. He was killed at Gettysberg, Va. on 7/2/1863. They had two children, Joel H. Whitten, Esq. of Lamar and Josephine Craven wife of George W. Wilson of Randolph Co. She remarried March 28, 1865 to Mr. R. Calhoun of Cleburne Co. by whom she had three children, Josephus M., Elizzie T. and John W. Calhoun, all who are now married. She is survived by her mother, brother, five children and several grandchildren.

    Mrs. Nevada E. Beck, wife of Thomas Beck and daughter of G.W. and V.E. Lovvorn, 20 years, 3 months 7 days, died January 23, 1897. She was married on 2/23/1896, and is survived by a babe only one month 10 days old.

8 January 1897

    Dr. William H. Mitchell was born in Randolph Co. 7/27/1862; married 3/19/1889 to Miss Bessie Willoughly; graduated from Medical College of Augusta, Ga. 2/28/1891; and died 1/1/1897. He was buried in the Masonic Cemetery.

12 March 1897

    Isham T. Weathers died at his home in Roanoke on Wednesday after a lingering illness aged 85 years. He was born in Rutherford Co., N.C. 10/31/1811, and is survived by his wife, 9 sons and 3 daughters.

19 March 1897

    Catharine W. Earnest was born in Clark Co., GA 11/28/1818 and died 2/29/1896. She was the daughter of Elisha and Pricilla Earnest. At 18 she joined the Methodist Church in Merriweather Co. She lived several years with her only sister, Mrs. Rhoda Ann Evans. Funeral services were conducted by her uncle Gooden Adcock and Rev. Mr. Grant and burial was in Green's Chapel Cem.

26 March 1897

    Thomas E. Arnold was born in Randolph Co. 10/29/1861 and died 11/11/1896 at his home 2 miles north of Roanoke. He was the son of T.D. and H.A. Arnold. His father died when he was a small boy. At 24 he married Miss L.A. Weathers. He is survived by his wife and 4 children.

CIVIL WAR PENSIONERS
OF
RANDOLPH COUNTY, ALABAMA

According to a publication of the State of Alabama entitled "Laws for the Relief of Needy Confederate Soldiers and Sailors" which was printed in 1907, the following Articles were drawn up regulating pensions for Confederate States of America servicemen:

ARTICLE I

Pensions for Confederate Soldiers and Sailors, 1995-2037

1995. Special appropriation for needy Confederate soldiers and sailors.- - -The sum of four hundred thousand dollars is annually appropriated out of the treasury for the additional relief of needy Confederate soldiers and sailors who are resident citizens of the State of Alabama, and their widows.

1996. Soldiers and sailors who are entitled to pensions. - - -Any resident citizen of this state at the time of filing his application, who, while in the military or naval service of this state or the Confederate states, lost a leg or an arm, or the use thereof, or who, from wounds received while in such service, or who, from sickness or old age, or who is blind or deranged, and unable at the time to make a living by physical labor by reason of his permanent disability, and who did not desert the service of the Confederate States or the State of Alabama, and who does not now own property to the value of four hundred dollars, and whose salary or income does not exceed three hundred dollars per annum, shall be entitled to the provisions of this chapter.

1997. The widow of soldiers and sailors who are entitled to provisions.- - -The widow of any soldier or sailor of this State or of the Confederate States, who has not married since the death of such soldier or sailor, and whose husband did not desert the service of the State or of the Confederate States, and who was a resident citizen of the State on the first day of January, 1899, and who is a resident citizen of the State at the time of filing her application, and who does not own property to the value of four hundred dollars, shall also be entitled to relief under the provisions of this chapter, as hereinafter provided.

CIVIL WAR PENSIONERS
OF
RANDOLPH COUNTY, ALABAMA

This ledger containing records of the Civil War Pensioners from Randolph County is located in the Court House in Wedowee. The information provided is as follows: The name of the soldier and/or his widow providing he died prior to January 1899. Then is shown his rank, company and regiment, date and place of enlistment and the date and place of discharge, reason for applying for the pension, age at taking this action and the Post Office nearest his home. The last column in the ledger entitled "Remarks" often provided the date of death of the pensioner.

CERT. # PENSIONER AND DETAILS

CLASS I

12801   MARTIN DUKE, Pri, Co. B, 10 Rgt, enlisted 4/1/62 in Montgomery, discharged 5/1/65 in Hew Hope, Ga., was blind, aged 65, Rock Mills P.O. Remarks: Is now dead.

12802   JESSE HULSEY, Pri, Co. C, Rgt 2, enlisted 2/7/62, New Hope, Ga, discharged 7/1/64, New Hope, Ga., was blind, aged 72, Abner P.O. Remarks: Is now dead.

12803   J.H. PARMER, Pri, Co. B, 10 Rgt, enlisted 8/63 Chicamauga, Ga., discharged 8/65, Resacca, was blind, aged 76, Sewell P.O. Remarks. Died 3/15/1904.

CLASS II

12809   J.F. CAPEHART, Machinist, enlisted 8/1/61 in Auburn, discharged 3/1/62 in Richmond, Va., loss of right leg, aged 58, Louina P.O.

12808   T.T. KILGORE, Pri., Co. C, 63 Rgt., enlisted 12/62 in Atlanta, discharged 4/26/65, aged 72, Roanoke P.O.

CLASS III

12817   D. BUTLER. No other information given.

12815   J.B. HANNON, Pri, Co. I, enlisted 11/62, discharged 4/26/65 in Ga., was wounded, aged 67, Sewell P.O.

CLASS IV

12821   MARY ABNER, widow of LEVI ABNER, Pri, Co. H, 38 Rgt, He died 4/31/1865.

12824   Mrs. DILE ADAMS, widow of D.T. ADAMS, Pri, Co. I, 22 Rgt., he died 12/16/94.

12820   H.J. ANGLIN, Pri, Co. F, 14 Rgt., enlisted 7/28/61 in Hickory Flat, discharged 4/9/65, aged 65, West P.O.

12819   HARRIETT ARNOLD, widow of F.D. ARNOLD, Pri, Co. E, 17 Rgt, he died 4/7/1862.

12823   VETURA ARNOLD, widow of JAMES M. ARNOLD, Sgt., Co. G, 47 Rgt., he died in May 1864. Remarks: Widow now dead.

12822   NANCY E. AUSTIN, widow of WILLIAM A. AUSTIN, Pri, Co. A, 21 Rgt., he died 8/21/1864.

12828   M.E. BAILEY, widow of J.C. BAILEY, Pri, Co. G, 9 Ga., he died 9/28/1879.

12850   W.D. BALDWIN, Pri, Co. I, 49 Rgt., enlisted 2/62 in LaFayette, aged 72, Haywood, P.O. Remarks: now dead.

12827   SARAH A. BANKSON, widow of W.W. BANKSON, Pri. Co. F, 8 Ga. Rgt., he died 2/25/1863.

12834   S.E. BAREFIELD, widow of W.P. BAREFIELD, Pri., Co. I, 13 Rgt., he died 6/26/1862.

12836   MARTHA C. BARTON, widow of ENOCH BARTON, Pri., Co. E, 17 Rgt, he died 1/20/1896. Remarks, she moved out of the state.

12829   J.J. BASS, Pri, Co. E, 6 SC Rgt., enlisted 6/1/61 in Charleston, SC, discharged 7/63 in Va., was wounded, aged 73, Remarks: now dead.

12849   MANERVA BENEFIELD, widow of ROBERT BENEFIELD, Pri, Co. C, Bell's Bat., he died 2/15/1898. Remarks: widow now dead.

12837   MARY BENEFIELD, widow of W.H. BENEFIELD, Pri, Co. I, 2 Ga., he died 5/17/1886.

12840   NANCY BENNETT, widow of J. BENNETT, Pri, Co. K, 9 Rgt., he died 2/3/1886. Remarks, Widow now dead.

12826   Mrs. M.F. BEVERLY, widow of W.C. BEVERLY, Pri, Co. I, 13 Rgt, he died 11/29/1884.

12851   WASHINGTON BIBB, Pri, Co. I, 29 Tenn., enlisted 6/1861 in Blue Springs, discharged 4/26/1865, debility, aged 62, McCaville P.O.

12825   SUSAN BIRD, widow of JAMES M. BIRD, Corp., Co. A, 4 Ga. Rgt., he died 7/29/1862

12832   S.B. BISHOP, Pri, Co. A, 10 Rgt., enlisted 3/1862 in Fredonia, discharged Kingston, Tenn., aged 74, Rock Mills P.O.

12831   M.S. BLACK, Pri, Co. F, 6 Rgt., enlisted 5/10/61 in Montgomery, discharged 4/9/64, diseased, aged 66, Rock Mills, P.O. Remarks: now dead

12848   Mrs. S.A. BLAIR, widow of J.W. BLAIR, Pri, Co. E, 17 Rgt, he died Dec.1889.

12838   V.T. BONNER, Pvi, Co. K, 14 Rgt, enlisted 8/1/61, discharged 3/24/62 in Atlanta, wounded, aged 58, Wedowee P.O.

12833   J.H. BOYD, Pri, Co. K, 12 Rgt, enlisted 8/19/61 in Montgomery, discharged 4/5/65, aged 61, Rock Mills P.O.

12842   M.E. BRADEN, widow of R.E. BRADEN, Pri, Co. F, 22 Rgt., he died 10/22/1899

12847   RICHARD M. BREED, Pri, M.D. ROBERTSON's Home Guards, enlisted Pine Hill, discharged Apr. 1865, aged 79, Lofty P.O. Remarks: now dead.

12851   ISAAC BROWN, Pri, Co. F, 59 Rgt., enlisted 5/18/62 in Roanoke, discharged 7/7/65 in Petersburg, Va., wounded, aged 64.

12835   Mrs. J.A. BROWN, widow of H.H. BROWN, Pri, Co. F, 59 Rgt., he died 12/12/64.

12830   W.A.D. BROWN, Pri, Co. K, 38 Rgt., enlisted 10/61 in Ga., discharged 4/9/65 in Pa., wounded, age 70, Sewell P.O. Remarks: now dead.

12844   W.R. BROWN, Pri, Co. K, 3 Rgt, enlisted 9/3/63 in Griffin, discharged 4/18/65, age 74, Lofty P.O.

12839   Mrs. E.B. BRYAN, widow of G.W. BRYAN, Pri, Co. O, 9 MS Rgt, he died 2/3/1886. Remarks: widow now dead.

12852   Mrs. F.E. BRYANT, widow of THOMAS BRYANT, Pri, Co. F, 59 Rgt, he died 1/9/64. Remarks: Widow died 3/16/1905.

12843   G.M.S. BURDETT, Pri, Co. H, 47 Rgt, enlisted 4/18/62, discharged 4/9/65 in Cedar Run, Va., wounded, age 67.

12841   W.J. BURROUGHS, Pri, Co F, 25 Rgt, enlisted 10/18/61 in Talladega, discharged 4/26/65, rupture, age 68, Abner P.O.

12846   T.W. BURSON (Mrs.), widow of W.J. BURSON, Pri, Co. G, 7 Ga. Rgt., he died 4/16/1891.

12845   D. BUTLER, Pri, Co. G, 2 Rgt, enlisted 6/28/61 in Mc Donald, discharged 4/9/65 in Chancellorsville, Va., wounded, age 65, Newell P.O.

12863   L.A. CANADY, Pri, Co. F, 59 Rgt, enlisted 2/15/61 in Wedowee, discharged 4/20/65, age 69, Hopkins P.O., died 4/2/1905.

12859   B.M. CARTER, Pri, Co. D, 19 Rgt, enlisted 6/10/61 in Newnan, Ga., discharged 5/25/62, paralysis, age 62.

12851   J.I. CHILDERS, Pri, Co. H, 60 Ga. Rgt, enlisted 10/62, discharged 1865 in Chancellorsville, Va., wounded, age 57, Driver P.O. Remarks: dead.

12864   Mrs. M.A. CHILDS widow of S.W. CHILDS, Pri, Co. B, 37 Rgt, he died 5/12/1897.

12865   NANCY A. COFIELD, widow of C.V. COFIELD, Pri, Co. C, 22 Rgt, he died 1/22/1894.

12862   J.T. COLDWELL, Pri, Co. I, 3 Rgt, enlisted 5/10/62 in Columbus, Ga., discharged 8/10/63 in Perryville, Ky., wounded, age 58, Tolbert P.O. Remarks: dead.

12867   J.K. COLE, Pri, Co. K, 38 Rgt, enlisted 10/1862 in Mobile, discharged 4/26/65 in Resacca, Ga., wounded, age 56, Graham P.O. Remarks: gone to Texas.

12858   M.E. COLLINS, widow of J.A. COLLINS, Pri, Co. E, 16 Ga. Rgt., he died 1/10/1896.

12869   SARAH L. COLWELL, widow of W. COLWELL, Pri, Co. B, 8 Rgt., he died 9/10/1896.

12871   Mrs. C.M. COOK, widow of J.W. COOK, Pri, Co. A, 1 Ga. Rgt, he died 4/11/1891.

12860   SARAH COOPER, widow of H.G. COOPER, Pri, Co. K, 38 Rgt, he died Dec. 1862.

12857   WILLIAM COOPER, Pri, Co. I, 41 Ga. Rgt, enlisted 2/62 in Franklin, Ga., discharged 4/29/65 Perryville, Ky., age 79, Lamar P.O.

12861   M.V.B. CORLEY, Pri, Co. K, 14 Rgt, enlisted July 1861, discharged 4/9/65 in Salem Church, Va., age 58, Rock Mills P.O.

12873   W.R. COX, Pri, Co. I, 4 Ga. Rgt, enlisted 10/26/61 Newnan, Ga., discharged 5/11/64, rheumatism, age 73, Potash P.O. Remarks: died 2/17/1904.

12870   AMANDA CRAFT, widow of D. CRAFT, Pri, Co. G, 22 Rgt., he died 2/3/1885.

12855   Mrs. M.E. CREED, widow of J.B. CREED, Pri, Co. I, 8 Car Rgt, he died 1/21/1899.

12868   MARTHA C. CREWS, widow of ANDREW J. CREWS, Pri, Co. F 30 Rgt, he died 5/24/1880.

12872   W.P. CREWS, Pri, Co. F, 20 Rgt, enlisted 4/61 Marion, discharged 4/65 Resacca, Ga., debility, age 63.

12866   DISIE CRISWELL, widow of JAMES CRISWELL, Pri, Co. F, 14 Rgt, Remarks: died 10/10/69.

12856   Mrs. C.E. CROOK, widow of EMORY CROOK, Pri, Co. C, 14 Rgt, he died 9/24/1870.

12876   Mrs. S.R. DALRYMPLE, widow of J.W. DALRYMPLE, Pri, Co. E, 17 Rgt, he died 8/4/1863. Remarks: widow died June 1903.

12877   Mrs. E.C. DANIEL, widow of W.D. DANIEL, Pri, Co. B, 10 Rgt, he died 6/9/1877.

12875   R.M.C. DAUGHERTY, widow of J.S. DAUGHERTY, Pri, Co. I, 2 Ga. Rgt, he died 5/19/1895.

12881   ALBERT T. DAVIS, Pri, Co. G, 37 Rgt, enlisted 3/1862 in LaFayette, discharged 4/26/65, ill health, age 56, Louina P.O.

12879   J.F.M. DAVIS, Pri, Co. A, 22 Rgt, enlisted Dec. 1862 in Oxford, discharged 4/9/65, debility, age 74, Rockdale P.O.

12874   Mrs. M.E. DAVIS, widow of J.B. DAVIS, Pri, Co. K, 37 Rgt, he died 3/9/1870.

12878   Mrs. S.A. DUNCAN, widow of A.J. DUNCAN, Pri, Co. A, 31 Rgt., he died 10/6/1863.

12880   Mrs. A.G. DUNSON, widow of JAMES M. DUNSON, Pri, Co. B, 37 Rgt, he died 8/30/1883.

12883   T.J. EDMONDSON, Pri, Co. F, 25 Rgt, enlisted 1/5/63 in

Talladega, discharged 4/26/65 in Franklin, TN., age 59, Tolbert P.O.

12881   MARY ELEY, widow of WILLIAM ELEY, Pri, Co. G, 7 Ga. Rgt, he died 8/2/1896.

12884   H.T. ESTES, Pri, Co. C, Ferrell's Bat., enlisted 5/5/63 in Hickory Flat, discharged 4/26/65, defective sight, age 62, High Shoals. Remarks: he died 4/30/1905.

12887   J.T. FINCHER, Pri, Co. I, 8 Rgt, enlisted 1863 in Wedowee, discharged 4/26/65, age 73.

12888   W.V. FOSTER, Pri, Co. G, enlisted 5/64 in Wedowee, discharged 11/1864, age 86, Christiana P.O.

12886   Mrs. S.E. FREELAND, widow of J.M. FREELAND, Pri, Co.E, 41 Ga Rgt, he died 4/26/65.

12889   J.J. FREEMAN, Pri, Co. A, 59 Rgt, enlisted 6/62, discharged 4/26/65, weakness, age 62, Omaha P.O.

12885   Mrs. S.E. FRENCH, widow of W.J. FRENCH, Pri, Lt. Walthall Bat.

12891   W.D. GANN, Pri, Co. G, 30 Rgt, enlisted 3/19/62 in Talladega, discharged 4/9/65 in Vicksburg, MS, wounded, Delta P.O. Remarks: now dead.

12893   JOSEPH GATLIN, Pri, Co. K, 46 Regt, enlisted 5/4/64 in Dalton, Ga., discharged 4/9/65, rheumatism, Wedowee P.O.

12895   Mrs. S.A. GATLIN, widow of JNO. E. GATLIN, Pri, Co. K, 46 Rgt, he died 11/25/1862.

12899   E.L. GAUNTT, Corp., Co. E, 17 Rgt, enlisted 9/1861 in Montgomery, discharged 5/10/65 in Mobile, age 66, Rock Mills, P.O. Remarks: is now dead.

12891   F.G. GERMANY, Pri, Co. A, 10 Rgt, Enlisted in Fredonia, discharged 1862, lung trouble, age 63, Corn House P.O.

12890   J.M. GILLEY, Pri, Co. F, 7 Ga Rgt, enlisted 9/1862 in Calhoun, Ga., discharged 4/10/65 in Ft. Harrison, Va., rupture, age 64.

12898   E.O. GRAY, Sgt., Co. K, 46 Rgt, enlisted 4/1862 in Level Road, discharged 6/1865, age 63, Level Road P.O.

12897   Mrs. F.M. GRAY, widow of W.W. GRAY, Pri, Co. K, 46 Rgt, he died 8/30/64. Remarks: Widow now dead.

12892   H.R. GRAY, Pri, Co. K, 46 Rgt, enlisted 5/2/62 Loachapoaka, discharged 4/26/65, age 64, Wedowee P.O.

12896   C.V. GREEN, Pri, Co. K, 14 Rgt, enlisted 3/63, discharged 4/9/65 in Gettysburg, PA, wounded, age 71. Remarks: now dead.

12917   W.H. HADAWAY, Pri, Co. A, 14 Rgt, enlisted 4/1861, discharged 4/1865 in Gaines Mill, Va., wounds, age 58, Omaha P.O.

12900   Mrs. C.F. HALL, widow of WILLIAM J. HALL, Pri, 10 Rgt, he died 8/21/1862.

12921   SUSAN HANCOCK, widow of J. HANCOCK, Pri, Co. E, 14 Rgt, he died 9/7/1864.

12913   T.L. HARDY, Pri, Co. D, 14 Rgt, enlisted 2/18/62 in La Grange, Ga, discharged 11/22/64 in Bears Station, Va., wounds, age 59, Rock Mills, P.O.

12903   MARTHA HARMON, widow of J.B. HARMON, Pri, Co. B, 17 Rgt, died 2/12/1887.

12923   ELBERT HARRIS, Pri, Co. H, 31 Rgt, enlisted 4/1862, discharged in Ga. 4/26/65, disabled, age 56, Byron P.O.

12922   G.W. HARRIS, Pri, Co. B, 10 Rgt, enlisted 4/1862 in Lamar, discharged 4/9/1865, piles, age 63, Napoleon P.O.

12914   JNO. HARROD, Corp., Bells Bat, enlisted 8/1864 in Albany, discharged 1865, crippled, age 50, Lofty P.O.

12901   JASPER HARRY, Pri, Co. G, 31 Rgt, enlisted Oct. 1862, discharged 4/9/1865 in Va., wounds, age 62, Roanoke P.O.

12912   R. HEAD, Pri, Co. E, 17 Rgt, enlisted 9/9/61 in Roanoke, discharged 4/26/65 in Shiloh, TN, wounds, age 60, Rock Mills P.O.

12916   Mrs. B.A. HENDERSON, widow of J.A. HENDERSON, Pri, Co. D, 17 Rgt, died 8/19/1889.

12910   J.A. HENDON, Pri, Co. A, 10 Rgt, enlisted 3/1862 in Fredonia, discharged 4/26/65 in Ga., wounds, age 61, Napoleon P.O.

12908   JAMES HENDRIX, Pri, Co. C, 25 Rgt, enlisted Jan. 1862 in State hill, discharged 4/26/65, age 72, Lofty P.O.

12919   M.L. HENLEY, Pri, Co. I, 16 Rgt, enlisted 4/1861, discharged 4/1865 in Seven Pines, Va., age 60, Wildwood P.O.

12902   Mrs. L.T. HENRY, widow of W.T. HENRY, Pri, Co. A, 2 Rgt, he died 2/25/1890.

12905   ELIZA HESTER, widow of JAMES L. HESTER, Pri, Co. F, 59 Rgt, he died 1864.

12915   M.M. HESTER, Pri, Co. F, 59 Ala. Rgt, enlisted 2/1863 in Big Spring, discharged 4/9/65, age 77, Omaha P.O.

12925   J.J. HODGE, Pri, Co. H, Walthall's Bat., enlisted 1/66 in Talladega, discharged 4/26/65, aged 72, Almond P.O.

12920   WILLIAM HODGES, Pri, Co. E, 17 Rgt, enlisted 4/17/62 in Roanoke, discharged 4/20/65 in Franklin, TN, wounds, age 62.

12911   TABITHA HOLLIDAY, widow of DAVID HOLIDAY, Pri, Co. A, 10 Rgt, he died 3/12/1863.

12907   J.H. HOOD, Pri, Co. A, 2 Rgt, enlisted 7/1864, discharged 4/26/65, rheumatism, Omaha P.O.

12904   SUSAN HORNSBY, widow of JAMES M. HORNSBY, Pri, Co. E, 17 Rgt, he died 12/3/1862.

12918   Mrs. M.L. HORTON, widow of J. HORTON, Pri, Co. K, 46 Rgt, he died 8/1863. Remarks: widow died 7/10/1903.

12909   T.M. HUDDLESTON, Pri, Co. D, 17 Rgt, enlisted 9/1862 in Lamar, discharged 5/1865 in Resacca, Ga., wounds, age 68, Sewell P.O.

12924   J.A. HUNT, Pri, Co. F, 59 Rgt, enlisted 5/1862 in Montgomery, discharged 4/26/65, age 72, Almond P.O.

12906   Mrs. P.A. HURLEY, widow of J.A. HURLEY, Pri, d. 3/1/83.

12926   B.V. IVERSON, Pri, Co. K, enlisted 5/1862 in Eufaula, discharged 5/1865 in Tenn., age 63, Lofty P.O.

12927   CLORINDA JAMES, widow of JNO. JAMES, Pri, Co. I, 3 Rgt, he died 3/22/1866

12928   JOHN JINKS, Pri, Co. A, 59 Al Rgt, enlisted 4/1862, discharged 4/9/65 in Drury Bluff, Va., wounds, age 64, High Shoals P.O.

12929   ELIZABETH JONES, widow of FREELAND JONES, Pri, Co. C, 3 GA Inf., he died Oct. 1864.

12930   Mrs. S.A. KELLEY, widow of ROBERT KELLEY, Pri, Co. C, 14 AL Rgt, he died 2/19/1896. Remarks: Widow died 1904.

12932   MARTHA KERR, widow of _____ KERR, Pri, Co. F, 50 AL Rgt, he died 5/16/1864.

12937   R.A. KEY, widow of G.W. KEY, Pri, Co. K, 14 Rgt, he died July 1862.

12934   ELIZA KIDD, widow of MOSES KIDD, Pri, Co. G, 22 Ala. Rgt, he died 1/24/1864.

12935   JAMES A. KIDD, Pri, Co. B, 8 Rgt, enlisted Sept. 1861 in Columbus, KY, discharged 4/26/65 in Gettysburg, PA, wounds, age 68, Newell P.O.

12933   S.J. KIDD, Pri, Co. K, 46 Al Rgt, enlisted 5/1862, discharged 4/26/65 Dalton, Ga., wounds, age 69, Level Road P.O.

12940   Z.M. KIDD, Pri, Co. F, 25 Rgt, enlisted Nov. 1862, discharged 5/22/1865, piles, age 63, Christiana P.O.

12939   FRANCIS KIRKLAND, widow of JOSEPH KIRKLAND, Pri, Co. B, 39 Rgt, died 2/8/1898. Remarks: widow now dead.

12931   MARY KITTLE, widow of THOMAS KITTLE, Pri, Co. B, 10 Rgt, he died 3/18/1863. Remarks: widow died June 1902.

12938   SARAH KNIGHT, widow of M. KNIGHT, Pri, Co. F, 25 Rgt, he died 5/28/1888.

12936   Mrs. E.J. KNOTT, widow of C.C. KNOTT, Pri, Co. I, 44 Ala. Rgt, he died 10/18/1862.

12944   DANIEL LAMBERT, Pri, Co. I, 22 Rgt, enlisted 4/1863 in Talladega, discharged 4/26/65 in Jonesboro, Ga, age 73, Goldberg P.O.

12943   J.H. LANDERS, Pri, Co. I, 2 Rgt, enlisted 6/1863 in Kingston, discharged 4/26/65, age 54, Lofty P.O.

12941   JAMES M. LANDERS, Pri, Co. C, 26 Rgt, enlisted 9/1863 in Carrollton, Ga, discharged 4/2/65, age 73, Wildwood P.O.

12956   ARRA E. McCLENDON, widow of SIMPSON McCLENDON, Pri, Co. H, 32 Ga. Rgt,,he died 4/18/83.

12960   J.P. McCLAIN, Pri, Co. E, 13 Rgt, 1864-1865, old age, age 85. Remarks: he died 2/19/1905

12962   A.J. McCONNIEL , Pri, Co. F, 14 Rgt, enlisted 8/12/61, discharged 4/3/65 in Seven Pines, Va., wounds, age 60.

12952   W.I. McCORD, Pri, Co. G, 47 Rgt, enlisted May 1862, discharged Apr. 1865 in Chicamauga, Ga, spinal trouble, age 59, Stonehill P.O.

12958   J.H. McCULLOUGH, Pri, Co. F, 59 AL Rgt, enlisted 4/5/62 in Wedowee, discharged 4/9/65 in Drury's Bluff, Va., wounds, Cornhouse P. O.

12961   KATIE McELROY, widow of HENRY McELROY, Pri, Co. H, 7 Car Rgt, he died 4/1/1880.

12942   L.A.M. McLEROY, widow of THOMAS J. McLEROY, Pri, Co. E, 16 Ga Rgt, he died 3/1/1896.

12953   WILSON MILLS, Pri, Co. D, 10 Rgt, enlisted March 1862 in Victoria, discharged May 1865 in Ky., wounds, age 71, Hilton P.O.

12948   A.L. MITCHAM, Pri, Co. K, 13 Rgt, enlisted 7/28/61 in Montgomery, discharged 4/1865 in Fredricksburg, Va., wounds, age 60, Stonehill P.O.

12949   LOUISA MITCHEL, widow of K. MITCHELL, Pri, Co. E, 13 Rgt, he died 11/14/1898. Remarks: widow now dead.

12946   Mrs. M.C. MOBLEY, widow of W.G. MOBLEY, Pri, Co. K, 46 Rgt, he died 3/19/1865.

12957   PHILLIPS MOONEY, Pri, Craft Arty, enlisted 3/13/61 in West Point, Ga., discharged 9/14/1864, afflicted, age 75, Rock Mills P.O. Remarks: he died Feb. 1905.

12955   A.J. MOORE, Pri, Co. B, 10 Rgt, enlisted 8/1862 in Sweetwater, TN, discharged 5/5/1865 in Ga., wounds, age 58, Sewell P.O.

12950   A.J. MOORE, Pri, Co. B, 10 Rgt, enlisted 4/13/62 in Lamar, discharged 4/26/65 in Ky., rheumatism, age 56, Sewell P.O.

12951   H.R. MOORE, Pri, Co. H, 31 Rgt, enlisted 3/10/62, discharged 4/26/65 in Powder Springs, Ga., wounds, age 56.

12954   J.B. MOPP, Pri, Co. L, 17 Rgt, enlisted 6/1862 in Mobile, discharged 4/26/65 in Ga., wounds, age 74, Rock Mills P.O.

12945   Mrs. M.A. MORTON, widow of T.F. MORTON, Pri, Co. I, 9 MS Rgt, he died 7/22/1892. Remarks: widow now dead.

12956   SARAH A. MOSTELLER, widow of C.C. MOSTELLER, Pri, Co. C, 51 Rgt, he died 9/30/1867.

12947   Mrs. E.A. MULLOY, widow of J.M. MULLOY, Pri, Co. F, 59 Rgt, he died Sept. 1864.

12964   H. NAPIER, Sgt., Co. K, 1 FL Rgt, enlisted 1861, discharged 1865 in Shiloh, wounds, age 63, Wedowee P.O.

12968   CATHARINE NELSON, widow of GUY NELSON, Pri, Co. K, 14 Rgt, he died 2/28/1862.

12966   W.H. NESBET, Lt., Co. K, 34 Ga Rgt, enlisted 5/13/62 in Yellow Dirt, discharged 7/1/65 in Ga., wounds, age 60, Graham P.O. Remarks: moved to Ga.

12965   Mrs. M.B. NIX, widow of G.W. NIX, Pri, Co. H, 31 Rgt, he died 8/8/1864.

12963   SHAW NIXON, Pri, Co. E, 17 Rgt, enlisted 9/13/62, discharged 4/26/65 in Resacca, Ga., wounds, age 62, Roanoke P.O.

12967   ELIZABETH A. NOLAND, widow of WILLIAM NOLAND, Pri, Co. C, 25 Rgt, he died 9/23/1880.

12969   J.W. NOLEN, Pri, Co. C, 14 Rgt, enlisted Aug. 1861 in Auburn, discharged 4/9/65 in Va., wounds, Christiana P.O.

12971   Mrs. T.S. OGLETREE, widow of M. OGLETREE, Pri, Co. F, 3 Rgt, he died 1/29/65. Remarks: widow died 8/6/1904.

12972   SARAH OMERY, widow of THOMAS OMERY, Pri, Co. E, 56 Ga Rgt, he died 5/17/1903. Remarks, widow is now dead.

12970   H.F. OWEN, Pri, Artifice (?), Co. C (William Key arm of service), enlisted 5/7/62 in Griffin, Ga., discharged 4/26/65, breast disease, age 67, Wedowee P.O. Remarks: pensioner is dead.

12973   O.S. OWEN, Pri, Co. K 13 Rgt, enlisted 7/23/61 in Montgomery, discharged 4/9/65 in Wilderness, Va., diseased, age 56, Gay P.O.

12975   Mrs. A.E. PITTMAN, widow of J.W. PITTMAN, Pri, Co. E, 17 Rgt, died June 1864. Remarks: Mrs. A.E. PITTMAN is dead.

12974   MARY A. PITTMAN, widow of JNO. R. PITTMAN, Pri, Co. E, 1 Ark Rgt, died 5/1/1864.

12981   J.M. RAGSDALE, Pri, Co. C, enlisted 1862 in Tallassee, discharged July 1865, age 64, Newell P.O.

12977   J.R. RAY, Pri, Co. F, 59 Rgt, Enlisted 6/1863 in Wedowee, discharged 4/26/65 in Chicamauga, Ga, wounds, age 52.

12978   SARAH RAY, widow of J.D. RAY, Pri, Co. F, 59 Rgt, he died 10/5/63.

12979   F.M. RICHARSON, Pri, Co. E, 19 Rgt, enlisted 6/10/61 in Ga., discharged 4/9/65 at Gaines' Farm, Va., asthma, age 67, Wedowee P.O.

12980   Mrs. M.J. ROBERSON, widow of JNO. ROBERSON, Pri, Co. I, 4 Ga Rgt, he died 8/8/93.

12984   NANCY RAGSDALE, widow of W.A. RAGSDALE, Pri, Co. A, Rgt 22, he died 6/10/1863.

12982   C.D. REEVES, Drummer, 13 Rgt, enlisted 7/17/62 in Montgomery, discharged 4/9/65, age 64, Rock Mills P.O.

12983   ANDREW ROBERTS, Pri, 22 Ga Rgt, enlisted 9/25/61 in Montgomery, discharged 4/26/65, wounds, age 62, Wildwood P.O.

13005   Mrs. H.A. SADDLER, widow of WILLIAM SADDLER, Pri, Co. K, 46 Rgt, he died 8/20/1862.

12997   S.E. SATTERWHITE, widow of W.J. SATTERWHITE, Pri, Co. G, 22 Rgt, he died Apr. 1863. Remarks: widow now dead.

13011   J.M. SCOTT, Pri, Co. A, 10 Rgt, enlisted 2/5/1862, discharged 4/9/65 in Chicamauga, Ga, wounds, age 53, Roanoke P.O.

13001   LOUISA SHAMBLEE, widow of S.W. SHAMBLEE, Pri, Co. I, 8 Car Rgt, he died 2/7/63.

12998   G.H. SHAW, Pri, Co. E, 9 Ga Rgt, enlisted 5/1/62 in Atlanta, discharged 4/9/65, rupture, age 64, Pencil P.O.

12995   NANCY L. SHAW, widow of A. SHAW, Pri, died 5/20/1873.

13009   JAMES T. SHELLNUT, Pri, Co. E, 17 Rgt, enlisted Sept. 1863 in Mobile, discharged 4/26/65, hernia, age 54, Peace P.O.

12988   JNO. SHELLNUTT, Pri, Co. K, 34 Ga Rgt, enlisted May 1861 in Blue Springs, Ga., discharged 4/26/65 in New Hope, Ga., age 69, Omaha P.O.

13002   BARBA GIBSON, widow of GEORGE GIBSON, Pri, Co. H, 31 Rgt, died 7/12/1863. Remarks; widow now dead.

13008   W.H. SIMPSON, Pri, Co. G, 22 Rgt, enlisted Nov. 1862 in Lamar, discharged 4/9/65, rheumatism, age 72, Lamar P.O..

12986   SARAH SKIPPER, widow of LEVI SKIPPER, Pri, Co. F, 21 Ga Rgt, died 1862.

12985   M.W. SLAY, Pri, Co. I, 13 Rgt, died 9/8/1867.

* 12992   ANDERSON F. SMITH, Pri, Smith's Co., 4 Rgt, enlisted 4/27/64 in Tuskegee, discharged 4/27/65 in Montgomery, Sickness, age 84, Hickory Flat P.O. Remarks: now dead.

* 13006   ELIZABETH SMITH, widow of J.C. SMITH, Pri, Co. B, 45 Rgt, died 1/17/1891. Remarks: widow now dead.

* 13010   JAMES A. SMITH, Pri, Co. C, 34 Rgt, enlisted 8/1863 in Newnan, Ga., discharged 4/26/65 in Atlanta, age 75, Napoleon P.O.

* 12994   J.L. SMITH, Pri, Artie Rgt, enlisted 9/1861 in Roanoke, discharged 4/26/65, age 63, Malone P.O.

* 12999   JORDAN SMITH, enlisted 4/1863 in Delta, discharged 4/9/65, crippled, age 65, Pencil P.O.

13000   Mrs. M.A. SMITH, widow of C.M.G. SMITH, Pri, Co. G, 30 Rgt, died 5/2/1898.

13007   W.F. SMITH, Pri, Co. C, 34 Rgt, enlisted 10/29/62, discharged 4/26/65 in Atlanta, age 72, Napoleon P.O.

12987   Mrs. P.H. SPEARS, widow of W. SPEARS, Pri, Co. F, 59 Rgt, died 11/1/1862.

12989   WILLIAM SPEARS, Pri, Ferrill's Arty, enlisted 4/16/62 at LaGrange, Ga., discharged 4/16/65, age 64, Haywood P.O.

13003   Mrs. M.M. STEPHENS, widow of JNO. STEPHENS, Pri, Co. F, 3 Rgt, died 12/19/1891.

13004   MARY STEPHENS, widow of J.F. STEPHENS, Pri, Co. G, 30 Rgt, d. 8/7/1863.

12996   J.H. STEVENS, Pri, Co. A, 56 Ga Rgt, enlisted 4/1862 in Big Shanty, Ga, discharged 6/1865, debility, Lamar P.O.

12991   H.W. STEWART, Pri, Co. C, 56 Ga Rgt, enlisted 4/1862 in Bowdon, Ga, discharged 4/9/65, bad cough, age 59, Graham P.O.

12993   G.W. DINGLER, Pri, Co. H, 3 Rgt, enlisted 1862, discharged 4/26/65 in Murphreesboro, Tenn. cough, age 58.

13017   Mrs. J.E. TARVER, widow of MARTIN TARVER, Pri, Co. F, 14 Rgt, he died 6/12/1894.

13021   J.G. TAYLOR, Pri, Co. F, 25 Rgt, enlisted Apr. 1862 in Wesobulga, discharged 4/26/65, bad sight, age 68, Roanoke P.O.

13013   LOUISA TAYLOR, widow of JNO. TAYLOR, Pri, Co. F, 25 Rgt, he died 1863. Remarks: Widow died 7/3/1903.

13014   W.M. TAYLOR, Pri, Robertson's Home Guards, enlisted at Carter's Store, discharged 4/1865, age 78, Lofty P.O.

13018   MARGARET TEAL, widow of WILLIAM R. TEAL, Pvt, Co. I, 41 Ga. Rgt, he died 10/23/1898.

13015   J.W. THOMASON, Pri.Co. G, 31 Rgt, enlisted Nov. 1861 at Cusseta, discharged 4/9/65 at Holders Run, Va., wounds, age 56, Hawk P.O.

13012   T.H. THORNTON, Pri, Co. K, 14 Rgt, enlisted Aug. 1861 in Auburn, discharged 4/9/65, rheumatism, age 65.

13016   D.C. TOWNSEND, Pri, Co. F, 2 Car Rgt, enlisted Apr, 1861 in Greensboro, SC, discharged 4/11/65 in NC, age 60.

13019   J.M. TRAYLOR, Pri, Co. B, 10 Rgt, enlisted 4/15/62 in Rock Mills, discharged 5/2/65, breast disease, 57, Lamar P.O.

13020   S.M. TRUETT, widow of C. TRUETT, Pri, Co. K, 60 Rgt, died 4/16/1867.

13022   T.F. USSERY, Pri, Co. F, 14 Rgt, enlisted 8/1/61 in Auburn, discharged 4/17/65 in Gettysburg, VA, disability, age 56, Rock Mills, P.O.

13023   T.Y.C. VINSON, widow of W.W. VINSON, Pvt, Co. E, 17 Rgt, enlisted 8/17/62 in Roanoke, discharged 1865, age 79, Cornhouse P.O. Remarks: widow now dead.

13024   Mrs. E.M. VINSON, widow of W.W. VINSON, Pvt. Co. E, 17 Rgt, he died 4/12/1894.

13038   B.A. WADE, Pri, Co. B, 22 Ga. Rgt, enlisted 8/1861 in Montgomery, discharged 4/65 in Shiloh, injuries, age 58, Peace P.O.

13045   REBECCA WADKINS, widow of JOSEPH WADKINS, Pri, Co. C, 14 Rgt, he died 5/2/1863.

13039   F.M. WAKEFIELD, Pri, Ferrell's Arty, enlisted 1863 in Columbus, Ga., discharged 4/26/65, age 74, Ofelia P.O.

13046   M.W. WATSON, widow of E. WATSON, Pri, Co. F, 22 Rgt, died 1861.

13028   PRUDY WATWOOD, widow of WESLEY WATWOOD, Pri, Co. A, 21 Rgt, died July 1892.

13033   Mrs. W.T. WEAVER, widow of S.D. WEAVER, Pri, Co. K, 14 Rgt, died 5/6/1864.

13031   F.W. WELLDAIN, Pri, Co. F, 59 Rgt, enlisted May 1862 in Wedowee, discharged 4/9/65 - Chicamauga, Ga., wounds, age 54, Wedowee, P.O. Remarks: now dead.

13044   JNO. H. WHATLEY, Pri, Co. F, 42 Rgt, enlisted 11/12/63 in Talladega, discharged 4/26/65 in Atlanta, age 75, Sewell P.O.

13027   JUDGE WHATLEY, Pri, Co. K, 9 MS Rgt, enlisted 1863, discharged 4/26/65, breast disease, age 52, Wedowee P.O.

13043   D.C. WHITE, Pri, Co. E, 17 Rgt, enlisted 10/15/62 in Roanoke, VA, discharged 4/26/65 in Atlanta, wounds, Roanoke P.O.

13026   MARTHA A. WHITE, widow of GEORGE WHITE, Pri, Co. K, 56 GA Rgt, died 11/10/86.

13032   L.D. WHITEHEAD, Pri, Co. B, 16 GA Rgt, enlisted June 1861, discharged June 1865, wounds, age 62.

13037   JAMES WHITLEY, Pri, Co. F, 42 Rgt, enlisted 11/13/62 in Talladega, discharged 4/26/65, rheumatism, age 70, Graham P.O.

13034   EMILY WILDER, widow of J.C. WILDER, Pri, Co. F, 14 Rgt, died June 1862.

13048   M.J. WILKINSON, widow of M.D. WILKINSON, Pri, Co. K, 46 Rgt, died 4/8/1895.

13036   Mrs. E.C. WILLIAMS, widow of WILLIAM WILLIAMS, Pri, Co. I, 44 Rgt, he died 3/24/1879.

13041   Mrs. L.J. WILLIAMS, widow of S. WILLIAMS, Pri, Co. I, 25 Rgt, died 3/21/93.

13030   ISAAC WHALEY, Pvt., Co. K, 9 MS Rgt, enlisted 11/62 in Wedowee, discharged 4/26/65, age 72, Wedowee P.O. Remarks: now dead.

13049   Mrs. F.J. WILLINGHAM, widow of W.D. WILLINGHAM, Pri, Co. G, 35 Rgt, died 12/12/62.

13040   L.J. WILLINGHAM, widow of K. WILLINGHAM, Pri, Home Guards, died 7/6/1898.

13035   PERMELIA WINDSOR, widow of W.A. WINDSOR, Pri, Co. F, 13 Rgt, died 4/20/1891.

13051   Mrs. F.A. WOOD, widow of W.D. WOOD, Pri, Co. K, 8 Car Inf., died March 1884. Remarks: widow now dead.

13029   LEDDA A. WOOD, widow of WILLIS WOOD, Pvt, Co. K, 4 Ga Rgt, died 6/9/1884.

13050   MARY J. WOOD, widow of J.W. WOOD, Pri, Co. B, 8 Rgt, died 1/24/85.

13025   J.P. WORKMAN, Pvt, Co. B, 3 SC Rgt, enlisted Apr. 1861 (?) in Newbury, SC, discharged Apr. 1865 in Richmond, VA, aged 60, Roanoke, P.O.

13047   Mrs. T.E. WRIGHT, widow of J.R. WRIGHT, Pri, Co. B, 10 Rgt, died 12/9/93.

13052   A.A. YOUNG, Pvt, Co. F, 25 Rgt, enlisted 9/1861, discharged 3/1865 in Resacca, Ga, paralysis, age 73, Christiana P.O.

13053   ELIZA YOUNG, widow of C. YOUNG, Pri, Co. F, 25 Rgt, died 4/22/1863.

12990   J.M. STEVENSON, Pri, Co. E, 21 Rgt, enlisted 4/2/62 in Flat Rock, discharged 5/10/65, age 70, Abner P.O.

CLASS II

12816   M.K. HOLLIS, Pri, Co. H, 44 Rgt, enlisted 5/1862 in Nacahapoka, discharged 5/15/65 in Cedar Run, lost a leg, age 71, Rock Mills P.O. Remarks, died 4/13/1905.

CLASS IV

13054   J.W. ADAMS, Pri, Co. K, 56 Ga Rgt, enlisted 8/1863 in Franklin, discharged April 1865 in Dalton, GA, wounded, age 55, Ofelia P.O.

13057   J.G. ADAMSON, Pri, Co K, 56 Ga Rgt, enlisted 5/1/62 in Franklin, discharged 4/12/65 in Nashville, wounds, age 57, Rock Mills P.O.

13056   S.M. ADAMSON, Pri, Co K, 14 Rgt, enlisted 8/1/61 in Auburn, discharged 4/26/65, debility, Level Road P.O. Remarks: now dead.   Age 65 at time of application.

13055   Mrs. E.M. ALMOND, widow of ELIJAH ALMOND, Pri, Co. E, 56 Rgt, died 4/26/75. Remarks: widow is now dead.

13058   HARRIETT BALL, widow of M.J. BALL, Pri, Co. G, 22 Rgt, died 2/6/96.

13060   J.M. BOGGS, Pri, Co. A, 10 Rgt, enlisted 3/10/62 in Hickory Flat, discharged 8/1863, heart trouble, age 68, Lofty P.O.

13061   G.W. BOYD, Pri, Co. K, 13 Rgt, enlisted 7/16/61 in Montgomery, discharged 4/9/65, debility, age 61, Rock Mills P.O.

13063   R.J. BREED, Pri, Co. A, 7 Rgt, enlisted 3/20/61 in La Fayette, discharged 7/25/61, debility, age 61, Rock Mills. Remarks: now dead.

13062   RACHAEL BRAND, widow of BRYAN BRAND, Pri, Co. F, 59 Rgt, died 11/12/1899.

13059   N.D. BRUMBELOE, Pri, Co. F, 14 Rgt, enlisted 7/1861 in Hickory Flat, discharged June 1865 in Gettysburg, PA, aged 68,

West P.O. Remarks: is now dead.

13064   Mrs. A.A. BURSON, widow of WILLIS BURSON, Pri, Co. G, 28 Rgt, died May 1864.

13065   J.E. COFIELD, Pri, Co. F, 26 Rgt, enlisted 1/4/1861 in Talladega, discharged 4/26/65, nervous, age 54, Lofty P.O.

13066   Mrs. T.C. COOK, widow of JEPTHA COOK, Pri, Co. F, 46 Ga. died 9/13/1884.

13067   J.L. DIXON, Pri, Co. I, 3 Rgt, enlisted 5/10/61 in Montgomery, discharged in Va. 4/9/65, wounds, age 59.

13068   J.H. DENNIS, Pri, Co. E, 46 Ga Rgt, enlisted 3/10/62 in Hamilton, Ga., discharged May 1885, age 62, Cambridge P.O.

13069   J.A. FERRELL, Pvt, Co. E, 19 Ga, enlisted Jan. 1863 in Franklin, discharged 4/20/65 in Ocean Pond, Fla., wounds, age 55, Sewell P.O.

13070   J.E. GARRETT, Pri, Co. F, 25 Rgt, enlisted 4/4/62, discharged 4/9/65 in Atlanta, debility, age 67, Dingler P.O.

13074   J.H. HAND, Pri, Co. A, 44 Ga Rgt, enlisted 5/4/62, discharged 4/9/65 in Gettysburg, Pa, age 65, Truett P.O.

13073   L.H. HARRIS, Pri, Co. K, 34 Rgt, enlisted Oct. 1861, discharged 4/26/65, eye, age 61, Lamar P.O.

13072   NANCY P. HERRAGE, widow of JAMES HERRAGE, Pri, Co. H, 7 Ga Rgt, died 5/25/93. Remarks: widow now dead.

13071   Mrs. M.J. HURSTON, widow of W.R. HURSTON, Sgt, Co. R, 13 Rgt, died 9/17/62.

13075   J.J. JONES, Pri, Co. F, 25 Rgt, enlisted 9/14/62 in Almond, discharged 4/26/65 in Franklin, Tn, wounds, age 60, Swann P.O.

13076   LUCINDA LIPHAM, widow of T.M. LIPHAM, Pri, Co. F, 2 Ga, died 4/9/1894.

13078   Mrs. N.A. McCULLOCH, widow of H.F. McCULLOCH, Pri, Co. H, 7 Rgt, died 6/20/96. Remarks, widow is dead.

13077   W.W. McDONALD, Pri, Co. B, 10 Rgt, enlisted 3/10/62 in Bacon Level, discharged 4/26/65, diseased, age 57, Christiana P.O.

13079   W.P. NOLES, Pri, Co. K, 34 Ga Rgt, enlisted 6/3/62 Big Shanty, discharged 4/26/65 in Resacca, rheumatism, age 69, Lamar P.O.

13080   J.H. OLDHAM, Pri, Co. B, 2 Rgt, enlisted 7/1861 in Camp Boone, discharged 4/9/65, age 66, Roanoke P.O.

13081   JNO. W. PERRY, Pri, Co. F, 25 Rgt, enlisted 9/1862 in Talladega, discharged 4/26/65, lung trouble, age 68, Wedowee. Remarks: is now dead.

13082   E.T. PHILPOTT, Pri, Co. E, 4 Ga Rgt, enlisted 3/4/1862 in LaGrange, discharged 4/9/65, debility, age 58, Rock Mills P.O.

13083   MARTHA PRESNAL, widow of JNO. G. PRESNAL, Pri, Co. F, 59 Rgt, died 2/10/1864.

13084   J.T. RANCY, Pri, Co. A, 1 Rgt, enlisted 4/1862 in Roanoke, discharged 4/9/65, lung touble, age 57, Roanoke P.O.

13085   W.J. RANSEY, Pri, Co. K, 12 Rgt, enlisted 4/9/64 in Wedowee, discharged 4/9/65, lung trouble, age 57, Lamar P.O.

13086   Mrs. M.A. ROBERTSON, widow of S.F.C. ROBERTSON, Pri, Co. E, 17 Rgt, died 2/18/1865.

13089   JOSEPH SWINT, Pri, Co. F, 8 Rgt, enlisted 8/10/62 in Camp Watts, discharged 4/9/65 in Petersburg, hernia, age 68, Roanoke P.O.

13090   NANCY C. SMITH, widow of W.B.F. SMITH, Pri, Co. G, 47 Rgt, died Oct. 1862.

13087   A.D. STARNES, Pri, Co. A, 1 Rgt, enlisted 6/1/1861 in Troy, discharged 5/20/65 in Atlanta, debility, age 71, Wedowee P.O. Remarks: gone to Texas.

13088   L.A. STILLWELL, Pri, enlisted 5/11/62 in Columbus, discharged 4/9/65 in Petersburg, heart trouble, age 61, Lofty P.O.

13091   J.P. STONE, Pri, Crofts Arty, enlisted May 1864 in Dallas Ga, discharged 1865, diseased, age 55, Almond P.O.

13092   JAMES A. SWAN, Pri, Co. E, 17 Rgt, enlisted 9/1862 in Mobile, discharged 4/26/65 in Cumberland Gap, wound, age 62.

13093   NANCY TRAYLOR, widow of WILLIAM TRAYLOR, Pri, Roberson's Militia, died 12/4/1899.

13094   J.C. WRIGHT, Pri, Co. K, 46 Rgt, enlisted 5/1/62 Loachapoka, discharged 4/26/65, age 72, Forrester School P.O. Remarks: now dead.

13095   Mrs. A.C. WILF, widow of J.A. WILF, Pri, Co. F, 13 Rgt, died 11/1/1861.

13096   W.W. YANCY, Pri, Co. B, 10 Rgt, enlisted 3/10/62 in Rock Mills, discharged 4/26/65, debility, age 55, Sewell P.O.

13097   MARY D. YOUNG, widow of ROBERT YOUNG, Pri, Co. A, 5 Rgt, died 4/18/1900.

CLASS II

12811   J.M. BELL, Pri, Co. G, 22 Rgt, enlisted 9/25/61 in Montgomery, discharged 1/22/65 in Murphreesboro, TN, paralysis, age 70, Wedowee P.O.

12812   B.H. LASITER, Pri, Enlisted 3/1863 in Carrollton, discharged 4/26/65, paralysis, age 79, Lime P.O. Remarks: now dead.

CLASS IV

13099   FRED ADAMSON, Pri, Co. K, 46 Rgt, enlisted 3/7/62 in Louina, discharged 4/26/65 in Bentonville, NC, age 67, Louina P.O.

13098   CHURCHILL ALLEN, Pri, Co. G, 46 Rgt, enlisted 3/15/62 in Lumpkin, Ga., discharged 4/26/65. rheumatism, age 77, Gay P.O.

13107   A.G. BOGGS, Pri, Co. A, 10 Cav, enlisted 1862 in Montgomery, discharged 4/26/65 at 1st Manasses, catarrh, age 67, Dingler P.O.

13105   W.H. BOWEN, Pri, Home Guards, enlisted 1863 in Wedowee, discharged 1865, rheumatism, age 53, Haywood P.O.

13106   E.M. BOYD, Pri, Co. E, 17 Rgt, enlisted 4/13/61 in Montgomery, discharged 4/26/65 in Shiloh, MS, wounds, age 75, Rock Mills P.O. Remarks: now dead.

13104   B.P. BREWER, Pri, Co. A, 10 Cav, enlisted 4/8/62 in Montgomery, discharged 5/18/65, age 67, Roanoke P.O.

13100   N.E. BROMBELOE, widow of N.D. BROMBELOE, Pri, died 5/21/1901.

13103   T.N. BROWNING, Pri, Co. K, 14 Rgt, enlisted 8/12/61 in Auburn, discharged 4/9/65 at Seven Days Fight, wounds, age 61, Roanoke P.O.

13101   P.K. BROOKS, Pri, Co. B, 10 Rgt, enlisted 3/11/62 at Rock Mills, discharged 3/6/65, rheumatism, age 58, Pencil P.O.

13102   W.L. BURK, Pri, Co. D, 17 Rgt, enlisted 1/15/62 in Mobile, discharged 4/26/65, rheumatism, age 65, Rock Mills P.O.

13111   Mrs. M.A. CHAFFIN, widow of MOSES B. CHAFFIN, Pri, Co. I, 8 Rgt, died 1/1865.

13108   E.B. COOK, widow of W.F. COOK, Pri, Co. K, 17 Rgt, died July 1894. Remarks: widow now dead.

13109   A.A. CREWS, widow of W.P. CREWS, Pri, Co. I, 26 Rgt, died 1/21/1901.

13110   J.M. CRUSE, Pri, Co. E, 2 Ga, enlisted 3/14/1864 at Botornion, Ga., discharged 4/65 in Savannah, Ga., rheumatism, age 56, Sewell P.O. Remarks: died 10/29/1904.

13114   G.J. DAVIS, Pri, Co. I, 59 Rgt, enlisted 2/15/62 in Roanoke, discharged 4/19/65, disease, age 65, Omaha P.O.

13113   T.E. DISHAROON, Pri, Co. G, 37 & 58 Rgts, discharged 5/16/65, age 66, Cambridge P.O. Remarks: died 5/1/1905.

13112   Mrs. ANN DUKE, widow of MARTIN DUKE, Pri, Co. B, 10 Rgt, died 1/8/1901.

13118   E.T. GAUNTT, Pri, Co. E, 17 Rgt, enlisted 4/1863 in Dalton, Ga, discharged 4/26/65, rhuematism, age 56, Ofelia P.O.

13116   M.E. GIBSON, SR, widow of G.B., Pri, Co. D, Cav., died 6/11/1890.

13117   MARY E. GIBSON, JR., widow of WILLIAM S., Pri, Co. C, 34 Rgt, died 8/27/1895.

13115   S.A. GUNN, widow of F.B. GUNN, 1st Lt., Co. I, 8 Cav., died 8/23/1876.

13119   WILLIAM HARPER, Pri, Co. I, 14 Rgt, enlisted 7/1861 in Auburn, discharged 4/9/65 in Seven Pines, Va, wounds, age 67, Rock Mills P.O.

13120   JAMES M. HEARD, Pri, Co. K, 34 Ga Rgt, enlisted May 1862 in Big Shanty, Ga., discharged 4/26/65, age 69, Newell P.O.

13121   ATHERILA E. JACKSON, widow of JNO. C. JACKSON, Pri, Co. E, 19 Rgt, died 10/16/1861.

13122   PETER KLINE, Pri, Co. K, 42 Rgt, enlisted 10/15/62 in Talladega, discharged 4/26/65, age 80, Cambridge P.O. Remarks: now dead.

13123   A.E. McCLENDON, widow of E.H. McCLENDON, Pri, Co. H, 47 Rgt, died 7/19/98.

13124   W.A. MOSES, Pri, Employed in Mining Bureau, enlisted 12/1/62 Shell Mound, TN; discharged 4/26/65, rheumatism, aged 71, Omaha P.O., Remarks: d. 2/6/1905. (Wife, MARY MOSES from Archives)

13125   N.M. POOR, Pri, Co. E, 17 Rgt, enlisted 8/1863 in Mobile, discharged 9/1863, age 68, Ocre P.O.

13126   T.A.E. RADNEY, widow of JAMES L. RADNEY, Pri, Co. B, 2 Ga Rgt, died 9/7/1900.

13128   Mrs. E.F. RICE, widow of E. RICE, Pri, Co. G, 22 Rgt, died 9/20/92.

13127   JAMES A. ROLLINS, Pri, Co. T, 59 Rgt, enlisted 2/15/62 in Wedowee, discharged 4/9/65, age 69, Corbin P.O.

13131   J.M. SAXON, Pri, Co. B, 7 Car. Rgt, enlisted 9/13/62 in Carrollton, Ga., discharged 4/26/65, age 68.

13129   JANE SMITH, widow of ANDERSON SMITH, Pri, Co. A, died 1/18/1900, Remarks: widow now dead.

13130   MARY A. SMITH, widow of ISAAC SMITH, Pri, Home Guards, died 6/9/1898.

13134   L.W. TOWNSEND, Navy, enlisted 9/18/64 in Wilmington, NC, discharged 4/26/65, lung trouble, age 60, Omaha P.O.

13132   J.H. TRUETT, Pri, Co. I, enlisted 1863 in Quincy, Fla., discharged 4/26/65. age 78, Roanoke P.O. Remarks: now dead.

13133   JOHN S. TURNER, Pri, Co. H, 1 Ky Cav., enlisted 10/8/61 in Hopkinsville, Ky., discharged 4/1865 in Murpreesboro, TN, wounds, age 73, Goldberg P.O.

13135   W.N. VOWELL, Pri, Co. O, 27 TX Rgt, enlisted 7/4/61 in Nesho, TX, discharged 4/1/65, eye trouble, age 76, Sewell P.O. Remarks: is now dead.

13136   J.M. WARD, Pri, Co. K, 14 Rgt, enlisted 8/7/61 in Auburn, discharged 4/9/65 in Gettysburg, PA, wounds, age 63, Roanoke P.O.

13137   W.L. WARD, Pri, Co. C, enlisted Dec. 1863 in West Point Ga., discharged 4/26/65, age 59, Roanoke, P.O.

13138   F.M. WHITE. Pri, Co. E, 13 Rgt, enlisted 1/19/61 in

Montgomery, discharged in Sharpsburg, Va., wounds, age 57, Happyland P.O.

13139   W.M. YATES, Pri, Navy, enlisted 3/1863 in Decatur, Ga., discharged 8/1863, paralysis of bowels, age 59, Ofelia P.O.

13042   T.M. WILLIAMS, Pri, Co. F, 21 Rgt, enlisted May 1861 in Ga., discharged Apr. 1865 in Wilderness, Va., stiff muscles, age 62, Rock Mills, P.O.

CONFEDERATE REUNION, 1907 —Banked before the side entrance of the First Baptist Church, Roanoke, are more than 100 veterans of the Aiken-Smith Camp, No. 293, gathered for the April 26 Memorial Day celebration 50 years ago. Unidentified is the foremost figure, seated on top step. Kneeling at left behind him is Bill Radney, at left is Jesse Faucett. Directly behind Radney, eyes closed, is M. R. Taylor. In first standing row, with scrambled tie, clutching bowler hat, is Capt. W. A. Handley. Second, behind him is clean-shaven Martin Pittman. Right of Pittman is J. B. Carlisle. Man with wooden leg, seated, front row, is Major Benjamin Walker. Holding light hat in right hand, front row, Coleman. Right of Coleman, kneeling, is G. O. Hill. F. D. Powing, with full beard, is Buck Weathers is seated fourth from left, front thers. Standing behind, white row, holding right knee. Readers beard against brick wall, is Gen. should be able to identify others B. F. Weathers. Head at corner of in this picture submitted by Rustained glass window is John H. fus Eichelberger. Oldham. Third from right, seated, is Mack Wood. Behind, at left, is

BONDS & WILLS I
RANDOLPH COUNTY

P. 13. LW&T of JAMES H. RADNEY of Randolph County. Names his wife, SARAH; son, JOHN W., daughter, ALICE MANLEY, wife of C.D. MANLEY, and NANNIE PRESCOTT, wife of C.M. PRESCOTT. Also names daughter SALLIE MITCHELL, wife of S.C. MITCHELL. JOHN W. RADNEY, only son, was appointed as Executor of the Estate. Signed 9/26/1894. Witnesses: A.M. AWBREY and F.P. NICHOLS. Filed 4/6/1898. A.J. WEATHERS, Judge of Probate.

P. 16. LW&T of JOHN P. MORROW, deceased. Names wife, GEORGIA ANN MORROW, and step-son, WILLIAM TRAYLOR, to share equally with his own children in the final distribution of property. Names his wife to be Executrix. Signed 6/30/1881. Witnesses: J.T. OWENS and C.A. PRESCOTT. S.E.A. REAVES, Judge of Probate.

P. 18. LW&T of WILLIAM HORNSBY of Roanoke. Names wife, SARAH, single daughters, BETSY, MARY and DORCUS HORNSBY, sons, WILLIAM and NOAH, married daughters, HARRIETT HORNSBY, MARTHA BETTS and SARAH SANDERS. Named WILLIAM and NOAH, sons, to be Executors of the Estate. Signed 10/1/1853. Filed 4/1/1854. Witnesses: JAMES WEAVER and J.M. WILF. JOSEPH BENTON, Judge of Probate.

P. 44. LW&T of MARTHA E. DISHAROON. Names daughters, ETTA, FANNIE, sister CLARINDA MICKLE, son J.T. DISHAROON. Named ETTA and FANNIE to be Executrix. Witnesses: B.F. WEATHERS and WYATT W. WOOD. Dated 6/28/1895. Filed 1/8/1900.

P. 55. LW&T of WILLIAM M. JOHNSON of Randolph County. Names wife, SARAH E. JOHNSON, minor children, HATTY A., WILLIS M., JR. and FRANK M. JOHNSON. States that he had 14 children and 1 grandchild, JINCY MARVIN JOHNSON. Named JOHN T. and JAMES M. JOHNSON as Executors. Signed 12/20/1886. Witnesses: JOSEPH R. HOOD and A.J. CHEEVES and R.S. PATE. Filed 11/12/1900. STELL BLAKE, Judge of Probate.

P. 73. LW&T of HIRAM E. FORBUS of Wehadkee. Names wife, SARAH A. FORBUS, nephew: MANLEY FORBUS, nephew, W.A. WHITAKER. Appointed S.D. LEWIS as Executor. Signed 1/8/1896. Witnesses, S.D. LEWIS and W.R. HEAD. Filed 8/11/1903.

P. 114. LW&T of C.J. USSERY, dated 1884. . ."Being in my 65th year and propose making a trip to Texas and not being very stout. . .appoint MILLARD F. USSERY and my wife, NANCY A USSERY, as lawful executors." He named his son, THOMAS USSERY, mentioning that he was wounded in the late war, names CALLIE, daughter of his son, CALVIN USSERY, granddaughters ELLA and IDA McPHERSON. Witnesses: J.T. SHELNUT and H.N. SHELNUT. Filed 8/7/1906, JOHN T. KAYLOR, Judge of Probate.

In the settlement of the Estate his widow's name is mentioned as NANCY ANN USSERY, and his next of kin, SUSEY VEAL, wife of WILLIAM VEAL of High Shoals, EMALINE MAYFIELD, wife of W.S. MAYFIELD of Roanoke, T(?). F. USSERY of High Shoals, LOUISA WALLER, wife of W.S. WALLER of Roanoke, NANNIE WEATHERS, wife of WILLIAM WEATHERS of High Shoals, W.F. USSERY of High Shoals, MOLLIE SPARKS, wife of J.M. SPARKS of Temple, Texas, MILLARD F.

USSERY of High Shoals, J.R. USSERY of High Shoals, BETTY WEATHERS, wife of I.B. WEATHERS of High Shoals, all over 21 years of age, and CALLIE USSERY, daughter of CALVIN USSERY, a son now deceased and she under 21. Filed on 8/15/1884.

DEED RECORD I
RANDOLPH COUNTY

State of Alabama) P. 2. An execution rendered in Circuit Court Randolph County) in favor of MARY SCHUESSLER as executioner of a judgement against the property of R.C. HAYNES bounded by lands of J.W. TRUETT & THOMAS PATE, JR., R. McCLURG in Randolph County. CHARLES SCHUESSLER became purchaser of said property in Dec. 1896. Recorded 12/21/96. R.H. HARRIS, Shff.

State of Alabama) P. 4. On 4/4/1892 SARAH R. MITCHELL & STEPHEN Randolph County) C. MITCHELL executed and delivered to the British & American Mortgage Co. 10 promissory notes. The Company appointed JOHN T. HEFLIN of Roanoke as their lawful attorney in foreclosing the mortgage. Filed 11/4/1896. Signed LIONEL H. GRAHAM & AWERK R. SHATTOCK, Directors of the Company.

State of Georgia) P. 10. JAMES W. CALLEY & wife, ITURA R. CALLEY Coweta County) of Coweta Co. sell, alienate and convey to EMMA M. SMITH of Randolph County that tract of land known as the JAMES M. SMITH lands deed to CALLEY 4/2/1891 by the SMITHS and now conveyed to EMMA M. SMITH. Signed 12/11/1896. Witnesses: OTIS E. SMITH & C.R. CLOWERS, Notary Public.

State of Alabama) Indenture made 8/5/1858 between CULLEN PEAVY Randolph County) and wife ELIZA PEAVY of Randolph Co. and JOSEPH M. SMITH of Coweta Co., Ga. for part of the above tract of land. P. 12

State of Alabama) P. 13. Indenture made 4/1/1859 between WILLIAM Randolph County) GRIFFIN and wife MARY A.L. GRIFFIN of Randolph Co. and JOSEPH M. SMITH for part of the land mentioned above on Page 10.

State of Alabama) P. 14. Indenture made 4/2/1891 between JOSEPH Randolph County) M. SMITH and wife EMMA A. SMITH to JAMES W. CALLEY, his heirs and assigns. Filed 1/2/1897.

State of Alabama) P. 16. Indenture made 12/10/1860 between Randolph County) WILLIAM W. SPEARS and wife PAROLLE H. SPEARS of Randolph Co. Wit: CULLEN PEAVY & EALOM SMITH. Filed 1/7/1897.

State of Alabama) P. 17. Indenture made 1/3/1893 between SYREL- Randolph County) DIA EDGE of Red Hill, Ala. and Mrs. G.A. FOL- SOM of the same place. SYRELDIA grants to granddaughter Mrs. FOL- SOM the old land plat of the provincial Act of Congress of 4/24/ 1820. A.B. BROOKS, J.P., certified to this transaction 6/3/1893. THOMAS M. BARCLIFT, the attending physician of Red Hill, Marshall Co., certified to the mental condition of Mrs. EDGE, dated 6/3/1893.

State of Alabama) P. 26. DEED- Mortgage executed by G. GAY and Randolph County) wife, M.J. GAY, and R.R. GAY to WHITE & AW- BREY as security on 4/20/1894. SAMUEL HENDERSON, Atty. for WHITE & AWBREY in Roanoke. Filed 12/16/1895.

State of Alabama) P. 28. DEED. MARTIN P. PITTMAN & ELIZA E. Randolph County) PITTMAN, in consideration of our natural love and affection for our daughter, LAURA V. STEPHENS, convey described property in Randolph Co. Dated 12/18/1896. M.J. MICKLE, J.P.

State of Alabama) P. 29. DEED. MARTIN P. PITTMAN and wife, Randolph County) ELIZA E. PITTMAN, for and in consideration of the natural love for our son, ESCAR A. PITTMAN and daughter LOLA E. WOOD convey described real estate 12/19/1896.

State of Alabama) P. 32. Indenture made 8/19/1894 by and between D.S. & M.S. JACKSON on the first part and G.O. KAYLOR of the second part for valuable consideration convey described real estate. Witness: J.W. BARKER.

State of Alabama) P. 34. DEED. Conveyed from J.D. McCRARY to Randolph County) his beloved wife, LELA C. McCRARY, described real estate 11/2/1895. W.P. NEWELL, J.P.

State of Alabama) P. 35. MAJOR SCHUESSLER & ROBERT L. SCHUESSLER Randolph County) LER comprising the firm of SCHUESSLER & CO. grant unto GEORGIA RAILWAY CO. for valuable consideration described lands. Signed 6/6/1896. Wit: T.J. EAST, Notary Public. (Also names MATTIE SCHUESSLER, wife of R.L. SCHUESSLER.)

State of Alabama) P. 38. Conveyance of described tract of land Randolph County) from J.B. CREED & wife, M.E. CREED, to J.D. THRASHER 12/12/1896. J.F. BOLT, Justice of Peace.

State of Alabama) P. 40. STEPHEN STEPHENS & ANDREW STEPHENS, Randolph County) Exec. of LW&T of ALSEY STEPHENS, late of Randolph Co., were authorized to sell described land after the death of decedent's wife. Wit: G.W. CLEGG & H.B. RADNEY

State of Alabama) Conveyance from W.M. BIRDSONG to THOMAS Randolph County) TREADAWAY of 2/4/1861. Wit: T.J. JOHNSON & B.F. PARKER, J.P. Recorded 3/6/1897. A.J. WEATHERS, J.P.

State of OHIO) DEED. ALEXANDER G. PATTON of Columbus, Ohio, Franklin County) a widower, for $7,500 sold to DAVID S. GRAY & ROBERT M. ROWND, described tract of land in Randolph Co. A portion of the property was known as the CHARITY A. CAMPBELL homestead (purchased from the U.S. Gov.) adjoining the ELIZABETH KAMP entry and sold to WILLIAM E. HORNE, THOMAS C. HILL & JAMES M. PHILLIPS. Part of the land known as the JOSIAH FARLEY homestead, and deed to same, part was originally State school land and deeded about 1855 by T.J. MORRISON & wife to the present owner, this land adjoining DOUGHERTY's HOMESTEAD, and land originally located by RICHARD E. BRADEN 4/25/1873 and conveyed to DUDLEY BRADEN. Dated 9/3/1888. Wit: FLORZEL SWINT & JOHN J. LENTZ. Above certificate by FLORIZET SMITH, Notary Public for Franklin Co., Ohio.

State of Alabama) P. 46. WILLIAM E. HORNE of Cleburne Co., AL Cleburne County) convey to CHARLES FOSTER of Ohio one undivided half of any and all realty mining and other interest heretofore owned by me in partnership with others and individually. 10/6/1883. Wit: B.C. GRIER.

State of Alabama) P. 53. DEED. From execution in favor of J.T. Randolph County) HALPEN and against R.E. BRADEN 2/9/1884 to recover described land sold to J.M. PHILLIPS, A.G. PATTON, THOMAS C. HILL & WILLIAM E. HORNE. 2/7/1884. M.V. MULLINS, Shff.

State of Alabama) P. 55. Original Deed of Conveyance from
Randolph County) WILLIAM E. HORNE, THOMAS C. HILL, JAMES M.
PHILLIPS to ALEXANDER G. PATTON recorded and dated 12/8/1883.
Names M.L. HILL, wife of THOMAS C. HILL, as relinquishing dower
rights. Wit: T.G. PARSONS & THOMAS M. CASSELS.

State of Alabama) P. 58. ELIZA HODGE, A.J. LANGLEY, J.M. LAN-
Randolph County) GLEY & W.W. LANGLEY in consideration of $265
convey described tract of land to R.N. WILLIAMS 10/24/1893.
Signed by ELIZA HODGE, ALICE LANGLEY, W.W. LANGLEY, A.J. LANGLEY,
M.E. LANGLEY, J.W. LANGLEY & M.L. LANGLEY. Wit: JAMES P. WIL-
LIAMS & E.A. GRAY, J.P. The latter examined HODGE, ALICE LANG-
LEY & M.E. LANGLEY separately & apart from their husbands.

State of Alabama) P. 59. DEED. THOMAS A. WALKER received judge-
Randolph County) ment against the Copper Hill Mining Co. in
Selma, AL on 6/13/1881 for $9,135.29 and on 6/22/1881, R.T. WIL-
SON, Received, recorded the judgement against same. The property
in Randolph Co. belonging to the company was conveyed to WALKER
& WILSON 11/7/1881. M.V. MULLINS, Shff. Wit: M.M. TEAGUE.

State of Alabama) P. 62. DEED. By virtue of Mortgage Deed
Randolph County) executed by ANDREW J. STORK & wife, MARTHA
C. STORK to JOSHUA BALLARD, described lands were sold at public
outcry at Omaha on 4/21/1888 to N.H. WILLIS.

State of Alabama) P. 63. Certificate of Redemption. On 6/1/
Randolph County) 1896 land sold to the State of Alabama for
payment of taxes was redeemed by W.G. MILLIGAN with deposit of
$14.82 being made. Wit: W.J. WEATHERS, Judge Probate 10/5/1896.

State of Alabama) P. 65. Conveyance from J.L. SMITH & MARY C.
Randolph County) SMITH to FLOYD PHILLIPS for described lands
10/39/1884. Wit: JOHN B. SMITH & THOMAS JOINER. Rec. 1/7/1897.

State of Alabama) P. 65. Conveyance made from JOHN B. SMITH
Randolph County) & ENDITH SMITH to J.L. SMITH for land in
above transaction dated 4/4/1876. Wit: A.H. AVERY & C.A. JACKSON.

State of Alabama) P. 66. Conveyance of L.C. SMITH & EMMA V.
Randolph County) SMITH to T.H. MORROW. 3/3/1897. Wit: J.H.
WHITTEN, J.P.

State of Alabama) P. 68. DEED. Indenture made 1/8/1873 between
Randolph County) G.G. PATE, as Adm. of WILLIAM WOOD, dec'd.
and SARAH KNIGHT, wife of JAMES KNIGHT. PATE sold on 11/6/1870
the real estate of decedent to purchaser. Survey made by F.A.
McMURRAY in 1870. R.H. BALL, Clerk Cir. Ct., A.J. WEATHERS,
Judge Probate Ct.

State of Alabama) P. 70. INMAN BUSBEE & wife, MARY J. BUSBEE,
Chambers County) did on 3/5/1886 execute and deliver to MARY
SCHUESSLER, Exec., a cert. mortgage on described land bounded by
the lands of MINUS RADNEY on the north, by the Tallapoosa on the
east, and lands of JAMES PUGH & JERRY WOOD on the west and on
the south by lands of R.H. HARRIS. As BUSBEE failed to pay indebtedness the property was sold at public sale to J.A. BINGHAM
on 3/30/1896. Dated 12/9/1896. Wit: E.M. OLIVER, N.P.

State of Alabama) P. 72. LaFAYETTE W. LILES on 7/6/1892 exec-
Randolph County) uted a cert. mortgage on described real estate
to National Mutual Building & Loan Assoc. of N.Y. to secure indebtedness. The mortgage was foreclosed and sold on 3/8/1897
with the Assoc. being the highest bidder.

State of Alabama) P. 75. W.A. HANDLEY and wife, H.H. HANDLEY,
Randolph County) in consideration of the "love we bear for the
prosperity of our town of Roanoke and our neighbor, ANDREW T.
AMOS" give, grant & convey to him the described land on the east
side of Roanoke and West Point Road adjoining his land and the
land of WILLIAM M. AMOS. Dated 12/14/1880. Wit: M.J. MICKLE.

State of Alabama) P. 76. CHARLOTTE JONES, an unmarried woman,
Randolph County) for $1.00 paid by H.D. SMITH, transfer this
instrument at any time in 30 months for $5.00 an acre all the
gold, gold ore and gold bearing rock, Feldspar, Mica, Kaolin and
all other valuable ores, metals or minerals on described land
and the use of all the waters and timber of said land necessary
in mining and manufacturing. Dated 3/29/1897. Wit: J.W. OLIVER
& J.C. SWANN.

State of Alabama) P. 77. Decree rendered in Chancery Ct. case
Randolph County) where JOHN T. HEFLIN was complainant and THOS.
J. GREEN, et al, defendants in October Term 1888. The Register
was authorized to sell described land known as the Mill place
sold by WASHINGTON TRAYLOR to JOHN T. HELFIN in Randolph Co. on
2/18/1891. H.T. HEFLIN, as Adm. of JOHN T. HELFIN, Deceased, was
the highest, best and last bidder for the land and title conveyed.
Signed 2/18/1889.

State of Alabama) P. 79. DEED. ROBERT T. WEST and wife W.L.
Randolph County) WEST conveyed to J.C. HURLEY and L.W. HURLEY,
JR. quit claim to described land on 5/11/1897. Wit: J.W. OLIVER.

State of Texas) P. 80. W.H.H. CANON & ARMINDA CANON conveyed
Brown County) to LEVI HURLEY described land in Randolph Co.
dated 5/23/1884. Wit: HENRY FORD, Co. Clk Brown Co. & J.T. MAYO.

State of Alabama) P. 81. Indenture made Jan. Term 1883 between
Randolph County) M.V. HUDSON, Exec. LW&T of C.D. HUDSON, dec.
of Randolph Co. to T.C. GOODWIN, individually and as guardian of
GUSSIE A. GOODWIN, a minor residing in Spalding Co., Ga. & R.H.
FALLON, husband of EMMA, formerly EMMA GOODWIN, in consideration
of compromise of several lawsuits by each of parties of 2nd part
as heirs of JAMES GOODWIN, dec. and as guardian of T.C., GUSSIE
A. & EMMA GOODWIN now EMMA FALLAN. Land to be sold for distri-
bution bounded on east by Tallapoosa River, on the south by
ALECK YOUNG & JOHN NIX, on the west by WILLIAM WHITE & SAMUEL Mc
MURRAY (originally known as JOHN REAVES place and now known as
the HUDSON place.) 1/2/1882. Wit: W.H. SMITH, JR.

State of Alabama) P. 82. Wedowee, AL. We, the heirs of C.D.
Randolph County) HUDSON, relinquish all interest in the land
mention above conveyed as heirs of HUDSON & wife, MATILDA. Signed
1/2/1883 by F.T. HUDSON, T.S. USSERY, J.T. HUDSON, W.C. HUDSON,
S.F. WORTHY, S.A. STRICKLAND, C.S. HUDSON, JR. & M.V. HUDSON.
S.E.A.REAVES , J.C.P.

State of Alabama) P. 84. F.H. FALLOW & EMMA FALLOW of Lee Co.
Lee County) apply through their attorney, THOMAS C. GOOD-
WIN to sell tract of land known as the HUDSON place. 2/16/1883.
Wit: JAMES R. GREENE & E.B. DUABITTE (?).

State of Alabama) P. 84. L.W. HURLEY, SR. & wife, NANCY HURLEY,
Randolph County) convey to J.C. & L.W. HURLEY, JR. the right
to described property on 4/5/1888. G.W. FRENCH, J.P.

State of Alabama) P. 86. In consideration of 17 bales of cotton

Randolph County) (1500 lbs. each) to be delivered 11/1/1884, 4 on 11/1/1885 and 5 on 11/1/1886, L.W. HURLEY, J.C. & L.W. HURLEY, JR. have cancelled promissory note to T.C. GOODWIN, A.(?)H. & EMMA FALLOW & T.C. GOODWIN as guardian of GUSSIE A. GOODWIN. Wit: W.H. SMITH & L.W. HURLEY. 2/19/1883. Filed 4/3/1897.

State of Alabama) P. 89. DEED. F.A. VAUGHAN & wife, T. COOPER Tallapoosa County) VAUGHAN, for valuable consideration paid by Z. JONES WRIGHT, JR. convey described land in Randolph Co. between land formerly owned by GREER & Mrs. ANDERSON, now owned by H.M. MICKLE & Mrs. ANDERSON on 4/2/1891. J. PERCY OLIVER, Register in Chancery.

State of Alabama) P. 91. For valuable consideration paid by Marshall County) JOHN C. DULIN described land in Randolph Co. conveyed by J.F. McCRELESS 1/5/1885. AARON WOODRUFF, Justice of Peace.

State of Georgia) P. 92. J.C. DULIN and wife A.E. DULIN, con- DeKalb County) vey to J.W. BOYD of Randolph Co. the rights to above land on 4/6/1897. JOHN W. McCardy, N.P. & CHARLIE GILHAM, Witnesses.

State of Alabama) P. 93. In consideration of valuable considera- Randolph County) tion paid by H.E. HESTER, A.J. & MARY A. GREEN conveyed described real estate in the fork of Franklin and Wedowee Road on 9/26/1881. Wit: A.W. DUKE, ALLEN HESTER & T.J. CAMP, J.P.

State of Georgia) P. 94. J.L. LOVVORN of Carroll Co. conveyed Carroll County) to JOHN C. DANIEL of Randolph Co. described property on 11/12/1896. Wit: W.F. HATFIELD & T.A.G. SMITH, N.P.

State of Alabama) W.A. HANDLEY & wife, ADELIA A. HANDLEY, for Randolph County) valuable consideration paid by W.D. MITCHELL, conveyed described real estate in Randolph Co. 4/28/1897. S.C. FAUSELL, N.P.

State of Alabama) P. 96. ELIZANN MAHULDA (also spelled MATILDA) Randolph County) ALMON, for love and affection for beloved son, WILLIAM ANDERSON ALMON, convey described real estate on 4/26/1897. J.H. WHITTEN, J.P.

State of Alabama) P. 97. JAMES B. LASHLEY for love & affection Randolph County) of daughter, AMANDY SERFRONY LAMBRETY and daughter, MATILDA R. MINDY LASHLEY, convey described land on 10/22/1895. Wit: H.H. BEARD.

State of Alabama) P. 99. R.E. TAYLOR, for valuable consideration, Randolph County) conveyed to HIRAM GIBSON all interest in described property. 1/7/1897. R.G. ROWLAND, N.P.

State of Alabama) P. 100. Agreement made 9/24/1896 between Randolph County) JOHN H. & wife, EMMA TEAKEE, of the 1st part and SAMUEL ANGLEY of the 2nd part. concerning mineral rights. A.J. BRADFORD, J.P.

State of Alabama) P. 103. ROBERT S. HEFLIN & M.P. HEFLIN for Randolph County) valuable consideration convey to C.M. CAMP all their interest in described land on 7/1/1876. GEORGE H. AUSTIN, J.P.

State of Alabama) P. 104. H.R. GAY, administrator of Estate of
_____ County) H.M. GAY, deceased, as duly appointed in Probate Court 10/13/1870, obtained an order to sell described real estate on 11/16/1870. Land was bought at public outcry by CALISTA M. CAMP, wife of HENRY C. CAMP. Sale was confirmed. 1/14/1871.

State of Alabama) P. 106. JAMES M. YATES & wife, SARAH F. YATES Randolph County) did on 12/28/1892 execute a mortgage on described real estate to National Mutual Building & Loan Assoc. of N.Y. Made a default in payment and on 1/20/1896 the Assoc. purchased the property. CHANDLER B. LEE, Pres. & GEORGE R. SUTHERLAND, Sec.

State of Alabama) P. 108. H.R. GAY, Administrator of H.M. GAY, Randolph County) deceased, sold real estate known as the HARKINS place on east side of Corn House Creek to MARY ANN CLEMENTS, wife of A.M. CLEMENTS 11/16/1870. S.E.A. REAVES, Judge Probate.

State of Alabama) P. 110. A.M. CLEMONS for valuable consideration Randolph County) tion convey to wife, MOLLIE A. CLEMMONS, described real estate on Corn House Creek, at a ford between ROBERT MERRILLS & D.G. WALDROPS. 1/25/1883. Wit: C.O. GROSS & J.B. RICHLAND.

State of Alabama) P. 113. OLIVIA BURKE of Montgomery Co. (Cert. Randolph County) #19084) deposited in the General Land Office in Montgomery full payment of described land 9/10/1885 signed by Grover Cleveland, Pres. on the certificate. Recorded in Randolph Co. 5/27/1897. A.J. WEATHERS, Judge Probate.

State of Alabama) P. 114. M. BURKE, trustee, for and in valuable Montgomery County) ble consideration of MARY A. SCOTT, conveyed described real estate in Randolph Co. 5/12/1897. Wit: WILLIAM D. GAY & W.E. CARMICHAEL.

State of Alabama) P. 116. JAMES G. SMITH & wife, E.J.M. SMITH, Tallapoosa Coynty) for valuable consideration convey to HELEN E. OLIVER all their interest in the land in Randolph Co. part of which was known as the JAMES GARNER lands. 1/21/1886. Wit: WILEY W. SMITH & J.R. WRIGHT, J.P.

State of Georgia) P. 118. Indenture made 8/22/1890 betwen JAMES Troup County) G. TRUITT of Troup Co. & Mesrs. SCHUESSLER & CO. of Randolph Co. convey the right to land in the town of Roanoke. Signed JAMES G. TRUITT & MARY E. TRUITT. Wit: C.D. HUDSON & W.J. McCLURE, Notary Public of Troup Co.

State of Alabama) P. 120. C.N. BAKER & wife, C.P. BAKER, on Randolph County) 9/13/1889 by their mortgage did convey to SCHUESSLER & CO. described land in Rock Mills, Randolph Co. The land was sold by SCHUESSLER & CO. to T.J. EAST on 1/30/1896. R.E. TAYLOR, N.P.

State of Alabama) P. 122. J.E. FIELDEN & EDWARD FIELDEN and Randolph County) their wives, M.D. FIELDEN & S.A.M. FIELDEN, on 5/1/1893, by mortgage deed conveyed described real estate in Randolph Co. to SCHUESSLER & CO. to be paid by 10/1/1893. Said land was sold 1/30/1896 to T.J. EAST.

State of Alabama) P. 124. MILLIE SCHUESSLER, Executrix of J.M. Chambers County) SCHUESSLER, deceased, in consideration of settlement of partnership of SCHUESSLER & CO. for valuable consideration conveys her rights to described land to MAJOR & ROBERT

L. SCHUESSLER. Signed 4/4/1894. W.E. BOSWORTH, J.P. Chambers Co.

State of Alabama) P. 126. L.S. SCHUESSLER and wife, SALLIE S.
Chambers County) SCHUESSLER, ZACK SCHUESSLER and wife, IDA
SCHUESSLER, CHARLES SCHUESSLER and wife, CARRIE SCHUESSLER and
MILLIE SCHUESSLER, as Executrix of J.W. SCHUESSLER, for valuable
consideration convey all right to described real estate, to A.F.
AMOS and S.S. WALLER land.

State of Georgia) P. 128. Conveyance was made 10/29/1890 by
Floyd County) Mr. J.R. CAMPBELL to E.J. McGHEE for his
interest in described land.

State of Georgia) P. 129. Indenture made 3/29/1897 between
Floyd County) J.L. CAMP, surviving partner of CAMP, GLOVER
& CO. and Mrs. EMMA J. McGHEE, sole heir of CAIN GLOVER, deceased,
of CAMP, GLOVER & CO. For valuable consideration they conveyed
to JAMES GLOVER McGHEE of Floyd Co. all interest in described
land. Wit: W.E. MEREDITH & T.W. SCOTT, Notary Public of Floyd
County.

State of Alabama) P. 131. Deed between POWHATAN G. TRENT, JR.
Randolph County) of Rock Mills and MARY IDA TRENT, wife, and
National Mutual Building & Loan Assoc. of N.Y., to be paid by
10/20/1893. Conveyance made 2/20/1896 for partial payment not
received on parcel of land in Rock Mills, formerly belonging to
P.G. TRENT, SR. Said land bounded by W.R. SHARMAN & W.D. BOWDEN.
Wit: R.E. TAYLOR.

State of Alabama) P. 134. Execution issued in Circuit Court
Randolph County) Fall Term 1893 against R.E. MERRILL in favor
of W.C. DODSON on a judgement levied on described property to
be sold 12/17/1894. Property was sold to J.R. MORRIS. ROBERT
WILLOUGHBY, Shff.

State of Alabama) P. 136. Contract made on 8/19/1895 between
Randolph County) PINETUCKY GOLD MINING & MINERAL LAND CO.
as lessor and HUGH McJUDOR of Chicago, Ill, as lessee, D.R. Mc
LAUGHRIN, President. Att: W.O. GRIFFIN, Sec. Protem and
HUGH McJUDOR.

BURSON SCHOOL - The old and "new" buildings. Courtesy of the Department of Archives & History, Montgomery, Alabama.

HARRISON GROVE SCHOOL - The old and "new" buildings. Courtesy of the Department of Archives and History, Montgomery, Alabama.

LIME SCHOOL, RANDOLPH COUNTY - The old and "new" buildings. Courtesy of the Department of Archives & History, Montgomery, Alabama.

ROANOKE NORMAL COLLEGE - Courtesy of the Department of Archives & History in Montgomery, Alabama.

SCHOOL IN DISTRICT 47, RANDOLPH CO. Courtesy of the Department of Archives & History, Montgomery, Alabama.

The old Wade Carlisle home in Roanoke, c. 1860. Located on the site of Handley High School, it was purchased by Dr. J.H. Sharman and moved to Albany, Georgia in 1962.

The old Judge John Reaves home, c. 1837. This Louisiana bayou home was purchased by George and Vernie Perry and moved into the City of Wedowee where it is listed on the Bi-Centennial Trail.

OLD ROCK MILLS JUG FACTORY - This business began probably in the 1840s by a Mr. Leaman who located a deposit of fine pottery clay in the vicinity. It later was under the proprietorship of W.O. Pounds and in 1937 was inherited by his son, J.W. Pounds, and at various times has gone by the names of Pittman & Pounds Pottery and Pounds Pottery.

WEHADKEE YARN MILLS - Historic marker erected by the Randolph County Historical Society next to the shoals in Rock Mills.

The Prescott-Burns home. Built about 1899 by Charles Alvin Prescott in Wedowee.

The Benefield Funeral Home in Wedowee. Built about 1905-1910 by John Carlisle who was in the mercantile business.

Originally built for Dr. Knight's Sanitarium, this building is now Yarbrough Commercial Printing Company.

The James McCosh Mill on Wehadkee Creek in extreme southeast Randolph County. It is one of the only (if not THE only) stone mill in Alabama. Is similar to the Pennsylvania mill architecture. c. 1889. Now protected from vandalism by a chain-link fence.

The Mark Awbrey home in Roanoke. Presently in the process of being restored. Early 1900s.

The Butler-Bingham home. Built in Roanoke by Morgan Butler in 1906. Presently being restored.

INDEX

ABBOTT, James 111
  W.H. 114
ABELE, Temperance 157
ABERNETHY, A.E. 124
ABLES, N.M. 105
  Thomas 148
ABEL, Rev. Ephraim 104
ABNER, J.F. 114
  Mary 165 Levi 165
ADAMS, D.T. 165
  Dile 165
  J.W. 177
  James 135
  Jiles J. 150
ADAMSON, F. 113
  F.A. 107
  Fred 179
  J.G. 109,113,177
  S.H. 113
  S.M. 113,177
  W.C. 113
ADCOCK, A. 153
  Eliza M. 126
  Gooden 163
  Goodwin, 126,140
ADDINGTON, __ 114
  J.W. 25
ADRIAN'S FERRY 19
ADRIAN, F.F. 24,27
ADRINE, F.F. 2,77,149
  F.R. 2
AIKEN, James 2,27,58,
  80,87,88
AIKINS, Sarah 119
AKENS, James 151
ALBRIGHT, Minnie 140
ALDRIDGE, Henry 114
ALEXANDER, James E.
  159
ALLEN, A.P., SR. 113
  Ben 136
  Bernettie 114
  Dr. C. 131
  Churchill 179
  J.H. 23,33,40
  James 27,148
  James F. 2
  James H. 77
  James W. 149
  Lelan 3
  Prof. 78
  U.R. 118
  W.R. 116
ALLISON, William 146
ALMON, E.R. 111
  Elijah 177
  Elizann Mahulda 188
  Elizann Matilda 188
  Wm. Anderson 188
ALMOND, E.R., 177

AMARINE, Henry 149
AMOS, A.F. 190
  A.J. 145
  Able 109
  Andrew T. 187
  C.M. 24
  J.B. 22,35
  James B. 105
  Jim 35
  Mary 133
  William M. 187
AMOS & DAVIS 145
ANDERS, Alem 120
ANDERSON, Mrs. 188
  Ann 89
  Jim 5
  Lewis 89
ANDREWS, E.D. 107,113
  Mrs. F.C. 146
ANGELS, Teula 116
ANGLEY, Samuel 188
ANGLIN, H.J. 165
ARBACOOCHE GOLD MINES
  19
ARINGTON, S.A. 114
ARM, W.J.N. 113
ARMSTRONG, __ 48
  Bill 50
  Henry 50
  Henry W. 27,88,151
  Jim 50
  John B. 150
  John R. 155
  Warren 24,50
  William 100,104
ARNETT, J.T. 114,145
  Jesse 114
  R.A. 26,65,114
  Rich 66
  Richmond A. 66
ARNOLD, F.D. 165
  H.A. 163
  Harriett 165
  James M. 166
  Levi 111
  T.D. 163
  Thomas E. 163
  Vetura 166
  William 2
ARNOTT, J.F. 146
ASHCRAFT, Catharine
  104,158
  R.C.A. 146
  S.J. 125 Thomas 104
  Thornton 143
ASKEW, J.M. 107,113
ATKINSON, N.L. 146
AUSTIN, A. 105
  A.C. 105
  George 113

George H. 188
Jane 128
L.B. 113
Nancy E. 166
William A. 166
AUSTON, J.C. 113
  Larkin 113
AVERY, A.H. 111,186
  Elizabeth 161
  John 111
  W.R. 107,111
AWBREY, A.M. 4,183
  The Awbreys 7 Mark
AWBRY, Ruth 118 199
BAGGETT, Sarah 136
BAGGS, Eady M. 123
BAILEY, Charles 129
  Eddie 116
  J.C. 113,166
  J.H. 113
  Lossie 130
  Lula Belle 121
  M.E. 166
  Manuel 136
  Maudy 138
  Maurice 137
  N.G. 144
  P.G. 144
  Perry BAILY 137
  Pollie Ann 131
  Mrs. S.H. 133
  T.P. 161
  W.F. 103
  Walter 117
BAIN, W.H. 129
BAIRD, Andrew N. 151
  H. 104
  Joseph C. 151
BAKER, Mrs. 4,88
  B.A. 112
  Busing 5
  C.A. 146
  C.N. 146,189
  C.P. 189
  Isaac 20,24,25,54
  J.M. 3,5
  Jean 4
  Jethro 156
  John 101
  Oscar 4
  T.D. 111
  W.A. 143
BAKER & HUTCHENS 4
BAKER & MICKLE 4,5
BALDWIN, W.D. 166
BALES, Burrell 157
BALL, A.C. 109
  Harriett 177
  J.D. 109
  M.J. 109,177

R.H. 186
BALLARD, E.E. 145
  Joshua 186
BALLDIN, W.D. 110
BANKS, Sylvia 132
BANKSON, Sarah A. 166
  W.W. 166
BARBER, E.S. 25,159
BARBER'S STORE 6
BARCLIFT, Thomas M.
  184
BAREFIELD, S.E. 166
  W.P. 166
BARKER, Miss Cattie 57
  E.S. 57
  J.W. 184
  W.M. 57
BARKER & HILL 57
BARNES, D.S. 110
  John 122
BARNETT, J.P. 100
  W.M. 118
BARNWELL, Daniel 150
BARRET, T.V. 110,119
BARRETT, W.J. 26,68
  William 110
  William J. 68
BARRITT, William 114
BARRON, Hiram 25,26,
  58,59,80,88,107
  J. Day 26
  J.F. 145
  Mrs. J.F. 146
  Joe Day 25,58,60
  John D. 24,58
  M.D. 27
  Matthew M. 58,60
  Milton D. 27,45,58,88
BARROW, Elizabeth 112
  J.D. 109
  W.J. 112
  William 122
BARSH, Alaxander 129
  J.H. 24
  Mrs. J.M. 137
BARTLETT, Ella Catherine 161
  Y.J.A. 112
BARTON, A.M. 161
  E. 110 Mrs. 128
  Enoch 137,166
  J.C. 110,161
  Lucinda 123
  Martha C. 166
  William 110
BASS, Claudia 137
  J.J. 166
  S.T. 111
BASSETT, James 101
  John 101
  Martha A. 101
  Richard 101

T. 106
Thomas 112
W.H. 101
William H. 101
BATTLE, Richard 127
BAVEN, J.H. 156
BAZEMORE, B.H. 25
  Blount H. 54
  Moore 148
BEAN, D.M. 112
  Wiley 112
BEARD, F.M. 114
  G.W. 112
  H.H. 188
  Joseph C. 149
BEARDEN, E.D. 109
  Richard 140
BECK, E.M. 138,139
  Nevada E. 163
  Thomas 163
BEECHER, Fielding 148
BELCHER, 5
BELL, A.S. 143
  J.H. 26,73
  J.M. 24,109,146,179
  James H. 61
  Lucinda 119
  M.R. 2
  Middleton R. 26,73
  Sarah 111
  W.C. 143
  Walter 109
BELL'S MILLS 61,73
BENAFIELD, William H. 116
BENEFIELD, Mrs. S.E. 113
  Funeral Home 197
BENIFIELD, Manerva 166
  Mary 166
  Robert 110,166
  W.H. 166
BENNEFIELD, Cemetery 138
  Lucinda 134
  Nancy E. 138
BENNETT, Bama A. 121
  J. 27,111,166
  Jenkins 22,35
  John R. 116
  Jones 122
  Mrs. L.M. 113
  N.C. 113
  Nancy 166
  R.D. 113
  Rachiel L. 125
  William L. Bennette 117
BENTON, Joseph 17,21,24,30,36,103,150,183
  Robert 148
BERRYHILL, T.N. 62
  Thomas N. 102

BETTS, Martha 183
BEVERLY, Rev. J.C. 100,101
  James 113
  Mrs. M.F. 166
  W.C. 166
BIBB, Wash 166
BIBLES (BIBBS ?),
  Jennie 126
BIGHAM, B.H. 110
BILLINGS, Josh 75
BILLINGSLEY, David 102
  G.W. 102
  Washington 151
BINDER, Laura 138
BINGHAM, J.A. 186
BIRCH, J.C. 105
BIRD, James M. 166
  Susan 166
BIRDSONG, Bob 55
  Elizabeth 104
  John 104
  Robert 39
  W.M. 184
BISHOP, S.B. 166
BLACK, Rev. Lewis J. 43
  M.S. 166
  Robert 150
BLAIR, J.W. 110,122,166
  John C. 103
  Mrs. S.A. 166
BLAKE, Deliah 76
  James 109
  John 102,112
  Mrs. John 69,77
  Stell 53,183
  Dr. 7
  Thomas 2,19,25,27,52,53,54,76,109
  Tom 140
  W.H. 143
BLAKE & GILES 143
BLAKE's FERRY 2,14,47,52,143
BLANTS, Mary Ann A. 124
BLEDSOE, Peachy 155
  Rev. W.C. 73
BOGGS, A.G. 180
  J.M. 110,177
BOLE, Esq. 162
BOLT, Benjamin 94
  Isham 109
  J.F. 107,184
  Lucinda 119
  R.H. 22,38,111
BONNER, J.W. 114
  T.H. 130
  V.T. 111,166
  W.H. 142
  Dr. W.W. 128,129,137
BOONE, H.C. 145

BORNBY, Miss 88
BOSWORTH, W.E. 190
BOWDEN, Frank, Jr. 70
  Mrs. Frank 70
  Mattie 119
  W.D. 146,190
BOWEN, Abarilla 130
  Alanson 63
  Henry 135
  Ibbervilla 121
  John A. 110
  John D. 21,28,47,150
  John D., Jr. 150
  Judge 33
  M.N. 106
  S.H. 110
  W.H. 180
  William C. 63
  Mrs. W.C. 63
BOWEN & WILLIAMS 150
BOWERS, Thomas J. 157
BOWLING, Minerva 140
BOYD, E.M. 180
  F.M. 146
  G.W. 177
  J.H. 166
  J.W. 188
  Robert Lee 119
BOYED, E.M. 114
  F.M. 114
  J.H. 113
  Jackson 109
BOYKIN, James 118
BRADEN, A.L. 108
  Dudley 184
  M.E. 166
  Nancy 109
  R.E. 109,166,184
  Richard E. 102,184
BRADESHAW, R. Alonzo 128
BRADFORD, A.J. 188
  John 112
  Nathaniel 112
BRADLEY, Ada 162
  J.L. 106
  Leatha C. 124
  M.B. 111
  M.E. 139
BRADSHAW, Mrs. C. 146
  F.M. 106
  J.W. 17,18,28,94, 134
  Mary Fletcher 118
  Mollie 106
  Monroe 115
BRAIDY, Nancy 120
BRADY, Simon D. 133
BRAND, Bryan 177
  Rachel 118,177
BRANAN, P.G. 110
BRANNON, Rev. A.S. 161
BRANON, B.O. 109

J.W. 109
BRAZIEL, F.M. 110
BRAZILE, J.P. 110
BRAZWELL, J.F. 112
  W.C. 112
BRAZZELL, James 138
BRECKINRIDGE, John C. 72
BREED, Joseph 114
  Larkin 22,34
  R.J. 146,177
  R.N. 109
  Richard M. 167
  W.A. 109
BREWER, B.P. 180
  Willis 109
BRICKELL, R.C. 2
BRIT, Charles 129
  Piney 130
BRITISH & AMERICAN MORTGAGE CO. 184
BRITT, Ella 132
  J.D. 132
BRITTAIN, W.H. 7
BROCK, J.C. 119
BROMBELOE, N.D. 180
  N.E. 180
BROOKS, Mrs. 137
  A.P. 184
  Adeline 116
  Cora 130
  James 117
  John R. 105
  P.K. 180
  Susie 130
BROWN, A. 63
  A.J. 113
  Abnor 113
  Adline 114
  Caroline 110
  Christopher 154
  E.A. 111
  H.H. 167
  Isaac 167
  J.A. 144
  Mrs. J.A. 167
  J.B. 106
  J.W. 43
  James 112
  John 112
  Lucy 120
  Marion 120
  Mrs. N.E. 113
  Nancy 154
  Ruthy 128
  Seaborn S. 118
  T.N. 26,63,64,112
  Thomas N. 64
  W.A.D. 167
  W.O. 113
  W.R. 167
  W.R.V. 113
BROWN & MCPHERSON 83

BROWNING, T.N. 180
BRUCE, George W. 112
BRUMBELOE, N.D. 177
BRUMBLAW, G.W. 122
BRUN, Sarah 113
BRYAN, Mrs. E.B. 167
  G.N. 111
  G.W. 167
BRYANT, Mrs. F.E. 167
  Francis E. 110
  Thomas 167
BUCHANAN, E.L. 109
  Joseph 109
  W.M. 22,36
  William 156
  William M. 148,149
BUCKALEU, L.L. 113
BUCKHANNAN, Sophia 118
BURCH, E.A. 112
  J.C. 112
  L.B. 112
BURDETT, G.M.S. 167
BURDEN, G.W. 114
  J.N. 114
  James 109,151
BURDON, James W. 103
BURGESS, Lt. 44
  E.M. 23,42,43,103
  Elias B. 159
  Elias M. 42,43
  G.W. 113
  Mrs. George 161
  J.F. 114
  Mrs. N.E. 113
  Nancy Jane 136
  Mrs. P.F. 114
  Pink BURGES 125
BURK, J.S. 113
  John L. 154
  W.L. 180
  Wiley 113
  William 113
BURKE, Olivia 189
BURNES, E.R. 111
  E.S. 107
BURNHAM, Dr. 28
  Andrew 21,23,28,40, 154, 155
  Andy 20
BURNS, Col. 129
  Isabella 116
  Mitchell 162
  W. 106
  William 117
BURRER, W. 111
BURRESS, G.W. 112
BURROUGHS, W.J. 143,167
BURROW, Amanda 121
  J.G. 112
  John J. 111
  P.B.M. 112
BURROWS, J.W. 144
BURSON, Mrs. 115

A.A. 178
Isaac 103
J.C. 23,45
J.C., Jr. 110
J.C., Sr. 110
J.J. 103
Permelia 112
T.W. 167
W.J. 167
Willis 178
BURTON, Mollie 74
 W.H. 61,104,113
BUSBEE, Inman 140,186
 Mary J. 186
 W.A.C. 23,46
BUSBY, F.F. 111
 Inmon 117
BUTLER, Clark 109
 D. 165,167
 Daniel 109,110
 James 109 Morgan 199
 Pickens 109
 Samantha 129
 W.H., Sr. 109
 Whit, Jr. 109
 William 109
BUTTS, R.J. 121
BYERS, Henry J. 153
BYERS, PHONICK & CO.
 153
BYRD, Phylis 132
 Phyliss 135
 Sarah 135
 William 135
CABANISS, Septimus D.
 2
CADENHEAD, Nancy 130
CALDWELL, Cary 101
 John R. 41 Laurene
 W.F. 23,40   99
CALHOUN, E.B. 138
 Elizzie T. 163
 Hassy 118
 John W. 163
 Josephus M. 163
 Joycey Anjaline 163
 Morgan 128
 Mr. R. 163
CALLEY, Itura R. 184
 James W. 184
CAMP, C.M. 188
 Calista M. 189
 Dr. E. 41
 H.D. 112
 Harriett 41
 Henry C. 189
 J.J. 114
 J.L. 190
 J.P.D. 56
 John 3
 Johnathan 22
 Jonathan 37
 Lew 128

Lula Collista 119
M.C. 114
Mrs. Mary 56
Rev. T.A. 161,162
T.J. 106,188
W.E. 58
W.L. 109
William 25,102
William E. 58
Wyatt 140
CAMP, GLOVER & CO. 190
CAMPBELL, "Bug" Bill
 47
 Charity A. 184
 J.R. 190
 James F. 108
 John 154
 W.B. 24,47
 W.W. 7
CANADY, J.T. 144
 L.A. 167
CANAL GOLD MINES 19
CANADA, Robert 131
CANON, Arminda 187
 W.H.H. 187
CANTRELL, A.C. 105
 T.A. 154
CAPEHART, J.F. 165
 John 122
 W.T. 113
CAPLIN, Mrs. E. 110
CARD, J.H. 131
CARDWELL, W.W. 114
CARLIE, Samuel Y. 26
CARLILE, Francis A.108
 Lucy J. 108
 Samuel J.Y. 108
 John 111
 W. 108
CARLISLE, J.B. 187
 John 7,197
 Samuel Y. 60
 Wade 195
CARMICHAEL, W.E. 189
CARPENTER, BARTO 58
 Berta 54,58
 Bud 54
 Eph 54
 Ephraim 153
 Ephriam 54
 Frank 54
 Ida 54
 Mallie 58
 Mally 54
 Mandy 127
 Mary 54
 Mattie 55,58
 S. 27
 Sam 40,56
 Samuel 22,23,25,40,
  54,151,152
 Sug 54
CARROLL, Shelly 134

CARSON, B.M. 167
 J.M. 113
 John M. 119
 John Henry 119
 Mary 131
CARTER, E. 27,64
 Enoch 26,65,91
 John 117
 Katie 122
 Leah 115
 Mary A. 158
 S. 111
 S.D. 111
CASKEY, R. 149
 R.W. 23,40
 Robert 22,33
CASPER, Rebecca 121
CASSELLS, Absalom 151
 Henry 151
 Mark 153
CASSELS, Elender 152
 Thomas M. 186
CASTLEBERRY, Laura 124
CASTLES, Absalom 150
 Henry 150
CASWELL, B.F. 114
 Noah 115
CATO, Nellie Lucille
 129
CHAFFIN, M.A. 180
CHAFIN,
 Martha 111
 Moses B. 180
CHANDLER, Frederick W.
 159
CHAPPELL, Jimmie 126
CHARLESTON CONVENTION
 3
CHATAM, J.M. 114
CHEAVERS, A.J. 51
CHEEVES, A.J. 24,107,
 183
CHE-WASTI-HADJO 18
CHEWNING, Willie Innis
 117
CHILDERS, E. 105
 J.I. 167
 P.A. 109
CHILDS, Lula Belle 123
 Mrs. M.A. 167
 S.W. 167
CHILES, S.W. 112
CHUNING, J.J. 102
CISSION, Charles P. 92
CLARADY, J.A.J. 112
CLARDY, J.A.J. 143
 Omi Stone 126
CLARK, Capt. 43,44
 James 101
 Lydia 111,128
 Marion 101
 Mary Ann 101
 Massie 126

W.J. 111
William M. 101
CLEGG, B.F. 143
  G.W. 184
  James 142,143
  K.L. 129
CLEMENS, Anderson 161
  Ben 52
  James 52
  James M. 25,52,56
  Jesse 52
  Prosser L. 52
  William 25,52,54,56
CLEMENTS, A.M. 189
  Benjamin A. 153
  James M. 153
  Jesse M. 153
  Mary Ann 189
  P.L. 153
  Prosser 149,152
  William 149,153
  Winfred 153
CLEMMENS, J.M. 25
  James W. 25
CLEMMONS, ___ 7
  Anderson 136
CLEPTON, Eugenia 125
CLEVELAND, Grover 69, 189
  Tom 74
CLIFTON, C.F. 102,111
  Ike 162
  J.T. 111
  Len 162
  W.N. 83,111
CLIFTON & SWAN 111
CLINE, Henry 121
CLOWERS, C.R. 184
COATS, J.C. 109
COCKERELL, T.M. 144
COCKRELL, Jonathan 112
  Lorenzo 127
  Martha 110
  T.M. 112
  W.H. 112
COFFEE, Langston 159
  N.A. 158
COFIELD, C.V. 167
  Crosby 126
  E. 110
  H.W. 163
  J.E. 178
  James 109
  L.E. 112
  Louella 133
  Mary 129
  Mattie 140
  Nancy 128
  Nancy A. 167
  W.H. 23,24,25,46,109
  W.J. 26,68,143
  W.S. 112
  William 123

COGHREN, J.M. 157
COGSWELL, A.B. 113
COLE, C.H. 73,107
  Columbus 117
  Earnest 137
  Harper 6
  J.K. 167
  J.R. 144
  James 80 W.R. 107
COLE & CASPER 144
COLEMAN, John 102
  Major 182
COLEY, A. 109
COLINS, Mary 112
COLLIER, Joshua 112
  Thomas 102
COLLINS, J.A. L67
  M.E. 167
COLQUITT, Gen. 41,42
COLUMBUS SENTINEL 19
COLWELL, Bard 140
  J.T. COLDWELL 167
  Mathew 140
  R.A. 111
  S.F. 113
  Sarah L. 168
  Tobe 140
  W. 168
  William 24,114,126, 147
CONAWAY, Jane 112
CONNALY, D.M. 153
CONNELL, Mary 110
CONNELLY, Ed 6
  Richmond 130
  W.E. 22,25,27,89,111
CONNER, Permelia 112
COOK, Allen 113
  Mrs. C.M. 168
  E.B. 180
  Jeptha 178
  J.W. 168
  T.C. 178
  W.F. 180
COOLY, J.B. 26
J.B. COOLEY 63
  John B. 63
COOPER, H.G. 168
  Sarah 168
  William 168
COPELAND, Frank 135
COPPER HILL MINING CO. 186
CORLEY, M.V.B. 168
CORMACK, William 156
COSKEY, R. 22
COSPER, Alice 41
  George H. 159
  J.G. 159
  James G. 159
  Joe 41
  Joel H. 103
  John 129

William 102,153
COSTON, John 24,50
COTNEY, A.W. 143
COTTLE, Lou 138
COX, Oliver W. 152
  W.R. 168
CRAFT, Amanda 168
  D. 168
  D.M. 109
  J.G. 109
CRAWFORD, Henry 132
CRAWLEY, Feraby 119,120
  George 109
CREAMER, David 159
CREED, J.B. 134,168, 184
  James 162
  M.E. 184
  Mrs. M.E. 168
  Rhoda L. 134
  Sam 162
CREEL, Caroline 112
  J.H. 112
  M.P. 130
  William 130
CREWS, A.A. 180
  Andrew J. 168
  Martha C. 168
  W.P. 168,180
CRIDER, D.V. 80
  David V. 25,100,102, 155
  Thomas S. 157
CRIM, Morris 115
CRISWELL, Disie 168
  James 168
  John 118
CROCKET, Mrs. M.A. 109
CROMPTON, William 149
CROOK, ___ 56
  Mrs. C.E. 168
  Emory 168
CROUCH, James, Sr. 110
  Mrs. James A. 134
  Jimmie 129
  Shadrick 114
  T.D. 114
CROW, Elizabeth 110
  Harrison 23,40
  "Jude" 40,77
CROWDER, C.F. 114
  D.G. 114
  W.Z. 114
CROWLEY, Feraby A. 132
CRUMLEY, G.W. 146
CRUSE, J.M. 180
CRUTCHFIELD, Thomas A. 120
CULBERTSON, Sarah 137
CULBREATH, Ira 149,150
  Ira P. 159
CULPEPPER, Barbara 133
  Bill 7

John 102
John J. 112
W.H. 63
Rev. W.H. 143
W.W. 112
William H. 63
CUMBIE, H.E. 114
  Samantha 114
CUMMING, Bailey 162
  J.W. 111
  Nancy 158
CUMMINGS, Cilla 136
  J.S. 113
  J.T.L. 112
  James 136,162
CUNNINGHAM, W.H. 18,
  22,24,25,36,37
  William H. 151,153
CUMMINS, Irene 136
  Thomas 136
  William 113
CURRY, Joseph 21,24,
  30,109
DABNEY, A.B. 100
  A.E. 113
DAILY EVENING NEWS 60
DALE, A.M. 110
  Mrs. A.M. 110
DALRYMPLE, J.W. 168
  S.R. 168
  Sarah R. 132
DANIEL, E.C. 168
  I.N. 162
  J.A. 110
  J.H. 130
  J.N. 112
  J.S. 145
  John C. 188
  Ketrel F. 151
  L.N. 102
  N.M. 112
  Nathan 124
  T.Y. 144
  W.D. 168
DANNELLY, Malinda 112
DANNER, John L.C. 37
DARDEN, George 154
  Sarah 154
  W.C. 146
  Z. 27,80
DARNALL, Catharine 100
  Joseph 101
• DAROUGHTY, J.S. 109
• DAUGHERTY, J.S. 168
  Joel Scott 128
  R.M.C. 168
DAVIS, Mrs. 90
  Pres. 3
  A.J. 146
  Albert T. 168
  Bill 5,6
  Bud 107
  Charles 26,65,66,112

Chesley 110
D.I. 107
D.L. 31,105,106
David L. 105
E.H. 100
Elbert 132
Francis 110
G.B. 100
G.J. 180
H. 106
J.B. 100,168
J.F.M. 168
J.H. 24,27,51,90,93
J.H., Jr. 22,37
Dr. J.H., Sr. 105
J.O. 112
Jeff 34,37
Dr. Joseph 89,90
Josie E. 132
Lem 31
M.E. 168
Mary 110
Mattie 118
Nath 6
Dr. S.J. 116,117,118
  119,120,123
Todd 37
DAWKINS, J.W. 109
DAWSON, Col. 43
DEAN, Elliott 132
  P.E. 125,126,127,
  128,129,130,131,
  132,133,136,137,
  138,140,141,142
  W.A. 105
  W.A., Sr. 113
DEFREES, ___ 6
  Ida 46
DELAMAR, Fannie 128
DEMPSEY, Roxilla 103
DENMAN, A.W. 2,27,34,
  59,80,86,87,100
  Abner W. 86
DENNIS, Eliza 163
  J.H. 178
  Joe 163
  Joycey Anjaline 163
DENSON, Col. J.H. 73
  N.D. 26,74
DERRETT, Francis 149
DEVAUGHAN, W.F. 143
DEWBERRY, Giles 113
DIAL, Jno. H. 113
DICKSON, Catherine 111
DICKSON'S MILL 19
DINGLAR, Leosier 120
  William 102
DINGLER, F.M. 112,144
  G.W. 175
  J.T. 143,144
DISHAROON, Docia A.T.
  126
  E.H. 106,113

Etta 183
Fannie 183
Dr. H.B. 115,116,117,
  118,121,122,127,
  131,137,138,139,
  140,141,142
Dr. H.B. DISHASOON
J.T. 183   ⁻146
Martha E. 183
T.E. 106,180
DIXON, Henry 126
  J.L. 178
  Rebecca 124
DOBBS, William 131
DOBSON, B.J. 105
  C.T.G. 105
  John 151,152
  Katie 105
  W.W. 147,162
  W.W., Jr. 111
  W.W., Sr. 111
  Wallace Washington
  126
DODD, Andrew 109
  J.W. 109
DODSON, Mrs. Benjamin
  P. 63
  Catherine A. 29
  Susan A. 41
  W.C. 190
  W.W. 19,21,27,30,
  72,89
  Wallace Washington
  89
DOLLAR, Brice 113
DONALD, Mr. 6
DONNER, John L.C. 22
DOROUGH, George 126
DORRIS, John M. 153
DOSTER, Jack 137
DOTHARD, T. 148
  W. 148
  William 112
DOUGHTERY, Bob 69
DOUGHTERY HOMESTEAD
  184
DOUGLAS, Stephen A. 72
DOWDLE, Congressman 37
  James F. 71
DOWDY, James 149
  Michael 149
DOWNS, D.S. 110
DRAKE, William O. 133
DREWERY, E.A. 109
DRIVER, A.J. 7
DUABITTE, E.B. 187
DUKE, A.W. 188
  Dr. A.W. 115,116,117,
  118,119,121,122,
  123,124,126,127,
  128,129,131,132,
  135,140,142,144
  Ann 180

Anna M. 125
D.J. Davis 130
Fannie 125
Gertrude 117
Dr. J.D. 115,116,117
    119,121,123,124,
    125,126,129,131,
    134,135,137,139,
    142,144
Isaac 139
James 23,40
John 120
Martin 114,165,180
R.H. 113
Rus 8
S.J. 150
William R. 103
DULIN, A.E. 188
    J.C. 188
    John C. 188
DUNCAN, A.J. 168
    S.A. 168
DUNN, Hilliard 125
    T.H. 113
DUNSON, A.G. 168
    James M. 168
    Jeff 134
    Jefferson 135
    Nancy 134
DURHAM, Jimmie 121
EARNEST, Catharine W. 163
    Elisha 163
    F.M. 107
    Katie 137
    Pricilla 163
    Walker 71
EASON, Frank 135
    Raichell 110
EAST, B. 113
    Benjamin 113
    Cordelia 121
    Joe 143
    Riley 134
    T.J. 24,51,113,184, 189
    Z.R. 112
EDGE, Sarilda 114
    Syreldia 184
EDMONDS, I.M. 146
EDMONDSON, J.H. 159
    John H. 156
    Martha 136
    Pollie 132
    T.J. 111,168
EDWARDS, G. 106
    Greenberry 111
    Simeon 113
    W.N. 110
EICHELBERGER, C.W. 23, 46
    Charlie 66
    Emma Trene 129

George 66
Jacob 19,66,159
Mary EICHELBURGER
    Rufus 182   129
EICHELBERGER & HOLLY 114
EIDSON, James 125
ELEY, Mary 169
    William 169
ELLIOTT, Mrs. 116,117
    Cynthia 138
    Emma 121
ELLIOTT'S GRAVEYARD 130,138
ELLIS, W.N. 107
EMBRY, Elizabeth 113
    J.H. 105
EMBY, James 105
EMORY, Jim 6
ENLOE, Agnes 62
    C.C. 25,114
    Harvey 7
    Hoyt W. 161
    W.B. 110
ENTERKIN, W.S. 109
ERDMAN, Prof. 6
ESTERS, Amanda 140
ESTES, H.T. 169
    Martha 128
ETHRIDGE, H.P. 109
EUBANKS, A.J. 105
EVANS, Rhoda Ann 163
    Susan 162
    Thomas J. 105
FAIR MILLING & MINING CO. 98
FALKNER, Franky 132
    Jeff 2
    Jeff, Jr. 69
    Jefferson 21,22,26,
        28,29,36,37,60,69,
        150,154
    Joel 154
    W. 27
    W.G. 23,25,33,40
    William 152
    Wilson 22,25,71,80,
        102,156
FALLAN, Emma 187
    R.H. 187
FALLOW, A.H. 188
    Emma 187,188
    F.H. 187
FANCELL, Samuel 41
FANNIN, Annis 154
    E. 154
    James C. 154
    John M. 154
    Joseph P. 154
    Nancy 154
    Sara 154 Mary 154
    William 153,154
    William M. 154

FARRIS, Margarett J. 158
FARROW, B.E. 112
FAUCETT, Jesse 113,182
    John 5
FAULKNER, Jeff 19,20
    Jefferson 36,148, 149
    W.G. 24,54
    Wilson 58
FAUSELL, S.C. 188
FAUSETT, Sam 6
    Manley Barron 117
FEARS, Judson 137
FERRELL, Mrs. 118
    F.M. 2,27,86
    J.A. 178
FERRILL, H.B. 112
    Martha 135
FETNER, G.A. 111
    Joseph S. 112
    William A. 112
FIELDER, E. 113
FIELDEN, Edward 189
    J.E. 189
    M.D. 189
    S.A.M. 189
FIELDS, Riley 6
FINCHER, J.M. 106
    J.N. 110
    J.T. 111,169
    Nancy 138
FINDLEY, George 159
    Jane 125
FINLEY, A. 149
FISHER, Henry 112
FLINN, B.A. 25,55
    Benjamin 157
FLOYD, Dr. W.G. 126, 127,128,138,142
FOLSOM, F.F. 114
    Frank Foldsom 122
    Mrs. G.A. 184
FORBUS, Hiram E. 183
    Manley 183
    Sarah 110
    Sarah A. 183
FORD, B.H. 146
    Capt. B.H. 38,60
    B.J. 22,38,106
    Henry 187
    R.H. 22,36
    Mrs. R.H. 162
    William 148
FORD & STEPHENS 113
FORESTER, George 27, 85,89,92,93
    Rufus 23
FORMBY, P.A. 114
FORRESTER, George 113
    Mary Frances 135
    Rufus 46
FORRESTER's CHAPEL

FORRESTER's Cemetery
  131
FORT SUMTER 3
FOSSETT, Samuel 107
FOSTER,   133
  Amsie 163
  Belle 141
  Charles 25,58,59,
    80,103,114,184
  Elizabeth 114
  F.M. 143
  G.B. 143
  Leander 123
  N.T. 114
  R.M. 107
  W.H. 114
  W.V. 169
FOWLER, Betsy 124
  Dempsy 109
  Miles 109
  S.B. 109
  W.C. 106
FRANKLIN, Henry 131
FREDWELL, R.A. 106
FREELAND, J.M. 169
  Lewis 153
  S.E. 169
FREEMAN,   16
  E.J. 110
  Eli 110
  Emma 104
  Ezekiel 104
  H.C. 110
  Hugh 103
  J.J. 110,169
  J.W. 112
  Jacob 104
  John F. 102
  John W. 104
  Martha J. 104
  Sallie 122
  Sophia D. 104
FRENCH, G.W. 26,109,
    129,187
  George 68
  George W. 68
  S.E. 169
  Samantha 110
  Unicey 109
  W.J. 169
FULLER, Betsy 131
  H.L. 112
  John 121
  Mary Ann 132
  Rebecca 121
FURGERSON, Hanah 132
  H. FURGURSON 139
  Neil 13
FURLOW, Jim 4
GAMBLE, T.E. 114
  W.H. 114
GANN, James 112
  Nathan 111

W.D. 169
GARNER, Hudson 157
  James 110,189
GARRENDEED, Sturdy 155
GARRETT, Florida 120
  J.B. 104
  J.E. 178
  Jane F. 104
  John 112
  Jonathan 102
  Marcus L. 104
  N.B. 100,159
  Nathan 104
  Thomas F. 71
GARRISON, Mr. 7
GASTON, S.B. 113
  David 114
  Frank 119
  Jane 136
  Mary 121
GATES, Henderson 129
GATLIN, Jno. E. 169
  Joseph 169
  S.A. 169
GAUNTT, Dr. 105,137
  E.L. 169
  E.T. 180
  Dr. E.T. 115,116,
    117,118,120,124,
    126,128,129,130,
    132,139,142,147
  Dr. W.T. 125,135
GAY,   86
  Dr. 117
  Mr. 71,81
  E. 113
  F.M. 113
  G. 184
  H.M. 27,65,92,189
  H.R. 113,189
  Mrs. H.R. 69,77
  Henry M. 2,26,70,71,
    72,85,92,93
  J.A.M. 112
  J.M. 26,66,67
  Julia 113
  Miss M.A. 113
  M.J. 184
  R.R. 113,184
  Robert 161
  Dr. S.J. 124,126,127,
    128,129,130,131,
    132,133,135,137,
    139,140,142
  Dr. Stonewall J. 139
  William 112
  William D. 189
GAZAWAY, Henry H. 156
  Jesse 156
GEORGE, Happy 113
  Marion, Jr. 138
  N.J. 145
  Nicholas J. 145

W.J. 113,140
GEORGIA RAILWAY CO. 184
GERMAN, William 158
GERMANY, F.G. 169
GHENT Dr. H.C. 87
GIBBS, John N. 114
  T. 111
  W.C. 146,147
  William 147
GIBSON, Barba 174
  G.B. 180
  George 174
  Henry 122
  Hiram 145,188
  Dr. J.A. 124
  Dr. J.B. 125
  M.E., Sr. 180
  S.B. 125 Wm. 135
  Mary E., Jr. 180
  William S. 180
GILBERT, Francis 113
  Francis E. 107
  Peggy 153
  Simon 153
GILES, Butler 144
  Nancy 112
GILHAM, Charlie 188
GILL, L.E. 145
GILLAND, Thomas 23,40
GILLELAND, Lucinda 158
GILLEY, J.M. 169
GILLISPIE, Miss 4
  Crawford 4
  Mary GILLESPIE 90
GIPSON, Hiram 113
  Dr. J.A. 125
GLADNEY, Noah 114
  Samuel 112
  T. 114
  Thomas 103
  Thomas N. 138
  William 100,102
  Graveyard 119,139
GLOVER, Miss 89
  Cain 190
  Emily 62
GOGGINS, Isaac 113
GOLD RIDGE GOLD MINE
    87
GOODIN, John 2,81,82,
    86,92,149
    71
  John GOODEN 159
  Thomas 149
GOODSON, Mary 126
GOODWIN,   11
  Emma 187
  Gussie A. 187,188
  John 27,71
  Macajah 40
  Micajah 23
  Polly 139
  T.C. 187,188

207

```
       Thomas C. 187          GREER,      188         HAMILTON, A.J. 28
GORDAN, Sarah M. 110           GREGG, Catherine 141     Jack 28,33
GORDON & MCKEE 155             D.S. 112                 James 112
GORE, J.B. 110                 G.W. 109               HAMMONS, J. 106
  J.P. 136                     M.M. 112                 Kissie 123
  Knatty 110                 GRESHAM, David E. 150,     Mary HAMMONDS 158
GOSS, Rev. B. 100                153                  HAMTON, Rev. C.J. 143
  Benager 4                  GRIDER, David G. 57      HANCOCK, J. 170
GOTIER, Anthony 131           GRIER, B.C. 184           Susan 170
GRAHAM, Abbe 162              GRIFFIN,      7         HAND, B.J. 24,25,27,
  Lionel H. 184                 Mrs. 88                   57,58,100
GRAN, James F. 20               Augustus 157            Brade 4
GRANT, Rev. Mr. 163             Cordelia 56             Britian J. 57
  Della 138                     Elbert 112              H.N. 110   J.H. 178
  P.J. 145                      Mary A.L. 184           John H. 104
GRAVETT, John 112               W.O. 190                Raulaughy 109
GRAY, Amelia 115                William 184             W.R. 109
  E.A. 186                   GRIMES, Lemuel 111,124  HANDLEY, Capt. 76
  E.O. 145, 169              GRISHAM, David E. 25,    Mrs. 75
  F.M. 169                       27,55,56              Adelia A. 188
  Franklin N. 121               J.T. 110               Bowden A. 74
  Isaac 135                     R.M. 110               F.M. 113,145
  J.J. 109                   GRIZZLE, Nora 116         Frank M. 74
  Mansfield 107              GROGAN, W.H. 26,60        H.H. 187
  R.O. 107                   GROSS, C.O. 189           Jack 74,75
  Dr. S.J. 123               GUANTT, E.E. 114          James M. 74
  Seaborn 2                     J.C. 114               John R. 74
  Seborn 26,69                  Luther 114             Mrs. John R. 74
  W.W. 169                   GUSAON, A.B.C. 94         Nancy 141
GREATHOUSE, Peggie 132       GUINN, Capt. 107          W.A. 26,57,187
  Peggy 134                    Mrs. Lt. 43,44          William A. 74
GREEN, A.H. 110                J.M.K. 5,9,10,11,25,  HANKS, Denia 118
  A.J. 26,67,110,145,           43,44,62,78,105,     HANLEY, F.N. 6
     188                        106,107                Guy 4
  Andrew Jackson 67            J.W. 21,36,55,103       Jack 6
  Anna 123                     James W. 21,29,103,     W.A. 6,7
  Betty 124                      153,155,156          HANNA, John 23
  C.A. 149                     Jim 46                 HANNAH, Ella 133
  C.V. 169                     John 29                  John 40
  Dick 73                      Josephine L.P. 37     HANNERS, N. 150
  Mrs. Dick 73                 L.H.W. 100,159        HANNON, J.B. 165
  E.L. 120                     Lee 78                HANSON, James 25,52
  Glen Addie 124               Rachel 29             HARCROW, David 153
  J.W. 110                   GUNN, F.B. 180            Hugh 152,153
  James 149                    S.A. 180                James 153
  Joshua 110                 GUY, Henry M. 55          Jane 153
  Josiah 110                 HADAWAY, W.H. 169         Lindsey 103
  Mary A. 188                HADLEY, Joe 121           Mary 153
  N.B. 110                     Monroe 131              Peggy 153
  N.B.S. 114                   Sarah 121               Rachael 153
  Peter 102,113              HAINES, T.C. 109          Samuel 153
  Richard 137                HALE, Steven 135        HARD & CO. 144
  T.C. 129                   HALL, Andrew J. 155     HARDNET, Burk 136
  T.P. 111                     C.F. 169              HARDNETT, Fannie 118
  Thomas 145                   L.F. 114                B. Hadnett 144
  Thomas J. 187                L.J. 113              HARDY, Cordie 136
GREEN's Ch. Cem. 131,          Otto 135                Dock 64
     138,163                   William J. 169          T.L. 170
GREENE, Jacob J. 157         HALLIS, Elias 112       HARKIN's place 189
  James R. 187               HALPIN, Huston 122      HARMON, B.G. 105
  M.A. 106                     J.F. 145                J.B. 170
  N.A. 106                     J.G. 145                Martha 170
  R.M. 6                       J.T. HALPEN 184       HARPER, David E. 128
```

Frank 5,7
Green 83
Green B. 114
Isaac G. 120
Joseph 109
William 114,181
Wyatt 114
HARPER & WYATT 146
HARRALSON, Hugh 110
HARRINGTON, Fannie 137
HARRIS, D.C. 111,114
  Dr. Daniel C. 53,102
  Mrs. Daniel C. 83
  Elbert 170
  G.W. 170
  Harriet 131
  Harriette 110
  Hugh 23,24,39,47
  Hugh W. 25,53
  J.H. 73
  John 102
  L.H. 178
  Little 159
  Martha 128
  Puss 132
  R.H. 184,186
  Thomas L. 122
  W.N. 106
HARRISON, Dr. J.M. 135, 137,138,140
  William Henry 68
HARRIST, John 153
HARROD, Jno. 170
HARROD & CO. 144
HARTON, Mattie 123
HARRY, Jasper 170
HARY, J.J. 114
HATFIELD, W.F. 188
HATHORN, Hugh 3,4,52, 98
  James 3,4,25,52,53, 54, 98,153
HAVENS, Jacob 106
HAWKINS, Isiah 113
  J.D. 105
HAY, L. 106
HAYES, B.F. 112
  B.W. 112
  J.C. 109
  John S. HAYS 154
  T.M. 112
HAYNES, Fletcher, 5,39
  Mrs. Fletcher 32,67
  Fletcher W. 126
  M.D. 106
  P. 103
  R.C. 184
HAYTON, John T. 144
HAYWOOD, Cyntha M.A. 104
  Domino 94
  Jesse 94
  Matilda C. 104

Mattie 129
Sarah A. 104
William A. 104
HAYWOOD Cemetery 138
HEAD, A.H. 162
  B.F. 110
  George 134,135
  John 141
  Nannie 125
  R. 170
  Richard 114,120
  Susan Jane 135
  T.E. 27,114
  Thomas E. 90
  Tom 90
  W.R. 183
  William Charlie 134
HEALLY, T.T. 146
HEARD, Fannie 133
  J.D. 103
  James M. 181
  John S. 155
HEARN, Mrs. 90
  Asa 17,34
  B.H. 114
  C.C.Adm. 112
  D.N. 112
  David N. 102
  J.J. 27,114,146
  J.M. 27,34,71,156
  Jason J. 90
  "Mouse" 34
  S.W. 90
  Tom 94
  Whit 90
HEARON, Fannie 130
HEATON, W.D. 27
  William D. 90
HEFLIN, Mrs. 70
  Bill 75
  Bob 81,82
  H & H 128,129,130, 133,135,136,137, 138,140,141
  H.T. 142,187
  J.L. 145
  James 77
  James W. 108
  John 113
  John T. 2,26,44,69, 70,72,77,82,114, 156,184,187
  M.P. 188
  R.S. 2,21,26,27,30, 59,72,75,80,83,197
  Rhoda 137
  Robert S. 77,188
  S. 69
  Sarah A. 108
  W.L. 102,116,145
  Dr. W.L. 69,73,75, 77,120,124,125,142
  Wiley 108

Dr. Will 98
Dr. William 120,121, 122
Wyatt 2,27,69,77,79, 108,116
Dr. Wyatt 121,122,147
HEFLIN FAMILY 8
HENDERSON, B.A. 170
  J.A. 170
  J.C. 111
  J.C.A. 119
  James A. 124
  John 92
  John W. 115
  Lizzie 119
  Samuel 27,92,184
  Wiley 131
HENDON, J.A. 170
  J.A.T. 110
  Sarah 125
  G.B. 114
  W.N. 114
HENDRICKS, John M. 24, 25,57
  Levi 112
  Lucindie 120
HENDRIX, James 170
HENLEY, M.L. 170
HENRY, Clarisa Jane
  J.T. 153   122
  Joe 33
  L.T. 170
  T.C. 106
  W.T. 170
  William 114,153
HENSON, The HENSONS
  Mrs. 123   94
  R. 127
  Sally 111
HERNDON, Salema 121
HERRAGE, James 178
  Nancy P. 178
HESTER, Allen 110,188
  Elsie 127
  Eliza 170
  G.R. 110
  H. 110
  H.E. 110,145,188
  J. 110
  James L. 170
  M.M. 170
  Matthew M. 110
  Tarpley 103
  W.A.J. 143
  Warren 120
  Welden 129
  William 137
HICKS, Mary 133
HIGGINBOTHAM, E.B. 111
  Eph. 94
  Homer B. 119
  Nelson 101
  Pucket 102

HIGGINS, B.F. 139
  Frank 140
  J.C. 139,140
  John 139
  M.E. 140
  M.R.J. 139
  Robert W. 13
HIGH PINE CO. 8
HIGHT, William 102
HIGHTOWER, Mrs. 86
  Sheriff 18,19,20
  A.D. 109
  Bill 31
  Uncle Bill 32
  I.M. 102
  J. 2
  Aunt Liza 32
  Joshua 27,60,86,87
  William 16,18,22,23,
    31,39,86,109,154,
    156
  William M. 86
HILL, Amanda 120
  Bud 64
  Dick 64
  Elmira 136
  Francis 109
  G.O. 25,182
  G.W. 113
  George 64
  I.G. 113
  J.J.92
  J.L.' 109
  Jeremiah 141
  John 64,141
  M.L. 185
  Malinda Jane 132
  Margaret B. 108
  Thomas C. 184,186
  William 108,121
  Mrs. William 161
HILL, HARDY & CO. 7,
  146
HINTON, Bradford 125
HODGE, Eliza 186
  H.P. 143
  J.J. 170
  J.M. 143
  Rev. J.M. 143
HODGES, Bennett 113
  C.C. 113
  J.M. 113
  R.T. 106
  Thomas 113
  William 170
HODNETT, B. 106
HOLAWAY, Mrs. James
  105
HOLDER, Arther Grubbs
  127
  Caroline 113
HOLLAWAY, John 109
  Lenard HOLLOWAY 138

Lucy HALLAWAY 140
Rena HALLAWAY 140
HOLLEY, Grover 124
HOLLIDAY, Tabitha 170
  David HOLIDAY 170
HOLLIS J.K. 115
  Susan M. 123
HOLLOWAY, Mrs. I.W.
  108
  John 111
  Myrtle 126
  Zechariah 151
HOLLY, Len 66
  T.C. 114
  T.T. 26,66
  Thomas T. 66
  Tom 66
HOLMES, A.J. 135
HOLPIN, T.D. 107
HOMAN, James, Jr. 121
  Hezekiah 121
HOOD, Dr. 105
  J.H. 170
  J.R. 18,111
  Joseph R. 183
HOOPER, Green 117
HOOTEN, A. 109
HOPGOOD, Dr. S.P. 123
HOPKINS, Judge 2
  Daniel 150,154
  Sara 154
HORNE, William E. 184,
  186
HORNSBY, Betsy 183
  Dorcus 183
  Harriett 183
  J.M. 40
  James M. 23,170
  Mary 183
  Noah 183
  Sarah 183 Susan 170
  T.M. 127
  William 183
HORTEN, E.H. 106
  J. 170
HORTON, Hardy 133
  John 113
  M.L. 113,170
  Martha 141
  S.P. 141
HOUSE, Amanda 154
  Annis 154
  Emeline 154
  Nancy 154
  Sarah 154
HOUSTON, George 3,121
  J. 105
  John 162
  Laura 141
  Lizan 113
  Martha 128
HOWLE, Peter M. 48
  William 102

HOWLES, M.G. 102
HOWLIN, James 150
HUCKEBA, H.H. 24
  Mrs. H.H. 63
  L.C. 37
  H.H. HUCKABA & CO.
    147
HUCKEBY, ___ 119
  Bettie 127
  Jerry 127
HUCUBA, S.A. 105
HUDDLESTON, T.M. 171
HUDSON, C.D. 2,27,80,
  111,187,189
  C.S., Jr. 187
  Cicero D. 80
  F.T. 111,187
  J.T. 114,187
  Mrs. M. 111
  M.V. 114,187
  Matilda 187
  Sanford 104
  W.C. 187
  Dr. Wesley 41
HUEY, John 152
HUFF, Lettitia 158
HUGHBANKS, Matilda 109
HUGHES, Mrs. M. 114
HUGHEY, Joseph 111
HULL, Bettie 124
  John 139
HULSEY, Jesse 165
HUMPHRIES, Elijah 23,
  24,40,47,71,81,82,
  153
  Presley 102
  T.M. 107
HUNT, Benjamin 156
  C.W. 110
  F.M. 112
  Gilbert 110
  Hansell 156
  J.A. 171
  John 2
HUNTER, A.P. 23,102,
  154,159
  Alman P. 33
  Almond P. 22,39,62,
    154,155
  Augustus 157
  Bob 61,62
  Emily 62,89
  J.B. 142
  J.D. 146
  John 109
  John A. 148
  R.S.M. 26,61
  Robert S.M. 61
  S.T. 113
  V.A.P. 107,112
  W.A.J. 143
HURD, Manda 106
HURLEY, J.A. 114,171

J.C. 187,188
L.W. 187,188
L.W., Jr. 187,188
L.W., Sr. 187
Levi 139,187
Nancy 187
P.A. 171
HURST, G.M. 109
  Gilbert 51
HURST, COX & CO. 153
HURSTON, M.J. 178
  W.R. 178
HUTCHENS, L.C. 106
  Z.M. 26
  Zachary M. 61
HUTCHENS, Z.M. 159
IDSON, Levi 122
INGRAHAM, Bryant 111
INGRAM, E. 25
  Edmond 55,56
  Gabriel 149
  William 23,25,45,46, 58,102
  William INGHRAM 112
IRVIN, John Y. 23,46
IRVINE, J.Y. 113
IVERSON, B.V. 171
IVERSON & CO. 114
IVINS, Elizabeth 158
JACKSON, Atherila E. 181
  Uncle Billy 65
  C.A. 105,186
  Charlie 105
  D.S. 184
  Elizabeth 152
  J.B. 113
  J.J. 155
  Jno. C. 181
  M. S. 184
  Mittie 132
  Nancy 116
  W.T. 112
  W.P. 26,64
  William P. 64,117
JACKSONVILLE REPUBLI-
  CAN 20
JAMES, Clorinda 171
  Jno. 171
JENKINS, Allen 159
JETER, Barny 113
  W.I.P. 111
  Jinkens, Allen 102
JINKS, John 171
JOHNS, James 117
  John 116
  J.B. 109
  T.F. 109
  William 24,48
  Z. 113
JOHNSON, Mrs. 127
  Augusta A. 121
  B.D. 145 Mrs. B.D. 145

Benton 110
Billie 161
D.T. 114
Dora 131
Eva 161
Frank M. 183
Gracie 121
H. 109
Hatty A. 183
Henry 115
Irvin 121
James M. 183
Jesse 149
Jincy Marvin 183
John C. 102
John T. 183
Joseph 113
M.A. 107
N.T. 114
Nancy 113
Nancy A. 133
Peter 153
Rachael 153
Sarah E. 183
Soloman 109
T.J. 184
W.L. 113
William 129
William M. 183
Willis M., Jr. 183
JOINER, Eli C. 148
  Frank 139
  King 127
  Thomas 111
JONES, Alexander 129
  Charlotte 187
  D. 105
  David 126
  Elizabeth 171
  Freeland 171
  George W. 158
  Grover 74
  J.J. 178
  James B. 15
  Jonathan 157
  L. 7
  Mattie 115
  Nancy 125
  Richard 23,39
  Sam 5
  Tom 87
  Tom Organized 73
JORDAN, Dr. C.A. 116, 119,142
  Jane 133
  S.B. 110
  S.E. 22,35,109
  William 102,109
JORDAN Graveyard 120, 138
KAMP, Elizabeth 184
KAYLOR, G.O. 184
  John T. 183

KEE, J.B. 113
  Rhoda 113
KEEBLE, Caroline 108
  James 124 J.H. 106
  James H. 115
  Jimmie 120
  John 108 J.H., Jr. 114
  Lessie 130
  T.S. 114
KELLEY, Alfred 124
  Lewis 110
  Robert 171
  S.A. 171
KELLIE, Frances 128
KELLY, Christer 36
  Martha 36
  Mrs. N.E. 126
  Shedrick 100
KEMP, W.H. 109
  Wiley M. 87
KENNEDY, Elizabeth 121
  R.D. 24
  Sallie KENEDY 135
  William C. 155
KENT, A.J. 145
  Frederic 113
  J.W. 110
KERR, Martha 171
KEY, George W. 102,155
  J.F.M. 106
  James A. 171
  John KEE 109
  W.W. 145
KIDD, E.G. 109
  Eliza 171
  J.M. 146
  James 112
  James A. 171
  Moses 171
  S.J. 171
  W.W. 24
  William 110
  Z.M. 171
KILGORE, T.T. 165
KIMBEL, E. 154
  Peter 154
KIMBELL, Miss J.A. 112
KING, Dock 87
  Ezekiel 133
  Joel 153
  Louisa 114
  Peyton 69
  W.R. 69
KIRBY, Etta 141
  Fannie 130
  Hanah KIRBEY 114
  W.T. 113
KIRK, Morgan 130
  Sarah Ann 112
  Thomas 112
  W.J. 112
KIRKLAND, Francis 171
  Joseph 171

KIRKLIN, Thomas 109
KITCHEN, ___ 146
KITCHENS, J.M. 24,26,
  37,52,63,110
  James M. 63
  Louisa 110
  Mary Ann 37
KITE, Caswell 102
  Shadrick 152
KITLEY, Mrs. S.B. 112
KITTLE, Mary 171
  Thomas 171
KLEGG, K.L. 139
KLINE, Peter 181
KNIGHT, A.M. 114
  Alexander 134
  Bud 117   Dr. 198
  Cynthia E. 128
  G.B. 112
  Henry 7
  J.A. 79
  James 186
  James A. 79
  M. 171
  Monroe 144
  Nancy 157
  Royer 124
  Sarah 37,79,171,186
  Thomas 122
  W.E. 113
  W.T. 112
  William 107
  William E. 118
KNIGHT, W. & CO. 113
KNOP, John 105
KNOPP, J. 102
KNOT, James 131
  Mandy 131
KNOTT, C.C. 171
  E.J. 171
KNOWLES, A.J. 109,110
  Ransom 158
  W.H.P. 112
KNOX, W.F. 109   171
LAMBERT, Daniel 112,
LAINTAIT, James 158
LAMBRETY, Amandy
  Serfrony 188
LANCASTER, J.W. 110,
  120
  Liddie 134
  Lydia 132
LANCE, John H. 158
LANDERS, H.D. 26,67,
  J.H. 171   109
  James M. 172
  Z. 114
LANDRUM, Samuel B. 155
LANE, C.A. 114
  H. 114
  J.M. 103
  Jesse 114
LANE'S CHAPEL 136

LANEY, Mr. O.B. 162
LANGLEY, A.J. 113,186
  Alice 186
  J.M. 186
  J.W. 186
  Jeff 137
  M.E. 113,186
  M.L. 186
  N.L. 110
  W.W. 186
LANING, William 157
LARON, M.D. 145
LASHLEY, James 112
  James B. 188
  Matilda R. Mindy 188
LASITER, B.H. 179
LATTEMORE, John 149
LAWLER, Levi R. 151
LAWLEY, Julius 140
LAWRENCE, S.C. 146
LAWSON, W. 113
LAY, Moses 127   149
LEDGER HORTON & CO.
LEE, Chandler B. 189
  Elizabeth 158
  Isham B. 103
  J.B. 114
  Jason 127
  James H. 159
  Milton O. 109
  Polk 127
  Gen. R.E. 87
  Wiley 131
LEFTWICH, J.H. 26,68
  Joseph 144
LEGON, Hon. D.G. 2
LEHANAN, John 114
LENTZ, John J. 184
LESLIS, J.D. 125
LEVERETT, Mrs. M.E. 110
  Mary E. 101
  Robert L. LEVRITT
    153
LEVINS, Jessee 110
LEVINS GRAVEYARD 161
LEWIS, Edward 114
  Carabel 122
  Rosa 123
  S.D. 183
  S.L. 110
LIGON, N.N. 24
LIKES, Samuel H. 148
LILES, Amos 113
  Dr. J.D. 115,116,118,
    119,120,121,122,124,
    127,128,135,140,142
  J.R. 143
  J.T. 143
  Lafayette W. 186
  M.D. 117,122,129,
    131,132,139,141,
    142,145
  Dr. M.D. Lials 145

  Mary 121,133
  Young DeKalb 139
LINCH, D.W. 112
  Elijah Y. 110
LINDLEY, Mrs. 127
  R.E.S. 127,132
LINDSAY, Robert 83
LINEVILLE, Bird 135
LINVILLE, Daniel B. 152
  Elender 152
  Elizabeth 152
  Lambird 152
  Merriam 153
  Rebecca 153
  Tom 137
  William 152
  Worly 152
  Worley 154
  Worley D. 154
LINLEY, James 110
  T.M. 110
  Rev. T.M. 163
LIPHAM, Bethania 124
  H.L. 127
  J.N. 26,66
  James 121
  James N. 67
  Lucinda 178
  R. 131
  Smiley M. 140
  T.A. 110
  T.M. 178
  Thomas A. 127
LIPP, Ann M. 110
  E.J. 110
  G.W. 135
  Sarah 110
LISLES, Stephen 110
LITTLETON, M.A. 106
LIVRETT, Robert 150
LONG, Matilda 158
  W.L. 105
  William P. 120,121
LONGSHORE, 3,4
  E. 103
  Euclidus 151
LOUINA, 1, 96
LOUINA EAGLE 60
LOVELESS, Caroline 110
  H.R. 109
  W.T. 129
  William 107
LOVENS, Harriet 110
LOVERN, James 116
  Lennie 117
  Mattie 115
  R.M. LOVORN 124
LOVVORN, G.W. 163
  J.L. 188
  J.N. 64
  John, Sr. 110
  John N. 65
  Nevada E. 163

Dr. R.M. 127,131
T.J. 139
V.E. 163
W.D. 25,26,27,63, 110
W.H. 90
William D. 64
LOWERY, Mr. 118
LUKE, Isaac 139
LUNDAY, Thomas T. 156
LUNDIE, T.F. 25
T.L. 25
Thomas F. 55,56,81
MABERRY, J.C. 155
MADDEN, Cornelia 127
Georgia L. 133
Ras 139
MADISON GAZETTE 2
MALM's GRAVEYARD 132
MALONE, Mrs. M.A. 112
MANING, J.T. 112
MANLEY, Alice 183
C.D. 183
Dave 4,5
David 61
Frank T. 122
Mary 122
MANLY & HANDLY 146
MANN, Annie Eloise 126
MANNING, Dr. J.T. 124, 125
MAPP, J.B. 101
MARABLE, D.J. 113
Matthew 151
MARILAND RISLEY & CO. 155
MARION, Maj. A. 114
MARROWS, The 94
Hugh 102
MARSHALL, Jessie 128
MARTIN, Judge 28
Dr. J.W. 127
Mary A. 103
Mary Ann 123
Sanders 122
Thomas 103
MARTIN & FOSTER 150
MASHBURN, Dovey 131
M.W. 111,119
Newton M. 119
T.B. 111
MATHEWS, Mrs. 134
Jane 114
Jim 130
Lucinda D. 119
Martinie 116
S.J. 105
Susan 140
MATHIS, Jim 129
MATTHEWS, J.F. 110
MAY, C.J. 106
Talbert Mills 83
Tolbert 135

MAYFIELD, A.B. 110
B.W. 107,110
D.M. 110
W.S. 26,64
William S. 65
MAYO, J.T. 187
MAYS, A. 106
Elvira 140
McArthur, James 159
McBRIDE's GRAVEYARD, 135,138,140
McBURNETT, Albert 150
McBURNETT'S GRAVEYARD 135,136
McCAFFREY, James 114
McCAIN, Nancy 112
McCALLOM, W.H. 112
McCARDEN, S.B. 113
McCARDY, John W. 188
McCARLEY, J.T. 113
John 140
Robert A. 132
Susan E. 118
Vinie 106
McCARTER, William 106, 114
McCASH, S.A. 159
McCLAIN, D.B. 112
J.P. 172
N.W. 112
McCLELLAN, William B. 2
McCLENDON, A.E. 181
Arra E. 172
E.H. 181
Dr. E.H. 119,120, 142,146
Simpson 172
W.H. 159
William 3
William M. 159
Wiley 3,4
Wiley Martin 151
Willie 3
McCLINTOCK, William R. 102
McCLUNG, Hiram 110
McCLURE, James W. 157
Samuel B. 151
W.J. 189
McCLURG, R. 184
McCOLLOUGH, C. 105
John 80
McCOLLUM, Jonathan 153
McCOMB, __ 6
McCOMBS, A.T. 113
McCOMIC, Elijah 112
James 112
McCONNELL, J.A. 172
Mary 158
McCORD, H.G. 106
W.I. 172
McCOSBY, James 102
McCOSH, J.E. 114

James 19,198
McCOWAN, Mr. 154
Mary 154
McCRARY, J.D. 184
Lela C. 184
McCRARY, N.E. & SON 143
McCREA, Ella 118
McCRULESS, J.A. 110
J.F. 110
J.F. McCRELESS 188
McCULLAR, Andrew 102
McCULLERS, ___ 157
James 112
McCULLOCH, H.F. 178
N.A. 178
McCULLOUGH, J.H. 172
Mallie 134
Sidney 126
McDANIEL, Matilda C. 104
McDONALD, Angus 156
Elizabeth 157
J.M. 114
Samuel 63
W.W. 178
McDONALD HOTEL 4
McDONOUGH, B.F. 114
J.M. 114
McELROY, Henry 172
John 158
Katie 172
McGANIGAL, R.L. 25
McGHEE, E.J. 190
Emma J. 190
James Glover 190
McGILL, J.E. 112
Thomas 139
W.R. 33,143
William 112
McINISH, Gilbert 112
McINTOSH, Chief 11
Chilly 17
Laughlin 148
Rolly 17
McJUDOR, Hugh 190
McKASKLE, George 14, 25,52
McKAY, John F. 60
W.E. 127
McKEE, John V. 22,33, 34,36
Lawson C. 152
Lindsey 34
Linsey 22
William 109
McKENZIE, A.F. 127
McKEY, John F. 26
Samuel 103
M'Kilroy, F.H. 105
McKinzie, W. 105
McKNIGHT, WILLIAM 19, 25,27,53,77,159
McLaughrin, D.R. 190

213

McLEMORE, ___ 133
   Caroline 131
   Charley 139
   James 115
   Solomon 135,139
McLENDON, Dr. E.H. 134
McLEROY, Henry 172
   J.M. McLEROAY 111
   L.A.M. 172
McMAHEE, W.C. 114
McMANUS, Dr. M.M. 116,
   119,120,121,129,
   132,139
   Mitchell 10
McMURRAY, F.A. 27,86,
   186
   F.M. 24
   Frank 86
   Franklin A. 86
   M.P. 106
   Marion Pearce 118
   Samuel 187
   W.H. 4
McMURRY, F.A. 113
   M.P. & Co. 113
   W.F. 113
McNEAL, William 157
McPHERSON, Coon 7
   Ella 106,183
   Grecie 123
   Ida 183
   James 24,153
   John 24,103
   Mariah 120
McQUERTER, F.E. 106
   W. 106
McQUORTER, Samuel S.
   151
McSWAIN, Daniel C. 102
McVEY, John 102
MEACHAM, J.A. 111
   Lydia MECHAM 111
   R.F. 105
   Robert B. 115
   W.B. 105
MEACHUM, Pvt. J.J. 43
   J.S. 114
   John J. 43,44
MEADOWS, Edward 131
   Nancy 112
MELLINS, M.V. 112
MELTON, D.A. 113
   Jane 133
MEMPHIS & CHARLES-
   TON R.R. 2
MEREDITH, W.E. 190
MERRILL, J.B. 114
   R. 114
   R.E. 190
   Robert 22, 114,189
MERRILL & TRAYLOR 114
MESSER, J.C. 112
MICKLE, Mrs. 5

Bill 5
Carrie 135
Clarinda 137,183
Docie 119
E.P. 146
Ed 5   188
H.M. 26,61,67,107,
J.M. 39
James 98
James M. 67,100,154
Jennie 93,94
Jury 113
Lillie 136
M.J. 5,6,61,67,145,
   146,184,187
Mallie MICKEL 133
Mary 93
Mary Ann 122
Polly 115
W.D. 5,98
William 93
MILLER, Eli 153
   Jeff 109
   John 150
   Sarah 153
   W.H. 25,58,159
MILLIGAN, W.G. 186
MILLS, Marcus A. 148
   Wilson 172
MILTON, J.C. 114
MISE, Louisa 110
   Reuben 110
Mitcham, A.L. 172
MITCHELL, ___ 109
   Charlotte 111
   D.D. MITCHEL 26
   Dan D. 61
   F.J. 111
   H.T. 112
   Hal 136
   J.C. 111,159
   Jackson 136
   Jane 137
   K. 172
   Louisa MITCHEL 172
   N.B. 111
   Peter 6,113
   Peter MITCHEL 102
   S.C. 183
   Sallie 183
   Sarah 108,111
   Sarah R. 184
   Stephen 108
   Stephen C. 139,184
   U.D. 143
   W.D. 188
   Dr. W.H. 126,127,
     128,130,131,132,
     133,134,136,137,
     138,139,140,141,
     142
   Dr. William H. 163
MITCHEM, ___ R.B. 114

MIZE, S. 106
   Wiley 27
MOATS, F.M. 109
   Mathew MOAT 141
MOBLEY, M.C. 172
   W.G. 172
MOFFETT, Linda 135
MOLTON, James 102
MONAGHAN, Martha 117
MONCUS, Alf MONKUS 51
   John C. 132
   William 116
MONTGOMERY, Hugh 23,25,
   28,29,40,54,155
MOODY, Mary 119
MOON Anderson 162
   Cornelia A. 123
   Ether 138
   J.A. 111
   Rev. Jesse 100
   Rauley 110
   Thomas 155
   W.M. 26,68,106
MOONEY, Phillips 172
MOORE, A.J. 172
   Ben 7
   Guy 55
   H.R. 172
   Henry 145
   Israel 4,5,55
   J.A. 103
   J.D. 7 John A. 5,6
   J.J. 106
   Mrs. John A. 46
   L.C. 132
   Lypson 55
   N.W. 107,109
   Polly 111
   Spencer 112
   Sygmon 55
   Sygmore 25,55,61,159
   Thomas 158
MOOTY, Ellen A. 161
   J.H. 112
MOPP, J.B. 177
MORGAN, E.M. 110
   J.F. 110
   John 161
   Lucinda 139
   R.M. 147
MORRIS, Emma 124
   J.R. 190
   J.W. 110
   Spencer 102,112
   Van. 114
MORRISON, J.T. 27,148,
   149,155
   Joel T. 22,33,34,151,
     155,156
   John T. 27
   T.J. 109,184
   W.E. 109
   W.P. 109

Rev. William 33
MORROW, Georgia Ann
    Jack 64   183
    John P. 183
    T.H. 186
    Zilphey 118
MORTON, M.A. 172
    T.F. 172
MOSELY, Harvey 137
MOSES, Mesdame 64
    Mary 181
    Susan 110
    W.A. 111,181
MOSTELLER, C.C. 172
    Sarah A. 172
MOTES, Mary Ann 115
MOTLEY, John 112
MUCKELROY, Elija 148
MULDREW, J.P. 114
MULLALEY, William 19,
    102
MULLALY, William 25,53
MULLINS, Green B. 27
    M.V. 22,24,35,106,
        184,186
MULLOY, E.A. 172
    J.M. 172
MUNCUS, James 112
MURPHEY, J.P.D. 111
    Jeremiah 2
    W.E. 109
MURPHY, J.C. 144
    Jerry 27,77
    John 25,55,56,154,
        155
    P.D. 162
MURRAY, F.M. 2
MUSICK, M.A. 106
    William MUSIC 110
NAPIER, H. 173
    Willie 134
NATIONAL MUTUAL BLDG.
    & LOAN ASSOC. OF
    N.Y. 186,189,190
NEAL, R.G. 109
    Susie 162
    William 162
NEELY, J.T. 149
    Mrs. N.S. 111
NELSON, Benjamin 113
    Catharine 173
    Guy 173
    M.C. 119
    Mrs. M.C. 132
    Mary 122
    S.E. 132
    William P. 152
NESBET, W.H. 173
NEWELL, J.C. 106,144
    James 129
    Lovie 129
    W.P. 2,22,27,33,34,
        71,184

William P. 81,153
ÑICAHARGO, 1
NICHOLS, C.B. 24,51
    Chris 51
    F.P. 183
    J.J. 110
    Park 4
    W.B. 4
    W.D. 5
NICHOLAS, George J. 145
NICKS, A.Q. 71
    Alvis Q. 151
    Bryon L. 25
NICKSON, John 130
NIX, A.O. 16
    A.Q. 33
    G.W. 173
    John 187
    Lucinda 130
    M.B. 173
NIXON, D.R. 113
    P. 106
    Shaw 173
    Stephen 100
NOEL, George W. 103
    J.A. NOELL 113
    Rhoda W. 103
    Richman 103
NOLAND, Elizabeth A.
    173
    Stephen 122
    William 173
NOLEN, Harriet 109
    J.W. 173
    Richard 154
NOLER, A.J., Jr. 144,
    145
NOLES, Caroline 111
    Dollie 119
    E.M. 138
    Ella 119
    John G. 124
    John W. 26,62,63
    W.P. 178
NORMAN, W.Y. 114
NORRED, Henry 130
    Joseph 107
    W.P. 113
NORRED & DAVIS 4
NORTON, S.E. 122
    Susan M. 128
    Young 128
NORWARD, William P. 105
NUNN, Elijah 157
    William R. 102
NUNNELLY, W.A. 111
OAKS, George 129
OGLETREE, M. 173
    Nancy 120
    T.S. 173
OLDHAM, J.H. 178
    John H. 182
OLIVER, E.M. 186

J.W. 25,187
    Martha 138
    P. Percy 188
    Rufus F. 121
OMERY, Sarah 173
    Thomas 173
ONEAL, E. 105
    M. 105
ORR, Guy 161
    John 102, 143
    R.D. 112
    Sallie 124
    T. 145
    Timothy 113
    W.J. 145
OSBORN, _____ 158
    W.H. 63,113
    William H. 64
OSLIN'S CHAPEL 141
OTWELL, Benjamin 158
OVERBY, Dr. 126,142
OVERTON, Elisabeth 131
    J.W. 105
    Jacob 110
    Mary E. 120
OWEN, John T. 54
    O.S. 173
OWENS, A.D. 111
    A.J. 161
    Alexander 110
    Andrew 56
    Bill 56   Emma 123
    Eucatan 161
    Mrs. F.E. 56,147
    Frances E. 128
    Henry 56
    J.T. 161,183
    James T. 124
    John T. 22,23,24,
        38,147
    Preston 56
    Samuel T. 27,40,77,
        79
    Tom 56   152
    William 25,27,37,56,
    Waller 102
    Yucatan 56
PARISH,   Comer 130
    M.E.R. 113
    Sherman PARRISH 124
PARK, Elizabeth 157
    Rev. Mose 45
    Rev. Moses 45,157
PARKER, B.F. 184
    Eda A. 107
    Ephraim 102
    Francis 113
    John 27
    Martha A. 107
    R.A. 25
    S.D. 111,145
    William 107,150
PARKS, Janie 124

Moses 113
Robert 123
PARMER, Fannie 124
　J.H. 165
PARRISH, Mary 132
PARSONS, T.G. 186
PATE, Mrs. 74
　Allen 135
　Bob 74
　Elbert 110
　G.G. (Bird) 73,79,
　　113,186
　James 73
　Lou 126
　Mary 37,79
　R.S. 26,147.183
　Robert S. 73
　Sallie Lou 117
　Samuel N. 109
　Sue 5
　T.F. 107,113,146
　Thomas, Jr. 184
　Thomas F. 73
PATILLO, Emma 137
PATRICK, Mallie 135
PATTERSON, Cicero 134
PATTON, A.G. 184
　Alexander G. 184,186
PAYNE, Isaac 152
PEAK, Tiney 137
PEARCE, William R. 109
PEARSON, D.R. 130
　J.M. 112
　J.S. 159
　James S. 103
　W. 146
PEAVY, Eliza 184
　Cullen 184
PECK, Paseline 113
PEELER, James 28
　Jacob 19,150,152
PELHAM, Charles A. 75
PERRY, George 195
　Rev. J.R. 143
　Jno. W. 178
　John W., Sr. 128
　Vernie 195
　Rev. W.W. 143
PERRYMAN, Esq. 45
　Cintha 110
　D.A. 23,26,27,48,
　　103,110,146
　Dave 161
　David A. 44,64,88,
　　89,104
　David P. 156
　E.M. 146
　F.M. 25
　Francis M. 20,102,
　　150,151
　O.H. 22,24,38,114
　W.M. 24　　135
PERRYMAN'S GRAVEYARD

PERSON, James 102
PETERMAN, George 112
PETTIT, John P.C. 152
PHELPS, Davy 127
PHILLIPS, Alsey 133
　Charles 150
　Daniel 32,67
　Floyd 186
　Floyed 111
　Isbell 106
　J.M. 184
　J.R. 114
　James R. 184,186
　John 120
　Rebecca 152
　Samuel 144
　Sarah F. 105
　Sopha 157
　T.M. 105,113
　Tyler 113
　Wilkins 153
　William 67
PHILPOTT, E.T. 178
PICKETT, W.D. 3
PIKE, Amanda 111
　Charles Edward 127
　Clara 125
　J.F. 114
　Simpsey 119
　W.A. 114
　W.F. 114
　Walter 121
　William 114
PINETUCKY GOLD MINES
　127,190
PINKARD, Mr. 7
　Ann 116
　M.J.F. 105
　John PINCKARD 153
　Mary 116
　Robert 118
PINKSTON, Rachel 119
PITMAN, Alf 118
　J. 120　T. 120
PITTMAN & POUNDS 196
PITTMAN, A.E. 111,173
　A.J. 147
　Alfonso 40
　Amburs 127
　C.C. 25,40,113
　Eliza E. 184
　Escar A. 184
　I.L. 40
　J.F. 111
　J.W. 173
　James M. 23,40
　John R. 173
　Joshua M. 111
　M.P. 23,47
　Martin 182
　Martin P. 184
　Mary A. 173
　Sarah 114

　T.L. 21,30,59,82,
　　83,103
　Tim 4
　W.A. 106,111
　W.W. 146
PITTS, Cora R. 120
　Ethel 119
　Grover 120
　Florence 120
POAGUE, James L. 120
POLK, W. 112
POLLARD, J.T. 114
　M.J. 162
　Mrs. Thomas 62
　Tom 77
"POLLY ANN" 50,51
PONDER, Bedford 7
POOL, Widow 4
　Bob 81
　George 113
　J.J. 111
　M.A. 113
　Mary 119
　N.B. 113
　Napoleon 81
　P. 105
　Pole 81
　Polk 81
　R.C. 27,80
　Rob 2
　Robert C. 80
　Thad 43,44,81
　Thasseus 81
　Dr. W.H. 113,115,117,
　　118,121,123,125,
　　127,131,134,136,
　　137,139,141,142
　W.P. 114,118
　Walter 123
　William P. 81,134
　Mrs. William P. 77
　William R. 139
POOLE, J.J. 146
　W.C. 146
　Mrs. W.P. 69
POORE, A. 112
　N.M. POOR 181
POPE, William 118
PORTER, Dr. C.C. 100
　John H. 149
　John S. 150　M.R.100
　Henry H. 150
POUNDS, W.O. 196
PORTHRO, Mathews 138
　Pinkie 138
　Shadrick 136
POSEY, James 101,137
　S.N. 111
POWELL, George C. 23,
　　24,39,47
　Peter 24
POWERS, F.D. 182
PRATER, E. 114

King 114
PRATHER, King 114
  S.O. 120
PRATT, Irvin 162
PRESCOTT, Mrs. 64
  Alice 38,125
  C.A. 26,64,147,183,197
  C.A. PRESCOAT 110
  C.M. 183
  Nannie 183
PRESNAL, Jno. G. 179
  Martha 179
PRESSNELL, Elizabeth 111
PRESTON, Rev. A.G. 143
  A.J. 105
  G.H. 112
  Hewland 129
  Mattie M. 143
  W.G. 26,68
  William L. 104
PRESTRIDGE, J.W. 111
PRICE, James 156
  Samuel 140
  William 150
PRITCHETT, W.F. 25
  W.J. 25
  Wiley J. 55
PROTHRO, James 25,52, 53,153
PROTHRO & McPHERSON's Mill 52
PROTHROW, Moses 111
PUGH, James 186
PULLIN,___ 109
PUTMAN, Matisin 149
PUTNAM, Howard M. 150
  Israel 159
  James M. 102
  Matthewson 148
  Simeon 150
RADNEY, Bill 182
  H.B. 184
  Herbert 140
  J.H. 23,24,46,51, 106
  J.S. 111
  James H. 115,183
  James L. 181
  James S. 52,56
  John 4
  John W. 183
  M.H. 112
  Minus 186
  Octavia 127,132
  Sarah 183
  T.A.E. 181
  W.A. 24,107
RAGAN, John R. 103
  M.A. 103
  R.G. 103
  Rhoda 110,130
RAGSDALE, J.M. 173

Nancy 173
W.A. 173
RAMPEY, B. 131
  Henry 103
  Nan 131
  William H.E. RAMPY 119
  Willie 133
RANCY, J.T. 179
RANDALL, F.P. 27,91, 146
RANDOLPH, John 1,96
RANDOLPH ENTERPRISE 60,75
RANDOLPH TOILER 10,135 136,138
RANSEY, W.J. 179
RAY, A.T. 150
  Andrew T. 25,54
  Frances 150
  J.D. 173
  J.H. 111
  J.R. 173
  John R. 54
  Mahala 111
  Murk 114
  Sarah 173
RAYBURN, Martha 139
REAVES, A.S. 25
  Lt. A.T. 43,44
  Angernon Sidney 87
  Benjamin 103
  E.W. 107
  Emily 107
  Gus 31
  Issabella 107
  John 21,22,25,27,29, 38,60,72,80,103, 111,122,159,187, 195
  John, Sr. 110
  Mentoria 72
  Polly 43
  Prior 102
  S.E.A. 21,24,27,75, 92,93,106,183, 187,189
  Steve 28,29,31
  Thompson 43,44
  William Elma 126
REED,___ 7
  B.J. 114
REESE, George 2,26,68
REEVES, A.M. 125
  C.D. 173
  E.P. 159
  John 2
  William 152
REYNOLDS, Zachariah 148
RICE, Aaron 109
  Alsia M. 122
  E. 181

E.F. 181
George 109
J.L. 109
James 109,125
Marion 140
Moses 109
W.S..107,112
RICHARD, E.G. 111
RICHARDS, R.W. 111
RICHARSON, F.M. 173
RICHLAND, J.B. 189
RICKE, F. 24
RIDDLE, G. 109
  Gideon 25,56,109
  Miss M.H. 100
  Rebecca 157
  S.W. 159
  Terry 148
  W.H. 109
RIEKE, Fred 162
  P. 105
RIGBY, S.J. 109
RILEY, Henry 113
ROANOKE COTTON MILL 7
ROANOKE COTTON WAREHOUSE 7
ROBERSON, Jno. 173
  M.J. 173
ROBERTS, A.J. 109
  Andrew 174
  J.H. 102
  R.G. 71,81
  Y.A. 113
ROBERTSON, A.P. 113
  Alice 41
  Bob 62
  C.W. 112
  Mrs. E.C. 111
  George T. 113
  Hardy 112
  Harriett 41
  J.D. 111
  J.H. 112
  J.J. 114
  J.M. 112
  J.W. 111
  James F. 41
  Jno. 114 John D.41
  Joseph W. 62
  Kate 161
  Kella 125
  Mrs. M.A. 113,179
  N.B. 144
  Dr. R. 80
  R.L. 23,41,46,62,101
  Rachell 112
  Mrs. S.A. 111
  S.F.C. 179
  W.C. 26,62
  W.C.S. 22,35,62
  William C. 62
ROBINSON,___ 68
  Capt. 87

J.J. 26
James J. 73
Jerry 130
John 114
Luke 113
M.D. 87
ROCK MILLS COTTON
  FACTORY 2, 196
ROCK MILLS MFG. CO. 114
ROCK MILLS JUG FTY. 196
RODAHAN, Charles 159
RODGERS, Henry 111
  Joe 141
  Mary 111
  Percilla 111
ROE, Jesse 162
ROGERS, Ann 158
ROLLINS, J.A. 144
  James A. 181
ROSE, Agga 6
  Aggie 94
ROSEMAN, Thomas 109
ROSS, Frederick 154, 155
ROUNDTREE, A.W. 111
  Mary A. 132
ROUSE, J.H. 159
  James E. 2
  James H. 100,103
ROWE, Kinian 114
  T.D. 114
ROWLAND, R.G. 146,188
ROWND, Robert M. 184
ROY, Earnest 129
RUSHTON, Joseph 103
  Martha 114
RUSSELL, Maggie 140
RUTTON, John W. 16
SADLER, Elizabeth 101
  H.A. SADDLER 174
  William SADDLER 174
SALTER, Edmond 156
SANDERS, J.M. 107
  Sarah 183
SANFORD GREENWOOD &
  CO. 149
SATERWHITE, Elizabeth 110
SATTERWHITE, S.E. 174
  Stella 140
  W.J. 174
SAUNDERS, J.M. 107
SAVAGE, Serg. J.L. 43
  Jeff 41
  Jesse 41,42
  Joseph 23,41
  Shelt 41,43,44
SAWYER, Archibald 13, 14,16,20,21,28,159
  Joe 21
  Judge 14,15
SAXON, A.C. 90,106
  J.M. 110,181

James 102,103
SCALES, Alexander 133
  James 74,103
  Joseph 133
  Sabe 138
  Sue 74
SCHUESSLER, Major 7, 184,189
  Bob 7
  Carrie 190
  Charles 184,190
  Ida 190
  J.M. 189,190
  J.W. 89
  L.S. 190
  Mary 184,186
  Mattie 184
  Millie 189,190
  Morgan 7
  Robert L. 184,189
  Sallie S. 190
  Zack 190
SCHUESSLER & CO. 184, 189
SCIPPER, Sarah E. 111
SCOTT, J.M. 174
  Mary A. 189
  T.W. 190
SCREWS, William Wallace 95,96
SCRUGGS, J.H., Jr. 159
SEARS, Agnes 131
  D.P. 145
  Feraby 132
  Gussie 133
  Mary C. 110
  Robert 134
SEEGAR, C.E. 162
SEERS, David 122
SELLERS, James 127
  John 110
SEYMOUR, Hattie 133
  S.A. 112
SHAFFER, Rev. J.P. 62
  John P. 7
SHAMBLEE, Louisa 174
  S.W. 174
SHARMAN, J.C. 146
  James, Jr. 123
  W.R. 68,146,190 195
  William R. 68
SHARP, D.C. 112
  Martha 133
STATTOCK, Awerk R.184
SHAW, A. 174
  G.H. 174
  George 109
  Nancy L. 174
SHEELY, Rube 132
SHELL, George 137
SHELLNUT, J.T. 161,183
  James 174 H.M. 111
  Jane 111   H.N. 183

John 174
T.J. 161
SHELLNUT, Andrew 139
SHELNUT, W.N. 114
SHELNUTT. Martha 136
SHEPARD, J.P. 114
  J. Truman 101
  Jerimiah 114
SHEPHERD, John 106
  Jeremiah 103
  Margaret 132
SHEPPARD, John 106
  O.W. 60
SHERMAN, J.C. 106
  James C. 93
  W.R. 26,114
SHERRER, Thomas 115
SHERRIAR, D.S. 105
SHIFLETT, Marion 139
SHIPP, Alma R. 131
SHIRD, Claudie 125
  Ella 125
  Walter 125
SHOCKLEY, L.G. 109
SHOCKLY, Nancy 157
SHORTER, Judge 28
SIKAS, Mary 114
SIMAS, W.A. 144
SIMINTON, Jno. 114
SIMM, 3,5
SIMPSON, Mary 134
  Thomas 114
  W.H. 174
SIMS, John 134
  Sewell 134
SINGLETON, Mrs. 123
  R.R. 150
SKINNER, 6
  Jim 6
SKIPPER, Levi 174
  Sarah 174
SLATHAM, C.W. 22
SLATON, Rebecca 111
SLAY, M.W. 174
SMITH, Gov. 37
  Mrs. 37
  Capt. 44
  Widow 5,138
  Dr.J.H.A.D. 98
  A.J. 134
  Albert 123
  Anderson 181
  Anderson F. 174
  Andrew J. 83
  Barnett 114
  Belle 105
  Bob 37,89
  C.A. 111,143,144
  C.M. 112
  C.M.G. 174
  Charles A. 83
  D. 98
  Dallas 83

218

David 83,84
David D. 83,102
Dolph 138
E.A. 112
E.B. 42,43,80,87
E.J.M. 189
Ealom 184
Elisabeth 132
Elizabeth 174
Emma M. 184
Emma V. 186
Endith 186
Florizet 184
H.D. 187
Hoyt 5,6
Isaac 181
J. 110
J.A. 110
J.C. 174
J.L. 174,186
J.M. 110,120,145,146
J.T. 110
James 151,153
James A. 174
James G. 189
James H. 102
James M. 83,184
Jane 181
Jeptha V. 19,37,83
John Anthony Winston 84
John B. 186
John F. 81
John O.D. 83,92,159
John T. 6,43,51,87
Jordan 27,112,174
Joseph M. 184
L.C. 186
Lee 110
Mrs. M. 112
M.A. 174
Martha 37,77,79
Mary A. 181
Mary C. 186
N. 105
Nancy 110,134,179
Nathan 123
Otis E. 184
P.M. 112
Puss 139
R.T. 22,27,79,111
Rial 110
Riley 118
Robert T. 37,83,125
S.S. 114
Sarah 118   37
Stephen A. Douglas
T.A.G. 188
Tea 127
Thomas 148
Touch 127
W.B.F. 179
W.F. 111,174

W.H. 2,25,27,59,61, 72,83,84,86,87,97, 111,187,188
Wade D. 122
Warren 129
Wiley W. 189
William H. 83
William H., Jr. 84
SNIVELY, Jim 94
SNOW, Sarah 157
THE SOUTHERN REGISTER 19   60
THE SOUTHERN MERCURY
SPARKS, J.M. 183
  Mollie 183
SPEARS, Amanda 103
  Daniel 103
  Daniel J. 103
  J.M. 111
  James R. 103
  Joshua 154
  Mary 111,158
  Mary A. 103
  Nancy 103
  Nancy L. 111
  P.H. 174
  Paralee 111
  Parolle H. 184
  W. 174
  W.H. 110
  William 175
  William R. 103
  William W. 184
SPENCE,   109
  Mrs. 116
  A.J. 111
SPRADLING, Seaborn 103
SPRAGBERRY, Uriah C. 102
SPRUCE, Johnnie 42
  Spark 42
  W.H. 23,25,42,100, 103
  W.M. 103
  W.R. 111
STABLER,   123
  Robert 123
STALLINGS, J.W. 24
  Jeremith W. 102
  Serg. J.W. 43
  W.J. 113
STARNES, A.D. 179
  Lizzie 140
STATBANE, C.W. 24
STATHAM, Charles W. 36,55,61,151, 153,154
STEEN, J.W. 127
STENFORD, Thomas 113
STEPHENS, Mr. 3
  Dr. A.R. 123
  Andrew 184
  D.L. 112

E.B. 107
E.H. 112   Henry 104
Harris 25,58,102
J.F. 109,175
J.H. 175
Jeremiah 26,59,60
John 120,175
Laura V. 184
Leah 115,121
Lydia 132
M.M. 175
Mrs. Mary 112,175
Maud 120
Mollie 138
O.T. 112   Overton 104
S.S. 143
Sarah 107
Soloman 107
Stephen 184
Thomas 114,124
William 111
STEPHENSON, Sallie C. 141
STEVENS, Mr. 6
  George 7
  Leola 125
  M.S. 146
  Prissie 134
  Mrs. W. 146
STEVENSON, Family 7
  Henry 8
  J.M. 177
  James B. 125
  John B. 7
  Leon 8
  Olin 8
  W.W. 8
  Worth 8
STEWARD, Cyrus Wilson 127
STEWART,   5
  Cyrus 110
  H.W. 175
  I.N. 111
  J.F.N. 113
  J.H. 112
  J.W. 22,25,38
  James 109
  John 128
  M.P. 23,47
  Martha 110
  Mary E. 106
  Mrs. S.W. 113
  W.H. 113
  W.L. 145   Willie 135
  William 158
  William D. 118
STIGLER, William 104
STILLWELL, John 109
  L.A. 179
STRICKLAND, Hardy 159
  Thomas 156
STRIPLIN, Elizabeth 158

219

John W. 155
STITT, J.T. 111
  James 130
  James Aikin 135
  Robert 111
  Thomas S. 140
  W. 111
  W.W. 26,66
  William W. 67
STONE, Calip 111
  J.P. 179
  Vida 138
STONED, James O. 107
STORK, Andrew J. 186
  Martha C. 186
STRAIN, J.D.W. 110
STRICKLAND, E. 101
  Eldon 141
  H.A. 114
  Hardy 71,101
  J.C. 114
STRIPLIN, Rev. Ben 41
  W.A. 23,25,41
STRONG, Carrie 130
  Emma 131
  Robert 131
  Thomas 109
STROUD, John 103
STUBBS, S.F. 105
  W.F. 113
SUDDOTH, Elbert
SUDDUTH, Candy 141
  William 141
SUMBERLIN, Benjamin 110
SUTHERLAND, George R. 189
SWAN, Charles 112
  H.E. 106
  James W. 112
  Jno. 112
  N.B. 113
  W.A.J. 145
  William H. 118
SWANN, Capt. 48,49
  Mr. 162
  Barney C. 138
  J.C. 187
  Dr. J.C. 126,127,
    128,129,130,134,
    136,137,139,142
  James A. 179
  W.A.J. 24,27,48,50
SWINT, Ann 114
  Edmon 121
  Flozel 184
  Joseph 24,114,144,
    179
SYKES, J.M. 111
TALLEY, L. 111
TARVER, ___ 128
  H. 114
  J.E. 175

Jno. 114
Martin 114,175
TATUM, Mollie 122
TAYLOR, ___ 114
  Amanda 139
  Bernice 125
  Dr. C.B. 27,72,91,
    122,123,147
  Dr. C.W. 125
  Charles 110
  Freeman 25,56,57
  Dr. G.W. 124,127
  Ibba 15 Mrs. G.W.
  J.G. 175   57
  James T. 115
  John 102,112,175
  John S. 150
  Lou 135
  Louisa 175
  M.J. 106
  Mrs. M.J. 133
  M.R. 182
  Mary A. 110
  Pearcy 112 P.H. 103
  Peter 111,147
  R.E. 188,189,190
  Sarah A. 134
  Sarah E. 114
  Silas 15
  Tilman 138
  W.M. 175 W.A. 112
  W.J. 24,62,106
  W.S. 26
  Wade 113
  William V. 67
  J.L.B.& Co. 146
  W.M. & Co. 147
TEAKEE, Emma 188
  John H. 188
TEAGUE, L.B. 112
  M.M. 186
TEAL, Margaret 175
  William R. 175
TENANT, C.W. 110
  Mrs. John 62
TERRILL, James 114
  John TERRELL 162
  Mary TERRELL 129
  Wash TERRELL 162
THARP, R.J.A. 114
THOMAS, Mrs. C.H. 110
  G.O. 107
THOMASON, Dr. F.G. 136
  J.W. 106,175
  John W. 57,64
  Lucy 141
  Martha 157
  Nan 57
  Nancy 57
  T.J. 21,31,57,72
  T.L. 25,114
  Thom 57
  Thomas L. 57

Wilson 141
THOMASTON, W.V. 100
  Wes 4
THOMPSON, Capt. 7
  Cordelia 125
  Mary 152
  Parish 152
  Thomas 112
THORNTON, Bath 4
  Isham 4,139
  J.M. 114
  L.C. 111
  T.H. 111,175
THRASHER, F.M. 110
THURSTON, Sarah 136
TIDWELL, Emily Ann 126
  J.H. 112
  Jack 126
  R.W. 112
TIPHAM, T.N. 145
TODD, B.S. 158
TOMBY, Miss 6
TOMLIN, W.J. 113
  Sarah TOMBLIN 118
TOMLINSON, Cynthia 42
  Texie 38
TOMPKINS, H.A. 162
TOWLER, Mrs. J.E. 114
TOWLES, J.M. 114
TOWNSEND, D.C. 175
  L.W. 181
TRAMMEL, Molley 119
TRAMMELL, Susan 133
TRAYLOR,Cordelia 128
  G.N. 127
  Dr. G.W. 126,127,128,
    129,130,131,132,
    133,135,137,138,
    139,140,141
  George 127
  Dr. George W. 127,
    129,142
  J.L. 139
  J.M. 175
  John, Sr. 110
  Larkin Tralor 123
  M. 126
  Mary 127
  Nancy 179
  Pete 135
  Robert 124
  W. 126
  W.B. 110
  Washington 110,134,
    187
  William 17,109,111,
    130,179,183
TREADWAY, Thomas D. 102
  Thomas TREADAWAY 184
TREADWELL, Angeline
  B.A. 113   141
  Stephen 151
TRENT, Dr. 7

220

Bone 87
Mary Ida 190
P.G. 26,59,60, 106, 114,115,116,117, 118,119,120,121, 122,123,124,125, 127,128,129,130, 132,133,134,135, 136,137,138,140, 141,159
Dr. P.G., Jr. 142
Dr. P.G., Sr. 142,190
Powhatan G., Jr. 190
Dr. W.S. 138
TRENT & SUDDOTH 114
TRIMBLE, Becky 136
  Nancy 136
  Ella 136
  Lama 136
  Violet 136
TRIPLETT, Hedgeman 14, 15,16,18,24,52
  Hedgeman Ferry 14, 15,16
TRIPLETT'S FERRY 2,97
TRUETT, C. 175
  Cassie 118
  Edmond 119
  J.H. 181
  J.W. 184
  Lilley 118
  S.M. 175
TRUITT, James G. 189
  M.O. 162
  Mary E. 189
TUCKER, Lucy 116
TURNER, B. 106
  Irvin 111
  J.C. 147
  John S. 181
  John T. 115
  Joshua 117
  Lucinda 117
  Noah 114
  Peter 111
TURNIPSEED, Andrew 149
TWILLEY, James M. 155
UMPHRIES, P.T. 109
UPCHURCH, Lucinda 123
USSERY, Bill 7
  C.J. 2,27,80,87,90, 106,111,183
  Callie 183,184
  Calvin 183,184
  Calvin J. 79,103,104
  Cora 121
  D.J. 105
  Dora 121
  F.F. 111
  Fannie 123
  Fed 116
  J.R. 144,183

M.F. 144
M.H. 144
M.J. 114,154
Millard F. 183
Milton J., Sr. 119
Nancy A. 183
Nancy Ann 183
S.E. 105
Susie 121
T.F. 175,183
T.S. 187
Thomas 183
W.F. 183
VANCE, Marcus D. 154
  Mary E. 154
  Matilda Ann 154
VANDIVER, Maj. 83
VARDEMAN, William 14, 21,36
VAUGHAN, F.A. 188
  Fred 7
  T. Cooper 188
VAUGHN, Mrs. E. 111
  Thomas 111
VEAL, Benjamin 110
  J.S. 107
  Jarrett 111
  Martha S. 138
  Susey 183
  T.R. 107
  William 183
VERDERY, A.N. 101
  John Eve 101
VICE, Abner 102
VINEYARD, J.L. 142
VINSON, E.M. 175
  H.W. 114
  T.Y.C. 175
  W.W. 175
  Wesley 127
VOWELL, Barbary 111
  W.N. 181
WADE, B.A. 175
WADKINS, Melia 106
  Joseph 176
  Rebecca 176
WADSWORTH, D.F. 134
  M.H. 154
WAFER, J.T. 25,54
  Thomas B. 149,153
WAFER's FERRY 54
WAGGONER, Mendy Nelson 126
WAGNER, Fred 7
WAH-KEE-HAH-NAH 17
WAH-WAH-SHEE 17
WAH-HAH-TAH-NEE 17
WAH-WAH-NEE 18
WAITE, G.W. 112
WAKEFIELD, F.M. 176
WALDREP, Alexander 111
  Thomas 111
WALDROP, D.G. 113,189

WALDRUP, E.P. 111
WALKER, B.F. 111
  Benjamin 182
  Burton 102
  F.W. 111
  James 25
  John 112
  Leroy Pope 2,3
  R.W. 2
  S. 111
  S.S. 114
  Sylvanus 22,23,33, 39,148,149
  Thomas A. 186
  W.H. 144
WALKER & WILSON 186
WALL'S GRAVEYARD 133
WALLACE, Burrel 125
WALLER, Amos F. 146
  Louisa 183
  O.C. 162
  S.A. 143
  S.S. 114
  W.S. 183
WALLIS, Elizabeth 111
WALLS, Henry 116
  Vincent 110
WARD, J.D. 109
  J.M. 113,181
  James H. 129
  Jane M. 113
  S.E. 106
  W.L. 113,181
WARE, Fannie 115
  Mary 157
WARE & CO. 148
WARREN, H. 155
  Emily A. 108
  O. 155
WAS-WAH-NEE 17
WASHINGTON, Ema Nail 138
WATERS, Arch 109
  Larkin 127,131
  Mrs. M.E. 162
WATLEY, Lula 139
WATSON, E. 176
  George 131
  M.W. 176
  Mary 110
  W.N. 107
WATWOOD, J.W. 110
  Prudy 167
  Wesley 176
WEATHERS, Judge 33
  A.J. 21,31,93,162, 183,184,186,189
  Gen. B.F. 1,5,6,27, 182,183
  Benjamin F. 93
  Betty 184
  Capt. B.F. 98,107
  I.B. 184 Buck 182

I.T. 26,65,93
Isham T. 65,70,98,
    163
J.D. 141
J.T. 111
Jack 31
Jennie 93
Jesse 114
Jessie 130
Miss L.A. 163
Nannie 183
Sarah 66,93
Sudie 162
Thomas 111
Tom 66,70,120
W. 112 Dr. Wm. 120
Dr. W. 119
W.J. 186
W.W. 24,48,49,102
William 144,183
Willis 114
WEATHERS & MICKLES 7
WEATHERS & PATE 7
WEAVER, G.F. 86
    Henry 86
    Isaac 27,59,86
    Isaac S. 2
    J.M. 111
    James 183
    O.B. 86,113
    S.D. 176
    Mrs. W.T. 176
WEBB, Milton 111
WEDOWEE, Chief 17
    HOTEL 152
    OBSERVER 147
WEHADKEE COTTON MILLS
    91
WEHADKA MFG. CO. 147
WELCH, Dr. J.M. 127,
    129,130,133,134,
    138,139,140,142
    Thornton 124
    W.A. 112
    William 102
    William H. 138
WELDON, Marth Ann 111
WELLDAIN, F.W. 176
WELLS, Carter 148
    Samuel 151
WEST, Capt. 27
    A.A. 27,88
    Augustus A. 88
    Eph 88
    Gus 88
    Ivin 111
    L.E. 112
    Lucinea 111
    R. T. 18,32
    Robert T. 187
    Stephen 111
    W.L. 187
    William 158

WHALEY, ___ 128
    Eliza Jane 131
    Isaac 176
    W. F. 111
WHATLEY, Bettie 138
    Jno. H. 176
    Judge 176
    Lula 139
    Willie 141
WHITAKER, W.A. 183
WHITE, A. 106
    Annie Mora 117
    Mrs. B.M. 110
    Capt. Boss 93
    Cora 118
    D.C. 176
    Daniel 113
    E.M. 109
    Emma 123
    F.M. 181
    H.M. 114
    J.F. 25,26,60,79,110
    J.T. 107
    James F. 23,40,58,
        59,149
    James Kennie 128
    John 114
    John A. 102,109
    John G. 102,159
    Josie 38
    L.L. 106,116,117,120,
        121,122,124,129,
        130,132,134,135,
        136,138,141,142
    N.R. 109
    Robert A. 123
    W.A. 146
    Dr. W.E. 4,5,6,38,
        92,115,116,118,
        119,120,121,146
    Wiley 4
    William 187
WHITEHEAD, L.D. 176
WHITFIELD, J.E. 102
    Robert 101
WHITLEY, James 176
WHITLOCK, Lula Bell
    134
WHITTEN, Craven Jen-
    kins 163
    H.H. 27,92
    J.H. 188
    Joel H. 163
    Josephine Craven 163
    Joycey Anjaline 163
    Juda 106
    Lucius C. 119
    Zuda 106   120
WHORTON, William C.
WIDNER & HEARN 144
WIER, T.P. 111
WILDER, Emily 176
    J.C. 176

Garrett 103,113
May L. 112
Waif 135
WILF, A.C. 179
    J.A. 179
    J.M. 183
    Tomlin 6
WILKERSON, Miss C.A.
    101
    Watson 127
    William 133
WILKINSON, B. 112
    Bartholomew 116
    Elkanah 152
    J. 112
    Levi 102
    M.D. 176
    M.J. 176
    Shadrach 152
WILLIAMS, E.C. 176
    H.M. 76
    Isaac WILLIAM 154
    J.L. 27,89
    J.N. 110
    James A. 148
    John 129
    L.J. 176
    Lula 137
    Mary Ann 104
    R.N. 186
    S. 176
    Seaborn 148
    T.M. 109,176,182
    W.M. 109
    William 151,154,176
WILLIAMS, WALKERS,
    LIKINS & HAMMONDS
    153
WILLIAMSON, ELIC 110
    H.M. 26
WILLINGHAM, Alice 138
    Amos 155
    Cash 107
    Elizabeth A. 107
    F.J. 176
    J.B. 150
    K. 177
    L.J. 177
    Martha 136
    Martha M. 116
    R.H. 107
    Sarah Jane 138
    Sophia 141
    W.D. 176
WILLIS, N.H. 186
    Sallie 122
WILLOUGHLY, Bessie 163
    J. 110
    Sheriff 32
    Robert 22,33,36,190
WILSON, B.F. 111
    Charles 111
    G.T. 143

222

George W. 163
Josephine Craven 163
R.T. 186
S.S. 110
Spencer 101
W.W. 24
William 110
WIMBERLY, Mr. 7
WINDSOR, Mrs. A. 128
  John D. 26,63
  Permelia 177
  W.A. 177
  W.W. 113
WINSTON, John A. 71
WISE, H.H. 22,26,38
  Hicks H. 73
WOOD, __32,67
  Mrs. 37
  A.C. 79
  Capt. Alford C. 49
  Alfred 37
  Ann 89
  Bill 5
  "Brister" 37
  Charles 153
  D.A. 114
  Dick 37,85
  Earnest 133
  Elizabeth 33
  Etta 130
  F.A. 176
  Henry 158
  Henry L. 102
  J.W. 177
  Jack 27,37,79,89
  Jerry 186
  Ladora 118
  Ledda A. 177
  Lola E. 184
  Lucy 113
  Lucy J. 127
  Mrs. M.L. 163
  M.W. 139
  Mack 182
  Martha 37,79
  Mary 79
  Mary J. 177
  Milton 163
  Ola 138
  R.J. 2,27,61,79,83
  R.P. 109
  R.T. 2
  Richard J. 84,85,92,
    104
  Robert S. 155
  Sarah 79
  Susan 122
  W. 24
  W.D. 176
  W.H. 22,37,79,113
  W.T. 23,26,45,72,97
  Wall 98
  Will 130

William 2,27,37,50,
  79,89,92,102,
  155,186
William W. 149
Willis 14,19,22,23,
  25,32,33,39,52,
  111,177
Winston 37,79
Wyatt W. 183
WOOD COPPER MINES 85,
  98
WOODRUFF, Aaron 188
  Irvin 102
WOODSON, J.M. 111
  Nancy 114
WOODWARD, E.L. 151
WORDSWORTH, Martin H.
  24
WORKMAN, J.P. 177
WORTHAM, A.M. 110
  Sarah Ann 125
  T.N. 110
WORTHY, J.H. 112
  S.F. 187
WRIGHT, A.J. 111
  Emma 141
  F.D. 105
  J.C. 7,26,65,114,179
  J.R. 146,177,189
  James 110
  Jefferson 132
  John C. 66
  John R. 126
  Lucinda 128,133
  Moses 102
  Nancy 119
  Ocie 137
  Susan 133
  T.E. 77
  W.H. 106
  William 110,137
  Z. Jones, Jr. 188
  Zachariah J. 141
WYATT, Jimmie 121
YANCY, W.W. 179
YARBROUGH, Billie 140
  Carrie E. 119
  William 110
YARNELL, Jane 137
YARBROUGH, Isaac J. 123
  Mary 111
YATES, Dr. 5,7
  E.M. 114
  Fannie 117
  James J. 112
  James M. 189
  Laura 131
  Marie 132
  Peter T. 111
  Sarah F. 189
  W. 112 Wm. James 112
  W.A. 106
  W.M. 144,182

YATES MOTOR CO. 4
YEARTA, Elisabeth 131
YEARTY, Elin 128
YOUNG,A.A. 112,177
  Aleck 187
  Asa 111
  C. 177
  Eliza 177
  Elizabeth 101
  Mrs. F.H. 132
  Ike 64,117
  Isaac 102,144
  J.F. 110
  J.H. 114
  J.W. 110
  John 54
  Leonard W. 19
  Mary D. 179
  Mary E. 158
  Nancy 124
  Richard 25,54
  Robert 111,179
  Samuel 111
  T.H. 110
  Virginia Harriett 101
  W.J. 114
  Westly 114
  William 101
YOUNG'S FERRY 2,97
ZACHARY, Ada 140
  Benjamin 13

Comm. Print. 198